JANUARY 1973

WATERGATE, ROE V. WADE, VIETNAM, AND THE MONTH THAT CHANGED AMERICA FOREVER

JAMES ROBENALT

CHICAGO REVIEW PRESS

Copyright © 2015 by James Robenalt
Foreword copyright © 2015 by John W. Dean
All rights reserved
Published by Chicago Review Press Incorporated
814 North Franklin Street
Chicago, Illinois 60610
ISBN 978-1-61374-965-4

Library of Congress Cataloging-in-Publication Data
Are available from the Library of Congress.

Cover design: John Yates at Stealworks
Interior design: PerfecType, Nashville, TN

Printed in the United States of America
5 4 3 2 1

To Joanna, whose love sustains me

CONTENTS

FOREWORD

Because Jim Robenalt, your author, is my friend, more than a brief note from me could be properly suspect. But the fact of the matter is that I truly enjoyed reading this book, so I am delighted he asked me to write a foreword to broadly introduce him and his work.

Together Jim and I teach a Continuing Legal Education (CLE) seminar for attorneys based on my experiences at the Nixon White House during Watergate, viewing them with the modern rules of legal ethics and professional responsibility. I suggested Jim join me in doing these seminars because I knew he was interested in history and he is a skilled trial lawyer. As such, I appreciated that not only is he good on his feet, but more important, he also understands information analysis and the techniques of effective presentations. These talents not only result in good CLE programs, which engage and entertain as they inform, but they are essential for a good book as well. Jim's ableness will become abundantly clear in the pages that follow.

I watched this book develop from its inception, so I can attest to the time, energy, and effort that was devoted to digging out the information underlying the extraordinary confluence of events he noticed occurring in January 1973, which are the basis of this book. This is Jim's third book. When his colleagues ask him how he finds time to practice law, teach CLEs, and write books, he often jokes that he doesn't play golf. In fact, he is a quick study, an experienced researcher, and an accomplished writer.

This book emerged from his study of Watergate and the Nixon White House for our CLE seminars. It was while digging into primary source material to develop our second program that he first noticed the unique intersection of a series of seemingly disparate events that occurred in January 1973, each event with varying degrees of connection to the Nixon White House: the ending of the Vietnam War and the beginnings of new problems for the Nixon Administration; the beginning of the ending of the Nixon presidency with the Watergate break-in trial; the beginnings of the debate over ending a woman's pregnancy, which was addressed by the US Supreme Court ruling *Roe v. Wade*; and finally there were the endings of the lives of two former presidents of the United States, Harry Truman and Lyndon Johnson.

These events, both the beginnings and endings, could not have occurred in a more appropriate month than January, a month named after a Roman god believed to have had two faces: one looking back and the other forward. Fittingly, Jim has similarly woven these stories together by looking back and then forward, as needed, blending past and future as it flowed through Washington, DC, to explain and report the events of this uniquely historic month. As a reader you will quickly realize you are in the hands of not only a good storyteller, but of a very sophisticated explainer who has a gifted knack for making the complex matters easily understandable, and the inexplicable, comprehensible.

I've always had a hunch that lawyers do better at gathering and analyzing historical evidence than most historians because of their training with the rules of evidence, their professional need to critically evaluate facts for their true value, and the ability to assemble reports that engage the listener or reader. I find full confirmation of my hunch in this book in two ways. First, readers will find wonderful thumbnail sketches of remarkably complex states of affairs that Jim has intertwined while revealing how they flowed through Washington in January 1973. Second, Jim has uncovered heretofore unreported (if not unknown) information about those events. It makes for a fascinating read.

While I do not disagree with any of the findings, in one instance we do not draw the same conclusions from the facts: I give the initial Watergate prosecutors, particularly former assistant US attorney Earl Silbert, more room for error than Jim has done, because I feel Silbert was in an impossible position at the time. As you will discover, Silbert relied on the testimony of former Nixon aide Jeb Magruder in the trial of the initial conspiracy to break in and bug the Democratic National Committee offices in the Watergate complex. Silbert was totally unaware that with Magruder he was dealing with a slick liar, not to mention Magruder was a member of the conspiracy that he was covering up. At the time Silbert had every reason to believe Magruder. Only recently with the transcription of more Nixon tapes for my latest book has it become clear that Silbert and his colleagues on the first

Watergate prosecution team were also being regularly undercut by their superiors at the Department of Justice. It was an impossible situation, and I have long thought Earl Silbert should do a book based on the contemporaneous diary he kept at the time, which is today located in the National Archives but only he can fully decipher.

There will be no spoilers in this foreword for insights to be found in this book. All I will say is that I challenged Jim to tell me something I didn't know about this month. Well he has done just that throughout this book, so I hope you enjoy it as much as I have.

John W. Dean
Author of *The Nixon Defense: What He Knew and When He Knew It*
Los Angeles, California
May 2015

INTRODUCTION

A Stand of Aspen

Walk among a stand of quaking aspen trees on a sunny, breezy day, and you will experience a sublime, surpassing sensation. The trees are alive with activity, silvery leaves glinting, twisting and trembling, whistling a soft melody, sounding like a voice of the beyond.

What you may not know is that all the trees you see are one organism, identical in DNA, carbon copies of one another.

That's because aspens grow in colonies from a single seedling that spreads through its roots. New stems, known as root suckers or ramets, pop up from the dirt at distances from the parent tree, creating a new tree, and then another, and then another. The entire clonal colony is interconnected below the surface through a single root system. The individual trees may come and go, but the root system remains, sometimes living for thousands of years.[1]

Studying American history is much like an examination of aspen trees.

The connections are not obvious unless one digs. And then it becomes clear that everything is mysteriously linked.

The White House, December 18, 1972

On Monday evening, President Richard Nixon sat down to a private dinner party in the family dining room in the upstairs residence. On the other side of the world, 129 giant B-52 Stratofortress bombers lumbered back in waves to bases around Southeast Asia from dramatic and intense raids over North Vietnam. Up to this point in the entire Vietnam War only one B-52 had been shot down in combat. Over the next two gut-wrenching weeks, fifteen of these jumbo planes would be blown out of the sky, including three on this night alone. Thousands of Vietnamese civilians would die on the ground. One week to the day before Christmas 1972, the infamous "Christmas Bombing" of Hanoi and Haiphong had begun.[2]

President Nixon's dinner guests on this historic night included his wife, Pat, daughter Julie, National Security Advisor Henry Kissinger, ABC News anchorman Howard K. Smith and his wife, and Alice Roosevelt Longworth, the daughter of the nation's twenty-sixth president, Theodore Roosevelt.[3]

Alice was Roosevelt's oldest child, born in 1884 to Alice Hathaway Lee, TR's first wife. Alice's mother died tragically two days after her birth from complications of undiagnosed Bright's disease, toxemia, or both. On the same day and in the same house, Theodore's mother, Mittie, died of typhoid fever. Within the year, a devastated Theodore retreated from the world in utter grief, heading west to the Badlands of North Dakota to hunt, write, read, and mourn.[4]

Baby Alice was left in the care of TR's oldest sister, Anna "Bamie" Roosevelt, until Theodore returned from North Dakota and later remarried. When Alice's father was propelled unexpectedly into the presidency in 1901 with the assassination of President William McKinley, she moved into the White House and became a national celebrity. From that time on, she always considered the White House her home. But unlike the historic mansion, her life was anything but staid. Alice became Washington's most notorious gossip, at times venomous, and a self-proclaimed hedonist.

"I can either run the country or I can attend to Alice," Roosevelt told a friend, "but I cannot possibly do both."[5]

Alice Longworth's surprisingly close relationship with Richard Nixon started before he became vice president. Nixon was a pallbearer at the funeral of Alice's daughter, Paulina, in 1957 (the death had been rumored a suicide), and Alice and Nixon stayed in touch through all of his electoral defeats and setbacks during the early 1960s.[6] Nixon returned her loyalty. Alice was an honored guest when Nixon's daughter Tricia married Ed Cox in June 1971 in a White House ceremony, which took place the day before the *New York Times* published the so-called Pentagon Papers, a top-secret study of the origins of the Vietnam War, leaked to the *Times* by Daniel Ellsberg.[7]

Nixon's obsession with leaks, fueled in large part by the release of the Pentagon Papers, became the spur for the creation of the White

House special investigative unit known colloquially as "the plumbers," which would be populated by the likes of G. Gordon Liddy and Howard Hunt, who later became the masterminds of the Watergate burglary.

One thing has a way of leading to another.

Undoubtedly Richard Nixon was looking to draw moral support and invoke historic connection when he invited Alice Longworth to dinner on the night the bombing started. The very dining room they sat in on the second floor of the family residence had once been Alice's bedroom. The room, like most in the White House residence, had been through various incarnations over time, having once been known as the Prince of Wales Room because that august personage had stayed there in 1860 during the Buchanan administration.

It was also the room where Willie Lincoln died, Abraham Lincoln was embalmed, and Alice had an emergency appendectomy. When Alice moved into the room in 1901, it had plain painted walls, two double brass-knobbed beds, and an ornately carved mahogany wardrobe. Jacqueline Kennedy converted the room into a family dining room in 1961 and installed antique wallpaper depicting scenes from battles of the American Revolution. The paper was still up in December 1972; Washington and Cornwallis looked down upon the Nixon party as they ate their meals.[8]

Nixon's fondness for Alice matched his admiration for her father. Alice's father had been an open proponent of the use of raw American power to shape world affairs. Nixon studied TR closely and took great pleasure in linking himself to this iconic president through his daughter. When the two spoke it was not unusual for Nixon to ask Alice what her father might think about something, or what comparisons might be drawn between Roosevelt's time and his own in the White House.

Camp David, November 13, 1972

Just a month before the mid-December dinner, Nixon and Longworth enjoyed a characteristically animated and entertaining postelection phone call, which (unbeknownst to Alice) was automatically recorded through a wiretap that Nixon had had installed on one of the phones in the Aspen Lodge at Camp David.

"Never was a better campaign!" Alice chirped on November 13, 1972, referring to Nixon's trouncing of Senator George McGovern a week earlier.[9] Like her first cousin Eleanor Roosevelt, Alice spoke in a high register, with a society affect that was distinctly patrician.

"Have you ever heard a president attacked as roughly as we got—as the Shriver-McGovern people who took us on?" Nixon asked her.

"I don't think I ever—" Alice started to say.

"I mean the names that they were calling me," Nixon interrupted. "I look back at the time that your father was in and they talked pretty rough in those days."

"Pretty rough," Alice agreed.

"But they used a term like *a rat* or something like that, but my God."

At this, Alice released a schoolgirl cackle.

"*World murderer?*" Nixon said in fake amazement.

"World murderer!" Alice repeated back in mock solemnity.

"As a matter of fact," Nixon said, "Taft used [the term] *rat* on himself when he said, 'Even a rat when cornered will fight!' " Demonstrating his broad reading and intimate familiarity with her father's career, Nixon easily pulled up from his prodigious memory this obscure reference to a quote from the tempestuous election of 1912, when Theodore Roosevelt abruptly turned on his own handpicked successor, William Howard Taft, splitting the Republican Party in two and opening the door to the presidency to Democrat Woodrow Wilson. Taft at first refused to believe that Roosevelt would run against him, but when reality settled in, he reached for something to say, finding an unfortunate metaphor to describe his need to fight back in spite of his reluctance. He painted himself as a cornered rat.

"Oh poor William Howard," Alice said, "even a rat when cornered will fight."

"Yeah, I'll never forget that," Nixon said, as if he had lived through the campaign of 1912 with Alice, who at the time was almost twenty-eight. Nixon wasn't born until two months after the election of 1912, on January 9, 1913.

"We behaved very badly," Alice admitted, "we did." Nixon mumbled something that sounded like agreement. "The Bull Moosers," Alice added, "we behaved dreadfully, we were dreadful—but never mind!"

"That language was nothing compared to what they used [against me]," Nixon sourly added.

"Well I *ache* to see you," Alice said, keeping the conversation from turning disagreeable. "Let me know sometime when you and Pat will be around." Only Alice Longworth could speak with such ease to Richard Nixon. He hated familiarity, but Alice was a rare exception.

A month later, Alice sat for dinner with the Nixons and Henry Kissinger. As Richard Nixon moved toward one of the most controversial and provocative moments of his already turbulent presidency, the jubilant mood following his stunning election win in November had faded and turned dark—and he had reason to worry anew about the charge of "world murderer."

The White House, Lead-Up to the Christmas Bombings

On the weekend before the bombing was to start, Nixon anxiously and compulsively called Henry Kissinger, going over details and obsessing about the planning for the bombing as if to buck himself up—to convince himself that what he was doing was justified and to strengthen his resolve in carrying out the attacks.

"When you really come down to it," he said to Kissinger during one of the calls on Sunday morning, December 17, "at the top of the heap, you've always got to have somebody that's willing to step up and hit the hard ones."[10] Kissinger was in full agreement and tried to put some context around what was about to happen. He told Nixon that the bombing raids to come—averaging one hundred B-52s per night—would be the equivalent of a four-thousand-plane raid in the Second World War.

"Goddamn," Nixon said in astonishment. He seemed to have scarcely realized the magnitude of the firestorm he was unleashing. The statistic caught him short.

"It's going to break every window in Hanoi," Kissinger dryly observed.

"You mean, just from the reverberations, huh?" Nixon asked.

"Yeah," Kissinger replied.

"Well that tends to shake them up a little bit, too, doesn't it?" Nixon said, with the slightest hint of a nervous laugh.

Despite the outward show of bravado for Kissinger, none of this was necessarily easy for Richard Nixon. His mother had been a devoted Quaker; her son wanted to be known in history as a pacifist, not a warmonger. "The greatest honor history can bestow is the title of peacemaker," he declared in his first inaugural address in January 1969.

The military plans in December 1972 were directed at the destruction of North Vietnam's power plants, its transportation hubs, and of course Radio Hanoi, but these targets were all in the vicinity of the densely populated cities of Hanoi and Haiphong. And B-52s, Nixon recognized, were not built for precision bombing. Yet the cloudy weather in December precluded the use of smaller planes with newly developed smart or precision-guided bombs.

There were pronounced risks. Nixon was troubled with the prospects of high civilian casualties, so much so that he had difficulty even verbalizing his concerns when he spoke of the raids with Kissinger. In a phone call to Kissinger placed just before Nixon attended worship services in the White House, he said, "With this blow," and then he grew silent. "I just hope to God, Henry," he haltingly continued, "I went over those—as you know, for the first time, I don't do target lists usually, but I went over that goddamn thing with [Chairman of the Joint Chiefs of Staff Admiral Thomas H.] Moorer and [Deputy Secretary of Defense Kenneth] Rush. Moorer swears this is everything they can hit that's worth hitting—I mean, without taking out too much civilian stuff."[11]

But Nixon was at bottom a fatalist. He said it often. Later on Sunday afternoon, in yet another call with Henry Kissinger, he said, "My point is, I'm just totally resigned to it. We have to be resigned to it, fatalistic as hell."[12] He was forever prompting his subordinates, Kissinger in particular, never to second-guess a decision once it was made.

"It's like Lot's wife," he would frequently say, referring to the biblical story. "You can't look back."

When the president, the First Lady, and daughter Julie Nixon Eisenhower escorted eighty-eight-year-old Alice Roosevelt Longworth to the ground floor of the White House to see her off into the chilly December evening, it was its own notable moment. The nation's thirty-seventh president, along with the daughter-in-law of the thirty-fourth president, said goodnight to the daughter of the twenty-sixth president. What Nixon had started that night would have consequences in Congress, in the nation, and around the world.

January 1973

What was coming was January 1973, a portal in time. It would turn out to be a month that would shake the American political system to its foundation and change the fundamentals that underpin the idea of consensus government. And the events of that month—great happenings—would pile one on top of the other with remarkable rapidity during the short span of thirty days or so.

A war would end, a new political movement would get its start, a burglars' trial would undo a presidency, the Supreme Court would establish a woman's right to an abortion, and two ex-presidents would drop dead. Such things do not happen in the ordinary experience of humankind—or do they?

Lyndon Johnson and family pay respects at the Truman Library. Within a month, LBJ would also be dead.

Harry S. Truman Library

The panorama of American history is dotted with clusters of periods of momentous occurrences and occasions, personal and national, that are strangely connected and surprisingly bunched together. On a timeline and in hindsight, they stand like the copse of trees at Gettysburg, the focal point of Pickett's Charge on the last day of that epic battle. Intersecting at moments in time, these events fuel and power historic change; they represent great turning points, pronounced markers in the life of the nation, though they are not necessarily recognized for their full significance at the time.

What are we to make of this phenomenon of simultaneity?

Jay Winik, in his brilliant book *April 1865*, wrote about the "breathtaking simultaneity" of the extraordinary events of April 1865, when Lee's army surrendered at Appomattox Court House just six days before President Lincoln was assassinated by John Wilkes Booth at Ford's Theatre. Winik marveled at how so many "tales of human drama," which produced such "far-reaching consequences," could be packed within "a simple span of some thirty days or so."[13]

The same can be said of other turning points in American history. The spring of 1968 saw two of the bleakest moments of the American republic unfold within nine weeks of one another: the assassination of Dr. Martin Luther King Jr. on April 4 and the assassination of Robert F. Kennedy on June 6. These murders had an overpowering impact on the American civil rights movement, to say nothing of the destiny of the nation for the next fifty years and beyond.

President John F. Kennedy's assassination happened during the same month, November 1963, as the assassination of President Diem of South Vietnam, both events having much to do with the expansion of America's involvement in the Vietnam War.

After coming to power at roughly the same time, Franklin Roosevelt and Adolf Hitler died within weeks of one another in April 1945, thrusting an inexperienced Harry Truman into the presidency and placing on his shoulders the momentous decision of whether to take America, and the world, into an age of nuclear weaponry.

Woodrow Wilson's first wife, Ellen, died in the White House on August 6, 1914, just days after the outbreak of general war in Europe. Her demise sent Wilson into a paralyzed state of depression at a time when the crisis in the world required his keen and undistracted attention. More important, Wilson's second wife, Edith Bolling Galt, whom he began courting within six months of his first wife's death, played to Wilson's faults, accentuating a tendency toward stubborn willfulness and stoking his messianic vision of himself, both traits that ill-served the world during and after the Paris Peace Conference at the end of the Great War. A second catastrophic war was all but guaranteed as a result of the flawed Versailles Treaty, over which Wilson had presided.

Yet is there any importance to assign to the fact that great events appear to occur in close temporal proximity? One answer may be found in what historians call "contingency." "For historians," Winik wrote, "it is axiomatic that there are dates on which history turns, and that themselves become packed with meaning." But, he asserted, history is neither fated nor a random sequence of events. "It was not inevitable that the American Civil War would end as it did," he wrote, "or for that matter, that it would end at all well. Indeed, what emerges from the panorama of April 1865 is that the whole of our national history could have been altered but for a few decisions, a quirk of fate, a sudden shift in luck."[14]

There is, Winik wrote, a great deal of "choice and uncertainty" that contribute to how things turn out. This is what historians call *contingency*. Take away one decision, one event, and everything changes.

Whether it was chance, luck, Providence, or something else, there can be little doubt that some force seemed to be activated during the eventful and traumatic month of January 1973.

And like a stand of aspen, it all was inexplicably and inextricably interconnected.

PRELUDE

"The Very Thought of Losing Is Hateful to Americans"

Spring 1970

If there is a prelude to January 1973, it is the spring of 1970. During this time, particularly in April, the storm systems that would converge to generate January 1973 began to coalesce. The war in Indochina took a critical turn. Henry Kissinger started his secret meetings with the North Vietnamese in Paris. And Richard Nixon, almost by accident, put the man on the Supreme Court who would become the author of the opinions in the abortion cases.

Like its successor in January 1973, it was a period of great simultaneity.

Choisy-le-Roi, France, January 1970

When Richard Nixon took office in January 1969, American deaths in Vietnam stood at roughly thirty-six thousand, a substantial number of which occurred during the shattering year of 1968. As a presidential candidate, Nixon promised to end the war, citing a secret plan. But the fact is that another twenty-one thousand Americans would lose their lives before the war finally came to an end for America four years later, in January 1973.[1]

On his first morning as president, Nixon discovered a thin folder tucked away in a safe in the second floor of the residence in the White House that contained the daily Vietnam situation report. The digest—the only thing left in the safe by Lyndon Johnson—had been updated through the final day of LBJ's administration. It showed that in the preceding week alone, 185 Americans were killed and 1,237 were wounded.

The losses in the preceding twelve months were staggering by any measure of war: 14,958 Americans had been killed. Almost as sickening, 95,798 had been wounded, many grievously and permanently.

"I closed the folder," Nixon wrote about this encounter in his memoirs, "and put it back in the safe and left it there until the war was over, a constant reminder of its tragic cost."[2]

There had been public peace negotiations in Paris with the North Vietnamese dating back to the time of the Johnson administration, but these efforts had been a study in futility. A year after Nixon took office, at the urging of his national security advisor, Henry Kissinger, secret negotiations were opened with the North Vietnamese in the last days of February 1970.[3] A brief stab at secret talks had been attempted in August 1969, but neither side moved to activate the consultations following an initial meeting.[4]

The site chosen for the renewed clandestine discussions was a modest residence owned by the Democratic Republic of Vietnam in Choisy-le-Roi, a commune in the southeastern suburbs of Paris. Careful measures were taken to keep the press off Kissinger's trail when he flew to Paris and, for a time, no one other than a select few knew that the back-channel discussions were under way. "The house in Choisy-le-Roi where we met with the North Vietnamese," Kissinger remembered, "might have belonged to a foreman in one of the factories of the district."[5]

Despite some hope of progress in private, little was accomplished. The North Vietnamese were uncompromising in their demands that America get out of Vietnam and that President Nguyen Van Thieu in South Vietnam be overthrown. "North Vietnam's sole reciprocal obligation would be not to shoot at our men as they boarded their ships and aircraft to depart," Kissinger sarcastically wrote of this time period.[6]

Hanoi's negotiating position did not even address the release of American prisoners of war.

The lead negotiator for the North Vietnamese was a man named Le Duc Tho, who went by the title "Special Advisor" to Hanoi's Paris delegation.[7] He outranked everyone in the Paris mission and was a member of Hanoi's Communist Party Politburo. He was described by Kissinger as "gray-haired, dignified," a dour man who "invariably wore a black or brown Mao suit." Although his dress was simple and his demeanor polite, these things could not mask his single-minded determination and his unbending resolve. "His large luminous eyes only rarely revealed the fanaticism that had induced him as a boy of sixteen to join the anti-French Communist guerrillas," Kissinger observed. He in fact had spent ten years in prisons under the French and as a result had become, in Kissinger's eyes, a professional revolutionary. He was a daunting opponent; "implacable" is the term Kissinger used most frequently in his memoirs.[8]

Meanwhile Nixon, true to his campaign promise, had begun a steady drawdown of American forces as part of his "Vietnamization" policy—a plan to turn over the defense of South Vietnam to its people and its army. But the reduction of American forces, so necessary to quell the domestic revolt in America, had an undermining effect on peace negotiations. Le Duc Tho told Kissinger that he believed that Americans no longer had the domestic will to continue to fight, and that Vietnamization was an illusion. "Before, there were over a million US and puppet troops, and you failed," he told Kissinger. "How can you succeed when you let the puppet troops do the fighting?"[9]

Given these conditions, the secret meetings in Paris in March and early April 1970 predictably bogged down.

In the spring of 1970, however, other forces would suddenly erupt and make the situation worse. The war, to the great surprise of the American public, would expand into Cambodia.[10] At a state university in a small college town in northeastern Ohio, four students moved inescapably toward their deadly rendezvous with national guardsmen.

Cambodia, Spring 1970

The Vietnam conflict had always had spillover influences in neighboring Laos and Cambodia. The North Vietnamese, like the French imperialists before them, had desires to establish hegemony over all of Indochina, so they perennially kept troops in both countries in support of local Communist insurgents. Recognizing the threat, the United States sent "advisors" and Special Forces to prop up the existing neutral governments, and engaged in secret bombing campaigns to try to maintain the uneasy equilibrium in each of these countries.[11]

In addition, the North Vietnamese made heavy use of the so-called Ho Chi Minh Trail, a path that extended from Laos down through Cambodia—running roughly parallel to the borders of Vietnam—as a supply line for its war in the south. Hanoi built up munitions and supply storage areas along this route that came to be known as "sanctuaries." From these havens, the North Vietnamese could infiltrate the south and launch cross-border attacks against South Vietnamese and US forces.

Cambodia at the time was ruled by a long-standing but unpredictable prince named Norodom Sihanouk. Sihanouk was crowned king of Cambodia in 1941, when he was only eighteen years old. He later abandoned the throne and became prime minister, and still later he became chief of state. He skillfully balanced all the conflicting forces within his country and avoided an open war with the North Vietnamese while maintaining his silence as American bombs fell on the Communist sanctuaries in the western part of his country.[12]

In January 1970 Sihanouk took an ill-advised vacation to the French Riviera. During the trip Cambodia's prime minister, Lon Nol, orchestrated a coup because of increasing displeasure with Sihanouk's inability to deal with the presence of the North Vietnamese in Cambodia. Cambodian Communists, with the support of the North Vietnamese, took advantage of the resulting chaos to step up their efforts to take over the country.[13]

Eventually the exiled Sihanouk, looking over the entire situation, concluded that he had no choice but to side with the Communists against Lon Nol's struggling government. In the process he blamed the United States for what was happening.

Kissinger saw that if Sihanouk returned to power in Cambodia, it would be under Communist domination and, as he put it, "all of Cambodia would become an enemy sanctuary."[14]

Minneapolis, Minnesota, April 1970

Nixon had other worries on his mind in the spring of 1970. He needed to find a nominee for the Supreme Court who could win Senate confirmation. The drama over the Supreme Court had started two years earlier.

In June 1968 the chief justice of the United States, Earl Warren, who was then seventy-seven years old, announced his desire to retire. He wrote to President Johnson: "I have been advised that I am in as good physical condition as a person my age has any right to expect. The problem of age, however, is one that no man can combat and, therefore, eventually must bow to it."[15]

The problem was that Johnson was a lame duck. He had astounded friends and foes alike when he declared in late March 1968 that he would not seek reelection. The war had worn him down, and he wanted to find a way to end it without the distractions of a presidential campaign.

Republicans, who believed they would win in 1968, were not about to approve Johnson's candidate for the most important position on the Supreme Court. Johnson nominated his close friend Abe Fortas to take Warren's place. Fortas had been Johnson's lawyer, and rumor was that even after Johnson secured a seat for Fortas as an associate justice of the Supreme Court in 1965, Fortas continued to consult with LBJ, assisting in the drafting of legislation and writing major addresses.

The Nixon campaign, in league with Senate Republicans, helped uncover some serious financial improprieties that traced back to Fortas.[16] He had accepted unusual fees to teach at American University.[17] After a bitter fight and filibuster, Fortas finally withdrew his name from consideration in October 1968.

Nixon's victory in November 1968 assured that he would select the next chief justice of the United States. But there was even better news for Nixon. Likely through the skullduggery of his staff, additional damaging information about Fortas surfaced.[18] This time, Fortas was forced to resign altogether from the court.

Thus by May 1969, four months into his first term, Richard Nixon had two seats to fill instead of just one. Fred Graham of the *New*

Justice Harry Blackmun.
Collection of the Supreme Court of the United States

York Times pointed out Nixon's good fortune in being able to remake the court so early in his presidency. The Fortas resignation, Graham wrote, offered the occasion for Nixon "to change the liberal cast of the Supreme Court by replacing Justice Fortas and Chief Justice Earl Warren, who will retire next month."[19]

Nixon's selection of Minnesotan Warren Burger to replace Earl Warren proceeded without incident. But the Democrats were out for revenge when it came to filling the Fortas seat. Two successive Nixon nominations were stalled and defeated in the Senate. Clement Haynsworth, a federal judge from South Carolina, was the first to be rejected.[20] Nixon tried again to nominate a Southerner, as part of his overall Southern Strategy. A Florida federal judge, G. Harrold Carswell, was suggested next.[21] He too flopped.

It was early April 1970—almost a year after Fortas stepped down—and Nixon had run out of patience. He angrily blamed the Senate for sectionalism and complained that it simply was not possible to get Senate confirmation for anyone "who believes in the strict construction of the Constitution, as I do, if he happens to come from the South."[22]

All of these unexpected events would inure to the benefit of an obscure federal judge from Minneapolis named Harry Blackmun.[23] He was one of the least likely candidates to be considered for the Supreme Court, but fate and serendipity were about to deal him a winning hand. The third person to be formally nominated by Nixon for the seat, Blackmun would later self-deprecatingly refer to himself as "Old Number Three."[24]

April 1970

As if synchronized, these various strands all came together in April 1970, taking place one on top of the other.

On April 2, the movie *Patton* was released. The not-so-subtle Vietnam message: America had never lost a war. "The very thought of losing is hateful to Americans," George C. Scott growls as George Patton addressing his Third Army in the movie's iconic opening scene, set in front of an immense American flag.

At virtually the same time of the movie's release, things were approaching the breaking point in Paris. Henry Kissinger and Le Duc Tho argued to a standoff on April 4.[25] The North Vietnamese charged that the Americans had financed and staged the coup in Cambodia. "I indicated that we would not be the ones to expand the war to

Cambodia," Kissinger replied to Le Duc Tho.[26] He returned to Washington, frustrated and uncertain of whether talks would ever resume.[27]

On Saturday night, April 4, Nixon hosted a dinner for the duke and duchess of Windsor in the State Dining Room. The guests included Chief Justice Burger and his wife, Fred Astaire, Charles and Anne Morrow Lindbergh, Alice Roosevelt Longworth, Arnold Palmer and his wife, George and Barbara Bush, and astronaut Frank Borman and his wife, in town from the NASA Manned Spacecraft Center in Houston, Texas.[28]

On the following morning, Sunday, April 5, Lyndon and Lady Bird Johnson returned to the White House to participate with the Nixons in Sunday worship services in the East Room, John Cardinal Krol of Philadelphia presiding. Barbara and George H. W. Bush and three of their sons, George W., Jeb, and Neil Bush, took part in the services.[29] Later the Johnsons joined the Nixons in a reception in the State Dining Room. The Johnsons were in town to attend a family wedding.[30]

That evening, after the Johnsons had gone, the president, First Lady, and Julie and David Eisenhower gathered in the White House theater in the East Wing to watch a private screening of *Patton*.[31] Nixon was mesmerized. In April 1970 he watched the three-hour film multiple times, at least once with Henry Kissinger.

It was the start of a manic period for Nixon.

Within the next few days, he was complaining to his chief of staff, Bob Haldeman, that individuals in his administration needed to "take the offensive." Nixon grumbled that the people around him "[didn't] radiate enthusiasm, because [they] really [didn't] feel it," Haldeman recorded. Nixon told Haldeman he should see *Patton* because the general "inspired people, charged them up." As his chief of staff, Nixon said, Haldeman needed to do the same. Haldeman took the sleight. "Pointed!" he wrote.[32]

On April 8 the Senate rejected Judge Carswell's nomination for the Supreme Court. "Carswell day," Haldeman noted in his diary, "and he went down the tubes!"[33] Haldeman cautioned a measured response. But Nixon was enraged. "Wants to step up political attack," Haldeman wrote. "Investigators on Kennedy and Muskie plus Bayh and Proxmire."[34]

On this same day, Nixon privately decided he would make a dramatic announcement of additional troop withdrawals from Vietnam in the upcoming week. He would redeploy 150,000 troops, stretched out over a year.[35] Suspicious of leaks, he told none of his cabinet officers of his plan. Instead, he had his press secretary, Ron Ziegler, leak to the *Washington Post* and *New York Times* that the withdrawal would be in the range of forty thousand troops, hoping to amp up the public relations bump he expected to receive after the announcement.[36]

On Thursday, April 9, Haldeman wrote that Nixon "turned into a demon." He impulsively "cut loose" in the White House press room late in the afternoon, appearing unannounced before startled reporters. Haldeman recorded that, Patton-like, Nixon went "looking for the offensive to counteract defeat."[37] He spoke for two minutes, rapid-fire, and concluded his remarks by asserting that the Senate, "as presently constituted," would not approve a southern conservative, so he would find a nominee from outside the South. Haldeman winced at the president's sharp demeanor. The *New York Times* headline the following day captured his mood: "President Bitter."[38]

After dinner in the residence that evening, Nixon retired to the Lincoln Sitting Room, settling into his favorite overstuffed, brown velvet armchair, a holdover from his New York apartment. He started placing a flurry of telephone calls—to Gerald Ford, George Bush, Tom Dodd, Harry Byrd, William Brock, Harry Dent, John Mitchell, Spiro Agnew, Henry Kissinger, Ron Ziegler, and Bob Haldeman. Finally, around 8:30 PM, he spoke with Chief Justice Warren Burger, who was vacationing in Palm Beach, Florida.[39]

Burger had floated the idea of his friend from childhood, Harry A. Blackmun, then a sitting judge on the US Court of Appeals for the Eight Circuit. Nixon went to the Executive Office Building bowling alley to blow off steam after his call with Burger.[40]

Burger's recommendation stuck. John Mitchell called Harry Blackmun to instruct him to get to Washington the next day to discuss his potential nomination to the Supreme Court.[41] At three in the afternoon, on Friday, April 10, Mitchell escorted Blackmun into the Oval Office for a "completely off the record" meeting with the president.[42] The interview lasted less than thirty-five minutes.[43] With lightning speed, just two days after the Carswell defeat, Nixon had settled on the slender, soft-spoken, sixty-one-year-old Blackmun as his nominee.

After this brief meeting with Blackmun, and just before hosting a formal state dinner in the East Room for the German chancellor Willie Brandt, Nixon took a moment to call the astronauts of Apollo 13 at Cape Kennedy. They were scheduled for liftoff the following morning.

Deep Space, April 13, 1970

Apollo 13 launched as scheduled on Saturday morning, April 11. The mission proceeded smoothly until Monday night, April 13. By then, the spacecraft was almost two hundred thousand miles from Earth.

Just minutes after signing off on a televised broadcast, the astronauts heard a loud *bang*. They immediately observed one of the command module's oxygen tanks venting into open space. The initial fear was that the spacecraft had been hit by a meteorite. "Houston, we've had a problem here,"[44] Commander Jim Lovell radioed back to earth in one of the greatest understatements of the space program.

By the time all this was transpiring, Nixon had retired for the night. Sometime after midnight, Henry Kissinger began placing panicky calls to Bob Haldeman, imploring him to wake the president to tell him "about problems of Apollo XIII on way to moon." Haldeman refused, "on the basis there was nothing [Nixon] could do."[45]

Early Tuesday morning, Nixon was briefed on the situation. With former Apollo 11 astronaut Michael Collins, he drove over to the Goddard Space Center in Maryland to find out more. The newspapers reported that he looked "taut and tired" when he arrived.[46]

The situation was dire. Frantic efforts to abort the mission and bring the men back to Earth were under way. Later in the day, Nixon phoned the families of the astronauts with a hopeful report. Haldeman's notes registered a different tone. "Whole deal is still pretty shaky," he recorded, "but there's apparently an even chance that they'll get back."[47]

In Phnom Penh, Cambodia, the harried government of Premier Lon Nol was being enveloped by Communists forces. He finally was forced to appeal for outside help. "The Salvation Government has the duty to inform the nation that, in view of the gravity of the situation, it is deemed necessary to accept from this moment on all unconditional foreign aid, wherever it may come from, for the salvation of the nation," Lon Nol pleaded in a national broadcast.[48]

For the next three days, Nixon's attention was focused on the plight of Apollo 13. He was awash in pent-up energy and could only wait and hope and plan for any contingency. He bounced from one idea to another, finally settling on a plan to fly to Houston if the astronauts made it back. There he would pick up family members and head for Hawaii to meet with the returning spacemen.[49]

Lost in all the commotion and drama of the week was the announcement on Tuesday morning, April 14, that Harry Blackmun had been nominated by the president to take the Fortas seat on the Supreme Court.[50]

On Friday, April 17, the president and an anxious world watched on television as the parachutes of Apollo 13 opened and gently dropped the stricken command module into the South Pacific. "Apollo XIII day," Haldeman wrote in his diary. "They made it back and *P* was really elated!"[51]

Honolulu, Hawaii, April 18 to 19, 1970

On Saturday, April 18, the president flew to Houston and presented the NASA ground crew with the Medal of Freedom, the nation's highest civilian honor. He collected the families and traveled to Hawaii, where he was greeted at the Honolulu International Airport by Admiral John S. McCain, commander of the Pacific forces. Later that day, he presented the astronauts with their own Medals of Freedom.[52] It was an emotional ceremony. "Very brief," Haldeman wrote, "touching and impressive."[53]

On Sunday morning, April 19, the president met with McCain and his top commanders in the Pacific to talk about the widening crisis in Indochina. This fateful conference would turn out to have momentous consequences for the nation and the course of the war in Vietnam. Without the Apollo 13 near-disaster, the meeting would never have taken place.

McCain warned that the sanctuaries in Cambodia needed to be removed immediately, especially given the pace of American troop withdrawals. The idea of invading Cambodia had not been under active consideration before this detailed, map-laden discussion. "The military briefing by Admiral McCain illuminated the perils we faced in Cambodia and its danger for Vietnamization," Kissinger wrote. "It magnified Nixon's restlessness and helped speed up his decisions."[54] Nixon, sleep deprived and wound up over the Apollo 13 excitement, would move forward with impulsive quickness, as he did with many of his momentous presidential decisions.[55] A day after the McCain briefing, he told Haldeman that he had made up his mind to "take over responsibility for the war in Cambodia."[56] He would largely leave his cabinet out of it.

At the same time, on Monday, April 20, Nixon improbably decided to move forward with his speech on troop withdrawals. He wrote that his intent in giving the speech was to "drop a bombshell on the gathering spring storm of antiwar protest."[57] He took the opportunity to repeat his now familiar Patton theme: "America had never been defeated in the proud 190-year history of this country," he warned the North Vietnamese, "and we shall not be defeated in Vietnam."[58]

Although Nixon knew the likelihood that he would expand the war into Cambodia, his troop withdrawal speech raised false expectations that Vietnamization was working and that the US involvement was finally moving toward its terminus point.[59]

The backlash was now guaranteed to be all the more intense.

Washington, DC, April 20, 1970

Nixon flew back to Washington late on the night of Monday, April 20, after delivering his troop withdrawal speech from San Clemente on national television. He arrived back in Washington around two in the morning, yet was up the next morning at 6:00 AM. By the time an exhausted Haldeman arrived in the Oval Office at 9:00 AM, he found Nixon "cranking in full gear."[60] Nixon's daily diary from this time shows he met regularly, for short periods, with this physician, Walter Tkach, making it likely he was being administered some sort of stimulant.

Nixon clearly was suffering from insomnia. Early Wednesday, April 22, he was up at 5:00 AM dictating his thoughts on Cambodia to Kissinger. "I think we need a bold move in Cambodia, assuming that I feel the way today (it is five AM, April 22) at our meeting as I feel this morning to show that we stand with Lon Nol," he ruminated. "I do not believe he is going to survive." Nixon was especially incensed over the State Department, labeling the American delegation in Cambodia "jerks in the embassy."[61]

"Another busy day, as P roars on, in his new energy, with little sleep," Haldeman observed later that morning.[62] Nixon attended Kissinger's National Security Council meeting in the afternoon, as he suggested he would, to discuss options in Cambodia. The consensus was against the use of American forces in any ground invasion. But then Vice President Spiro Agnew spoke up. He scolded the group, saying they needed to "stop pussyfooting about the American role" in the invasion.[63]

Kissinger believed that Agnew's challenge pushed Nixon to authorize American air support for the cross-border invasion by South Vietnamese troops, and eventually to authorize the commission of American soldiers in the invasion. "I have no doubt," Kissinger wrote, "that Agnew's intervention accelerated Nixon's ultimate decision to order an attack on all the sanctuaries and use American forces."[64]

Nixon himself later wrote that he understood the domestic risks he was taking. "I never had any illusions," he wrote, "about the shattering effect a decision to go into Cambodia would have on public opinion at home."[65]

Nixon's overexcited state of mind was obvious to his closest advisors. Kissinger later recounted Nixon railing at him about a press leak concerning the provision of rifles to Lon Nol's soldiers by the United States. "He flew into a monumental rage," Kissinger wrote. "On the night of April 23 he must have called me at least ten times—three times at the house of Senator Fulbright, where I was meeting informally with members of the Senate Foreign Relations Committee. As was his habit when extremely agitated he would bark an order and immediately hang up."[66]

By week's end, Nixon came to his ultimate decision to commit US ground forces in the Cambodian invasion, but not before exhibiting more bizarre behavior. He met with Kissinger at Camp David on Saturday, April 25, but then decided to go for a cruise on the presidential yacht *Sequoia* down the Potomac. John Mitchell and Bebe Rebozo joined the two men. Kissinger wrote that during the voyage the "tensions of the grim military planning were transformed into exaltation by the liquid refreshments." The men got drunk, Kissinger remembered, "to the point of some patriot awkwardness when it was decided that everyone should stand at attention while the *Sequoia* passed Mount Vernon—a feat not managed by everybody with equal success."[67]

The group returned to the White House that evening, where Nixon insisted that they all watch *Patton*.[68] "It was the second time he had so honored me," Kissinger wrote with sarcasm. "Inspiring as the film no doubt was, I managed to escape for an hour in the middle of it to prepare for the next day's NSC meeting."[69]

On Sunday evening, April 26, the final decision was made to invade Cambodia after an emergency NSC meeting.[70] It had been exactly one week since Nixon had been briefed by Admiral McCain in Hawaii.

"We would go for broke," Nixon wrote of his decision.[71] Melvin Laird, secretary of defense, and William Rogers, secretary of state, expressed strong disagreement.[72] Many of Kissinger's top lieutenants, including Morton Halperin and Anthony Lake, resigned in protest.

After laboring over the draft of his address to the nation into the small hours of April 30 (from 1:15 AM to 5:30 AM), Nixon had breakfast at 8:50 AM and then worked twelve hours straight before briefing congressional leaders in the White House theater, just minutes before going on the air to tell the nation that the United States had invaded Cambodia.[73] According to Nixon, the leaders, including "doves" like Ted Kennedy and William Fulbright, stood and applauded as he left the room. Ironically, the briefing was carried out in the same White House theater where Nixon had spent so many hours watching *Patton*.[74]

Things were about to go haywire.

Kent State University, May 4, 1970

The night Nixon announced the Cambodian incursion, Chief Justice Warren Burger showed up at the White House to deliver a note of support. When Nixon learned that the chief justice was at the gates, he insisted that he be shown up to the Lincoln Sitting Room. "I didn't want to disturb you, Mr. President," Burger said when he arrived, "but I wanted you to know that I think your speech tonight had a sense of history and destiny about it." Burger proceeded to sit with the president until just after midnight, as he took calls in response to the announcement.[75]

The nation was stunned. Students in campuses across the country came out in mass protest. Following an early morning visit to the Pentagon the next day, on Friday, May 1, Nixon made the volatile situation much worse by off-handedly calling some of the student protestors "bums."[76]

On Saturday, May 2, the ROTC building at Kent State University in Ohio was burned to the ground in protest by students. The town's mayor asked Ohio's governor to declare an emergency and call out the National Guard. Two days later, at just past noon on Monday, May 4, the guardsmen wheeled unexpectedly on a hill and began shooting into a crowd of unarmed demonstrators. Four students, two of them young women, were killed.[77] The stricken father of one of the young women killed could only say to the press, "My child was not a bum."[78]

"When dissent turns to violence, it invites tragedy," Nixon said in a provocative statement released the day of the shootings. Vice President Agnew callously called the killings "predictable and avoidable."[79] Privately, Nixon told his chief of staff, H. R. Haldeman, that he hoped the "rioters had provoked the shooting," but Haldeman wrote that Nixon knew "there was no real evidence they did, except throwing rocks at the National Guard."[80]

The situation approached chaos on the campuses. One by one, colleges and universities shut down. Students suddenly with nothing else to do began to descend upon Washington by the tens of thousands. Nixon was under siege as masses of students assembled on the Ellipse, an open park adjoining the White House grounds.[81] Troops were stationed at government buildings around the capital, including soldiers from the Third Army (Patton's former army) in the basement of the Executive Office Building.

Tom Wicker, a *New York Times* columnist, wrote that Nixon's and Agnew's attacks on the Kent State victims "could have no other purpose, and no other result, than to set generation against generation and class against class for the calculated political purposes of the Nixon Administration."[82]

There was an overwhelming sense of drama and tension in the capital. Jittery cabinet members leaked stories to the press that they had expressed misgivings about the Cambodian operation.[83] The secretary of the interior, Walter Hickel, wrote a stinging letter to Nixon, which was released to the press. Hickel charged that Nixon was consciously alienating young people and ignoring his cabinet.

By Wednesday, May 6, the president was completely isolated and seemed unsure how to respond. "As day went on, concern from outside about campus crisis built rapidly," Haldeman wrote. "All of us had lots of calls and memos, etc. P came to grips with it this afternoon. Obviously realizes, but won't openly admit, his 'bums' remark [was] very harmful."[84]

In desperation, Nixon announced he would hold a news conference at 10:00 in the evening on Friday, May 8. (The late hour was to accommodate Game 7 of the NBA Finals, between the Knicks and Lakers.) It was a huge gamble. Visibly nervous, though apologizing for nothing, the president appeared before a hostile group of reporters. "I could feel the emotions seething beneath the hot TV lights as I entered the East Room," Nixon remembered.[85] His tone was quiet and restrained. He said he shared the objectives of the student protestors. He too wanted an end to the killing, an end to the war, and an end to the draft. The difference was that he thought his moves in Cambodia would hasten the end of the war.[86]

Nixon returned to the residence and began working the phones, still tense. "I was agitated and uneasy as the events of the last few weeks raced through my mind," he wrote.[87] After an hour of fitful sleep, he began to make phone calls, including one to a startled Helen Thomas of United Press International (UPI) at nearly 4:00 in the morning.[88] The president's valet, Manolo Sanchez, hearing loud classical music coming from the Lincoln Sitting Room, entered to find Nixon staring out the window at the Ellipse, where students were camped out for the night.

Rashly, Nixon suggested that he and Sanchez visit the Lincoln Memorial, where a smattering of students were slumbering in sleeping bags. Eight or nine students awoke around 5:00 AM to find Richard Nixon and his valet standing at the base of the Lincoln statue. Nixon engaged in a rambling, disoriented "rap" session with the astonished students. As word spread, a small crowd of about fifty formed. Almost an hour into the encounter, the president's staff and the Secret Service maneuvered him into a limousine to be taken back to the White House. [89]

But Nixon instructed his chauffeur to drive instead to the Capitol building, where the president insisted that Mr. Sanchez take the rostrum in the House chambers to give an extemporaneous speech as Nixon watched and applauded. The two men then left and went to the Mayflower Hotel to have breakfast at the Rib Room.[90]

A dazed Nixon finally arrived back at the White House, bleary-eyed, around 7:30.

"The weirdest day so far," Haldeman wrote in wonderment. "I am concerned about his condition. The decision, the speech, the aftermath killings, riots, press, etc., the press conference, the student confrontation, have all taken their toll, and he has had very little sleep for a long time and his judgment, temper and mood suffer badly as a result."[91]

New York City, May 8, 1970
On Friday, May 8, in New York City, construction workers attacked and beat antiwar protesters in the Wall Street area, "chasing youths through the canyons of the financial district in a wild noontime melee that left about 70 persons injured."[92] The hard hats then "stormed City Hall, cowing policemen and forcing officials to raise the American flag to full staff from half staff, where it had been placed in mourning for the four students killed at Kent State University on Monday."[93]

Dallas, Texas, May 22, 1970
Two weeks later, on May 22, a hearing was held in the federal district court in Dallas on a woman's right to an abortion. The case was entitled *Roe v. Wade*. No witnesses would appear; no experts were called. Instead, the case was taken under advisement by a three-judge panel after just two hours of oral argument by the lawyers. [94]

The hearing in Dallas took place exactly ten days after Harry Blackmun was unanimously confirmed by the Senate.[95]

The scene was set for January 1973.

1

"We've Got to Still Shoot Some Sparks"

The Oval Office, January 1, 1973

Richard Nixon welcomed the New Year in quiet solitude. He arose early and made his way to the Oval Office, arriving shortly after 7:30 AM, surprising the security guards who had to scramble to find keys to open the office for the president. First Lady Pat Nixon was in Pasadena, California, the guest of honor in the eighty-fourth Tournament of Roses Parade, which was scheduled to begin later that morning. Nixon was by himself in the White House. He scribbled notes about his second term on one of his ubiquitous lawyers' yellow pads and dictated some personal letters for his secretary, Rose Mary Woods, to transcribe whenever she finally made it to her office on that holiday morning.

Nixon had rare time to reflect. As he looked out over the next four years, his immediate focus was to put an end to America's involvement in the war in Vietnam, something he promised to do in the 1968 campaign. Time was running out on his first term and his ability to keep that pledge. He desperately wanted a peace agreement before his inauguration on January 20.

He knew that he was at the end of the rope with Congress—he had tested its limits in December with his bombing campaign in North Vietnam, and he was alert to the fact that the new Congress set to convene later in the week was likely to vote to cut off further funding for the war.

The ex-presidents club, such as it was, had decreased to one with the passing of Harry S. Truman, the nation's thirty-third president, the day after Christmas in Independence, Missouri.[1] The only living ex-president, Lyndon Baines Johnson, was seen popping nitroglyc-erin capsules to relieve acute angina at a civil rights symposium he had hosted in Austin in the middle of December, but Johnson had survived several previous heart scares, and he was only sixty-four years old.

Despite the fact that Nixon was trying to dismantle many of the reforms of the Great Society, he needed Johnson's support in his han-dling of the war, and he intended to respect LBJ's legacy with an end to the war that was something more than an abrupt pullout. "Peace with honor," Nixon called his plan. Johnson and Nixon had developed a peculiar relationship, at times bordering on friendship.

As 1973 dawned, the domestic calm that prevailed was a thin veneer. The stock market was reaching new highs, but within a year, after another devastating Middle East war and an oil embargo, the economy would be in real trouble. The cutoff of oil would touch off both a severe recession and trigger high inflation—"stagflation"—a vexing condition that would persist well into the 1980s. For this and other reasons, the stock market would start a long downward spiral after reaching its high in January 1973.[2]

Under the surface ominous forces were churning. The trial of the Watergate burglars was scheduled to begin in the second week of January, casting a menacing shadow that Nixon could not ignore. He was bedeviled by this scandal—this "third-rate burglary"—that simply would not go away, even in the face of his landslide victory in November.

By January 1974, only one year later, Judge John J. Sirica would be on the cover of *Time* as the "Man of the Year," and Richard Nixon would be scrambling to explain an eighteen-and-a-half-minute gap in a White House tape recorded several days after the break-in.[3] By then, Nixon's presidency would be in a death spiral.

All of that seemed unfathomable as January 1, 1973, began. Most of the president's advisors were out of town, still on holiday vacations, enjoying the fruits of their hard work in the 1972 reelection campaign. Everyone assumed that the worst was behind them and that the sec-ond term would be less tempestuous than the first.

★   ★   ★

Steve Bull, the president's thirty-one-year-old aide, was in the West Wing when he heard the buzzer in Rose Mary Woods's office going off, indicating a call from the president. Bull responded, telling the president that Woods had not yet arrived; he asked if there was anything he could do, as nobody else seemed to be around.

Nixon replied that only Woods could help with his personal letters. But he told Bull to be on the lookout for Washington Redskins quarterback Billy Kilmer and Coach George Allen and his family, whom Nixon had invited to come to the White House later that morning.

The day before, the Redskins had surprised Tom Landry's Dallas Cowboys, winning 26–3 in a sensational NFC Championship Game, propelling the Redskins to a berth in Super Bowl VII.[4] They would face the AFC champion Miami Dolphins, who were undefeated.[5]

Bull told the president that he had attended the Redskins game and the two then compared notes on the gutsy performance of their home team, which had shut down the defending Super Bowl champion Cowboys, led by quarterback Roger Staubach. Nixon was a huge football fan and had spent big chunks of his weekends in December by himself watching the NFL playoff games at Camp David, Maryland (in part because the NFL at the time blacked out all home games, whether or not they were sellouts).[6]

Soft-spoken and deferential, Steve Bull coordinated the president's schedule and appointments. Bull had lost his father when he was thirteen years old, and he came to see Nixon as something of a father figure. Though Bull was from a well-off New York family, he enlisted and served in Vietnam as a second lieutenant in the marines and later found work as an executive with the Canada Dry Corporation. He signed up to be an advance man for the Nixon campaign in 1968. Impressed with Bull's skills, Nixon's chief of staff, Bob Haldeman, asked Bull to stay on after the campaign. Bull rose in responsibilities as others left the administration. A Marlboro chain-smoker with a stylish razor haircut and fashionably long sideburns, Bull had regular access to Nixon, coming and going ten to twenty times a day for brief scheduling discussions.[7]

On that morning, Bull politely reminded Nixon that he had to make a decision about whether he would attend Harry Truman's memorial service at the National Cathedral, planned for the end of the week on Friday, January 5.[8]

Nixon groaned. "Can we get out of it?" he asked.

"It appears it would be rather difficult," Bull quietly responded.

Nixon and Truman had never been on good terms. Truman thought Nixon was a congenital liar, and Nixon resented Truman's attacks on him during the Alger Hiss investigation when Nixon was a congressman.[9] But Nixon's uneasiness about the Truman memorial was driven less by his poor relationship with Truman than by his total disdain for the man who was scheduled to deliver Truman's eulogy: Francis B. Sayre, the dean of the National Cathedral.

"He's such an ass; he's been an ass for years," Nixon seethed about Sayre to Bull.

Bull responded that Sayre had been seen "wandering around with his marchers [there] on Saturday."[10] Francis Sayre was one of the foremost opponents of the war in Vietnam. On Saturday, December 30, Sayre had led a peaceful walk to the White House in protest against the Christmas bombing of North Vietnam.[11]

Sayre was no stranger to the White House, and not just because he would occasionally show up to protest. Francis Sayre had been born in the White House fifty-eight years earlier, in January 1915. He was Woodrow Wilson's first grandchild, the son of Jessie Woodrow Wilson, the president's second daughter.

"President Wilson made no effort to conceal his joy when informed that the child was a boy and that Mrs. Sayre was well," the papers reported on the occasion of Sayre's birth. "His face was wreathed in smiles for hours afterward," the press wrote of the proud grandfather. Wilson had three daughters, and reports were that the child might be named for his grandfather, but Wilson vetoed the idea and the baby was named for his father, Francis.[12]

Sayre's antiwar sentiment was inextricably linked with the civil rights movement of the 1960s. He had marched with Martin Luther King Jr. in Selma in 1965, and it was Sayre who invited King to preach a sermon at the Washington National Cathedral on Sunday, March 31, 1968.[13]

King's appearance with Sayre in March 1968 was in response to concerns that his Poor People's Campaign, scheduled to descend upon the capital later that spring, might turn violent. Just a week before in Memphis, at a massive rally that King helped to organize in support of striking sanitation workers, chaos had erupted and one young man had been shot and killed by police. King promised those who came to hear him at the National Cathedral that his marchers would not "tear up" Washington.[14]

By this time, though, King was as concerned with the Vietnam War as he was with civil rights. In this, his last Sunday sermon, entitled "Remaining Awake Through a Great Revolution," he denounced the war. "I want to say," King said with Sayre sitting nearby, "one other challenge that we face is simply that we must find an alternative to war and bloodshed." To ignore this reality was to be untrue to the movement. "Anyone who feels, and there are still a lot of people who feel that way, that war can solve the social problems facing mankind is sleeping through a great revolution."

King had become convinced, he said, that the Vietnam War was "one of the most unjust wars that has ever been fought in the history of the world." The war, he said, wreaked havoc with the country's domestic agenda, sucking up precious national resources, and it "put us in the position of appearing to the world as an arrogant nation."

"The judgment of God is upon us today," he thundered at the climax of his talk. "It is either nonviolence or nonexistence."[15]

Four days later he was dead.

King's stance on the war put him at odds with President Johnson, who had done so much for the movement with the passage of the Civil Rights Act of 1964, the Voting Rights Act of 1965, and the Fair Housing Act of 1968. But the war was destroying Johnson's Great Society reforms and his war on poverty. "This day," King said on March 31, "we are spending five hundred thousand dollars to kill every Vietcong soldier. Every time we kill one we spend about five hundred thousand dollars while we spend only fifty-three dollars a year for every person characterized as poverty-stricken in the so-called poverty program, which is not even a good skirmish against poverty." There simply was not enough money to pay for the war and the Great Society programs. And minorities, King knew, were dying in disproportionate numbers in Vietnam.

Johnson felt the sting. On the very evening that King spoke at the National Cathedral, he appeared on national television to speak to the country about his hopes for peace in Vietnam, but then, citing "division in the American house," announced that he would not run for reelection in 1968. "I shall not seek," Johnson said, "and I will not accept the nomination of my party as your president."[16]

Johnson's abrupt exit from the race opened the door to the White House for Richard Nixon. In 1968 Alabama governor George Wallace split the South and the Democratic Party, taking votes that in another year would have gone to the Democratic candidate. (Wallace received 13 percent of the vote.) As it was, Nixon barely won in a three-way race between himself, Wallace, and Johnson's vice president, Hubert Humphrey.

President Johnson and Dr. Martin Luther King Jr. in Cabinet Room, White House, March 18, 1966.
LBJ Library photo by Yoichi Okamoto

In 1972 things were very different. Nixon ran away with the election. But the election result was mixed, explaining in part Nixon's sour attitude about Dean Francis Sayre and his other perceived enemies on the morning of January 1, 1973.

Executive Office Building, November 7, 1972

Nixon's contrary reaction to his stunning landslide began on election night. Henry Kissinger observed it; he wrote that Nixon had been "seized by a withdrawn and sullen hostility that had dominated his mood since his electoral triumph." Kissinger thought it was a "strange mood," given the scale of Nixon's victory over Senator George McGovern. But there was no question that Richard Nixon seemed depressed and angry after his reelection.[17]

His election night address to the nation on television on November 7, 1972, was subdued. "The greatest landslide in history means nothing unless it is a victory for all America," he said, his upper lip showing the heavy perspiration he could never quite control or conceal, even with the best powder applied by his personal makeup consultant, Ray Voege. There was another reason Nixon looked grim on TV. That evening he had lost a cap on one of his front teeth while eating dinner that had to be replaced with a temporary cap. Nixon remembered that he was in considerable pain as a result and worried that if he smiled too broadly during the broadcast the cap might fall off. He wondered later if that tooth pain could account for the unusual "melancholy that settled over [him] on that victorious night."[18]

Privately, he was furious with what he believed were disrespectful remarks made by George McGovern in his concession speech. "We shed no tears," McGovern told an emotional group of his supporters at his headquarters in Sioux Falls, South Dakota, "because all this effort I am positive will bear fruit.

"There can be no question at all," he contended against the seeming facts, "that we have pushed this country in the direction of peace."[19]

To Nixon, McGovern was jutting out his jaw, acting defiantly despite having just lost the election by near historic proportions. "This fellow to the last was a prick," Nixon complained to Henry Kissinger on the phone shortly after McGovern's speech. Nixon said he was having trouble coming up with anything polite to say in a telegram that tradition required him to send to his defeated opponent. Kissinger, at his toadying best, responded that McGovern had been "ungenerous, petulant, unworthy."[20]

The election had been called by the networks at around 7:00 in the evening, but McGovern held out until almost midnight before formally conceding. Nixon was peeved.

After McGovern's concession, Nixon was driven from the White House to the Shoreham Hotel to deliver his victory speech. The five thousand supporters who had gathered at the hotel were taken aback by Nixon's abruptness. He was in and out. He shook few hands and fought through the boisterous crowd to make a curt ten-minute speech. Shortly after he returned to the White House, he returned the call of Nelson Rockefeller, governor of New York, and he was still smoldering about McGovern. "Did you ever see such an irresponsible campaign as this clown put on?" he asked.[21]

Nixon met with Bob Haldeman in his hideaway office in the Executive Office Building (EOB) that night to review the national election results. The two men summoned Chuck Colson, special counsel to the president, to come sit with them to analyze the strange returns that were beginning to emerge from around the country. Nixon had scored a landslide, that was for sure, but his party had been largely rebuffed in the congressional elections. During his entire first term, both houses of Congress had been Democratic. Now the Senate had added two Democrats (one being Joe Biden) and the House remained firmly in Democratic control. Nixon knew this meant trouble for his second term, despite his personal mandate.

On what should have been the greatest night of Richard Nixon's life, Chuck Colson recalled that the atmosphere in the EOB felt strangely funereal.[22] Nixon, through his valet Manolo Sanchez, ordered up from the White House mess plates of fried eggs, bacon, and toast for the three men as a sort of celebratory meal sometime before he retired to the White House residence at 3:00 AM.[23]

Nixon tried to find some positives. When talking with Governor Rockefeller, he confidently predicted that the end to the war in Vietnam was near. McGovern, he said, had been all wrong when he charged that in the waning days of the campaign the administration had played politics with the war, that peace negotiations had been a charade. In fact, Nixon revealed, Henry Kissinger had received a wire from the North Vietnamese just three days before the election advising that Hanoi was ready to return to the negotiating table, without conditions, in one week.

"It's all done," Nixon triumphantly reported to Rockefeller, and later to Hubert Humphrey.[24] He said he had deliberately held the news in his back pocket. "We never said it, see."

The problem was that it wasn't all done. Henry Kissinger had announced prematurely on October 26 that "peace is at hand," when in fact the United States was having trouble with both North and South Vietnam, for different reasons. In reality, Nixon and Kissinger were fighting for peace on three fronts: the South Vietnamese wanted to scuttle any peace that left North Vietnamese troops in the South, the so-called "cease-fire in place" concept; the North Vietnamese wanted a peace agreement that allowed them to control the formation of a coalition government in the South, with President Thieu jettisoned; and Congress wanted the United States out of Vietnam at almost any price.

Hanoi and Washington had all but reached fundamental agreement on terms in early October, but Saigon became the impediment. On the evening of October 25, the frustrated North Vietnamese publicly announced that an agreement had been hammered out with the Americans, and it was supposed to be signed by the end of October. The United States, they charged, was dragging its feet.[25]

Kissinger felt the need to respond.[26] His "peace is at hand" comment during a press conference the next day was meant to reassure Hanoi that the United States was not reneging on its promises, while allowing Saigon an opportunity to negotiate face-saving changes.[27] The comment backfired, raising false expectations that an announcement was imminent. By this time, Nixon had determined that he did not want any news out of Vietnam, pro or con, because his lead in the polls had become overwhelming. He wanted Kissinger to stop talking about the peace negotiations until after the election, when he believed he would have a window to address negotiations without congressional interference or concerns about electoral impact.[28]

The mixed election results made things highly complicated. When the new Congress convened in January 1973, the Democrats would hold a significant majority in the Senate—fifty-six seats against forty-two for the Republicans in the Senate, with one Independent.[29] In the House, Republicans picked up twelve additional seats, "far short of the 41 it needed for control," the *Times* wrote. Nixon's win was "an empty landslide."[30]

Given the massive split-ticket voting, Nixon recognized that his victory was more a reflection of disagreement with McGovern and his "bug out" peace strategy than a decisive vote of confidence for him. And the election results shifted momentum in negotiations to the North Vietnamese. Nixon miscalculated that he would have more leverage to negotiate peace *after* the election than before. He was wrong.

He would have been better off forcing the settlement before the election.

The Roosevelt Room, November 8, 1972

Despite retiring after 3:00 in the morning, Nixon was up and in the Oval Office at 8:00 AM. One of his first calls was to Harry Dent, another of his White House Special Counsel. Nixon was trying to sort out what had just happened. He also was looking for scapegoats.

Harry Dent started in politics as a top political aide to Senator Strom Thurmond of South Carolina, a states-rights Democrat who had bolted to the Republicans in 1964.[31] Dent was a lawyer by training and a lay preacher. (He was instrumental in establishing a prayer group in the Senate.) He also became one of the key architects of Nixon's "Southern Strategy." It was Dent who had urged Senator Thurmond to leave the Democratic Party after the civil rights laws were passed under Johnson in 1964. Thurmond supported Goldwater for president and joined the Republican Party, helping to start the great realignment of the "solid" Democratic South.[32]

Dent supported Nixon in the 1968 primaries when he pledged to appoint "strict constructionists" to the Supreme Court, a code for moving cautiously with desegregation and reversing public school forced busing. For his efforts, Dent was welcomed into the Nixon White House as an important advisor.[33] Though Dent had announced he was leaving to return to his law practice at the end of 1972, Nixon wanted to know from him why the congressional elections had gone so badly for the Republicans.

Nixon thought the national Republican Party, run by Kansan Bob Dole, had been a disaster. "But I just can't understand," Nixon said to Dent on the morning of November 8. "Isn't it really necessary to build a new party, I mean just to be quite candid."[34]

"Yes sir," Dent replied.

"The word 'Republican' is an anathema in the South, isn't it?" Nixon asked.

"No question," Dent replied.

Nixon spent considerable time following the election contemplating a new party, which included Southerners, the working class, labor union families, Catholics, and others who had never before voted Republican. He talked with John Connelly—his favorite to succeed him in 1976—about creating a new Republican Independent Party.

Nixon commented on how the "assholes" in the liberal press were already misinterpreting what had just happened in the election. He told Dent that he had privately lectured reporters, off the record, on the five-hour plane flight across the country on the day of the election. (He had started the day in California, where he and the First Lady voted, before flying back Washington.)

Nixon said he had told the captive reporters, "You guys are now blaming McGovern's *tactics* for losing this." But that was simply not true, he said. "His tactics didn't lose it; his *issues* lost it."

"That's right," Dent agreed.

"He lost the election the day of the nomination," Nixon said. "I mean Eagleton hurt him and things like that, but I said, 'you want to remember, he stood for busing, he stood for amnesty, he stood for acid, he stood for bigger welfare, and all of you [in the press] stood for that.'" Dent could not have agreed more.[35]

In this one sentence, Nixon had deftly captured the meaning of the 1972 election. McGovern had lost because he stood for *busing, amnesty, acid, and welfare.* These were the wedge issues, the reasons the country was dividing into two nations. A strong counterrevolution was under way, one based on fear and anger—anger over forced desegregation, busing, and Supreme Court activism; rage over draft dodging and the antiwar movement; fear of the drug culture and crime; and fury over the "freeloaders" in society who took the money of hardworking Americans.

And in the South especially, which had been the bedrock of the Democratic Party, these perceived attacks on the traditional way of life were quickly becoming the cause of a massive shift away from the Democratic Party—Strom Thurmond was the prophet in this tidal change. Though Nixon was correct that the Republican Party was still anathema in the South—and there indeed may have been a need for a new party—things were undeniably shifting.

In Nixon's mind, all of these threads—busing, amnesty, acid, and welfare—were wrapped around one overriding issue: *patriotism,* the defense of America and its values.

"Now, I said, 'take the South,'" Nixon continued with Dent, recalling his talk with the reporters aboard the *Spirit of '76,* the name he gave Air Force One in anticipation of the nation's bicentennial. "'You are going to try to write this as if this is a question of race.' I said: 'Hell, it's not a question of race, it's a question of *patriotism.* It's a question of moral values.'"[36]

All of this contributed to Nixon's already dark mood on the day after the election. It is difficult to fully account for his descent into seclusion after such a stunning victory, but one theory advanced by Henry Kissinger was that he had reached the ambition of his life and that "standing on the pinnacle, Nixon no longer had any purpose left to his life."[37]

His life always had been about the fight, hurtling from one crisis to another. Nixon's first book, written in 1962, bore witness to his predilection for catastrophe in its title: *Six Crises.*[38] Kissinger wrote that Nixon almost "craved disasters."[39]

Nixon's gnawing concern right after the election was that he needed to avoid a mediocre second term. He knew from history that second terms could be lackluster at best, scandal-ridden at worst. He had been carefully studying Robert Blake's nearly 845-page biography of Benjamin Disraeli, the Conservative British prime minister and author.[40] Disraeli observed in one of his speeches that the frenzied activities of a first term often leave government officials drained, without resolution or drive—burned out. Disraeli, according to Blake, was reminded of how he once spoke of governments being like "marine landscapes not very uncommon on the coasts of South America. You behold a range of exhausted volcanoes."

Nixon did not want his second term to be populated with "exhausted volcanoes."[41]

Thus, the morning after the election, twenty minutes after wrapping up his call with Harry Dent, Nixon met with his White House officials in the Roosevelt Room, the conference room just off the Oval Office. He told the story about Disraeli and exhausted volcanoes, and then left the room, leaving it to Haldeman to ask for everyone's resignation.

Haldeman recorded the gist of the encounter: "Then he went into his Disraeli story about the exhausted volcano," Haldeman wrote. "He said that it didn't apply to individuals, but it does apply to the entity, and that it's the responsibility of the leader to be sure we don't fall into that situation. We can't climb to the top and look down into the embers, we've got to still shoot some sparks, vitality, and strength, and that we get some of that from new people, both in the Cabinet and here in the staff."[42]

Haldeman followed the president's somber message by distributing mimeographed forms to everyone so they could list the documents in their possession as part of the resignation process.[43]

Henry Kissinger called the experience "wounding and humiliating." The president's audience was dumbfounded. The very people who had just worked so hard on his reelection campaign were being unceremoniously shoved out the door. "Victory seemed to have released a pent-up hostility so overwhelming that it would not wait even a week to surface; it engulfed colleagues and associates as well as opponents," Kissinger wrote.[44]

One of the people in the Roosevelt Room that day was John W. Dean, the White House Counsel. He was one of the few given advance word of the impending request for mass resignations. Haldeman assured him not to worry. The administration needed Dean to hold things together as the Watergate cover-up entered a critical stage, with the trial of the burglars scheduled to begin in January 1973.

November 8, 1972, the morning after the landslide reelection, in the Roosevelt Room with Ron Ziegler, Bob Haldeman, Henry Kissinger, Rose Mary Woods, John Dean, Charles Colson, Herb Stein, and other White House staff.

White House Photo Office, Nixon Library

Oval Office, January 1, 1973

Steve Bull left the Oval Office and Nixon returned to the dictation of his letters. "Dear Tom," he started his consolation note to Coach Tom Landry of the Cowboys. "As one who always pulls for the home team, [long pause] I was, ah, naturally rooting for the Redskins on Sunday. Period. Paragraph."

His chair squeaked as he leaned back, gripping the mike to the Dictaphone, which was attached by a twisting coil to the recording machine sitting on a small table next to his desk. "As a football fan, however, I want you to know that [long pause] the whole nation has enormous respect for you and the Dallas Cowboys. Period."

He reflected for a moment. "Ah, you were great when you were the champions last year, and you acted like champions when you had to absorb what I know was a bitter defeat"; then he corrected himself, "a tough loss this year." He commented on the marvel of defensive tackle Bob Lilly's performance, playing through serious injuries, and then brought his note to its conclusion: "The dignity and poise which you and all of the Cowboys demonstrated [pause] throughout the game [long pause] were in the best traditions [pause] of competitive athletics in America. Period. Sincerely."

It took him almost five minutes to dictate this short letter.[45]

Having attended to his correspondence, the president called Bull back in and asked him to locate Chuck Colson. Colson showed up minutes later, chipper as usual on that holiday morning. The conversation was about to turn conspiratorial, something both men enjoyed tremendously.

Colson had news to dish on Henry Kissinger.

2

"You Have Shown You Are Not Someone to Be Trifled With"

The White House, Mid-Morning, January 1, 1973

"So I see you survived," Nixon said to Chuck Colson as he entered the Oval Office. As usual, Nixon started with chitchat about football. Colson, who had been told by Nixon the night before that Coach George Allen had been invited to the White House, wondered if the coach, who was due to show up any minute, might not arrive a little hungover from the postgame celebrations.

"Oh, he doesn't drink," Nixon said.[1]

"Oh, is that right?" Colson responded. "I didn't know that."

"Well, he said he was going to buy a bottle of champagne, but he never takes part," Nixon continued. "He's the all-American square."

"Yeah, he really is," Colson instantly agreed.

Nixon said that his press aide, Diane Sawyer, pointed out in a morning press briefing left on his desk that the Washington media finally would have to recognize George Allen for his coaching talents; after all, his team had defeated both the Green Bay Packers and the Dallas Cowboys to advance to the Super Bowl.[2]

"It was an Allen victory," Nixon said, "a victory, as he put it last night, for square Americans and for the square types."

"Right," Colson replied.

"Not that [quarterback Billy] Kilmer is a square—he's a hell of a swinger"; Nixon quickly corrected himself, "but on the other hand, he doesn't wear his hair long, you know."

"He looks neat," Colson completed the thought.

"He's basically a UCLA type from the fifties. He's tough, strong."[3] Kilmer was drafted out of UCLA in 1961 by San Francisco. After a few years with the expansion New Orleans Saints, he was traded to the Redskins in 1971. (The Saints drafted Archie Manning to replace him.) Kilmer was known to be a fierce partier; he had a habit of falling asleep at the wheel and ditching his car into a body of water.

Not surprisingly, Kilmer would not make it to the White House on this morning.

The football preliminaries completed, the two men got down to the matter about which Colson had been called to report. Nixon had asked Colson the night before to find out if Henry Kissinger had been unfaithful with the press. Nixon wanted to know if Kissinger was behind a story that had appeared in the *New York Times* over the weekend implying that Kissinger had privately—and vigorously—opposed the Christmas bombing of North Vietnam.

Colson was the perfect guy to do a little investigating. He had no compunction about acting as the White House snitch. It would not be the first or last time Nixon would ask for intelligence on Kissinger. They had a history.

November 1972

Richard Nixon and Henry Kissinger had a codependent relationship that churned with tremendous backwater turbulence. Nixon resented the fact that the press saw Kissinger as a darling of the administration; Kissinger knew the media loved him. Worse from Nixon's standpoint, Kissinger hobnobbed with the reviled Georgetown set—he was too cozy with the intellectuals and socialites Nixon despised.

Yet Nixon needed the former Harvard professor. Though he spoke often of firing him for disloyalty or insubordination, he recognized Kissinger had geopolitical instincts that matched his own and that no one else in his administration had the breadth of vision that Kissinger possessed when it came to understanding the intricate balance of powers around the world and the international landscape that daily shifted under their feet.

Kissinger could be highly emotional—he was, Nixon knew, subject to wide swings in his moods. Surprisingly, there were times when it was Nixon who provided stability in the relationship, though the president was subject to his own sizable share of bouts of anger and rage.

But more than anything else, Nixon, with his petty jealousies and his genuine concern about Kissinger's insatiable need for media attention, worried about Kissinger courting the press. Nixon understood that Kissinger regularly painted himself as *the* rational actor in a White House dominated by an unbalanced president. Nixon was partly to blame. At times he encouraged Kissinger to portray him as a madman president, capable of almost anything. This theme, though, spilled over into Kissinger's dealings with the press and at Washington cocktail parties. Kissinger told people he was the check, Nixon the loose cannon.

As a consequence, Nixon absolutely forbade Kissinger from speaking with certain journalists whom Nixon considered hostile or untrustworthy. And Kissinger repeatedly violated the ban.

He had done so in dramatic fashion just after the election, as he was preparing to return to Paris in mid-November to try to conclude the peace negotiations. The day he was to fly out, a profile of Kissinger appeared in an Italian magazine (and the next day in American newspapers) written by an Italian attack journalist named Oriana Fallaci. With Kissinger's permission, Fallaci, who was known for her confrontational journalism, had shadowed him just before the election—and what she ended up writing was anything but flattering. Kissinger came off as preening and self-important. "I paid a price for my naïveté," Kissinger wrote. The interview was "the single most disastrous conversation I have ever had with any member of the press."[4]

In one of their exchanges, Kissinger seemed to casually agree with Fallaci that the Vietnam War was a "useless war." If that weren't enough, he supposedly said that he always acted alone in his diplomacy and that Americans found that appealing. "Americans like the cowboy who leads the wagon train by riding ahead on his horse, the cowboy who rides all alone into the town, with his horse and nothing else," he said. "This amazing, romantic character suits me precisely because to be alone has always been a part of my style or, if you like, my technique."[5]

Kissinger later told Haldeman that he had been joking but that Fallaci had written as if he were serious.[6] Joke or not, the gist of Kissinger's remark about being a lone ranger was not lost on Nixon.

Haldeman caught hell the next day. At home on Sunday, on a rare day off with his family, his phone would not stop ringing.[7] "P had some very strong reactions [about the Kissinger article]. He obviously is extremely displeased by it, in particular all the stuff Henry kept coming up with." In an unguarded moment, the president instructed Haldeman to tell Kissinger that he had recorded all of their conversations. "He later in the day told me I should let Henry know that obviously the EOB [Executive Office Building] and the Oval Office and Lincoln Room have all been recorded for protection, so the P has a complete record of all of [their] conversations."[8]

Nixon was concerned that Kissinger was planning to rewrite history and portray himself as the hero, the craftsman of all the important foreign policy decisions of the Nixon years. "He made the point [in the past] to Henry that he doesn't make the decisions," Haldeman wrote, "and when they are made, that he wavers the most." Nixon told Haldeman to tell Kissinger that he had already "written the total China story for his own file."[9]

Given the secrecy that Nixon insisted upon in connection with the White House taping system, it is revealing, but still surprising, that he would risk acknowledging its existence just to threaten Kissinger about his future writing of history. It is unlikely that Haldeman relayed to Kissinger that the taping system existed. Haldeman had an uncanny sense of knowing when to ignore some of Nixon's more impulsive orders, especially when he thought that the president would later regret them.

In the days following publication of the Fallaci article, Nixon continued to pester Haldeman. He ordered him to retrieve from Kissinger's office all of his memoranda to and from the president and to "get them into the P's files, especially all of his handwritten stuff, originals, physically move it into the P's files now."[10]

Thus, as Kissinger was entangled in some of the most delicate and intense negotiations with the North Vietnamese in the Paris talks, his boss was obsessing over who should get the credit and wantonly raiding his subordinate's files. It was one of the more telling episodes in the Nixon/Kissinger relationship.

More important for history, the Fallaci fiasco elevated a player who had been a junior actor—an important one to be sure, but subordinate in the broad scheme of things. Al Haig, an army general from West Point whom Kissinger brought onto his staff to assist with military matters, was singled out by Nixon to become his own personal mole within the Kissinger camp. After the Fallaci article, Nixon instructed Haldeman to set up a social engagement with Haig and his wife "as cover" so that he could have a frank talk with Haig about Kissinger.[11] From then on, Haig would report directly to Nixon about Kissinger's comings and goings—and about Kissinger's emotional and mental state. Early on, Haig observed that he thought Kissinger was paranoid, that he went through severe up and down cycles, and that as soon as negotiations were completed, he needed to have a serious psychiatric evaluation, or at least a very long vacation.[12] "In some ways, it's worse than you think it is," Haig told Haldeman.[13]

Kissinger was isolated and in bad grace with the president as he entered the critical stage of negotiations with the North Vietnamese. Nixon refused to see him before he left for Paris. "And as Nixon and I headed into the turbulent waters of a new negotiation," Kissinger remembered, "a steady course was not aided by the latent disaffection between the helmsman and his principal navigator."[14]

The rift between the two men was a harbinger of problems to come.

With Kissinger in Paris in mid-November, Nixon became somewhat of a recluse. The day following the election, he headed for Key Biscayne to get away from Washington and to enjoy the sun and water with his friend Bebe Rebozo. He then spent most of November secluded at Camp David, returning to the White House for short visits. While at Camp David, he enjoyed short swims in the heated outdoor pool, strolled the grounds, watched scores of movies and college and pro football games, and spent hours chattering on the phone. He, Haldeman, and Ehrlichman worked on his reorganization plans and hired and fired for the second term.

Nixon got out little. The public rarely saw him. He took his family to New York City for the Thanksgiving holiday, but they avoided people, staying at the presidential suite at the Waldorf-Astoria, privately dining at Trader Vic's at the Plaza Hotel, and taking in a performance of *Much Ado About Nothing* at the Winter Garden Theater on Broadway. While in New York, Nixon and his family were driven around Midtown, where he would occasionally instruct the driver to stop the presidential limousine to allow his wife and daughters to jump out and conduct some high-speed window-shopping for Christmas.[15]

During this trip, Nixon also met with John Mitchell at their old Wall Street law firm, Mudge, Rose, Guthrie and Alexander. The topic of Watergate and the secret cash being paid to the burglars to assure their continuing silence likely came up, though Nixon and Mitchell had become somewhat expert in studiously avoiding direct discussions of Watergate.

Mitchell had only recently been forced to become more deeply involved in arranging for more money to be paid to the burglars, who had grown restless as the trial before Judge Sirica was on the immediate horizon.

While holed up at Camp David, the president held a series of time-consuming interviews with members of his cabinet and other top administration officials to deal with resignations or offer new positions. Hating as he did any direct personal confrontation, Nixon developed an etiquette with Bob Haldeman. Haldeman would meet with the official first, soften him up, praise him for his service, and if a resignation was desired, instruct the official to "be a big man" and ask the president to do him the favor of releasing him from further duty. The official in question would then be shown in to see the president and would compliantly ask for his resignation to be accepted. Following the script, Nixon would agree, with great reluctance.[16]

In this fashion, Nixon moved Richard Helms out of the CIA, offering him the ambassadorship to Iran. Bob Dole was removed as chair of the Republican Party, replaced by George H. W. Bush. Nixon's secretary of state, William Rogers, was told he would have to resign, but Rogers insisted on staying for some decent period of time after the second inauguration so that it would not look as if he were being pushed aside by Henry Kissinger (with whom he had major differences during the first administration).

Few balked at the treatment, although Donald Rumsfeld double-crossed Haldeman. After agreeing with Haldeman to be a "big man" and step aside as the counselor to the president, he told Nixon he would not go when he was shown in to see him. "Typical Rumsfeld," Haldeman wrote in his diary, "rather slimy maneuver."[17]

The Oval Office, December 14, 1972

Kissinger's negotiations in Paris in November were a catastrophe. After five fruitless days, he was instructed to return to the United States, threatening the North Vietnamese with the resumption of unspecified military activities if they continued to stall in negotiations. He was sent back to Paris on December 4 for a second round, a last stab at resolution, but the North Vietnamese were going backward, withdrawing points that had been agreed upon and playing what Kissinger called a "cat and mouse game."[18]

Meanwhile, Haig had been dispatched to South Vietnam to convince President Thieu to accept whatever terms the United States could negotiate. In return, Thieu was given an ironclad promise from Nixon that, if he agreed to the settlement, the United States would respond with "swift and severe retaliatory action" should the North Vietnamese violate the terms of any final agreement.[19]

That critical promise subsequently would evaporate because of Watergate and Nixon's removal from office.

Kissinger returned from his second round of talks in Paris on the night of December 13, dejected and demoralized. As Kissinger was flying back in a windowless air force supply plane, Haig warned Nixon that Kissinger was in a particularly low frame of mind.

"I think we ought to send Henry away, frankly, for a rest, and get him the hell away from the press and everybody else," Haig said in a phone call to Nixon.[20]

"Oh, I couldn't agree more," Nixon said. "Where do you want to send him?"

"I think he goes to Mexico or any place else where it's hard to get on the telephone," Haig responded.

The next morning, Thursday, December 14, Nixon met with Haig and Kissinger in the Oval Office in one of the most important

(From left: Nixon, Haig, Kissinger) President Nixon meeting in Oval Office with Henry Kissinger and Major General Alexander Haig Jr., just after Kissinger returned from Paris, December 14, 1972. This is the meeting where the three men decided to bomb North Vietnam.

White House Photo Office, Nixon Library

conferences of his presidency. Nixon started the conversation by con-
soling an obviously despondent Kissinger. "You have no goddamn
reason to be discouraged about it," he said. "We are dealing here with
maniacs on both sides, to use your term."[21]

Kissinger, who had been up all night, described for Nixon the
"roller coaster" he had been on with Le Duc Tho, the lead negotiator
for Hanoi. His conclusion was that Le Duc Tho wanted to maintain
the appearance of negotiating while at the same time keeping a final
settlement just out of reach. He said he had good days and bad days,
but in the end, when it looked as if everything was about to be settled,
the North Vietnamese would change a translation or revoke a term
that had been agreed to the day before. They were trying to apply
pressure, he said, to cause the ultimate break between the United
States and Thieu, which would undermine Thieu's position and result
in his downfall.

But at the same time, Kissinger said, the North Vietnamese were
"terrified of what we [would] do."

Kissinger was in a strange and agitated state. "They're shits," he
said of the North Vietnamese. "They are tawdry, miserable, filthy
people." Their negotiating style, he bitterly quipped, "made the Rus-
sians look good."[22]

Nixon knew what was causing the problem. With Congress set
to reconvene in January 1973, the North Vietnamese strategy was
to string things along, hoping for the best possible settlement terms,
even perhaps the unilateral abandonment of South Vietnam by the
United States. "This is what those bastards know," Nixon said. "They
think the Congress will say 'To hell with the war.'"[23]

Nixon even wondered aloud whether "the left wing in this country" had secretly communicated with the North Vietnamese, advising
them to wait and hang tight for Congress in order "to screw those bastards" in the White House. He ventured that "our friends in the press"
likewise were pulling for a stalemate because they simply could not
bear the idea that he, Richard Nixon, could end the war with honor.

Faced with these odds, Nixon nevertheless thought that the war
could be ended in a way that avoided a "bug out." "We still have
chips," Nixon—the once expert poker player—said to Kissinger and
Haig. "They aren't many, but we still have some. And what we've got
to decide is how to use those damn chips."

With the time running against them, Nixon, Kissinger, and Haig
all agreed that the only thing left to do was deliver a "terrific wallop"

with a renewed bombing campaign that would target all the power plants and transportation infrastructure in the North. This attack would include reseeding of the mines in Haiphong Harbor. Because the seasonably bad weather prohibited the use of surgical strikes with smaller planes and smart bombs, Nixon suggested the use of the massive B-52s, which could fly above the weather and drop enough bombs to destroy large targets in the North.

Nothing would be said publicly about the bombing—it would just start. Kissinger would give a "low-key" press conference on Saturday, December 16, to explain why the talks had reached an impasse and that the United States stood ready to conclude an agreement whenever the North was willing to deal in good faith. And then, within forty-eight hours of the press briefing, the United States would begin, in Kissinger's phrasing, "to bomb the bejesus out of the North."[24]

Haig convinced Nixon that there should be a truce on Christmas Day, but otherwise the campaign would last for approximately two weeks, until Congress reconvened in the new year. If by that time the North had not buckled and agreed to finish negotiations, Nixon and Kissinger would then consider simply bargaining for the return of American POWs in exchange for the cessation of the bombing, letting the South go it alone.

"Remember," Nixon told both men as the meeting was concluding, "we are going to be around and outlive our enemies."[25]

And then, as if in a grade school classroom, the president reminded Kissinger: "And also never forget, the press is the enemy, the press is the enemy, the press is the enemy; the establishment is the enemy; the professors are the enemy, the professors are the enemy. Write that on the blackboard one hundred times and never forget it."[26]

Kissinger had his press conference on Saturday, December 16. The bombing started on the following Monday, December 18, the day Alice Roosevelt Longworth dined with the Nixons and Kissinger in the White House, exactly one week before Christmas. National and international reaction was fierce. The United States was painted as barbaric, and Nixon was portrayed as insane.[27] "Faith in reason and civilization has been one of the intangible victims of Richard Nixon's Christmas bombing offensive against North Vietnam," Anthony Lewis of the *New York Times* wrote. "If the elected leader of the greatest democracy acts like a maddened tyrant, and not one person in his Government says the feeblest nay, it is hard to argue against the view that ours is a lunatic society."[28]

In the incredible whirlwind that followed, Nixon and Colson became all the more concerned that Henry Kissinger would crack, bowing to pressure and criticism from the media, his former Harvard colleagues, and the "Georgetown set," and that he would privately speak against the very bombing program he had so strongly recommended when he returned from Paris.

Kissinger was told to go to California for a vacation to get him out of the eye of the storm. Unfortunately, California, unlike Mexico, had lots of telephones, and Kissinger had access to them.[29]

Nixon escaped to Key Biscayne for Christmas, saying nothing as the pressure built. Colson actually believed that the average man on the street was not particularly concerned about the bombings, but the international community was outraged, and the *New York Times* was flaying the administration. "Air raid sirens scream day and night," the editors of the *New York Times* wrote. "The earth trembles with the violence of an earthquake, and whole sections of the city crumble in a roar of flames and flying jagged steel. . . . This is Hanoi under attack by American B-52s, as described by Westerners who have been there."[30]

The reports not only claimed that there were thousands of civilian deaths, including a direct hit on a thousand-bed hospital, but also confirmed an alarming loss of American B-52s, owing to the skillful employment of Russian surface-to-air missiles by the North Vietnamese and their Russian advisors. In a condensed period, twenty-eight aircraft, including fifteen B-52s, costing nearly $8 million each, were shot down. Thirty-one pilots and crew became POWs, and ninety-three were declared missing in action. The columnist James Reston wrote that this was "war by tantrum."[31]

The White House, December 26 to 31, 1972

Nixon returned to the White House from his Florida vacation the day after Christmas. His first call was to Chuck Colson. Both men felt it was fortuitous that Harry Truman had died earlier that morning. Nixon said he planned to travel to Independence, Missouri, the next day to pay his respects to the Truman family.

"Oh, that helps, actually, Mr. President," Colson said.[32]

"Yeah, to a certain extent, it diverts [attention] to another story," Nixon agreed.

Better, Colson thought, Nixon's trip to Independence would show him "out front," representing all of the American people at a memorial service for a dead president. Colson was concerned that during the bombing "the public [hadn't] seen [Nixon] active quite enough." He added, "It's a good feeling for the public to see the president, and they know the president is there, and he's in charge."[33]

The Truman story and documentaries about his life would dominate the news for a day or two, Colson guessed, and then the New Year's weekend would bring football to capture people's attention.

"The weekend, you know damn well, is going to be football," Nixon said.

"Totally," Colson responded.

"And this one even more with the Rose Bowl," Nixon replied. "You see the bowl games come on New Year's Day. So you've got Sunday [New Year's Eve] and Monday [New Year's Day] both blocked." They figured they would have at least until midweek following the long New Year's weekend before Nixon had to say anything about the bombing, and by then hopefully there would be some sort of breakthrough with the North Vietnamese.

Nixon told Colson there was a reason for his silence about the bombing. "There are things, frankly, that we can't talk about," he said. "Right now, we're playing a very tough poker game. If we can avoid saying anything, it's better."

Colson pushed him to say something about the bombing soon if nothing broke by the middle of the first week of January 1973. "The American people need some explanation as to why we are continuing to bomb," he counseled.

As the conversation began to wind up, Colson dropped news on Kissinger, who Colson had learned had met with Senator Charles Percy of Illinois in his office in the White House just before leaving for Palm Springs. Colson knew that sprinkling this juicy tidbit would provoke a sharp reaction from Nixon. Percy was persona non grata at the White House, a liberal Republican who could be an opponent of the administration (and someone Kissinger probably anticipated would be a presidential candidate in 1976).

"I can't believe it!" Nixon snarled in astonishment. "For God's sake," he said, "we have *a rule* he is not supposed to see Percy. We have *a rule!*"

"Henry is positively compulsive this way," Colson responded, "and then when anything is said negative . . ." He didn't need to complete his thought—he had accomplished his goal: Nixon was ablaze.

The conversation shifted momentarily to the most recent Harris public opinion polls, but Nixon quickly circled back to Kissinger. "On this business of Percy, I can't believe it," he said. "Can you find out how much time he spent with him?"

"Yes sir, I can find out," Colson dutifully responded.[34]

Six minutes later, Colson called Nixon back. "It was forty-five minutes, Mr. President," he reported.

Nixon was flabbergasted: "This is it; this really breaks it off."

Colson commented that the problem with Kissinger was that he wanted to please everyone. Nixon granted the point. "You've got to have some enemies," Nixon said, "and he's playing the wrong kind of people."[35]

After dinner, Nixon obsessively called Colson again. He told him to tell Bob Haldeman, who was also on his way to California for a vacation, to call Kissinger and tell him the president was shocked. "Bob's got to scare him within an inch of his life. . . . Raise hell," Nixon said. "Henry has got to shut up now." He was especially leery that Kissinger would "screw up" the delicate negotiations with the North Vietnamese by pandering to "the goddamn columnists" and to the social crowd out in California, like the "Jill St. Johns and all those bitches, because they will leak to North Vietnam; let's face it."[36]

"I'll get ahold of Bob tonight when he gets in, sir," Colson promised.

"You have a little fun with it, too," Nixon cackled, "OK, boy?"

As a result of the savage bombing, secret communications with the North Vietnamese opened through back channels on Friday, December 22. The North Vietnamese were told that the United States would end the bombing within thirty-six hours if they agreed to return to serious negotiations and to complete the agreements.

After a daylong trip to Independence, Missouri, for a wreath-laying ceremony at the Truman Presidential Library and a very brief condolence meeting with Bess Truman and the rest of the Truman family at the Truman home on Wednesday, December 27, Nixon flew back to Washington and was in the White House by 6:30 PM.[37] That evening he called Henry Kissinger in California to get an update on the bombing situation.[38] There was not the slightest hint of the Percy incident.

Kissinger told Nixon that the North Vietnamese had given him a message canceling the technical meetings that day, but they had reaffirmed their offer to meet with him on January 8 in Paris. Kissinger said he responded that if Hanoi confirmed with specific dates for restarting the technical meetings and his meeting with Le Duc Tho

Pat and Richard Nixon walk past the casket of former president Harry
S. Truman as it lies in state at the Truman Library in Independence,
Missouri, December 27, 1972.
Cleveland Press

in Paris, the United States would end the bombing. Kissinger felt sure
they would know by the weekend. Both men wanted to end the bombing before January 1, 1973.

Nixon was adamant: "We gave them a hellava good bang. We are
punishing the hell out of them, aren't we?"

Kissinger responded that "there was no question about it."

"We've got our message across, Henry, and that's the important
thing," Nixon said.

"We've gotten our message across, Mr. President," Kissinger
replied in his dour German monotone, "and we've gotten it across
before all hell breaks loose here [meaning the return of Congress], and
we've faced down these people again, and you have shown you are not
someone to be trifled with."[39]

The United States officially called off the bombing on Friday,
December 29, but there were some serious fireworks still to come
within the administration.

Almost as if on cue, the *New York Times* ran an article on Sunday, December 31—New Year's Eve—written by columnist James Reston, that asserted that Henry Kissinger had opposed the bombing. "It may be, and probably is, true," Reston wrote, "that Mr. Kissinger as well as Secretary of State Rogers and most of the senior officers in the State Department are opposed to the President's bombing offensive in North Vietnam. . . . But Mr. Kissinger is too much of a scholar, with too good a sense of humor and history, to put his own thoughts ahead of the President."[40]

The fawning portrayal of Kissinger left little doubt that he had been one of the sources, if not the sole source of Reston's statements.

Camp David, Sunday, December 31, 1972

Nixon spent most of New Year's Eve at Camp David essentially by himself, watching the two NFL championship games. While he was cheered immensely by the Redskins' win, he was in a cold anger over the Reston article in the *Times*. Nixon called Colson five times during the day from Camp David before flying by helicopter back to the White House after the football games had concluded.

That night, Nixon called Colson again from the Lincoln Sitting Room.[41] Sipping a drink and audibly crunching his ice, he asked Colson if he "had given any more thought to the Kissinger problem." Colson said he had and that he didn't think "there was any damn question where that article came from." Kissinger had to be the source. "Can you trace that?" Nixon asked. "It would be very important to know that."

Colson thought he could.

"From now on," Nixon demanded, "I want a record of every one of his calls. Let's have that, huh?"

Colson said they could check the billings of Kissinger's phones.

"To hell with the billings," Nixon snapped. "Let's get the Bureau [FBI] on it, by God. Let's get in on his private lines. The hell with it." He was ordering wiretaps of his own national security advisor.

"We don't want to do anything to hurt his morale," Nixon backtracked. "But on the other hand, we've got to restrain him from making his debating points now; let him make them later." He wanted to bring Kissinger to heel—he would not be allowed to get out in front of the president when it came to wrapping up the Vietnam War.

"We mustn't let him shoot too soon," Nixon said. "*I've* got to do the shooting."[42]

The Oval Office, January 1, 1973

On New Year's morning, the first day of January 1973, Colson was ready to report on his further investigation of Kissinger.

He confirmed from the White House phone logs that there had been no calls to Kissinger from Reston. But that didn't mean Kissinger hadn't spoken to Reston from a private phone. And Colson speculated that Kissinger may have spoken with Max Frankel, the Sunday editor of the *New York Times*. This made some sense to Nixon. He thought there may well be a "Jewish connection" between Kissinger and Frankel, and that Frankel had passed on Kissinger's comments to Reston. Colson told Nixon that Kissinger frequently had breakfast with Frankel at the White House. Nixon was once again thunderstruck. *"How can he do that*, Chuck?" Nixon sputtered. "With everything the *New York Times* has done to us?"[43]

Though Colson delighted in reporting on the transgressions of Henry Kissinger, he would find himself that very week manipulated and compromised by his friend Howard Hunt and his lawyer.

And before the week was out, Chuck Colson would drag Richard Nixon further into the Watergate cover-up, sowing some of the very seeds that would result in the ignominious end of his hero's presidency—and his own trip to prison.

3

"Human Adversaries Are
Arraigned Against Me"

The Rose Garden, January 1, 1973

The president and Colson were in the middle of their conversation about Henry Kissinger when assistant Steve Bull entered the Oval Office to report that Coach Allen of the Redskins had finally arrived. Bull also informed the president of the news, just filtering in, that baseball star Roberto Clemente was on a plane that had crashed after taking off from the San Juan International Airport late the night before.

"Was he killed?" Nixon asked.

"They don't have confirmation yet," Bull replied.[1]

Clemente, the popular outfielder for the Pittsburgh Pirates, had boarded a rickety four-engine DC-7 plane that was overloaded with relief supplies for the victims of a massive earthquake in Nicaragua. The earthquake was believed to have resulted in the deaths of more than seven thousand people. Most of the deaths had occurred in the capital city of Managua, which had taken the brunt of the 6.2 magnitude shock at midday on Saturday, December 23.[2] The city was leveled.

The lumbering plane that Clemente was on nose-dived into heavy seas shortly after takeoff from San Juan. Clemente was thirty-eight years old and had been a perennial All-Star, four-time winner of the National League batting championship, defensive genius, and MVP in 1966. He led the Pirates to two world championships, one in 1960 and the other a decade later in 1971. "Mr. Clemente was the leader of Puerto Rican efforts to aid the Nicaraguan victims and was aboard the plane because he suspected that relief supplies were falling into the hands of profiteers," the *New York Times* reported after his death was presumed.[3] Clemente was scheduled to meet Anastasio Somoza, the military dictator of Nicaragua, at the airport, one of the very grafters he was attempting to circumvent with his personal mission.

Clemente's body was never recovered. It was a bad omen for the start of 1973.

George Allen and his family were shown into the Oval Office and Chuck Colson took his leave as the president greeted his visitors and directed them outside to the Rose Garden to pose for pictures in the bright sunshine. An ebullient Nixon proudly held an autographed football the coach had brought with him as a souvenir. The morning was unusually warm; temperatures would jump into the mid-sixties before the afternoon was over. No one needed an overcoat for the photo op.

Redskins football coach George Allen and family (including his in-laws) outside the White House Oval Office on Rose Garden steps with President Nixon, January 1, 1973.

White House Photo Office, Nixon Library

Though Colson had said nothing about Watergate in his morning meeting with Nixon, he was anxious about developments that threatened to boil over into an uncontrollable situation. With the start of the Watergate burglars' trial exactly one week away, Colson knew a moment of truth approached. That very day, a highly emotional personal letter written by E. Howard Hunt was on its way to his office. Howard Hunt was a desperate man.

The past three weeks had been beyond tragic for Hunt. For Colson, there was deep shame in how he had behaved in response to the incredible turn of events. His shame would cause him to finally get involved in Hunt's plight. A showdown loomed; commitments needed to be clarified and finalized before the trial started.

The time for endless vacillation had come to an end.

Colson's EOB Office, November 13, 1972

Chuck Colson first met Howard Hunt in the middle of the 1960s, when both men served as officers of the Brown University Alumni Club of Washington, DC. The two enjoyed each other's company and met occasionally for lunch or dinner, but they did not become close until early in the Nixon administration, when Hunt decided it was time to retire from the CIA.

After a promising start to his career in the CIA in 1949, Howard Hunt fell from grace as a result of his leadership role in the Bay of Pigs, the failed effort to overthrow Fidel Castro in Cuba. Hunt never recovered from the 1961 fiasco. He was ostracized and unhappy, eventually concluding that he would take early retirement in 1970 and look for work outside the agency. He asked Colson for guidance on what he might do in his post-CIA life. Hunt found a job at Mullen & Company, a public relations firm that had deep ties with the CIA and offices located just across the street from the White House.[4] Colson began to call on Hunt for occasional advice on matters related to spying and national security.

Then Daniel Ellsberg leaked the Pentagon Papers, a top-secret study of America's involvement in Southeast Asia, to the *New York Times* and other newspapers in June 1971. This was a turning point for Hunt and the start of the so-called White House Plumbers.

Nixon at first perceived the Ellsberg leak as someone else's problem; after all, the Pentagon study was directed mainly at his Democratic predecessors, Presidents Kennedy and Johnson, and how *they* had drawn the nation into Vietnam based on deception and dishonesty.[5]

"It really blasts [former secretary of defense Robert] McNamara, and Kennedy and Johnson," Haldeman wrote in his diary the day after the papers were published.[6] But it did not take long for Henry Kissinger and others to convince Nixon that the government needed to prosecute Ellsberg and his cohorts for espionage and to sue the *New York Times* and the *Washington Post* to enjoin them from further damaging publications. If the United States could not safeguard its national security secrets, Kissinger argued, nations like Vietnam and China would refuse to continue to deal with the United States in private talks.[7] Ellsberg was charged with espionage and other crimes and surrendered to federal authorities.[8]

The president and top administration officials became consumed with Ellsberg and the threat he posed to national security over the next several weeks. Colson later testified that Nixon suggested that someone be hired by the White House to focus exclusively on the Ellsberg case so higher-ups could return to running the government. Colson recommended his friend Howard Hunt in a memo to Bob Haldeman within weeks of the publication of the Pentagon Papers. "The more I think about Howard Hunt's background, politics, disposition and experience, the more I think it would be worth your time to meet him," Colson wrote to Haldeman on July 2, 1971. "I had forgotten when I talked to you that he was the CIA mastermind on the Bay of Pigs. He told me a long time ago that if the truth were ever known, Kennedy would be destroyed."[9]

The special investigative unit that Hunt and G. Gordon Liddy, a former FBI agent, would set up in Room 16 in the basement of the Executive Office Building became known as "the Plumbers," because they were addressing leaks for the chief executive.[10]

At the time of Colson's recommendation, Hunt was fifty-two. He had married Dorothy de Goutiere, a woman he met in Washington after the Second World War. They had four children: Lisa, Kevan, Howard St. John, and David. The two oldest, daughters Lisa and Kevan, were college-age in the summer of 1971. The boys were younger: St. John was seventeen and David just eight. Despite the appearance of a family that enjoyed a glamorous international lifestyle, the Hunts had known their share of personal calamity. Lisa and Kevan were in a severe car accident with friends in high school and Lisa, the eldest, suffered brain trauma that left her emotionally troubled and at times suicidal. She was hospitalized for her own protection for more than two years, "draining our financial resources," Hunt later recorded.[11] Rumors, likely true, always circulated that Dorothy Hunt was on the CIA payroll.[12]

After Hunt was arrested for his participation in the Watergate break-in in June 1972, Chuck Colson made it clear that he did not want to have any further direct dealings with him. Hunt actually showed up in the waiting room of Colson's office in the EOB early on the Monday morning following the break-in to warn that a safe he maintained in an office on the third floor of the EOB "was loaded." Colson was not yet in, so Hunt left the message with his secretary.[13]

Hunt's safe was indeed "loaded." He had stashed in it some of the electronic eavesdropping equipment from the Watergate operation after he escaped arrest in the wee hours of Saturday morning. The safe also contained evidence of multiple crimes and near-crimes that he and Gordon Liddy had participated in as part of their work as Plumbers. For good measure, Hunt's safe included a loaded .25-caliber Browning pistol.[14]

Despite frantic efforts by Colson to put daylight between himself and Hunt, he was instantly linked with Hunt in the newspapers in the days following the Watergate break-in, as it quickly became known that Colson had been Hunt's sponsor in the White House.[15] Try as he may, Colson was never able to fully disassociate himself from Howard Hunt or the taint of scandal.

Hunt, G. Gordon Liddy, and the five men who were arrested in the Watergate all needed money—money for bail, attorneys, and family support. The five who were arrested in the Watergate—Hunt and Liddy were in a nearby hotel room and were not apprehended at the scene, but were later arrested—were caught in business suits, wearing rubber gloves and toting sophisticated surveillance equipment and cameras, their pockets stuffed with brand-new hundred-dollar bills, and they all had, it turned out, significant CIA links. They were easily identified after being fingerprinted.

James McCord, the electronics specialist among the burglars, had only recently retired from the CIA and had officially signed on to work as a security consultant for the Committee to Re-Elect the President (CRP). The four other burglars were all associated with the Cuban expat community in Miami. (Frank Sturgis was Italian American but a soldier of fortune in the battle against Castro.) Except for the locksmith, Virgilio Gonzalez, all of the men had worked for Hunt in the Bay of Pigs operation.[16]

The men arrested understood that they were to act as soldiers in a war, saying nothing about who ordered the break-in or its purpose. The money paid to them would become known later as "hush money."[17]

Tony Ulasewicz, a former New York City cop who worked as a private investigator for the White House, was tasked with the job of delivering cash to Howard Hunt's wife, Dorothy, who in turn would distribute it to the lawyers and the others.[18] Ulasewicz supplied money in brown paper wrappers at drop points, including lockers at the National Airport in Washington. On the phone, he identified himself only as Mr. Rivers when he called Dorothy Hunt, and she became known simply as "the writer's wife."[19] Howard Hunt's hobby was writing cheap spy novels.

In the end, Dorothy Hunt became the pay mistress for the hush money.

Though Howard Hunt received assurances in late August through Colson's secretary that everything would turn out all right after the election, Hunt and his wife grew apprehensive that the opposite was true. The delivery of the money had become irregular and there was not enough of it to go around. The Hunts became convinced that they would be all but forgotten after the election.

On Sunday, October 22, 1972, two weeks before the election, Dorothy Hunt called Joan Hall, Chuck Colson's personal secretary, on an unlisted, private number that had been given to Howard Hunt when he worked at the White House to use in the event of an emergency.[20] Hall was surprised by the call; it instantly became clear that Dorothy Hunt was very upset. The money had slowed to a trickle, she complained. "I'm sorry to have to bother you," she told Hall, "but there is no one else to call. There are commitments that have not been met. We are trying to do our best but we need help; there are retainers for the lawyers—and all of this is creating terrible frustration." There was also an implied threat. "This makes for a very bad situation," Dorothy added. "Everyone wants to hold firm, but . . ."[21]

Chuck Colson did not want to hear about the call when his secretary tried to tell him about it the next Monday morning. He was engaged in his own campaign of willful ignorance. He instructed her not to give him any details about the call and to refer everything to John Dean, who was handling those matters as counsel for the White House.

Six days after Nixon's landslide election win in November, Howard Hunt had had enough. In utter frustration he called Colson
directly on November 13 to insist that commitments made to him
and his men *had to be kept*.[22] With the election behind them and a trial
scheduled to start in just two months, Colson decided to risk taking
the call. Without telling Hunt, he secretly recorded the conversation
on his office Dictabelt machine, hoping to get Hunt to confirm once
and for all that he, Colson, had nothing to do with the planning of the
Watergate caper.

Colson also later testified that he wanted protection—he hoped
he could secure evidence from Hunt's own mouth that could be used
later, if necessary, to rebut any attempt by Hunt or his attorneys to
implicate Colson by claiming he had ordered the break-in.[23]

After some introductory pleasantries, Hunt's call with Colson
turned semi-confrontational. Though Colson repeatedly tried to stop
him from going into details ("OK, don't tell me any more"), Hunt
unloaded on him. He complained bitterly that commitments were not
being kept and threatened that if "the ready" (meaning "money") was
not forthcoming, grave consequences would follow. "This is a long-
haul thing, but the stakes are very, very high," Hunt insisted. "And I
thought that you would want to know that this thing must not break
apart for foolish reasons," he menacingly said.

He set a firm deadline of November 25 for the "liquidation of
everything that's outstanding."[24]

Colson should have burned the Dictabelt. Instead, he called John
Dean, pleased that Hunt had not implicated him in the planning and
execution of the Watergate break-in. Somehow Colson had missed the
fact that, by virtue of this conversation with Hunt, he had just been
reeled into the conspiracy to obstruct justice.

To be sure, Colson was troubled by Hunt's unmistakable threats
against the administration. Dean took possession of the Dictabelt,
made his own copy of it on a cassette tape, and took the copy to
Camp David to play it for Haldeman and Ehrlichman, who were
working on the reorganization project for the second term. The two
listened impassively and recommended that he bring the tape to the
attention of John Mitchell, who had returned to private law practice
in New York.

Dean caught the next shuttle to New York and met with the former attorney general at the staid Metropolitan Club in Midtown.

Mitchell heard him out, listened to the tape, and left without recommending any action.[25] "You ever have any good news?" he sarcastically asked Dean.

The lights finally went on for John Dean as he listened to the ominous tape. During this time he opened his criminal law books for the first time and quickly discovered that he and the fellow conspirators were knee-deep in an obstruction of justice—they were paying defendants in a criminal case to maintain their silence.[26]

Shortly after the Colson-Hunt phone conversation, a long memo written by Howard Hunt was delivered to one of the attorneys for the Committee to Re-Elect the President named Ken Parkinson. It was even more direct in its threats. "The Watergate bugging," Hunt wrote in the memo, "is only one of a number of highly illegal conspiracies engaged in by one or more of the defendants at the behest of senior White House officials. These as yet undisclosed crimes can be proved."[27]

Among other things, Hunt referred to the September 1971 break-in at Daniel Ellsberg's psychiatrist's office in Beverly Hills, perpetrated by Liddy, Hunt, and two of the Miamians arrested in the Watergate—Bernard Barker and Eugenio Martinez. John Ehrlichman, Hunt knew, had approved the covert operation in writing on a "national security" basis.[28] The psychiatrist operation was a bust: Ellsberg's file, if one existed, was not located, and the burglars left the place in shambles. But the people who undertook the operation for the White House had to remain silent, and not just because of the Watergate break-in. The White House now had its own reason for paying the defendants to keep quiet.

This was becoming an extortion situation for the White House.

Hunt demanded that the administration keep its part of the bargain in return for the continuing silence of the defendants. In his memo, he laid bare their collective demands: financial support, the payment of legal fees, job rehabilitation, and eventual *pardons*. And pardons, they knew, had to come from the president himself.

Thus by late November, Howard Hunt and his wife, Dorothy, had become a major threat to the second term of Richard Nixon. All of the heavy fundraising, the brilliant campaigning, and the votes of more than 60 percent of those who went to the polls—all these things were being placed in jeopardy by two people who seemed determined to blow the lid off the Watergate cover-up if their blackmail demands were not met.

How to send a message in response was the question that must have obsessed the increasingly nervous people within the White House.

Chicago, Midway Airport, December 8, 1972

December 8, 1972, was a Friday. The weather in Chicago was overcast, with low clouds and a light to moderate freezing rain falling. United Flight 553 was scheduled to depart from Washington National Airport for Chicago at ten minutes before 1:00 in the afternoon. The plane was to make a stop at Chicago–Midway Airport at 2:30 PM, CST, then continue on to Omaha, Nebraska. There were fifty-five passengers aboard the Boeing 737-222, including five children and two infants, along with a crew of six.

Dorothy Hunt was flying in first class.

For some reason, she purchased a $250,000 life insurance policy from a vending machine in the National Airport before boarding.

After takeoff, the plane climbed to a cruising altitude of twenty-eight thousand feet. The flight proceeded on instruments in accordance with its flight plan.[29] Once the plane entered the Chicago Air Route Traffic Control area it began its descent at established radar vectors and leveled off at four thousand feet. At this point a problem arose. Another smaller aircraft had missed its approach to Runway 31L at Midway and had been instructed to execute a maneuver known as a "go around," which required it to circle around to try to land again. As a consequence, United Flight 553 was told by air traffic control to slow down to allow the smaller aircraft time to land first.

At the last minute, just as United Flight 553 was in its final descent, the controller at Midway began to worry that the smaller aircraft ahead of it would still be on the runway when Flight 553 landed. He told the United aircraft to execute its own missed approach and go around. United Flight 553 did not respond to the instruction.

The cockpit voice recorder captured what happened next.

"Ah, thousand feet," one of the pilots said, indicating the plane was one thousand feet above the ground. The sound of clicks can be heard as the crew went through its final landing cross-checks.[30]

And then, seconds later, as the plane broke through the five-hundred-foot ceiling of clouds, a sound arose that must have terrified the pilots. The stick-shaker activated. They were in a stall.

A stick-shaker is an alarm that violently rattles the pilot's control stick, like the vibrations of an unbalanced steering wheel of a car, when aircraft sensors measure an air speed that is too slow for the angle of attack. A pilot needs to take immediate corrective action to lower the nose, level off, and then apply thrust to power the aircraft out of the stall. But the pilots on Flight 553 must have intuited that they were too close to the ground to recover. If they knew enough about their aircraft and its weight, they could have guessed that when the stick-shaker activated at such a low altitude there was only one outcome: the plane was going to crash. There was nothing they could do.

Still, according to witnesses on the ground, the engines roared just before impact.[31] This desperate attempt to power out of the crash likely only exacerbated the situation, because the plane had its flaps down and its nose was up. The additional power would only have served to cause the plane to slam even harder into the ground.

The plane was about two miles from Midway Airport. After clipping off the tops of several trees and scraping the roofs of some homes, it plowed into a row of bungalows on West 70th Place. Two women in one of the homes hit, a mother and daughter, were killed instantly. Not everyone on the plane perished. Forty-five of the sixty-one persons aboard were killed, many from the toxic fumes of the intense fire that broke out inside the forward cabin, but seventeen in the coach section of the plane and one flight attendant in the front of the plane miraculously escaped, some walking out of the rear of the broken plane in a complete daze.

Dorothy Hunt, in her first-class seat, was burned beyond recognition. Her purse, containing $10,000 in hundred-dollar bills, somehow remained intact and was discovered by investigators in the wreckage.[32]

Theories of sabotage abounded and were stoked by a Chicago pathologist's report that indicated that one of the first-class passengers near where Dorothy Hunt sat was killed "by burns and apparently some explosive force." The pathologist was later questioned about his choice of words and made to clarify that "he had found no evidence of effects typical of an explosive device or charge." It was "a bad choice of adjectives," he explained.[33]

There was also later a very public debate between the head of the FBI and the chairman of the National Transportation Safety Board (NTSB) about what seemed to be highly inappropriate interference by FBI agents in the crash investigation. According to letters exchanged between John H. Reed, chairman of the NTSB, and William Ruckelshaus, director of the FBI, a hoard of FBI agents, approximately fifty, descended on the scene, taking "a number of non-typical actions relating to this accident within the first few hours following the accident." One FBI special agent actually went to the control tower to listen to the tower tapes before the NTSB investigators had done so.

Ruckelshaus defended his agents, writing that "the fact that Mrs. E. Howard Hunt was aboard the plane was unknown to the FBI at the time our investigation was instituted." Yet the authority he cited for the FBI intrusion was a federal statute that gave the FBI primary investigative jurisdiction in the event of the "willful" damaging, destroying, or disabling of a civil aircraft. Ruckelshaus conceded that his agents terminated their investigation within twenty hours of the accident.[34]

The accident eventually was ruled "pilot error."[35]

The Oval Office, December 11, 1972

The night of Dorothy Hunt's death, Richard Nixon was at Camp David. He and his daughter Julie, the one most like him, watched a private showing of *The Candidate*, a film starring Robert Redford.[36]

The next morning, Saturday, December 9, 1972, Nixon talked by phone with Chuck Colson, who had driven to Princeton to pick up his son for his winter break. The conversation was recorded via a tap on the Camp David phone. After chatting briefly about politics, Colson told Nixon of Dorothy Hunt's death the day before.

"I just got a terribly tragic bit of news," Colson said. "That plane crash—Howard Hunt's wife was on it." Nixon seemed surprised. "His wife is dead?" Nixon asked. "Yes, sir," Colson responded. "She was killed in that plane crash in Chicago."[37]

"Oh my God!" Nixon replied, his voice registering true shock.

"It's a tragedy," Colson continued. "I don't know whether the man can survive it, with all he's gone through. She was an *extraordinary* woman, just extraordinary. I think *any* judge who has *any* compassion will call that trial off."

"You mean call it off permanently?" Nixon asked. "Not permanently?"

"Well, maybe separate him out, or delay the trial or something, because she was a tower of strength to him," Colson said. "She was a rare, gifted woman, multi-linguist. Brilliant. A lot of charm."

"They have children?" Nixon asked.

"Four children, beautiful children. So it's a tragedy. Devout Catholic."

"God," Nixon sighed.

"Probably—" Colson started to say.

Nixon interrupted, "He's a Catholic?"

"Probably saves him from committing suicide," Colson finished his thought.

Nixon asked again about Hunt: "Is he a Catholic?"

"Yes, sir," Colson said.

"Yeah," Nixon replied.

"That's life, I guess," Colson said. "A real shocker."[38]

The following Monday, December 11, there was talk in the Oval Office of using the plane crash as an excuse to delay the upcoming burglars' trial, or at least to separate out Hunt's case for a later trial. This was seen as a benefit to Bob Haldeman because much of the evidence gathered at the Watergate pointed to Hunt but not Liddy. The case against Liddy was circumstantial and mostly came through his association with Hunt. Thus, Haldeman reasoned, if Hunt's case were tried separately, the case against Liddy just might collapse. This would be "very much to our interest," Haldeman said.[39]

Nixon was intrigued about the money that had been found in Dorothy Hunt's purse. He wanted to know if it could be tracked back to the White House or the Committee to Re-Elect the President.

"Do they have any reading yet on the traceability of that $10,000 bag?" Nixon asked.

Haldeman said that John Dean had spent most of the weekend trying to answer that question. The story Hunt was telling was that Dorothy had traveled to Chicago to meet a first cousin, deliver holiday gifts, and invest in Howard Johnson motels with some of their savings. Dorothy Hunt's cousin, Hunt pointed out, was married to a man who had "substantial investments in motels in the Chicago area."[40]

"I've been unemployed for six months now," Hunt said to the press, "and I have to find a way of providing for my family and children."[41]

"Apparently she and her family have some investments in Howard Johnson restaurants around out there," Haldeman reported to Nixon in the Oval Office. "She was going out with the money for investment," he said. "It was a business thing. They have a pattern of dealing in cash. That's the way the family moved it. When they carry stuff out, they carry it in cash." The bills, according to Haldeman, were expected to be returned to Howard Hunt that day by the Chicago police. Haldeman reported that Dean didn't know for sure if the money was traceable, but that Dean was "not particularly concerned about it" and didn't think it was.[42]

Hunt was a broken man. He turned to journalist and syndicated columnist William F. Buckley, who had first met Hunt as his case officer in Mexico City when Buckley joined the CIA fresh out of Yale. The relationship became a close one; Buckley eventually became the godfather to several of Hunt's children. Now, in this moment of crisis, he would be named executor of Dorothy Hunt's estate.[43]

Judge Sirica's Chambers, December 15, 1972

As if following the script set out in the Oval Office, Hunt's lawyer, William O. Bittman, filed a motion to separate Hunt from the upcoming trial based on Hunt's personal tragedy. Just a week after the crash, Bittman appeared before Judge John Sirica to argue for the severance. He had submitted a letter from Hunt's family physician, who opined that Hunt was unfit to stand trial.

Judge Sirica found Bittman's request unpersuasive. "Some people recover quickly and others it bothers quite a bit," he callously observed. He wanted an independent report from "an outstanding doctor" before he would consider the motion.[44]

In the following week, Bittman and Earl Silbert, the prosecutor for the government, were back in front of Sirica to address Silbert's request that the judge order Hunt to return from Florida, where he and his children had gone to escape the prospect of facing the holidays in the family home. Silbert demanded that Hunt come back so he could appear for two examinations by two government-retained physicians: one a neurologist and the other a psychiatrist. Again, Sirica was hard-hearted. "I was emotionally upset when my mother and father passed away," Sirica said to Bittman, "but I went back to work very soon—before a month went by—and I don't think anybody could be any closer to a person than a mother and a father, and that includes wives sometimes."[45]

Hunt was ordered to return to Washington on the day after Christmas—the day Harry Truman would pass away in Independence, Missouri—to be examined by the government-appointed physicians. "If he is just emotionally upset," Sirica told Bittman, "that, in my opinion, is not a valid excuse [for postponing the trial]." Sirica thought that Hunt could simply take breaks during the trial if he was overcome by his grief. "We have a very fine first aid setup downstairs and two trained nurses," he said. "Mr. Hunt will be given every advantage. If he gets tired during the day I will arrange for him to go down and take a rest for two or three hours if he wishes."[46]

Hunt complied with Sirica's order, seeing the physicians in two separate examinations on December 26 and 27. Both found him fit to stand trial. "Although he cried while relating some of the details of the events which followed the recent death of his wife," one of them wrote, "he almost immediately regained his composure without significant interruption in the examination."[47]

The trial would go forward. It would start one month to the day after Dorothy Hunt's death.

Potomac, Maryland, December 31, 1972
On New Year's Eve, Howard Hunt sat down at his desk at home to type out a letter to Chuck Colson. Colson had failed to show up for Dorothy Hunt's funeral. In his place, he sent his secretary, Joan Hall. He did take a few moments to scratch out condolence letters that he gave to her to deliver to Hunt and his children.

"The children and myself were touched by your letters," Hunt started his letter, "and we deeply appreciate your sympathy." Hunt wrote that he was still in shock. "I am unable to reconcile myself to Dorothy's death, much less accept it."[48]

He wrote that his wife's death had changed his "personal equation." His first concern had to be his children, especially his nine-year-old son, "who was unusually dependent upon his mother, particularly since last June's tumult began." He asked Colson to meet immediately with his attorney, Bill Bittman. He felt alone and abandoned by his friends. "I can't tell you," he wrote, "how important it is, under the circumstances, for Bill Bittman to have the opportunity to meet with you, and I trust you will do me that favor."

The letter was filled with pathos. "There is a limit to the endurance of any man trapped in a hostile situation and mine was reached on December 8th," Hunt wrote in his concluding paragraph. "I do believe in God—not necessarily a just God but in the governance of a Divine Being. His Will, however, is often enacted through human hands, and human adversaries are arraigned against me."

Colson sent the letter to John Dean on January 2, 1973, with a cover memo containing one simple inquiry: "Now what the hell do I do?"[49]

4

"The Abortion Cases"

The Oval Office, January 2, 1972

On the morning of the second day of January, Richard Nixon picked up the phone in the Oval Office and asked the operator to get the chief justice of the United States on the line. "Thank you," the operator politely responded.[1] Minutes later, she called back: "I have Chief Justice Burger. Here you are."[2]

"Hello?" Nixon called into his telephone.

"Good morning, Mr. President," Burger replied in his highly recognizable, melodious baritone voice. With a full head of white hair, square jaw, and commanding presence, reporters had worn out the phrase "straight from central casting" when referring to Burger as the quintessential chief justice. He assuredly looked the part.

"Well, I understood you called yesterday on the New Year, and I should have called you," Nixon apologized.

"Well not at all," Burger demurred.

"My gosh, did you go to the game, by chance?" Nixon asked, referring to the Redskins game.

"No," Burger responded, "I haven't been to a—"

Nixon cut him off. Intensely shy at times and never comfortable with small talk, even with presumed friends and allies, Nixon had a need to dominate a conversation, particularly at the outset, and especially on the phone, where any momentary pause in the dialogue seemed to be painful to him.

"I never go to those games," Nixon said, "and I'll tell you why I don't, is that, whenever they're sellouts—I went to one, Oklahoma, I mean, Texas and Arkansas, about three years ago—and the problem was that, it really caused so much commotion, because over one hundred people have to go when I go—sixty press and forty Secret Service. Well, that just takes a hundred seats away from people *that just die* [to go to the game]."

Burger mumbled something in response, but Nixon pressed on, saying that he was perfectly happy to watch the game on television. "So I went up to Camp David," he said of the Redskins game, "and I just saw it up there."

Again, Burger tried to get a word in: "Well you—"

"I was working up there anyway," Nixon defensively interjected.

"Well, the instant replay is much better," Burger blurted out.

"It's the *only* way to see a game," Nixon quickly shot back. "Of course there's something to the excitement of hearing the crowd," he added wistfully, a football fan trapped in a president's job.

Finally, Burger had an opening to squeeze in a few sentences. "Well, I haven't gone to [a game] for years. I spent yesterday just the way you did, I was down here at 9:00, worked all day, even missed the game [on television]."

"This is the time," Nixon said, "in these periods like this, when the people are all gone, I've just been in the office today and yesterday, and you get a lot of the paperwork done that you have just put aside." Like all successful men of his generation, work defined him.

"I wanted to start the year with a clean, empty box," Burger declared.

"I do it every time," Nixon agreed. "And my box is just as clean as it can be."

"I unfortunately didn't get out all my opinions," Burger conceded, "but I got all the little stuff tucked away, so now the decks are cleared for other things." As chief justice, Burger's duties included not only writing opinions but also all the administrative work of the court, including facilities, renovation projects, and personnel decisions. It was a major burden.

"Now you've got your mind cleared," Nixon encouraged him, "so that you can make *the big* decisions." Both men laughed.

"We'll have some pretty big ones coming out soon, too," Burger warned.

"Oh boy," Nixon exclaimed.

"I'm struggling with this pornography thing. I don't know whether—"

"Oh-oh," Nixon said upon hearing the word *pornography*.

"I don't know how we are coming out, but I'm coming out hard on it myself, whether I get the support or not," Burger said, referring to *Miller v. California*, a pending case that involved the unsolicited mass mailing of booklets containing graphic adult images in California. The case presented a First Amendment challenge to California's criminal obscenity statute.[3]

Burger told the president that he thought the then-prevailing "without redeeming social value" test for obscenity was senseless, "emanating from some of the campuses in this period." He said that to his mind, the standard meant "that if they have one of these outrageous orgies, then if they mention Vietnam or the condition of the ghettos, *it redeems the whole thing.*" Burger wanted to change the law, tying it to local community standards of obscenity and not allowing proof of what Burger believed was a more permissive national standard.

Nixon knew something about First Amendment law, having argued *Time, Inc. v. Hill* as a lawyer in the Supreme Court in 1966, during his wilderness years between the vice presidency and the presidency. Nixon represented a family whose kidnapping story had been fictionally portrayed in a book and then a 1955 Broadway play. *Life* magazine (owned by Henry Luce's *Time*) wrote about the play but failed to conduct appropriate fact-checking, according to the family.[4] The family thought the article portrayed them "in a false light," and they did not want to be in the public eye in the first place.

It was an invasion of privacy versus freedom of press quarrel, and Nixon lost.[5] Nixon had nothing but scorn for *Life*—which, to his delight in January 1973, was in the process of folding. "I read those [obscenity] cases when I did the Hill versus *Time* thing," Nixon reminded Burger, "because it relates to the whole freedom of the press thing, and let's face it, they've just gone overboard, that's all; it's always a question of balance. . . . I'm a square, I'm like [Coach George] Allen. I'm a square on [pornography]."

Nixon inquired about what other cases might be coming down, asking about busing in particular. "No, that's way down the road," Burger assured him, seemingly unaware of his propensity that morning to engage in unintended puns.[6] What Burger failed to disclose was that he was struggling mightily with an issue that dwarfed busing or obscenity. He faced the monumental question of when life begins, arising from two companion cases that had become known in internal court memos as simply "the abortion cases."

Bethesda Naval Hospital, September 1971

The road to *Roe* began with the unexpected resignations of two Supreme Court justices in September 1971. On September 17 (two weeks after Liddy and Hunt's break-in to the Beverly Hills office of Daniel Ellsberg's psychiatrist), the White House was informed by Chief Justice Burger that Justice Hugo Black would resign at 3:00 that afternoon. A senator from Alabama when he was appointed to the court by Franklin D. Roosevelt in 1937, Hugo Black had been a surprise to many liberals in his opinions; after all, he had once been a member of the Ku Klux Klan. Black became a stalwart of the Warren Court, an activist who cared deeply about social justice and the rights of the poor and the oppressed.[7] Nixon disliked him almost as much as he did Earl Warren.[8]

That same afternoon, Burger called again to tell Bob Haldeman that he was meeting with Justice John Marshall Harlan II, who, like Justice Black, was in the hospital. Harlan, too, he said, was likely to resign in short order due to his sharply deteriorating health. Black and Harlan had both been in the Bethesda Naval Hospital, though Harlan had just recently been moved to the George Washington Hospital as his condition worsened.

Harlan, a former Wall Street lawyer whose grandfather and namesake had been on the court, was in rough shape. He had been going blind for more than a year, requiring his clerks and his wife to read all his papers to him. He was also suffering from spinal cancer. Yet when he had heard that Justice Black was likely to retire, he held off his own announcement, telling one of Hugo Black's sons, "I do not want to do anything to detract from the attention that your father's retirement will get; he is one of the all-time greats on the Court."[9]

The prospect of two retirements must have been the source of wonderment to President Nixon. With a suddenness he could never have hoped for, the opportunity arose to completely make over the Supreme Court during his first term. Nixon had already replaced Earl Warren with Warren Burger and Abe Fortas with Harry Blackmun. Just a year after seating Blackmun, he had two new appointments within his grasp—all before the court and its composition could become the stuff of political fodder in the 1972 election. It was a remarkably good turn of fortune for any president, especially one who envisioned the emergence of a new conservative majority on the court.

The remaining liberal block of William O. Douglas, William Brennan, and Thurgood Marshall would be isolated. They could be outvoted by the four Nixon appointees when joined by either one or both of the two less predictable justices on the court—centrist Potter Stewart, who had been appointed by Eisenhower, and Byron White, one of two Kennedy appointees. (The other Kennedy nominee had been Arthur Goldberg, who was replaced by Fortas, who was in turn replaced by Blackmun.) White, a Colorado native and football star, graduated from Yale Law School. He met Kennedy in the service when he wrote the navy intelligence report on the sinking of *PT-109*. But "Whizzer" White, as he was known, turned out to be surprisingly conservative in his opinions. He dissented, for example, in *Miranda v. Arizona*, the case that established a criminal suspect's constitutional right to be advised of his right to remain silent and to have counsel before questioning by the police. Potter Stewart, a lawyer from Cincinnati, was also a frequent dissenter in the Warren Court, including in *Miranda*.

Nixon thus had reason to be optimistic about a major conservative shift in the Supreme Court, a change that he hoped might last for decades.

As it happened, Hugo Black died just more than a week after the announcement of his retirement. Nixon had been told by Burger that Justice Black was too sick to take visitors, so Nixon sent a solicitous handwritten note. Two days later, Black suffered a massive stroke, and six days later he was dead. When he retired, his thirty-four years on the Supreme Court were the third-longest in the nation's history.[10]

In the following week, President Nixon and Attorney General John Mitchell appeared without prior notice at Justice Black's funeral at the National Cathedral in Washington. Characteristically, and per his wishes, Black's remains were placed in a simple, unpainted pine coffin, and mourners were given free copies of the pocket-sized Constitution that he always kept at hand. But there was a problem for the president. "Mr. Nixon sat impassively in the front row of the National Cathedral," the newspaper reported, "as the Rev. Duncan Howlett [a close friend of the late justice] . . . said that Justice Black 'had little patience' with strict constructionists."[11] The direct jabs at the president and his attorney general were noted by the press—and even more so by Nixon. He had been humiliated.

This incident, though not directly involving the cathedral dean, Francis B. Sayre (he contributed only the concluding prayer), stuck in Nixon's craw. It was the main reason that sixteen months later, in the first days of January 1973, the president was so vexed about attending the Truman service, over which Sayre was to preside. Nixon continued to regret his spontaneous decision to pay his respects in person at Justice Black's funeral, and his loathing for Francis Sayre only increased as Sayre's antiwar activity intensified.

The topic surfaced in several discussions by Nixon in the first days of January 1973. He worried that if he attended the Truman service he would once again be sucker-punched from the pulpit. He told Steve Bull on the morning of January 1 that he had no doubt Sayre would try to make political hay at his expense while delivering the Truman eulogy.

"Like at Justice Black's?" Bull asked.

"Remember that?" Nixon responded. "Eewe!"[12]

The next day, talking to Rose Mary Woods as they unwrapped mounds of Christmas gifts that had been sent to the White House (including a case of wine from California governor Ronald Reagan), Nixon circled back to the theme. "I wish we had some excuse for not going to that darn cathedral. That Sayre is going to deliver the eulogy of Truman, and I'm probably going to get lectured."

Woods replied, "You'll get a police talk."

"My gosh, I don't want to get lectured, not at a funeral. Remember when they got me to go to Black's funeral? That Episcopal priest was *so* bad."

"Oh, I know," Woods commiserated.

"Remember, Hugo Black, right out there [in his coffin]. I tell you if I ever have any say in the matter, nothing would be done at that Washington National Cathedral. Absolutely *nothing*. First, I don't like the damn place."

"Well, Sayre's no good," Woods observed.

"Sayre's no good," the president agreed, "but, you know what I mean, they're just not our people, *not our people*." Nixon searched for a comparison. "I thought the [John F.] Kennedy [funeral service] at St. Matthews was much better. Much better."[13]

True to his word to wait for Justice Black's resignation, Justice Harlan let almost a week pass after Black's announcement before submitting his own notice of resignation on September 23, two days before Black died.[14] Harlan himself would not live out the year, dying on December 29, 1971.

Nixon officially had in hand what his staff referred to as a "double play." He could fill two seats at once, playing one off the other. The situation afforded him some true leverage in his selections.

Nixon, however, would dig himself a hole before the selection process was over. His initial picks, as Haldeman had described the earlier Haynsworth and Carswell nominations, would "go down the tubes."[15] And Nixon would react in exactly the same way as he had to these past rejections. He would respond in anger, and hastily. Like Harry Blackmun, the two men eventually chosen were second thoughts, the results of impetuous decisions.

But one of the picks in 1971, no doubt to Nixon's surprise, would come to play the decisive role in the outcome of *Roe v. Wade* and its companion case, *Doe v. Bolton*.

Supreme Court of the United States, October 1971

One thing that Nixon worried about as he moved to fill the Black and Harlan vacancies was a concern that his Department of Justice, run by a former bond lawyer, John Mitchell, had not been very adept at vetting candidates for the Supreme Court. They had missed badly on Carswell in particular, failing to note his high rate of reversal, among other things. So Nixon set up a second avenue for obtaining information about the people proposed by Mitchell. He asked his chief domestic advisor, John Ehrlichman, to have his team assist in the investigations of candidates.

Enter John W. Dean.

Dean was told by Ehrlichman on the day of Black's resignation that the president wanted him, as White House Counsel, to conduct his own independent background checks on the people whose names would be circulating.[16] He would end up working in parallel with the main person in the Justice Department who had been tasked with screening candidates—a young Arizona lawyer named Bill Rehnquist, who was in charge of the Office of Legal Counsel.

With two nominations in play, a surprising idea surfaced: why not a woman? Pat Nixon and her daughters lobbied Nixon to think seriously about a woman.

Resistance to the idea of a female on the Supreme Court was to be expected in a profession that was still almost totally male-dominated, but the strongest pushback actually came from the chief justice himself. Warren Burger expressed his adamant opposition, and before the shouting was over he threatened to resign.[17]

Nixon, though he was rankled by Burger's presumptiveness, privately expressed his understanding for the chief justice's position. "I don't think a woman should be in any government job whatsoever," he privately told Haldeman. "I mean, I really don't," he said. "The reason why I do is mainly because they are erratic. And emotional. Men are erratic and emotional too, but the point is a woman is more likely to be."[18]

And then there was the problem of males and females working side by side in close quarters with one another. Nixon told Haldeman that, given the cloistered nature of the Supreme Court and how it conducted its business, "it's like living with somebody inside a spaceship." It was uncomfortable for him to even think about the awkwardness for the two sexes under the circumstances.[19]

Nonetheless, Nixon wanted a woman as a nominee based on the political calculus of it all. "It just comes down to cold turkey," he said to his advisors. He did not think that anyone would vote against him just because he had nominated a woman for the Supreme Court. On the other hand, he might actually change some minds if he at least tried to place a woman on the court. And in the fall of 1971, when he was making his decision, Nixon assumed he needed every last vote to win come November 1972.[20] He had no way at that point of projecting that he would score a landslide.

The names of two women jumped to the top of the list for consideration. Judge Sylvia Bacon was a thirty-nine-year-old trial judge on the Superior Court for the District of Columbia, but she turned out to be too young and inexperienced to be a serious candidate. Justice Mildred Lillie of California, however, had the credentials. She had been a federal prosecutor and then a judge for more than two decades. She was currently serving on the California Court of Appeals in Los Angeles. She was "tough on crime" and had the support of both Governor Reagan and Sam Yorty, the maverick mayor of Los Angeles. Her political credentials were diverse: a Democrat, she had been appointed to the bench by Republican then-governor Earl Warren. And for bonus points, she was married to a Catholic.[21]

Nixon liked it all. It was just the kind of contrarian politics that he relished.

For the other seat, Nixon had first tapped a conservative congressman from the South, Virginian Richard Poff, but he soon enough withdrew his name from consideration, allegedly over concerns that an adopted son would find out about his adoption through the grinding confirmation process he would face in the Senate, especially as a Southerner.[22]

Next up was Hershel Friday, a bond lawyer from Little Rock, Arkansas, who had been recommended by Warren Burger and John Mitchell. John Dean and David Young, a former Kissinger aide who was also involved with the Plumbers, were dispatched from Washington to interview both Hershel Friday and Mildred Lillie.

What they saw of Hershel Friday was profoundly troubling. He was a competent business lawyer and had represented the Little Rock School Board on questions of school prayer and busing, but he had no thoughts about any of the other major issues facing the court. "He's like a blank sheet of paper," Dean reported to John Ehrlichman by phone from Little Rock.[23] John Mitchell's vetting process once again had failed spectacularly.

Justice Mildred Lillie was a different story. Dean and Young landed in Los Angeles on John Dean's thirty-fourth birthday, October 14. They met with Justice Lillie (Court of Appeals judges are called "justices" in California) the next day. Dean was highly impressed. "John, she's terrific," he reported back to Ehrlichman. "She is articulate, well read, knows the criminal justice system from the bottom up, and the civil justice system from the top down," Dean said. "She's had vast experience. She knows her way around the Constitution. While she's had no civil rights cases, she thinks busing hurts children. She doesn't like it. She's a deeply religious woman, and very active in her community. The president will do himself proud naming her."[24]

At just that time, Chief Justice Burger told John Mitchell that he would resign if Nixon appointed a woman.[25] And to the president's great consternation, someone within the American Bar Association (ABA) leaked the names of the six candidates that the White House had forwarded for screening. The *New York Times* and the *Washington Post* ran articles featuring the six, including profiles of Hershel Friday and Mildred Lillie.[26] Nixon was furious over the leak, fearing that the advance notice would allow his enemies time to "tear to pieces" his selections.[27]

He was right. Senator Edward M. Kennedy said, "Surely the compilation and submission of this list will rank as one of the greatest insults to the Supreme Court in its history." Indiana senator Birch Bayh added, "The president apparently will not announce his nominee until he sees which balloons rise to the top and which will burst."[28] Friday and Lillie were dead on arrival at the ABA—Friday because he was not qualified and Lillie because she was a woman. While the ABA Committee on the Federal Judiciary split 6–6 on a motion to record a rebuffing "not opposed" to Friday, they voted 11–1 that Justice Lillie was "unqualified" to serve on the court.[29]

Nixon appeared before the National Federation of Republican Women a few days later and disingenuously complained that Justice Lillie might have gotten "a better break" if the ABA committee had not been composed of twelve men. The committee "should at least have one woman on it," he said. He instructed Mitchell to terminate forthwith the agreement with the ABA to permit pre-nomination reviews.[30]

Nixon then had to pivot. It was already late October. He thrashed around for alternatives. One idea was Tennessee senator Howard Baker, the same man who would become the minority chair of the Senate Watergate Committee in 1973. But Baker hesitated to commit and lost the opportunity when Nixon moved on.[31]

It was the Harry Blackmun situation all over again. Nixon's first choices were shot down and he was forced to scramble to find new candidates. John Dean has written about the lightning quickness with which Nixon moved to find two new contenders. "On Tuesday, October 19, he had nobody vetted or ABA-approved, let alone ready to take either of the two open seats," Dean wrote. "By Thursday, the 21st, he would announce two nominations."[32]

October 21, 1971

John Dean first suggested the name of Bill Rehnquist on October 4, early in the selection process. He mentioned it to White House insider Richard Moore, who in turn discussed it with Ehrlichman and Mitchell. Dean himself continued to keep the idea of Rehnquist alive. The problem for Rehnquist was that nobody saw the political advantage in naming him as the choice. Though the forty-seven-year-old from Phoenix was considered a constitutional expert, he himself told a reporter, off the record, "I'm not from the South, I'm not a woman, and I'm not mediocre."[33]

Rehnquist's strengths were many from John Dean's standpoint. He was the editor of the *Stanford Law Review* and graduated at the top of his class, which included John Ehrlichman. He had youth on his side. And he had clerked on the court for Justice Robert Jackson (who had once stepped down from the court to become the chief prosecutor at Nuremberg). Rehnquist was as conservative as they came. Dean knew of him even before his White House years through his connection to Barry Goldwater's son, Barry Jr., who had been a swimmer with Dean at prep school in Staunton, Virginia. "Bill Rehnquist makes Barry Goldwater look like a liberal," Dean quipped to Dick Moore.[34]

The other name that emerged was that of Lewis Powell, a well-off, pro-business lawyer from Richmond, Virginia. Powell had been a respected president of the American Bar Association. He was appointed by President Lyndon Johnson to a presidential commission on crime, where he established himself as a thoughtful but fervent opponent of the Warren Court on the question of the rights of criminal defendants. He also had been chosen by President Nixon to work on a blue-ribbon panel that reviewed waste in the Defense Department and the Pentagon.

To be sure, Powell had skeletons in his closet. As the president of the Richmond City School Board he was roundly criticized for moving at a glacial pace with integration and busing. He belonged to all-white clubs and had written derisively about Martin Luther King Jr. and his civil disobedience philosophy. Powell believed in respect for the rule of law. He thought American life in general was suffering from "excessive tolerance."[35]

The White House first contacted Powell just two days before Nixon announced his selection to the nation on national television. Powell told John Mitchell and the president that he worried about his eyesight and his age—he was sixty-four. His reluctance made him all the more appealing to Nixon. Like Harry Blackmun before him, Powell's vetting was sparse to nonexistent; the ABA would not be consulted.[36]

Rehnquist likewise was told of his consideration for the court just before Nixon made the announcement. The man doing the vetting suddenly became the vetted (or more accurately, the non-vetted). Nixon took advantage of his "double play" to send both names to the Senate at the same time. Powell would take Black's seat, Rehnquist Harlan's. The president's TV appearance on Thursday night, October 21, came just twenty-four hours after the ABA formally rejected Judge Lillie and Hershel Friday.[37]

Nixon asked for a quick confirmation of both men.[38]

Fortunately for Powell (and critical to *Roe*), Rehnquist took most of the fire during the confirmation process. Powell's liabilities and personal beliefs were mainly overlooked. His age was actually seen as an advantage during his confirmation—he was not expected to last long on the court. Neither Powell nor Rehnquist was asked by anyone in the process about his views on abortion. The "abortion question" had not yet become a litmus test for Supreme Court nominees.

In convincing Powell to take the nomination, Nixon made note of how impactful justices can be in shaping the course of the nation over long periods of time, almost as if he sensed that such would be the case during Powell's tenure. "Time moves a lot faster than it used to," Nixon told Powell during a phone call the night of October 19. "I mean opinions, decisions will be made in the next five years that are enormously important, you know, on many of these issues," he said. "The whole concept of our system for many years to come may be determined in this period, and I just want you to know that the attorney general and I feel that, if you can see your way clear to do this, that we'll take the responsibility on the political side and all the rest."[39]

Court Chamber, December 1971

As the Rehnquist and Powell nominations were wending their way through the Senate, the two abortion cases came up for oral argument in the Supreme Court. *Roe v. Wade* was a Texas case; *Doe v. Bolton* was out of Georgia. They were scheduled to be argued back-to-back on Monday, December 13, 1971. Attorneys representing Texas and Georgia moved to delay arguments, thinking that Rehnquist and Powell, if confirmed, would be more sympathetic to the right of a state to regulate abortions.

Chief Justice Burger appointed Potter Stewart and Harry Blackmun to screen the pending cases to decide which of the cases should be deferred until Rehnquist and Powell joined. Blackmun later wrote that Potter Stewart pressed for *Roe* and *Doe* to be argued without delay because he thought they would be decided on narrow jurisdictional grounds. "How wrong we were," Blackmun later observed.[40] The request for a postponement of oral arguments was denied.[41]

The arguments went forward as scheduled on December 13, just days after Powell and Rehnquist were both confirmed by the Senate, though they would not be sworn in until January.[42] Because they did not participate in the oral arguments, they would not be permitted to take part in the decision. As it stood, it appeared that one of the most important decisions in the history of the United States Supreme Court would be decided by seven men, not even a full court.

That would all change.

President Nixon presents framed commissions of office to newly confirmed
Supreme Court Justices Lewis F. Powell Jr. and William H. Rehnquist,
December 22, 1971.

White House Photo Office, Nixon Library

On the night that President Nixon told the nation that he had
selected Powell and Rehnquist, he pointedly noted, "Presidents come
and go, but the Supreme Court through its decisions goes on forever."[43]

The Oval Office, Morning of January 2, 1973

Before wrapping up his phone call with Nixon on the morning of January 2, 1973, the chief justice made sure to let the president know that
he was very pleased with Associate Justice William Rehnquist. "By the
way," Burger said, "this young fellow—young now for you and me—
Rehnquist, he's a real star."[44]

"Isn't that great," Nixon responded. "Well, we'll try to give you—
one day if we ever get a chance—another one."

"Get another fella," Burger added, undoubtedly trying to reinforce his conviction that Nixon should never again start thinking
about a female nominee.

"You remember General McArthur's famous statement when he
spoke to the Congress?" Nixon asked, referring to McArthur's melo-
dramatic line that "old soldiers never die, they just fade away." Nixon

said that he would put it a little bit differently when it came to Supreme Court justices. "Supreme Court justices never die," Nixon quipped, "and they never fade away."

Both men laughed heartily.

"You've got to get some young fellas up here, and not any more in their sixties," Burger admonished.

"You guys are all right," Nixon responded. "My guys in their sixties are great—the Burger, Blackmun, Powell triumvirate."[45]

That proposition was about to be put to the test in the *Roe* and *Doe* cases that would come down in January 1973.

5

"I Just Feel the Torture You Are Going Through on Vietnam"

The Oval Office, Tuesday, January 2, 1973

It was later in the day on January 2 when Nixon finally hit upon how he might tactfully avoid the Truman memorial. He would look to his predecessor for cover, calling Lyndon Johnson in Texas at a quarter to 5:00 in the afternoon. It would be their last conversation.

With Kissinger, Ehrlichman, and Haldeman all returning late in the day from their holiday vacations, Nixon spent large chunks of his day with Chuck Colson. They talked about Nixon setting up a memorial fund for Roberto Clemente, with a personal contribution from the president and Mrs. Nixon. They talked about Kissinger. And they talked about the end of the bombing in Vietnam. But throughout the day Nixon obsessed over the Truman memorial service and Francis Sayre. He told Colson that Sayre, a confirmed pacifist, was going to have a difficult time eulogizing the president who dropped the atomic bomb to end the Second World War and then started the Korean War.[1] They began to circle around the idea that maybe former president Johnson wouldn't be going to the Truman service, and this could be Nixon's excuse for his own absence.

Nixon asked his assistant Steve Bull to check on Johnson's plans.[2]

Before this could all be buttoned down, however, Nixon had to meet with the man who had replaced LBJ in the Senate as majority leader, the mild-mannered and lanky senator from Montana named Mike Mansfield. At 3:30 PM, Nixon left his EOB office, where he had been conferring with Colson, and returned to the Oval Office to meet with Mansfield.[3]

This promised to be a critical meeting for the president. The two great adversaries over the war—Nixon and Mansfield—would meet one-on-one, and this was Nixon's chance to convince Mansfield to hold on, just a while longer, so Nixon and Kissinger could finally complete the peace negotiations with the North Vietnamese. He knew he had fences to mend and that his silence during the bombing had truly provoked the members of Congress who opposed the war. Mansfield was among the leading proponents in the Senate for ending America's involvement in Vietnam as soon as possible.

Mansfield was not a dove by nature. Born in New York City to Irish immigrants in 1903, he was sent when he was just three years old to live with an aunt and uncle in Great Falls, Montana, shortly after his mother died. He later lied to recruiters about his age so he could join the navy (he was just fifteen) during World War I. He enlisted in the marines after the war and was sent to the Far East, which started his lifelong interest in that part of the world. He became a recognized expert on Indochina.[4]

He was elected to Congress in 1942, where he served for a decade. He and young Nixon, as newly minted western congressmen, got to know each other during this time. In 1952, Mansfield won election to the Senate. In 1961, when Lyndon Johnson was elected to the vice presidency, Mansfield took his job as the majority leader of the Senate.[5] He would hold that powerful position for the next sixteen years, eventually becoming the longest-serving majority leader in history.

Mansfield at first supported President Kennedy's policy of increasing US involvement in Indochina, but after the Diem coup and Kennedy's assassination, he became the foremost critic of the war.[6]

Quiet and self-effacing in style, Mansfield was a dynamo in the Senate. His immense skills helped President Johnson pass the Civil Rights Act of 1964 and the Voting Rights Act of 1965.[7]

After greetings and photographs by the press, who were ushered in and out of the Oval Office, Nixon and Mansfield got down to business.[8] The first topic was how Nixon hoped to conduct regular meetings with the leaders in Congress. Nixon conceded that the government had a "split personality," as it had for his entire presidency, with the Democrats controlling both houses of Congress and the Republicans the White House. "We just have to learn to live with it, I guess," Nixon said. But he wanted to find ways to reduce partisan

President Nixon and Senate Majority Leader Mike Mansfield with press corps members in Oval Office, January 2, 1973. The microphones that will pick up their conversation are located in wall sconces on each side of the fireplace in the Oval Office; one is visible behind Mansfield.
White House Photo Office, Nixon Library

conflict, suggesting that he and the majority leader meet on a "fairly regular basis," particularly when it came to foreign policy.

"Well, Mr. President, speaking of foreign policy," Mansfield interjected, having found his opportunity to speak after an almost-fifteen-minute monologue by Nixon, "there's a feeling of great unrest among the members on the Hill on the Senate side." Mansfield warned that there were strong forces building to end the war. "I would be less than frank if I didn't call it to your attention."

"Who is it?" Nixon asked.

Mansfield would not name names. "I'm afraid if this war is not settled in some fashion, that it's going to be [a problem]," Mansfield said. "People are very disturbed around the country, too. And it's a matter which, in my view at least, they seem to tie to you personally. I was hoping for some way that the last inch could be covered, and be breached, not only in Vietnam—that's the primary source—but Laos and Cambodia as well. And I hope and pray that it would be possible that this could be done before the 20th of January [when Nixon would be inaugurated for his second term]."[9]

Mansfield said the Senate Foreign Relations Committee, on which he sat, had met that morning and discussed what they should do about the war. "I found the committee very restrained, very concerned, very disturbed," he said. Even Nixon's friends on the committee were alarmed over the unexplained bombing, Mansfield asserted. Though many were relieved over what appeared to have been a decrease in the bombing, at least temporarily, "they just [didn't] know what to do," Mansfield said. "And that's a dangerous situation to be in, because they're going to strike out in all directions."[10]

The president sat silently, patiently listening to a man he admired. Mansfield spoke in a deliberate, sometimes halting way. He was carefully picking and selecting his words. It seemed clear that he had not been in the habit of speaking so frankly with Richard Nixon. "I don't usually talk about these things with you," he said, "but I was feeling so deeply concerned personally, I just felt I needed to say it. This is the end of the line."

Nixon responded. "Mike, let me say that, as I'm sure you are aware of, no one is more aware of this than I am, and no one has perhaps a greater stake in bringing it to an end as quickly as possible, as [I do]," he said. Nixon then laid out for Mansfield what he thought would unfold once peace negotiations resumed in the following week. It would take, he thought, three to four days at a maximum to reach an agreement. And, he warned, "it would be very detrimental to what is now a situation where we are on the one yard line to the goal—to getting a goal—if anything were done, if anything were said. When I say 'said,' I don't mean people can't criticize what we've done, but to suggest *how* the thing ought to be settled [would be unacceptable]."[11]

Nixon did not want Congress dictating peace terms when he had come so far in his efforts to wrap things up. Congressional interference would serve no purpose other than to undercut his bargaining position—a position that he believed had just been established with the costly and risky air campaign over Hanoi.

"This is not a dodge," Nixon said. He conceded that it might be useful to go on television and make his case to the country as to where everything stood, but he thought that would "destroy the whole thing." They were very close to a deal and he was hopeful. What he needed was just a little more time.

He offered to make Henry Kissinger available to meet with Mansfield confidentially to provide a complete but "secure" briefing on the status of the negotiations. Then, after obtaining Mansfield's agreement to keep what he was about to say private, Nixon outlined in broad strokes why he thought negotiations could be brought to a conclusion in short order.

Nixon started with a brief history of the most recent talks. There had been a basic agreement on October 8, he said, but it wasn't completely worked out. Kissinger's October 26 "peace at hand" statement was true but unfortunate. It created a false impression that they were about to announce a deal. Kissinger had a deal that was "at hand," but it was not yet "in hand."

The North Vietnamese, he said, pulled back in the weeks before the election. And then, three days before the election, said they would return to the table.

Three or four big issues still remained when negotiations restarted after the election, all of which, Nixon thought, were bridgeable. They had reached basic terms on a cease-fire in Vietnam, but there was a hope they could achieve a cease-fire across Indochina, including Laos and Cambodia. The terms of the demilitarized zone (to prohibit future infiltration from the North) remained to be completely worked out. They also had to iron out some of the details on the return of prisoners. And they still had to work on the protocols for elections in the South.

South Vietnam continued to waver, he said, over an agreement that left North Vietnamese forces in the South. This was a vexing problem, and the South Vietnamese were proving to be quite stubborn over the point. They perceived this as a life-or-death issue.

Kissinger found that when he returned to Paris after the US election, the North Vietnamese engaged in "dilatory" tactics, "which would have meant not just weeks, but months more of negotiation." Hanoi wanted to keep talking but not reach agreement, he stressed. In the meantime, its forces stepped up their infiltration of the South, hoping to grab as much land as possible before the cease-fire.

"That's what happened," Nixon concluded, without saying a word about the bombing itself, or the use of B-52s, or why the bombing had abruptly ended.

The North, Nixon said, needed to come back to the negotiating table while still saving face. It could not appear that the bombing had been the cause of the renewed talks. This is why Nixon had said nothing.

It was a sensitive and delicate situation, and Nixon's message to Mansfield could not have been plainer: "Don't let the Senate screw this up."[12] Mansfield left the Oval Office at 4:19 PM. It was not clear if Nixon had made his case.

LBJ Ranch, January 2, 1973
Nixon called for William Timmons, his assistant for legislative affairs. He filled him in on his meeting with Mansfield and asked for Timmons's assessment of the likelihood that Congress would pass resolutions to end the war in the coming days.[13] "They're in a dangerous wicket here politically," Nixon said of the antiwar advocates in Congress. "This war is going to end," he said to Timmons, "and when it does, we're going to take their damn hides off."[14] Timmons gave his appraisal and left.

It was time to bring Colson back in. During the afternoon, there had been tentative confirmation from LBJ's people in Texas that he was unlikely to come to the Truman service. When Nixon asked Colson if this was still the case, he said it was, "with a caveat." Apparently, Colson said, "Johnson loves funerals and memorial services." Nixon moaned.[15]

"Why don't I just call Johnson and tell him that I'm not going," Nixon finally said.

"That's one of the suggestions I was going to make," Colson responded.

Nixon picked up his phone. "President Johnson, please," he requested of the White House operator.[16]

Minutes later, Lyndon Johnson was on the phone from his ranch near Johnson City, Texas.

"Happy New Year!" Johnson beamed.[17]

"Happy New Year," Nixon responded. "How you feeling?"

"I feel pretty good," Johnson replied in his flat Texas drawl.

"Ah, well, by golly, we think of you," Nixon said. "I saw our friend Bebe [Rebozo] and I told him that you were waiting for him to come out and call on you."

"You tell him that that's your Christmas present to me," Johnson said.

Nixon roared. "Hey listen, that's something. He's feeling very low now, because he was sixty years old the other day."

"Oh," Johnson quietly exclaimed.

"And you know how Bebe . . ." Nixon continued. "I said, Bebe, you can't talk about being a young gay blade anymore," Nixon said, giggling clumsily.

"Oh, no he isn't," Johnson said. Johnson was sixty-four, having been born in central Texas in 1908. Nixon was just about to turn sixty—his birthday was exactly one week away, on January 9. Like Johnson, Nixon had been born and raised in rural poverty. Nixon grew up among the lemon groves of Southern California, where his father built the family's tiny mail-order home in Yorba Linda, using a kit he bought from a catalogue in 1912. Richard arrived a year later, the second son of Frank and Hannah Nixon. Like his brothers Harold, Edward, and Arthur, he was named for a famous king of England—in his case, Richard the Lionhearted, though his 1973 critics saw him more as Shakespeare's villainous Richard III.

"But I said don't worry about being sixty, it isn't all that bad," Nixon continued about Bebe Rebozo. "But he's in good shape," Nixon said self-consciously, "good shape."

The conversation tailed off for just an instant and Johnson jumped in. "Well, I just feel the torture you're going through on Vietnam," he said, referring to the Christmas bombings. "I wish'd I could do something to help you."

"Don't you worry about it," Nixon replied. "It's going to come out all right. We, ah, these people are now coming back to the table in a very, we think, constructive frame of mind."

"Good," Johnson said.

"And they *better*," Nixon insisted. "As you know, and I'm sure you feel the same way, we've got to get this finished in the right way and not the wrong way. That's what you tried to do; that's what I'm trying to do."

"You're doing it," Johnson muttered in an almost inaudible tone, "and I just wish for you the best."

Then Nixon was ready to get down to the real reason for his call. "Let me ask you—tell you one thing I particularly wanted to call about," he began. He said his staff had been in touch with the Truman family to see if they planned on coming to Washington. He reminded LBJ that they both had visited Independence the day after Truman died to lay wreaths and pay their respects to the family at the private services. "Under those circumstances," Nixon said, "it was not my intention to attend the public memorial service here, which is mainly for the diplomatic representatives and for, of course, members of Congress who could not go to the private service."

He mentioned nothing about his animus toward Francis Sayre. "Now on the other hand, I have understood you were not planning to come; if you were coming, I didn't want it to appear that I was not going. Could you tell me what your plans are?"

"No, I have no plans to go there at all," Johnson said.

Nixon could have stopped there—he had gotten the answer he wanted, but he continued to marshal his arguments. "It would seem to me, I think you agree, that we both have basically attended the service and it would look, I rather thought, as if we were exploiting it if we just went again, you know what I mean? Or how do you feel? I don't want anyone to think that we were affronting President Truman."

"Well, Bird and I talked that over," Johnson said, "and we thought that what we ought to do was to go the day you did and pay our respects."

"Good," Nixon responded. "Well, you did exactly the same, and therefore, that way we did it in a very personal way: you, Mrs. Johnson, and Pat and myself. And you feel as far as I am concerned that, ah, as far as you're concerned, you will not be there, and I will follow the same line here."

Johnson agreed, but he was sounding weaker as the conversation progressed. Nixon switched topics to the memorial service for House Majority Leader Hale Boggs from Louisiana, who was missing and presumed dead from a plane crash in Alaska in October 1972.[18] His mysterious disappearance was immediately linked to his membership on the Warren Commission. A memorial mass was planned in New Orleans for January 4.[19]

"Now I will not be at the Boggs thing," Nixon said. "I just can't get away there, but Pat will be there, so she may see you there. Are you going to that?"

"It depends on my condition," Johnson said.

"Right," Nixon responded, not really understanding the gravity of what Johnson was saying.

"I went to the ball game yesterday and I stayed up all night and had the doctor out from San Antonio," Johnson said. LBJ had traveled to Dallas the day before to attend the Cotton Bowl Classic, where Texas beat Alabama in a tight game.

"Look, your team won," Nixon said, still not getting what Johnson was saying.

"Yes, we had a wonderful game."

"I saw that game on television, Texas came back and won," Nixon said.

"I pay for it every time I do it," Johnson softly replied.

"You yell, don't you?" Nixon said.

"A little bit," Johnson said, laughing like a shy boy.

"Yeah, yeah, yeah," Nixon said distractedly.

"And then I stayed up, I had heart pains all night," Johnson said.

Nixon finally grasped what LBJ had been saying. "Oh, boy, *have you?* Goodness I called you at the wrong time."

"Not at all," Johnson graciously replied.

"Well—"

"I'm cheered," Johnson said. "I wanted to hear from you."

"Let me tell you this: I still have that invitation for you to go down and use that place in Florida, 'cause old Bebe is a great guy to have around; he cheers people up, you know, he never brings up any unpleasant subjects."

"[Tell him to] come see me, or I may go see him," Johnson responded.

That was it. The conversation lasted four minutes and thirty seconds. Johnson ended with his best wishes, saying, "Let me know if I can help you in any way. I know you're doing the best you can."

"Oh, it will come out," Nixon assured him.[20] Once he hung up the phone, Nixon turned to Colson, who had been quietly sitting there through the entire call. "He doesn't even know if he's going to the Boggs thing; he went to the ball game yesterday and he's had heart pains all day," Nixon said. "He's a hypochondriac," he said. "He's unbelievable."

Colson, as usual, agreed. "He's so pathetic."[21]

It was the last time that Richard Milhous Nixon and Lyndon Baines Johnson would speak. Exactly twenty days later, Johnson would die of a massive heart attack.

Fall 1968

The relationship between the nation's thirty-sixth and thirty-seventh presidents was strange, to say the least. Nixon had torpedoed Johnson's efforts to end the Vietnam War in October 1968, as the election hung in the balance, by telling the South Vietnamese leadership, through intermediaries, to hang tight until after the election rather than participate in Johnson's last-ditch effort to bring both sides together in Paris. Johnson found out about it and called those acts "treason."[22]

For his part, Nixon always believed that Johnson had bugged his campaign plane in 1968. In January 1973, as Watergate seemed more and more to threaten his presidency, Nixon would desperately search for some corroborating evidence of Johnson's wiretapping.

Despite the bad blood, Johnson was not altogether unhappy with Nixon's election in 1968.[23] LBJ's vice president, Hubert Humphrey, who became the Democratic nominee, sided late in the campaign with those who favored a bombing halt and a cease-fire in Vietnam.[24] Johnson did not want everything he had done, and all of the lives sacrificed, to have been for nothing. He knew Nixon favored a peace through strength over a "sellout."[25]

In 1972, Johnson gave lukewarm support to George McGovern. "It is no secret that Senator McGovern and I have widely differing opinions on many matters, especially foreign policy," Johnson said through a press release just after McGovern was nominated. "The Democratic Party can accommodate disagreement."[26] By October, Johnson said that his health prevented him from taking part in the presidential campaign.[27] The most Johnson would say was that he intended to vote for McGovern.

Nixon later portrayed his relationship with Johnson as intimate, though that was never really the case. Nixon wrote in his memoirs that Lyndon Johnson was "uniquely able to understand some of the things I was experiencing, particularly with Congress and the media over Vietnam, and we became quite close."[28]

The difference between the two men was that Johnson was tormented by the Vietnam War. It haunted him and drove him from office—and it was quickly killing him. Nixon, on the other hand, was a fatalist about his use of power. He had not started the war and he thought he was best equipped to end it, so he did not suffer from the same sense of anguish and remorse that LBJ experienced. His philosophy of never looking back and never second-guessing major decisions allowed him to escape the problem of being frozen by indecision, but this also kept him from engaging in serious introspection about what he was doing.

Nixon preferred to think of his role in the presidency as a "glorious burden." He wrote on Christmas Eve, 1972, at 4:00 AM, as the last bombs dropped in Hanoi before the Christmas Day halt, that he had to "get away from the thought of considering the office at any time a burden." To the contrary, he wrote, "I actually do not consider it a burden, an agony, etc., as did Eisenhower and also to a certain extent Johnson. As a matter of fact, I think the term glorious burden is the best description."

By his reckoning, God had given him the "great gift" to "exert leadership, not only for America but on the world scene."[29]

US Congress, January 3, 1973

As Mansfield predicted, Congress began striking out in all directions. "Congressional opponents of the war in Vietnam threatened today to try to cut off appropriations for the war if the Nixon Administration did not quickly obtain a peace settlement," the *New York Times* reported the next morning.[30]

The House Democratic Caucus voted 154–75 to declare its commitment to the termination of American military operations immediately, with the only provisos being that there be arrangements for the safe withdrawal of US forces and the return of all American prisoners of war.[31]

The Senate Foreign Relations Committee, chaired by Arkansas senator J. W. Fulbright, expressed its determination "that the legislative powers of the Congress should be brought to bear" if peace had not been negotiated by January 20.[32] By Thursday, January 4, the Senate Democrats voted 36–12 for an antiwar resolution almost identical to the House resolution.[33]

Mike Mansfield said the day after meeting with the president that the Nixon administration "had failed to make peace by negotiation." Mansfield was defiant: "The time has long since past [*sic*] when we can take shelter in a claim of legislative impotence."[34] Nixon obviously had failed to convince his old colleague to give him some additional time to finish off the peace negotiations.

The president was on the clock.

Lincoln Sitting Room, Evening of January 2, 1973

Nixon met with Henry Kissinger, back from California, just after dinner that night. It was the first time the two had a chance to meet face-to-face after the Reston article claiming that Kissinger opposed the bombing. They met for almost two hours.[35]

When Kissinger left, Nixon called Colson. "Well, I just had a long talk with Henry," he said, "and his dauber is a little down, so tomorrow— I told him that you and Haldeman are the two members of the White House staff that stood by him, and he said, yeah, you were really great and Haldeman was great—and so I would sort of cheer him up tomorrow and lay off of the past, and say, 'Now just be strong' and all that sort of thing."[36]

Colson didn't seem to blink at the notion that he had been one of the staff who had stood by Kissinger in recent days. "Was his dauber down because of the articles or was he just . . ."

President Nixon with Henry Kissinger in the Lincoln Sitting Room in the White House residence. The telephone line from the phone in this room was recorded.

White House Photo Office, Nixon Library

"Yeah, the articles," Nixon said. "Basically, the articles you and I pay damn little attention to."

Nixon marveled at how he had to be the one to keep everyone centered. "It's really something that I seem to have the responsibility of keeping our own people on their . . ." he said.

"I know," Colson interjected. "I was thinking what an incredible thing, the amount of work you've had to put in just to keep that fella's morale up, or anywhere near normal level."

"Well," Nixon said, "he just sees it all in such personal terms, Chuck."

Nixon instructed Colson to tell Ron Ziegler that he had met with Kissinger upon his return from California, and that they had talked for two hours, so that Ziegler could pass this information on to the press. Nixon didn't want any more stories about a rift between the two men.

It fell, therefore, to Chuck Colson to meet with Kissinger the next day to assist in keeping his dauber up. Colson, though, was about to face his own moment of truth with a visit from Howard Hunt's lawyer, Bill Bittman.

6

"Every Tree in the Forest Will Fall"

March Air Force Base, Riverside, California, January 2, 1973
On the same day that Nixon spoke with LBJ, a group from his White House staff boarded a brand-new, customized Boeing 707 at March Air Force Base in Riverside, California, to return to Washington from their holiday vacations. The 707 was commissioned to become the new Air Force One, and this was one of its very first flights. "It smelled like a new car," John Dean wrote, "and there were sheets over all the seats because the Air Force brass didn't want any passenger to leave a blemish before the President flew in the plane."[1]

At March Air Force Base, Dean received a frantic call from Paul O'Brien, a lawyer who was working for the Committee to Re-Elect the President on the Watergate investigation. "One of our boys is off the reservation," O'Brien said, referring to Howard Hunt. The phone call was hurried because the plane was about to take off.[2]

Elaboration on this bad news was waiting for Dean when he arrived back at his home in Alexandria, Virginia, that evening. He called O'Brien and was told that Hunt was despondent and wanted to plead guilty, but before doing so he wanted assurances of executive clemency. "O'Brien told me that Hunt would only take the assurances from Colson," Dean later testified, "and that Bittman had been trying to reach Colson." Dean promised to talk to Colson about it in the morning.[3]

Executive Office Building, Wednesday, January 3, 1973
The next day, January 3, Dean was back in his spacious office in the Executive Office Building. Colson called him to ask if he had seen Hunt's "human adversaries are arraigned against me" letter, and

while on the phone, Dean pulled from a large stack of papers Colson's "Now what the hell do I do?" memo, which had attached to it Hunt's letter of December 31. "I told Colson that I was aware of the fact that Bittman wanted to discuss the matter of Executive clemency for Hunt and that Hunt would only take assurances from him—Colson," Dean testified.[4]

Dean and Colson consulted with John Ehrlichman, Dean's predecessor as White House Counsel and now Nixon's top advisor on domestic affairs. Ehrlichman thought Colson should hear what Hunt's lawyer had to say, as long as he made no commitments.

Colson called Bittman and invited him to come to his office in the EOB later that afternoon.[5]

Colson received an earful from Bittman. Hunt was ready to crack, Bittman said, and suicide was not out of the question. Hunt thought he had been treated miserably and abandoned by the White House and the CIA. There had been pressure to revoke Hunt's CIA pension, and the White House stood silent. The prosecutors and FBI had been merciless with him. Not long before his wife died, FBI investigators showed Dorothy Hunt letters that were found in Hunt's safe in the EOB that suggested he had had an affair with another woman.[6]

All of this weighed heavily on Howard Hunt, Bittman said. He had leaned on his wife for emotional support after his arrest, and now she was gone. He had no interest in fighting the criminal case, but he knew, as did Bittman, that Judge Sirica was likely to impose a long sentence if he pled guilty. Howard Hunt did not want his children to become orphans. He worried especially about his nine-year-old son. Hunt needed rock-solid assurances that he would be out of prison and reunited with his children within a year at most.

Bittman made overt threats. He told Colson that he intended to pursue the White House's handling of Hunt's safe. He contended that the forcible opening of the safe in the White House basement by the Secret Service and a team from the General Services Administration just days after the Watergate break-in was an unauthorized search by the government. As a result, Bittman had filed a motion to suppress the evidence found in the safe. He said no one could locate several notebooks that Hunt said were in the safe that would show that higher-ups were involved. If Hunt was forced to go to trial, Bittman warned, Dean and Colson would be called to testify about the safe.[7]

Bill Bittman was an intimidating force. He made his name while a very young prosecutor in Bobby Kennedy's Department of Justice. In the summer of 1964, Bittman led the prosecution team that convicted Teamster president Jimmy Hoffa on mail and wire fraud charges in connection with his misappropriation of the union's pension funds.[8] Bittman was just thirty-two years old when he tried the case. During the trial and for months thereafter, there were so many death threats against Bittman that he had to have two bodyguards with him around the clock.

The press described Bittman as the archetypal prosecutor. "He looks and acts like a man who can take care of himself," the *New York Times* reported. "He is thick-necked and powerful looking and six feet tall. He weighs 195 pounds and has a bulldog jaw."[9] He was known for his aggressive, "swarming" style of cross-examination.

Further burnishing his reputation three years after the Hoffa conviction, Bittman led a Department of Justice team that convicted LBJ's protégé and onetime powerful secretary of the Senate, Bobby Baker, on charges of tax evasion.[10]

John Dean described Colson as "extremely shaken" after his meeting with Bittman on January 3. Colson huddled with Dean and Ehrlichman to recount what Bittman had said. "Colson spoke in gasps as if he'd been doing his old Marine exercises," Dean remembered.[11] Colson said that Bittman "came at me like a train." In response Colson was coy, saying he would do everything he could for his friend, but he stopped short of expressly promising to assist in seeking clemency.[12]

Bittman reported his conversation with Colson to Howard Hunt that night, and Hunt was not satisfied. He insisted Bittman meet again with Colson to nail down an understanding about clemency.[13] The next day, on January 4, Bittman met a second time with Colson in his EOB office. This time Bittman made it clear he would not leave without some sort of guarantee. According to Howard Hunt, Colson responded to Bittman in code. He told Bittman that if Hunt received a lengthy sentence, "Well, Christmas comes around every year."[14]

His reference was unmistakable. Richard Nixon had commuted the thirteen-year sentence of Jimmy Hoffa—the man Bittman helped put behind bars—right before Christmas in 1971.[15] "This was the type of subtlety and care that was often invoked," Hunt later wrote. "The words sound innocuous, but they contained a specific reference to the prior prosecution by Bill Bittman of Teamster boss Jimmy Hoffa, who had been paroled at Christmastime approximately two years earlier. It was generally known that Colson was the man behind the scenes who arranged Hoffa's pardon."[16] This was sufficient to satisfy Bittman and Hunt.

Bittman told Colson he would withdraw his motion to suppress.

Oval Office, January 3, 1973, Noon Hour

In large part because it was known that Colson had been Howard Hunt's sponsor at the White House, Colson had been gently nudged to leave the White House just after the election. Colson was scheduled to depart sometime after Nixon's second inauguration, hoping to score an overseas junket, at taxpayers' expense, as a reward for his faithful service before he officially resigned.

Colson had reason to be nervous on January 3, and not just because he had been all but physically accosted by Bill Bittman. At virtually the same time that arrangements were being made to set up the meeting between Colson and Bittman, Bob Haldeman, just back from his California vacation, met with Richard Nixon in the Oval Office. He had intelligence for the president about Colson and his involvement with Watergate.[17]

The discussion about Colson arose when Nixon bemoaned the loss of Colson at a time when he expected multiple fights with Congress. Colson was tough and knew how to play the game, Nixon said. No one in the White House could take his place. "I wonder if we shouldn't extend Colson by a couple of months?" Nixon proposed.

"I think it's better to let him go," Haldeman responded. "I tell you, I found out some things that—even though he is going to be missed—there's more to his involvement in some of this stuff than I realized."

"Which parts?" Nixon asked.

"Watergate," Haldeman replied.

"Colson?" Nixon responded. *"Does he know?"*

"I think he knows," Haldeman said.

"Does he know you know?" Nixon asked.

"I don't think he knows I know," Haldeman replied.

"What do you mean, through Hunt or what?" Nixon probed.

"Yes, through Hunt and Liddy," Haldeman said. "And if Liddy decides to pull the cork, Colson could be in some real soup. Liddy can do it under oath and then Colson is in a position of having perjured himself. See, Colson and Mitchell have both perjured themselves under oath already."

"You mean Colson was aware of the Watergate bugging?" Nixon again asked. "That's hard for me to believe."

"Not only was aware of it," Haldeman said, "but was pushing very hard for the results from it."

Colson had admitted to a meeting with Liddy and Hunt in the winter of 1972, prior to the approval of the multiple Watergate break-ins. Hunt and Liddy came to Colson's EOB office late in the day to complain that Jeb Magruder, the second in command at the Committee to Re-Elect, was dragging his feet on approving their budget and operations. Colson, with Liddy and Hunt sitting in his office, picked up the phone and called Magruder, telling him to "get off his duff" and approve the plans. The implicit threat was that Colson would take matters into his own hands if Magruder and Mitchell failed to move forward with Liddy and Hunt's intelligence plans.[18] The prospect of Colson taking action was enough to goad Magruder into finally convincing John Mitchell (who had moved from attorney general to campaign chairman on March 1) to approve the bugging plans at the end of March 1972.

Colson claimed he did not know of the specifics of Hunt and Liddy's plans, but now Haldeman had reason to think Colson's role had been greater than one phone call to Magruder.

Haldeman said that he didn't know any of this information firsthand—and he didn't want to know more—but his source, undisclosed to Nixon, was Jeb Magruder. Haldeman met earlier that day with Magruder for the first time since the weekend of the break-in back in June 1972. Magruder told Haldeman that Colson had played a significant role in ordering Watergate.[19]

"Who was he pushing?" Nixon inquired, wanting to know more about Colson's involvement.

"Magruder and Liddy. And that's why we have to be awful careful to take—Liddy we're taking care of in one way. We've got to be very careful to take care of Magruder the right way."

"How can you do that?" Nixon asked.

"I don't know. But I'm going to make sure he has the feeling that he's—John Dean's been doing a superb job of just patting him on him, covering all facets."[20]

The two discussed how to handle a nervous Jeb Magruder, who was on the list of witnesses to testify in a week before Judge Sirica. Magruder was already working as the director of the inaugural festivities, and Nixon suggested that maybe he could become involved with the Bicentennial Commission after January 20. "The main thing is he's got to feel in his own mind, in his own heart, that we're on his side," Haldeman said.

Nixon returned to Colson's knowledge of the break-in. "I can see Mitchell," he said, "but I can't see Colson getting into this thing."

"The stupidity," Haldeman replied.

"What the Christ was he looking for?" Nixon asked.

"They were looking for stuff on two things. One, on financial [information]," Haldeman said.

"Yes," Nixon said.

"And the other on stuff they thought they had on what [the Democrats] were going to do at [their convention] in Miami to screw us up, because apparently—a Democratic plot. And they thought they had it uncovered. Colson was salivating with glee over the thought of what he might be able to do with it."

Haldeman then ticked off the main areas of concern as the burglars' trial loomed. There was little danger of Liddy flipping, Haldeman thought. He felt the same way about Hunt, but he didn't know of the developing situation that day between Bittman and Colson. Haldeman believed that Jeb Magruder would hang tight, but he worried about Hugh Sloan, the treasurer of the Committee to Re-Elect, who was also being called to testify. Sloan had provided Liddy with the money for his operation but had not been told the reason that Liddy needed the money. Sloan, per Haldeman, "doesn't know enough, apparently, to matter; although he suspects a lot, and if they start him wandering along in his suspicions he could make a lot of news."[21]

Nixon hoped that the entire group would just plead guilty and get it over with. "All in all, it's better if they plead guilty, frankly," he said.

"I would think so," Haldeman agreed. "It may just all go away."

But Haldeman was resolute about one thing: Colson had to go.[22]

Rockville, Maryland, Late December 1972

There was another defendant who was showing signs of acute distress. Jim McCord, the former CIA security man who planted the bugs in the Watergate, was turning out to be quite the loose cannon. His behavior was becoming more and more bizarre.

McCord had tried to hire the flamboyant Boston attorney F. Lee Bailey to represent him in the Watergate case. At the time, Bailey was one of the most controversial and celebrated attorneys in the United States. He won fame when he was just twenty-eight, representing Sam

Sheppard, a Cleveland physician who had been convicted of killing his wife in 1954. Bailey convinced an Ohio federal trial court in 1966 to overturn Sheppard's conviction because of the media circus created by "massive, pervasive and prejudicial" pretrial publicity, and the unrestrained courtroom antics of journalists and news reporters during the trial.[23]

In 1971, the year prior to Jim McCord's arrest, Bailey had successfully defended Captain Ernest Medina, the army commander of the American troops who had brutally murdered hundreds of civilians in raids conducted in an area of tiny hamlets known as My Lai, in South Vietnam, in 1968.[24] Medina had been the supervising officer of a unit headed by platoon leader Second Lieutenant William F. Calley.

F. Lee Bailey, however, would never see the inside of a courtroom on behalf of McCord. He handed the case off to his partner, Gerald Alch, with whom McCord met. "I told him that I advised Mr. Bailey of my appointment with him," Alch later testified, "and that he, Mr. Bailey, was not interested in representing any defendants in this particular case." McCord hired Alch.[25]

Jim McCord was a strange man: ponderous, independent, stubborn, and standoffish. He had an impressive military résumé and had been employed in federal law enforcement and intelligence agencies, but he was something of a loner. A World War II veteran of the Army Air Corps and lieutenant colonel in the Air Force Reserves, he worked for the FBI and later the CIA, from 1951 to 1970, as a security officer. He retired from the CIA in August 1970 and formed his own consulting firm, McCord Associates, eventually signing on to become the chief of security for the Committee to Re-Elect the President (CRP), starting part-time in September 1971, full-time in January 1972.[26] As part of his duties, he also picked up responsibility for providing protective services for the family of John Mitchell, namely, watching after the unpredictable and irascible Martha Mitchell.

McCord saw himself as a patriot fighting against radicals and antiwar traitors. He believed, based on hearsay from Liddy and Hunt, that his actions had been sanctioned by John Mitchell and John Dean, so he did not question the legality of what he was doing.[27] McCord's lawyers early on worried about the level of his intelligence. One of Gerald Alch's associates, in meeting with prosecutor Earl Silbert in September 1972, told Silbert "that McCord might be willing to talk, that McCord wasn't too smart, was a super-patriot, thoroughly convinced that what he was doing was right, that he had not cooperated before at any time because he thought there would be intervention on his behalf."[28]

The White House knew that McCord was a wild card, but because all his information came through Liddy or Hunt, they were not concerned that he could effectively implicate anyone higher up in the CRP or at the White House. No court, they thought, would allow his testimony under the established rules of evidence that excluded hearsay statements.

Within the White House it was decided that a man named Jack Caulfield would become McCord's handler. Caulfield had been a distinguished New York City police detective, first meeting Vice President Richard Nixon in the 1960 campaign when Nixon visited New York and needed VIP protection. Caulfield later joined the Nixon campaign in 1968 and was hired in 1969 by the administration to work on the White House staff as a security consultant and liaison between the White House and law enforcement agencies.[29] He worked briefly as John Mitchell's bodyguard at the CRP in March 1972 but then took a job with the Treasury Department as acting assistant director for enforcement, Bureau of Alcohol, Tobacco, and Firearms.[30]

It was Caulfield who recruited another New York City detective, Anthony Ulasewicz, to join the White House staff. Ulasewicz would become the infamous "Mr. Rivers" in the hush-money scheme—the man who delivered cash in brown paper bags to Dorothy Hunt and others.[31]

Caulfield was also responsible for the CRP's hiring of McCord in 1971. Caulfield discovered Jim McCord through an inquiry of Al Wong, the assistant director of the Secret Service, when the security position for the Republican National Committee opened up. Caulfield later recommended McCord for the job at the CRP. The two men became personal friends, thereafter staying in touch.[32] Caulfield testified that he thought McCord "felt quite beholden" to him based on everything he had done for his career.

After he was arrested, McCord began to worry deeply that Watergate was going to be blamed on the CIA. He suspected that the new FBI acting director, L. Patrick Gray, was a Nixon loyalist, having succeeded J. Edgar Hoover after his death in May 1972, a few weeks before the Watergate break-ins. McCord thought that the Watergate investigation under Gray had been a complete charade; he was not about to let the CIA become the convenient scapegoat. "I would not turn on the organization that had employed me for nineteen years,"

McCord later testified, "and wrongly deal such a damaging blow that it would take years for it to recover."[33]

Starting in July, Caulfield began calling McCord, out on bail after his arrest, at a pay phone near his home in Rockville, Maryland, to reassure him that he was watching out for him. "No one asked me to make this call," Caulfield testified, "and I was motivated entirely by my own personal concern for his condition and that of his family."[34]

On December 28, 1972, with the trial about to start, McCord's ruminations and suspicions came to a head. McCord claimed that he was under intense pressure to "use as my defense during the trial the story that the Watergate operation was a CIA operation."[35] He decided he needed to write to Caulfield to warn of the consequences if this pressure continued. The note McCord wrote was anonymous, but it was clear to Caulfield when he read it that McCord had been the author. "Dear Jack," McCord scrawled, "I am sorry to have to write you this letter, but felt you had to know." He sent the letter to Caulfield's home.[36]

McCord had only recently seen the news that President Nixon had removed CIA chief Richard Helms from his position as director.[37] The papers reported that Helms had been named ambassador to Iran. Though Helms's departure was described as a voluntary "retirement," it was obvious that Nixon had forced him out. Helms was a "careerist" at the CIA, the first insider to be named director of Central Intelligence. His replacement was James R. Schlesinger, the forty-three-year-old chairman of the Atomic Energy Commission. Schlesinger, a systems management type, was expected to be faithful to Nixon.[38] McCord was troubled that this signaled the start of an all-out attack on the CIA by the Nixon administration. He thought "the White House was turning ruthless," he later testified.[39]

"If Helms goes," McCord wrote to Caulfield in his December 29 letter, "and the Watergate operation is laid at CIA's feet, where it does not belong, every tree in the forest will fall." McCord was emphatic in his threat. "It will be a scorched desert," he wrote. "The whole matter is at the precipe [sic] now." He asked Caulfield to relay his note to the people in charge of the cover-up. "Just pass the message that if they want it to blow, they are exactly on the right course," he wrote. "I am sorry that you will get hurt in the fallout."[40]

This letter found its way to John Dean on January 4.[41]

McCord later told Caulfield that he had hatched a harebrained scheme earlier in the fall to obtain his freedom. From his work for the CIA, McCord knew that certain foreign embassies were being wiretapped by the US government. He therefore decided to call two of those embassies, one in September and another in October, and he told the persons who answered the phone that the embassy was being wiretapped by the United States. He then identified himself as one of the Watergate defendants looking for a visa or other traveling papers.[42] "It was Mr. McCord's theory," Caulfield testified, "that if the government searched its wiretap records, it would find records of the two calls." The US attorney, McCord believed, once aware of this information, would "be forced to dismiss the case rather than reveal that the two embassies in question were the subject of national security wiretaps."[43] Jim McCord had created his own ace in the hole.

The plan made little sense and, as might be expected, went nowhere. McCord would face a trial, but no one was sure what he would do next. Reports were that he had stopped cooperating with his lawyer. He thought Alch was in on the White House ploy to blame the CIA.[44]

The Lincoln Sitting Room, January 3, 1973, 8:30 PM

The night of January 3, Nixon had some drinks delivered and settled into his overstuffed chair with its ottoman in the corner of the Lincoln Sitting Room. As had become his practice of late, he called Chuck Colson to unwind and catch up on the day's events. Though just that afternoon he had heard shocking news from Bob Haldeman about Colson's role in Watergate, Nixon said nothing of it. He possessed a remarkable ability to compartmentalize the information he received.

"Hello?" Nixon said, noticeably slurring his words.[45]

"Yes, sir, Mr. President," Colson verbally saluted, oblivious to the fact he had been stabbed in the back by Haldeman that day.

"Well, how'd your day go today?" Nixon asked.

"Well, I thought it was a good day," Colson responded, "except that, God, having those jackasses in the Congress back in Washington makes a difference, doesn't it?"

"Oh, well," Nixon laughed. "It doesn't bother you, does it?"

"No," Colson said. "It's just really amazing. I talked to our legislative people this afternoon and they said that, 'God, it is just so painful to go up [to the Hill] and have to listen to these people whine around, and they want briefings, and they want fact sheets.' "

"Well, don't let them get you discouraged, Chuck," Nixon said.

He and Colson spoke about Jerry Ford's leadership, or lack thereof, in the House. "He plays by the rules," Colson said in disparagement. Nixon told Colson that he had dined with Al Haig that night, and that Haig said that after talking to Kissinger it was his sense that Kissinger knew his cover had been blown with respect to the Reston article on the bombing. Colson had also talked to Haig. "We both agree that Henry means well, but he does get taken in by these people," Colson said.

Colson reported that even the cantankerous Edward Bennett Williams, who represented the hated *Washington Post*, had called him to ask for help with challenges to some FCC licenses for TV stations owned by the *Post*. Nixon recommended that Colson meet with him. "Just cold turkey it with him," Nixon said. "He's a cold turkey guy."[46]

The world was coming around. The market was up (to 1,040), the war was winding down, and China had been opened with Nixon's historic trip to Peking. Congress was an annoyance, yet things all seemed to be going in the right direction. Colson read to Nixon an excerpt from an editorial that was headlined "1972 Belonged to Richard Nixon."

"I think we pay too much attention to the Congress," Nixon said. "Let's not worry that much about them."[47]

For his part, despite a rambling twenty-minute call, Colson said nothing of his meeting with Bittman that day, or of the desperate plea for a promise of clemency for Hunt. Within a day, though, racked by guilt over Hunt's predicament, Colson would raise the issue with Nixon.

7

"The Pregnant Woman Cannot Be Isolated in Her Privacy"

The Oval Office, January 2, 1973

At the conclusion of his call with Chief Justice Warren Burger on the morning of January 2, Nixon reminded Burger that he would see him in a few weeks at the inaugural ceremonies.

"Well, we'll see you on the inauguration," Nixon said. "I mean, you're the guy that has to swear me in, you know."[1]

"Yes, I talked to the vice president the other day," Burger said of a discussion with Vice President Agnew. "I guess that tradition has varied with the vice president, but he called me, asked me if I'd do it, and I said, 'Yes, I will do two for the price of one.'"

Nixon tried to remember who had sworn him in as vice president and could only bring up the name of William Knowland, a senator from California who administered the oath in January 1953.[2] Always the student of the presidency, Nixon pointed out the difference between the oath taken by the president and the oath taken by the vice president. The president's oath is enshrined in the constitution ("I do solemnly swear [or affirm] that I will faithfully execute the Office of President of the United States, and will to the best of my Ability, preserve, protect and defend the Constitution of the United States"); Congress had to come up with one for the vice president.[3] And because the vice president also serves as the president of the Senate, it was decided that he (or she) should take the same oath as that administered to senators, representatives, and other government officers.[4]

"One of the beauties of my oath, you know, it's very short," Nixon said to Burger. "His [meaning Agnew's] is quite long. Did you notice the difference?" he asked. Burger said he did. "But mine is very short," Nixon continued. "I just swear to uphold and defend the Constitution of the United States."

"It's about seven lines long," Burger said. (It is actually thirty-five words.)

"*Even I* can remember that," Nixon joked. Both men chuckled.

Within ten months of this phone call, the nation faced the real prospect of a double resignation. Spiro Agnew resigned on October 10 under the shadow of an imminent indictment for taking bribes while governor of Maryland, and even during his term as vice president. At the same time, Nixon was embroiled in the desperate fight for his White House tapes. It is difficult to find a parallel in the history of the presidency for such a precipitous fall. And clearly there was something defective about Burger's administration of the oath—neither one seemed to take.

The United States Supreme Court, December 16, 1971

Warren Burger had larger issues to ponder than the giving of oaths in January 1973. Looking back over the last year, he knew he had made a critical error in the handling of the abortion cases, and he was wrestling with how to deal with the aftermath. His decision to push for a re-argument of the cases had backfired badly. Burger faced one of the great decisions of his life. Would he join the majority in both the Texas and Georgia cases?

When the justices met in conference to discuss the abortion cases after the first oral argument in December 1971, it became clear that they were iffy as to how to vote and uncertain as to the bases upon which the cases should be decided. Powell and Rehnquist, just confirmed by the Senate, did not sit for the oral arguments and were not entitled to take part in any of the deliberations over the cases.[5]

Sarah Weddington, a recent graduate of the University of Texas School of Law, argued the Texas appeal on behalf of her client, Jane Roe (whose real name was Norma McCorvey), and several other plaintiffs on December 13, 1971. At twenty-six, Weddington's total experience in a courtroom consisted of the two-hour argument before a three-judge panel in the proceedings below. Few lawyers with such meager résumés find themselves arguing before the US Supreme Court. She was, by her own admission, "petrified" about presenting the case in trial court and had broken down when she learned she was going to argue in the Supreme Court. "I mean, just wept," one of her friends recalled.[6]

Roe had been decided in the trial court on a facial challenge to the constitutionality of the Texas abortion statute, and it had been appealed directly to the Supreme Court, bypassing the usual review in a court of appeals. The record was incredibly sparse. No witnesses had been called. The three-judge panel relied on the papers submitted and the arguments of counsel.[7] The Texas criminal abortion statute dated back more than a century and allowed abortions only upon medical advice "for the purpose of saving the life of the mother."[8] The panel below found the Texas statute unconstitutional.[9]

The companion case, *Doe v. Bolton,* concerned a Georgia law, considered a reform statute. Passed in 1968, it reflected, as Justice Harry Blackmun would later write, "the influences of recent attitudinal change, of advancing medical knowledge and techniques, and of new thinking about an old issue." The Georgia statute outlawed abortions except when performed by a duly licensed Georgia physician based upon "his best clinical judgment" that a continued pregnancy "would endanger the life of the pregnant woman or would seriously and permanently injure her health," or for reasons of rape or a gravely defective fetus.[10]

The Georgia statute also set forth certain conditions for the authorization of an abortion: the woman had to be a Georgia resident, the physician's decision had to be written down and confirmed by at least two other licensed physicians, the procedure had to be approved in advance by a committee of the medical staff of the hospital, and the abortion had to be performed in a properly accredited hospital licensed by the state.[11] *Doe* was argued by Margie Pitts Hames, a Georgia attorney who had a decade of experience arguing civil rights and labor cases.[12]

The justices' conference for *Roe* and *Doe* took place on Thursday, December 16. Procedural issues dominated much of the discussion. Several questions revolved around the legal concept of *standing.* Though a complicated doctrine, the essence of standing is that the person or entity suing must show that they had been directly affected by the law, presenting for the court a real and existing controversy. A major question in abortion cases was whether a woman who was no longer pregnant by the time of a hearing or appeal—as had to be the case with both Jane Roe and Jane Doe—still had "standing" to continue the case. Or did the case become moot once the woman gave birth (or had an abortion)? Did the other plaintiffs in the case, like a physician prosecuted under the Texas statute, also have standing to challenge the statute?

The justices worked through these knotty procedural issues and decided they could address the underlying merits of the cases. On a woman's right to an abortion—the substance of the cases—there seemed to be a consensus that the Texas statute was unconstitutional but that the Georgia statute might be upheld, or at least sent back to the court below for a fuller exposition of the facts. The reasons for each justice's position were far from clear and certainly not yet set in stone.[13]

Chief Justice Burger decided that the best thing to do under the circumstances was to assign one of the justices to draft opinions in both cases and see if the writer could "command a court," that is, attract enough votes with his reasoning to establish a majority position. This was fairly unusual. Normally, a majority is identified at conference and the chief justice, per time-honored tradition, has the authority to make the assignment for writing the opinion *if* he sides with the majority. If the chief does not agree with the majority, the power to assign the opinion shifts to the next-most-senior justice who is in the majority.[14]

Burger chose his friend Harry Blackmun to draft opinions in both *Roe* and *Doe*. Burger's selection probably arose from his hope that Blackmun, a fellow conservative, would decide the cases on the narrowest of grounds, giving the greatest deference to legislative determinations made by the states involved. Burger also was aware that Blackmun had substantial experience grappling with complex medical quandaries and dealing with hospital committees, because he was cognizant of Blackmun's representation of the Mayo Clinic.

Burger's actions in making the assignment to Blackmun caused a sharp controversy within the court. Justice William O. Douglas, appointed by Franklin Roosevelt in 1939, considered it his right to assign the cases, because he believed he was the most senior justice in the majority.[15] Douglas sent a note to Burger disputing his assignment to Blackmun. Burger disagreed and responded that "there were not enough columns to mark up an accurate reflection of the voting in either the Georgia or Texas cases," and that these cases therefore had "to stand or fall on the writing." Burger hinted that, in any event, the cases might be candidates for re-arguments once Powell and Rehnquist joined the court.[16]

For the moment, Douglas took his objections no further. Blackmun, the day after receiving the assignment, sent a letter to the medical librarian of the Mayo Clinic asking for literature on the history of abortion.[17] He would make it his business to fill in a record that was all but nonexistent on the medical issues surrounding this most complicated and emotional of constitutional questions.

New Haven, Connecticut, 1965

The question of a woman's right to an abortion arose like a prairie fire in the last years of the 1960s. Out of the societal tumult stirred up by the Vietnam War, the sexual revolution, the women's movement, and the civil rights movement, women began to organize around reproductive health issues. Initially the debate centered on birth control and the use of contraceptives.

The group from which Sarah Weddington emerged was a case in point. The women with whom Weddington joined had been an offshoot of the antiwar Students for a Democratic Society (SDS) at the University of Texas. The women were offended by the sexist attitudes of the male leaders of SDS (which many SDS female members had experienced) and so formed their own weekly discussion group. They became active in promoting birth control on campus. "The group did not initially intend for the birth control project to deal with the question of abortion," scholar David Garrow found.[18] Nonetheless, over time, counseling on abortion became part of the mission. Sarah Weddington was asked to assist with legal counseling on issues facing the group.[19]

Nationally, efforts to reform highly restrictive abortion statutes, which had been fashioned in an era when antiseptic measures were unknown—and when any abortion threatened the life of a woman—cropped up in state legislatures. But results were slow in coming and mixed.[20] A few states, like Hawaii and New York, legalized abortions on request of the woman, up to a certain point in the pregnancy. In New York, for example, the legislature repealed its 1830 law in 1970 and allowed abortions up to the twenty-fourth week of pregnancy.[21] But activists impatient with the pace of legislative reform saw the courts as a better answer.

One reason was a case decided by the Warren Court in the spring of 1965. That year, William O. Douglas wrote the opinion of the court in *Griswold v. Connecticut*.[22] Estelle Griswold was the executive director of the Planned Parenthood League of Connecticut in New Haven. The league's medical director, Dr. C. Lee Buxton, was a licensed physician and professor at Yale Medical School. Griswold and Buxton were arrested for providing information, instruction, and medical advice to a married couple on how to prevent conception.[23] The Connecticut law made it a crime for any person to use "any drug, medicinal article or instrument for the purpose of preventing conception." It also made it a crime for people like Griswold and Buxton to assist or abet another in violating the law.

The Supreme Court overturned the convictions. Though Douglas conceded that the court should not "sit as a super-legislature" to "determine the wisdom, need, and propriety of laws that touch economic problems, business affairs, or social conditions," the Connecticut law in question, he thought, operated "directly on an intimate relation of husband and wife and their physician's role in one aspect of that relation."[24]

In deciding *Griswold*, Douglas set down a theory that sparked a revolution in constitutional thought, especially in the area of privacy. Finding no express right of privacy anywhere in the US Constitution, Douglas looked to various rights as expressed through the Bill of Rights and found that these rights gave off "penumbras," in the sense of shaded areas surrounding the core rights. Think of an eclipse. The core right—like freedom of assembly under the First Amendment—would be the black core that is the eclipse. A closely related right—freedom of association, for example—would be the lighter area surrounding the dark core—its penumbra.[25]

The right to privacy, Douglas conceived, was one of the penumbral rights that emanated from a host of core rights set forth in the Bill of Rights. "Various guarantees create zones of privacy," he wrote.[26]

"In other words," Douglas wrote to illustrate his point, "the First Amendment has a penumbra where privacy is protected from government intrusion." The right of privacy thereby was established as a peripheral right to other express rights, such as freedom of speech, freedom of assembly, and the right to be free of unreasonable searches and seizures by the government. "The present case, then, concerns a relationship lying within the zone of privacy created by several fundamental constitutional rights," Douglas wrote.

The Connecticut law was struck down.[27]

Griswold inspired a burst of creative and pioneering scholarship and thinking about privacy and the decision to bear children. If it applied to contraception, why not abortion? If it applied to married couples, why not unmarried women?

Roy Lucas, a New York University Law School graduate, published in 1968 one of the more influential law review articles on abortion rights.[28] Lucas proposed a federal constitutional basis for invalidating state criminal abortion laws, relying heavily on *Griswold*. In an idea that was later crucial to *Roe*, Lucas argued that women of means had ready access to "therapeutic" abortions—abortions performed in hospitals for supposed medical reasons—whereas women of poverty had few good choices and faced grave risks to end unwanted pregnancies. "To the poor the choice is between self-induced abortion and the accompanying danger or increased poverty and powerlessness in the face of the government mandate." Lucas started a new litigation group in New York City, the James Madison Constitutional Law Institute, which specialized in the development of model litigation papers and briefs on abortion and provided support to attorneys around the country who were starting to file cases challenging state abortion laws.[29] He would work with Sarah Weddington on *Roe* and Margie Pitts Hames on *Doe*.

Another landmark writing came from former Supreme Court justice Tom Clark, who stepped down in 1967 from the court when his son Ramsey became Lyndon Johnson's attorney general. (Thurgood Marshall took Clark's seat.) Entitled "Religion, Morality, and Abortion: A Constitutional Appraisal," his eleven-page article appeared in 1969 in the Catholic *Loyola of Los Angeles Law Review*. The paper was widely cited by pro-abortion attorneys in legal briefs. Justice

Iconic photo of Judge Sarah T. Hughes swearing in LBJ on the day of the Kennedy assassination, November 22, 1963. Seven years later, she would be one of three judges to decide *Roe v. Wade* in the federal district court.

LBJ Library photo by Cecil Stoughton

Blackmun footnoted it in his later opinions. Clark argued in favor of a modern right to abortion.[30] "Our society is in the midst of a sexual revolution which has cast the problem of abortion into the forefront of religious, medical, and legal thought," Clark wrote.

Sarah Weddington and classmate Linda Coffee were two of forty women, out of sixteen hundred law students, at University of Texas School of Law in the mid-1960s. Weddington began classes at the law school in the summer of 1965, just months after the *Griswold* decision came down.[31] Linda Coffee was later recruited by Weddington to assist in the challenge to the Texas abortion statute, mainly because of her familiarity with federal procedural rules and laws.

After graduation, Coffee had taken a clerkship with a federal judge, Sarah T. Hughes, who was already a legend. She was the judge who administered the oath of office to Lyndon Johnson on Air Force One on November 22, 1963, the day Kennedy was assassinated, and as a consequence held the distinction of being the only woman ever to administer the presidential oath.[32] Seven years after the tragedy in Dallas, Judge Hughes would be one of the three judges to hear and decide *Roe v. Wade* at the trial level.

The Supreme Court, Justice Blackmun's Chambers, May 1972

The *Roe* and *Doe* decisions were not the first abortion cases considered by the Supreme Court. In the spring of 1971, the court decided *United States v. Vuitch*. The case involved a District of Columbia abortion statute that prohibited abortions "unless the same were done as necessary for the preservation of the mother's life and health." The court held that the word "health" was not so vague that the statute was unconstitutional. The court was not required to reach the question of a constitutional right of a woman to an abortion.[33]

Harry Blackmun was one of the justices who voted to uphold the District of Columbia's abortion statute in *Vuitch*. Yet his initial reaction to the Texas statute in *Roe* was to strike it down based on a vagueness argument. Doctors would not know, Blackmun argued, when they could safely perform abortions because of the imprecision of the exception in the Texas statute that permitted abortions "for the purpose of saving the life of the mother." What did this mean to a physician? "Does it mean that he may procure an abortion only when, without it, the patient will surely die?" he wrote. "Or only when the odds are greater than even that she will die? Or when there is a mere possibility that she will not survive?"[34]

Blackmun's first draft of *Roe* was circulated on May 18, 1972, coincidentally ten days before the first Watergate break-in. After identifying his theory that the Texas statute was "unconstitutionally vague," he wrote to the other justices in a private memo: "I think that this would be all that is necessary for disposition of the case, and that we need not get into the more complex Ninth Amendment issue."[35] His first inclination, as Burger had hoped, was to solve the case by deciding it on a basis that was very narrow. He did not need to address the right of privacy.

Roe would hardly have been significant had it been issued in this form.

Far more important than Blackmun's initial reaction to *Roe* was his take on how to handle the companion Georgia case of *Doe v. Bolton*. "The Georgia case, yet to come, is more complex," he wrote on May 18. Though he reiterated his hope that *Doe* would be reargued to a full court, he proceeded to draft an opinion that was of singular importance in the outcome of *Roe*.[36]

Justices Brennan and Douglas reacted to Blackmun's *Roe* draft with letters that encouraged him to address "the core constitutional issue" of a woman's right to an abortion rather than invalidating the Texas law on the narrow ground of vagueness.[37] Both recalled that the majority had agreed to invalidate abortion statutes "save to the extent they require that an abortion be performed by a licensed physician within some limited time after conception."[38] These notes found favor in Blackmun's first draft of *Doe v. Bolton*.

On May 25 Blackmun sent around his draft of the *Doe* opinion.[39] It contained the seeds of the later *Roe* decision, as parts of it would be lifted and placed in the second and third drafts of *Roe*. But there was one very important and vital distinction about this May 1972 draft opinion: though Blackmun found a right of privacy in the decision to abort, he did not believe that the court could or should draw the line as to when life begins.

His analysis was obviously informed by his experience in the medical field. He started off by disposing of several of the Georgia restrictions and preconditions for obtaining an abortion—like the hospital committee preapproval requirement and the need for two consenting physicians to agree—concluding that these precautions were unnecessary. He wrote to the other justices that he found it difficult to sweep aside such safeguards, because he had seen for himself how these hospital committees routinely interdicted unnecessary surgeries—yet he believed such measures interfered with the sacrosanct relationship between a physician and his or her patient. By the same token, he wrote, he had "seen abortion mills in operation and the general misery they have caused," so he was ready to uphold some minimum requirements, namely the need for the approval of an attending licensed physician and for the procedure to be performed in a state-licensed hospital.[40]

These pronouncements, though debatable, were not particularly controversial.

But Justice Blackmun crossed over into a new frontier in his draft of the *Doe* opinion when he expressly recognized a woman's fundamental right of privacy in making the decision to have an abortion. He started by agreeing with *Griswold* and like cases that "a woman's interest in making the fundamental personal decision whether or not to bear an unwanted child is within the scope of personal rights protected by the Ninth and Fourteenth Amendments."[41]

The Fourteenth Amendment was a post–Civil War amendment that over time has been used to apply the Bill of Rights to the individual states. Within the Fourteenth Amendment is the Due Process Clause, which provides, "nor shall any State deprive any person of life, liberty, or property, without due process of law." This language had been interpreted by the Supreme Court to create not only procedural due process rights (fair trials and so forth) but also substantive rights—rights related to life, liberty, and property. In the abortion context, Blackmun was pointing to the word "liberty" in asserting a woman's right to make her own abortion decision. This liberty, it was argued, included a fundamental right of privacy to make such an intimate choice.

But crucially Blackmun was not prepared to allow a woman's decision to terminate her pregnancy to be entirely her own. "Appellants' contention, however, that the woman's right to make the decision is absolute—that Georgia has either no valid interest in regulating it, or no interest strong enough to support any limitation upon the woman's sole determination—is unpersuasive."

This is where Blackmun first penned one of the most famous lines that would make its way into *Roe*. "The pregnant woman cannot be isolated in her privacy."[42] There was another interest involved, one that the state could also protect: that of the fetus. "This situation, therefore, is inherently different from marital intimacy, or bedroom possession of obscene material, or marriage, or the right to procreate, or private education with which [*Griswold* and other cases] were respectively concerned."[43]

And at this point in his draft Blackmun reached his decisive turning point. When was that moment when this other interest obtained its rights? He needed to set a marker for when a fetus's rights assumed *protected* status. In this draft, however, he made it crystal clear that he was not about to do so. He backed away from entangling the Supreme Court in such line-drawing.

"The heart of the matter," he wrote, "is that somewhere, either forthwith at conception, or at 'quickening' [an English common-law concept of the time when a fetus first discernibly moves in the womb], or at birth, or at some other point in between, another being becomes involved and the privacy the woman possessed has become dual rather than sole. The woman's right of privacy must be measured accordingly. It is not for us of the judiciary, especially at this point in the development of man's knowledge, to speculate or specify when life begins."[44]

Blackmun did not want to draw the line.

By the end of May, he made another plea for rearguments in both *Roe* and *Doe*: "I believe, on an issue so sensitive and so emotional as this one, the country deserves the conclusion of a nine-man, not a seven-man court, whatever the ultimate decision may be." Blackmun said he wanted the summer to think it over. His plan, unexpressed to others, was to go back to the Mayo Clinic to conduct his own independent study of the history of abortion and the medical questions involved.[45]

The Supreme Court, Justice Douglas's Chambers, June 1972

The court voted to reargue. Justices Powell and Rehnquist, on the court for almost an entire term by June 1972, finally decided to abjure their own self-imposed neutrality and intervene, and they both voted to reargue. Their votes were decisive.[46]

At this point, Justice Douglas erupted, still smarting from the assignment by Burger to Blackmun of the writing of the *Roe* and *Doe* opinions. Justices Douglas, Brennan, Stewart, and Marshall all smelled a conspiracy.[47] They were convinced that Chief Justice Burger, having read Blackmun's drafts, had twisted Blackmun's arm and importuned him to ask the other justices for rearguments.

Douglas and his brethren were not far off in their suspicions. In Burger's May 31 memo to the conference, he argued strongly for reargument and wrote in a way that openly displayed his unhappiness with Blackmun's drafts. "I have had a great many problems with these cases from the outset," he wrote. "They are not as simple for me as they appear to be for others. The States have, I should think, as much concern in this area as any within their province; federal power has only that which can be traced to a specific provision of the Constitution." Burger even complained that the lawyers who argued the cases had provided "mediocre to poor help" to the court, and he hoped additional briefing might be solicited from interested parties, *amici*, or friends of the court to assist in rearguments in the fall term.[48]

The purpose of Burger's actions was obvious to Douglas: the chief justice wanted the two new conservatives, Powell and Rehnquist, to take part in *Roe* and *Doe* in the hope that they would vote to uphold the state statutes and undo Justice Blackmun's even limited recognition of a right of privacy in the abortion context.

Justice Douglas wrote an especially scathing and personal dissent to the decision to reargue the cases—a rare breach of court etiquette and civility and highly unusual in connection with a decision to reargue. But his personal diatribe against Burger was less significant than the fact that Douglas disclosed in his dissent that a majority of the justices had in fact already agreed on the outcome: five had accepted Blackmun's opinions, as they were. "Perhaps the purpose of the minority [referring to Chief Justice Burger] in the *Abortion Cases* is to try to keep control of the merits," Douglas wrote in the sixth draft of his dissent, dated June 13, 1972. "If that is the aim, the plan has been unsuccessful. Opinions in these two cases have been circulated and each commands the votes of five members of the Court. The decisions should therefore be announced."[49]

Records show that Blackmun did have a majority for both of his decisions as written in May 1972. Brennan, Douglas, Marshall, and Stewart all expressed agreement with Blackmun's drafts, leaving only Burger and White in dissent.[50] The 5–2 vote, had it come down, would have created a very different legal and political landscape from the one that was to come.

Justice Douglas, with some time to think about it, and after being coaxed by some of the justices, abandoned his sneering dissent and did not publish it. The nation would not know until much later how close the court had come to issuing very limited decisions in *Roe* and *Doe*.[51]

But Douglas did have one thing right: politics seemed to be playing a role in the reargument debate. "The *Abortion Cases* are symptomatic," Douglas wrote. "This is an election year. Both political parties have made abortion an issue. What the political parties say or do is none of our business. We sit here not to make the path of any

President Nixon and Chief Justice Warren Burger in Oval Office, June 14, 1972, a day after Justice Douglas penned his dissent in *Roe* and two days before the second disastrous break-in at the Watergate.

White House Photo Office, Nixon Library

candidate easier or more difficult. We decide questions only on their constitutional merits."

Three days after penning this dissent, late on the night of June 16, 1972, Gordon Liddy, Howard Hunt, Jim McCord, and a team of burglars broke into the Democratic National Committee headquarters at the Watergate for a second time.

This time their luck ran out, and in the early hours of Saturday, June 17, the burglars were arrested.

The nation's long national nightmare was just starting.

8

"Harry's Lovely Farewell"

The Oval Office, January 3, 1973

A heaviness settled in on the subject of Vietnam during the first week of January 1973. The press and members of Congress were asking the tough questions: Why did the president bomb North Vietnam? Why did the bombing stop? What exactly was the policy of the administration? What had been accomplished? And what would happen if future negotiations failed?

Nixon's private discussions with Henry Kissinger and press secretary Ron Ziegler that week show he was in a box. As Nixon pointed out to Ziegler in preparation for a midweek press conference, they had to be careful about saying anything to the American people or members of Congress about what their true intentions had been. "The purpose of the bombing was to break the deadlock [in Paris]," he said to Ziegler, "but you can't say that." Why were the North Vietnamese coming back to the table? "Because we bombed them," Nixon said, "but you can't say that."[1]

Nixon even found it necessary to dissemble with congressional leaders. Carl Albert, the Democratic speaker of the house, asked Nixon just after returning from the holiday what Nixon would do if his bombing strategy didn't work and future negotiations were unsuccessful. Would he go back and level Hanoi? Would he use nuclear weapons? Nixon refused to say. He was not going to be wrangled into taking a position that would limit his future actions. All he could say was that there would be "serious negotiations" in Paris.[2] By implication, he left open the door to the use of nuclear weapons.

The reality was that his options were extremely limited. His requirements for peace with honor were fairly straightforward: return of American prisoners of war, establishment of a cease-fire, and assurances of free elections in the South. The rest was window dressing. But getting there was something else altogether.

Congress was undercutting his leverage. The votes to choke off further funding for the war appeared to be lining up. The Democrats passed resolutions in "emotion-packed" conferences calling for an immediate end to the war.[3] One reporter wrote that "the new 93d Congress had pounced on Washington . . . with the fury of a January storm." Inauguration Day, January 20, was the deadline: settle or else.[4] Kissinger concluded that it would be a "bad idea" under these circumstances for him to meet privately with Mansfield and other leaders before returning to Paris because there was not much he could tell them. Ron Ziegler framed the dilemma succinctly in a draft statement he read to Nixon in a pre–press conference briefing: "Congress has to ask itself," Ziegler read from his text, "whether it wants to assume the responsibility of creating doubt in the enemy's mind about the US position or if Congress wants to raise doubts of what they will do and the effect that that will have on the negotiations—in delaying negotiations."[5]

South Vietnam's president Nguyen Van Thieu stepped up his efforts to intermeddle directly in American politics. He remained for Nixon a serious obstacle to ending the war. Nixon was not happy to read in the papers that Thieu had sent a delegation of South Vietnamese legislators to Washington during the first week of January 1973 to "persuade Congress to keep providing and even increase American military and economic assistance to South Vietnam if there is no peace soon."[6] Nixon told Kissinger to speak very plainly to the South Vietnamese ambassador about the folly of the mission. The ambassador must be told, Nixon said, that any attempt by South Vietnamese emissaries to lobby Congress would miscarry. "If these people come, it is the president's view, that it would be . . . very disastrous—a backfire," Nixon told Kissinger to say. "This Congress deeply resents any pressures, and particularly foreign pressures—they'll go right up the wall." The hazards for South Vietnam were grave—they risked not only the immediate withdrawal of American troops but also a total cutoff of all US aid, military and otherwise.

"He's demented," Kissinger said of Thieu.[7]

The public relations battle over the bombing also was hitting some very rough spots. Kissinger reported that the Pentagon was asked whether or not the pilots of the B-52 whose bombs destroyed the Bach Mai Hospital in Hanoi would be punished. The Pentagon response showed how difficult it was to control messaging, especially in the bedlam of war. The Pentagon spokesman said it was unclear that the pilots would be punished because it was not certain that the hospital had been destroyed by American planes.[8]

"Well, that's stupid on two counts," Kissinger pointed out to Nixon. "One, it was clearly done by American planes—"

"Second, it admits there might be punishment," Nixon said, completing the thought.

"That's right," Kissinger replied.

"Well, a hospital, for Christ's sakes," Nixon said, "things of that sort, it's not done deliberately, you know damn well, but these things happen, that's part of the problem."[9]

Nor could Nixon and Kissinger count on the Soviets for much help. Kissinger described a "very poor" meeting he had with Ambassador Anatoly Dobrynin during the first week of January 1973. "He didn't have a great deal to say on Vietnam," Kissinger told Nixon. Though Brezhnev desperately wanted to follow through with a summit on nuclear disarmament, the Soviets were in their own bind. It was especially difficult for them, in their relations with Communist leaders around the world, to appear to be assisting the United States, even in peace negotiations, when the United States had bombed North Vietnam so brutally.[10]

And meetings in Paris among the technical experts were not showing particular signs of progress. There were still "huge differences," Kissinger reported, over the structure and makeup of an international commission that would monitor post-settlement elections. The best Kissinger could say was that the differences "were not frivolous," as they had been before the December bombings. But there was no guarantee that a settlement could be worked out once he returned to Paris.

The plain truth of the situation was that the alternatives to peace were not just exceedingly limited; they were virtually nonexistent. In an especially revealing conversation with Kissinger on January 3, Nixon analyzed what would happen if peace talks failed. "Option Two," as they called it, had been drawn up by Nixon and Kissinger to address the contingency of unsuccessful negotiations. The plan was simple: if negotiations fell apart, the United States would resume its bombing campaign for the sole and limited purpose of forcing the return of American POWs. It may take six months, but the goal would be drastically reduced.

This prospect of backtracking was not only demoralizing and humiliating but also based on a centrally flawed theory, as Nixon frankly admitted to Kissinger. Option Two was based on the assumption that Congress would support renewed bombing if it was to compel the return of American prisoners of war. In the cold light of day, Nixon recognized that he and Kissinger were unlikely to "get away with it," that pressures at home would be too much to support any further bombing, even for POWs. "The domestic strain would be enormous," he observed. It was a remarkably sober and pessimistic assessment by the president. He was telling his lead negotiator that there really was no other course but peace.[11]

It was all or nothing—Kissinger had to bring home a peace agreement.

The National Cathedral, January 5, 1973

"Sometimes it must seem to every president as if the path ahead is blocked by some impenetrable wall, a river impassable," Francis Sayre read from his eulogy of Harry Truman. "The mendaciousness of man

Dean Francis B. Sayre in front of the Washington National Cathedral.
Archives of National Washington Cathedral

in all his affairs makes a prisoner of that leader who must see beyond; who may not allow the world to quench the spark of truth God has given to his keeping."[12] Sayre's voice boomed throughout the soaring Gothic structure, which was packed with mourners.

Richard Nixon remained in the White House, roughly four miles away. He started the day meeting with a bipartisan group of congressional leaders for breakfast in the State Dining Room. The breakfast ended a little after 10:00 in the morning so the leaders could make their way to limousines and cars for the fifteen-minute ride to the Truman service, which started at 11:00. President Nixon, as he had planned, stayed behind and went to the Oval Office for some fairly inconsequential and largely repetitive meetings with Haldeman, Ziegler, and Kissinger. Vice President Spiro Agnew, along with most of Nixon's cabinet, represented the president at the official state funeral.

Leaders assembled from around the country and the world to pay their respects to Harry Truman. Nearly two thousand people crowded into the cathedral, with representatives from thirty-five nations, including the prime minister of Ireland, the president of Israel, and the premier of South Korea. Former chief justice Earl Warren sat near all the Democratic and Republican leaders from the House and Senate. Chief Justice Warren Burger, Harry Blackmun, Lewis Powell, William Rehnquist, and the other justices of the Supreme Court were also present. Margaret Truman Daniel, Harry and Bess Truman's only child, and her husband, Clifton Daniel, associate editor of the *New York Times*, had come from Missouri with their four boys; Bess Truman, eighty-seven, the former president's widow, was too frail to travel. Mamie Eisenhower drove from her home in Gettysburg, Pennsylvania, to attend.

Bess Truman reportedly selected Dean Sayre to deliver the eulogy.[13] Francis Sayre spoke in hallowed space, for the nation and himself personally. The remains of Sayre's grandfather, Woodrow Wilson, were interred in a crypt, next to his second wife, Edith Bolling Galt, in one of the bays of the nave. Wilson was (and still is) the only President of the United States buried in the National Cathedral, or for that matter within the boundaries of the District of Columbia. Certainly Sayre must have been thinking of his grandfather, in addition to Truman, and likely Richard Nixon, too, when he composed the line in his eulogy that the presidency "makes a prisoner of that leader."

Just as surely, in his own passion to see an end to the Vietnam War, Sayre's prayer for presidential insight probably was directed at

Mamie Eisenhower, Clifton Daniel, Margaret Truman Daniel, Judy Agnew, and Vice President Spiro T. Agnew, attend Truman's memorial service in the Washington Cathedral, January 5, 1973.
Cleveland Press

President Nixon—that he be allowed to "see beyond" and "not allow the world to quench the spark of truth God [had] given to his keeping."

Harry Truman's accomplishments changed the course of humankind. As president, he acted distinctly on the world stage. He brought an end to the Second World War and in the process shouldered the burden of making the decision to use atomic weapons. His support was crucial to the birth of the State of Israel. He led America and the United Nations into the Korean conflict, and presided over the start of the harrowing Cold War and the costly plan for the containment of Communism. And yet Sayre chose his moment in praise of Truman to point to the straightforward character, honesty, and decency of the nation's thirty-third president. "Many of us remember still," Sayre said, "the dark days that Harry Truman faced, the loneliness of his responsibility, and the generous impulse he ever brought to it." He called Truman "a fearless son of simple soil, our brother Harry."

In Truman's ordinariness was extraordinariness. Sayre spoke of the demands of history, of the need to be prepared when great crises erupted. "In the eyes of his countrymen, Harry Truman was found to be such a man," Sayre said. "Earthy plain, there were no wrinkles in his honesty; when the time came, he stepped to the anvil humble but not afraid, relying always in his independent way upon the goodness of the Lord, in whose hand is the hammer of our fate."

Sayre prayed in thanksgiving, "By what good Providence Thou didst raise him to be our leader in time of peril, by what plain and honest grace did he respond."

James Reston, the *New York Times* columnist who had written the article that so upset Nixon (alleging that Henry Kissinger did not support the December bombing), wrote about the Truman services in a piece he titled "Harry's Lovely Farewell." Reston was moved. "Every once in a while, something happens in the capital of the United States which reminds us of the continuity of American life, heals our tragic misunderstandings, and connects our religious past to our modern secular age."

Knowing of Sayre's lineage, Reston remembered a moralizing quote from Woodrow Wilson about dying, its solitariness, and its ultimate connection to the choices, mistakes, and principles that form the basis of an individual's life. "We do not die separately," Reston wrote, quoting Woodrow Wilson. "We do not die by corporations. Every man has to live with himself privately, and it is a most uncomfortable life. He has to remember what he did during the day, the things he yielded to, the points he compromised. And this lonely dying is the confession of our consciousness that we are individually and separately and personally related to the ideals which we pursue, and to the persons to whom we should stand loyal." Perhaps Reston meant this as a glancing blow at the current occupant of the White House.

Reston was stirred by the simple dignity of the forty-minute Episcopalian service in the great cathedral, the prayers for Harry Truman, the prayers for the nation, and the "quiet civility" of it all. "Who says we are not still touched by the echoes of the old American religious heritage?" he asked. "You could see it in the faces of the silent throng in the Cathedral. Somehow, though nobody said so, the past seemed to be rebuking the present."

"O God, Our Help in Ages Past" they all sang at the recessional, as Margaret Truman Daniel, to use Reston's words, "led the congregation out into the grey January light."[14]

The Aspen Lodge, Camp David, Maryland, Friday Evening, January 5, 1973

That night, Richard Nixon made a series of phone calls. He had spent most of the afternoon meeting in the Oval Office with visiting dignitaries and heads of state who had come for the Truman memorial. He hosted a late reception for freshmen congressmen in the East Room and then flew by helicopter from the south grounds of the White House to Camp David. Once ensconced in the Aspen Lodge, he ordered a drink and called Chuck Colson.

He was hopping mad about two things. The *Washington Star* had misquoted him from his breakfast meeting with congressional leaders. Nixon told the leaders that he was "neither optimistic nor pessimistic" about the upcoming negotiations in Paris to end the war. The *Star* headline read that the president was "not optimistic" about the talks. "Raise hell," he told Colson.

But Nixon was more upset about the Senate Democrats adopting a resolution calling for an end to the war. "The Democrats have to be brutally attacked for this," Nixon said. He bemoaned the fact that no one in his camp was being more aggressive. Colson responded that during the campaign he had an attack apparatus in place but that he disbanded it after the election. "Our people really are a sad bunch of sacks," Nixon said of Republican leaders in the Congress. "We can do better than that." Nixon thought they must reexamine the need for a continuous attack apparatus. "You need eight or ten gut fighters around here," he said. "Let's not let our little boys sit down here and sort of play substance and reorganization and not fight the real battle." It was time, he said, for his people to start "fighting the Congress, kicking their balls."

Colson couldn't end the call without reporting some news on his secret surveillance of Henry Kissinger. "One other point, Mr. President, after we started keeping the log on Henry's calls—this is in total confidence, because Henry should never know—"

Nixon's interest was piqued. "What'd you find out?"

"After we started keeping the log, we found evidence of [syndicated columnist] Joe Kraft and Jerry Schecter [of *Time*]."

"Joe Kraft! Was Joe Kraft on the list?" Nixon was incredulous. Kraft would be one of the journalists to make it to the enemies list. He was a major critic of the Vietnam War and the December bombing.

"Oh yeah, January 2nd," Colson said. Kissinger had called him, he reported.

"And you saw his column today," Nixon said as the lightbulb went on. Kraft's article in the *Washington Post* was titled "Twelve Days of Bombing" and praised Kissinger as "perhaps the only instrument for effective foreign policy available to President Nixon."[15]

"Yeah, and how," Colson said of the Kraft article. "So you know where that comes from."

"Right," Nixon said, elongating the word for emphasis.

"We have not yet found the *New York Times* [meaning evidence of calls between Reston and Kissinger]," Colson said. "The problem being that we didn't keep a log until I ordered it on January 1st."

"Well, just keep the log from now on," Nixon ordered.

"They're going to keep the log on people and phones," Colson stressed.

"Incidentally, I want it on his private phone too. We can get that, can't we?" Nixon asked.

"I think we can," Colson tentatively responded.

"Well, sure, goddammit, we get it through the FBI!" Nixon shot back.

"Oh yeah, right, yeah, yeah," Colson sputtered in reverse.

"The FBI is to keep the log on his phone. He's not to know it," Nixon barked.[16]

In addition, Nixon wanted Colson to test Kissinger. "Just say, 'Henry, did you talk to Kraft?'" he instructed Colson to ask Kissinger. "And if he lies on that, I want to know it," Nixon said. "It's very important that I know that."

After a quick dinner with daughter Julie, Nixon called Henry Kissinger. As usual, not a word was said about Joe Kraft or Colson's surreptitious activities. Kissinger was getting ready for a dinner party at the home of columnist Joseph Alsop. Seething over Mansfield's open support of the Democrats' end-the-war-now resolution, Nixon told Kissinger to confront him. "I want you to play a very hard line with him," Nixon said. "I want you to say to him, 'Senator, I regret to say that your resolution has torpedoed the negotiations and I have reluctantly advised the president to go on national television next week and tell the nation.' Scare the shit out of him."[17] Kissinger happily agreed to deliver the message.

After a bruising week Nixon needed escape, and his thoughts turned to his friend Bebe Rebozo, whom he reached by phone in Key Biscayne. Rebozo said he happened to be with "our friend" John Mitchell. Nixon invited Rebozo to join him at Camp David for the weekend. "If you didn't have anything else planned, you might get a plane and come up tomorrow," Nixon solicited. "Sure!" Rebozo cheerily replied. "Be here Saturday night and Sunday," Nixon explained. "See a few movies and have a few jokes."[18]

All the tough talk, though, didn't change the central problem Nixon faced that first weekend of January 1973. He could step up his political attacks on Mike Mansfield and Congress, spy on his own national security advisor, and even hint to the speaker of the house that nuclear weapons might well be an option in Vietnam, but the hard calculus of the situation he had placed himself in was unforgiving. He knew he had to finish off the peace negotiations. And even then, his best judgment was that any peace agreement he could negotiate would likely spell doom for South Vietnam.

"Look, let's face it," he said to Henry Kissinger on January 3, after they had spent several hours going over all of the pros and cons of Option One (peace now) and Option Two (continued bombing for return of POWs), "I think there is a very good chance that either one could well sink South Vietnam."[19]

The continued existence of South Vietnam was fast becoming beyond the point. The severe domestic unrest that the war had engendered, as well as the inability to pay sufficient attention to other major world problems and developments, made the administration's past myopic attention on the survival of South Vietnam seem illogical. It simply was no longer worth the drag on America's domestic or foreign policy. "You also have to realize, too," Nixon said to Kissinger, "that I have responsibilities far beyond those [to Vietnam alone] and I just can't devote all this time to it. We cannot let Vietnam continue to blank out our vision with regard to the rest of the world. Thank God we did [détente with] Russia and thank God we [opened] China. But my point is, at the present time, as far as that damn Congress is concerned, and the lousy media are concerned, that's all they will talk about—all they will talk about."

The reality was sinking in. "Let me put it this way, I am going to be quite candid," he said to Kissinger. Though his numerous qualifiers showed that Nixon was having trouble verbalizing his thoughts, his message was clear: a bad result, the fall of South Vietnam, was now preferable to continuing the war. "Frankly, taking Option One, which we know has admitted potential risks—although not certain—[there are] risks of the collapse of South Vietnam, I think it's better than going to an Option Two, with all of the pressure and pain that we've had to go through. In other words, there comes a point in war when, not defeat—because that isn't really what we are talking about, fortunately, in a sense—but where an end which is not too satisfactory, in fact is very *un*satisfactory, is a hellava lot better than continuing. That's really what we come down to." A bad result had become better than continuing.

Nixon was worn down by the criticism and the outcry. Though the bombing did, in a true sense, bring the North Vietnamese back to the bargaining table, to what end? Congress was more active than ever. Nixon's options were more limited than ever. There was nowhere else to turn. And Henry Kissinger had lost all patience with President Thieu, who had blocked the October agreements, which in turn led to the December bombing. Nixon and Kissinger believed that if Thieu fell, he had only himself to blame.

"You know I was always for Option One, Mr. President," Kissinger said, "for all the reasons you gave. For the reason that I knew domestically we would wind up in something like this position sooner or later. Sooner or later the doves were going to come out and say we will have to pay ransom to the Soviet Union and to Communist China just to keep a war going in Southeast Asia, which we can no longer win because of the errors of your predecessors. And certainly [I was for Option One because it] fulfills your May 8 objectives, it exceeds them, and if the guy [meaning Thieu] collapses, it is his fault."

Kissinger believed Nixon's authority would have been unchallenged—in America and around the world—had he settled the war in October or even November, untied to the election. But Thieu raised objections because of his own domestic "brawl"—needlessly extending the war and forcing the bombing. "The war was well designed," Kissinger said. "We had achieved our objectives, and suddenly he raised objections he had never raised before." Kissinger called Thieu "insanely obstinate."

Henry Kissinger had his marching orders: end the war now.

But as with so many actions taken by Richard Nixon, his rash decision to use raw power and military force to bring about peace negotiations opened Pandora's Box. Not only was Congress galvanized to end the war, members like Mike Mansfield and Sam Ervin began to see that it was past time for Congress to reassert its authority and return balance to the constitutional balance of powers. Nixon took his election landslide as a mandate for his policies, but Mansfield and others saw the election results in a different way. "Mr. Mansfield said that the voters had given the Senate Democrats a mandate distinct from the President's in increasing the Democratic majority by three members, to 57 of the 100 Senate seats, in the Nov. 7 elections," the *New York Times* reported on January 4. "The clearest mandate, he added, involved the war. In the absence of a negotiated settlement, Mr. Mansfield said, 'it remains for the Congress to seek to bring about complete disinvolvement.'"[20]

But the assertion of this new authority would not end with mere protest over the war. This had become a much broader fight between the Congress and the president. A Missouri lawsuit filed at the end of 1972 by the Democrats challenged the president's right to refuse to spend highway trust funds appropriated by Congress. "Senator Sam Ervin, Jr., of North Carolina made it clear that the legal step was but a symbolic prelude to an effort to demonstrate that the power of the purse belongs exclusively to the Congress under the Constitution."

Singularly focused as he was on ending the war, Nixon failed to see the seriousness of related moves by Mansfield, which were reported in the *New York Times* during the first week of January 1973: "The Senate Majority Leader urged committee chairmen to start at once readopting measures that Mr. Nixon had vetoed since Congress adjourned on Oct. 18. And he called for investigations into alleged espionage and sabotage by the Republicans during the Presidential campaign."[21]

Oblivious to the threat to his presidency that the Christmas bombings had sparked, Nixon wrote in his diary over the weekend: "Colson told me Friday that he had tried to do everything he could to keep Hunt in line from turning state's evidence. After what happened to Hunt's wife, etc., I think we have a very good case for showing some clemency."[22] The implications of his involvement in discussions of clemency for a Watergate criminal—one who was about to go on trial—would turn out to be catastrophic.

Unlike Harry Truman, Richard Nixon had "wrinkles" in his honesty. His tangled web of untruths, and his stubborn reliance on stealth and power and intrigue, set up the very conditions that would lead to his own eventual collapse. Fortunately Bebe Rebozo was on his way to make it all go away for just one weekend, with some movies and a few jokes.

9

"I Wanted the Young Prosecutor to Know Just How Whitewashers Are Engineered"

The US District Court for the District of Columbia, December 4, 1972
Four days before Dorothy Hunt was killed in the plane crash in Chicago, Judge John Sirica held a pretrial conference with the lawyers in the Watergate burglars' case. Attorney Bill Bittman appeared for Howard Hunt; Henry Rothblatt was there on behalf of the four Miamians; Peter Maroulis for Gordon Liddy; and John Johnson of F. Lee Bailey's Boston firm Bailey, Alch & Gillis sat in for James McCord.

Three prosecutors, Earl Silbert, Seymour Glanzer, and Donald Campbell, were also present representing the United States.

"Are you going to offer any evidence in this case on the question of how the $25,000 check got into the possession of Mr. Barker?"[1] Judge Sirica inquired of Silbert.

Sirica had read about the check in the newspapers. He told the lawyers that he had been carefully monitoring what was being printed about the case as part of his consideration of a motion to change venue, based on an argument that the defendants could not get a fair trial in Washington because of all the publicity. In fact, John Sirica was gripped by the reporting of Bob Woodward and Carl Bernstein at the *Washington Post,* and he harbored his own strong suspicions that the truth behind the break-in was more likely to be found in newspaper accounts than in the presentation that the government was intending to make during the trial in his courtroom in January 1973.

The reason was simple. From Judge Sirica's viewpoint, Earl Silbert, the lead prosecutor for the government, was in a conflicted situation. An assistant US attorney in the Department of Justice, Silbert owed his job and his loyalty to his boss, the attorney general of the United States, Richard Kleindienst. Kleindienst in turn reported to the president. Sirica believed that Silbert was under pressure, whether overt or not, to confine his proofs in the case to the seven men who had been arrested and indicted. Sirica had come to his own conclusion that higher-ups had to be involved. He was obsessed with the origin of the money found on the defendants, thinking that this could be the trail leading back to more important people at the CRP, or even the White House.

As a consequence, Judge Sirica injected himself into the case in a way that was very unjudgelike. Rather than presiding as a neutral and impartial arbiter of the dispute, Sirica began to act as another prosecutor—one who, by his own lights, would not be tainted by association with the president or the Department of Justice. "I like Earl Silbert," Sirica later wrote. "I think he is a good lawyer. I wanted to be helpful, to share with him some of my experiences which I felt might give him some guidance through what was obviously a tough situation."[2] Sirica would push Silbert time and again to do more than Silbert was intending to do.

The $25,000 check that Judge Sirica asked Silbert about was a case in point. The check had been discovered by Miami authorities shortly after the arrests of the Watergate burglars in the summer of 1972. One of the men arrested, Bernard Barker, maintained a bank account for his real estate business in a Miami bank. The Dade County district attorney in Miami opened his own investigation after the break-in and searched Barker's Miami bank records, uncovering evidence of several large checks that had passed through his account, including a cashier's check made out to a man from Minneapolis named Kenneth H. Dahlberg in the amount of $25,000. Dahlberg, a heavily decorated WWII fighter pilot, ran a hearing-aid company in Minneapolis called Miracle-Ear (later sold to Bausch & Lomb), wintered in Boca Raton, and was an active fundraiser for the Republican Party in Minnesota.

Dahlberg, it turned out, was acting as a front for another wealthy Minnesotan, Archer Daniels Midland's CEO Dwayne Andreas, who wanted to give money to Nixon's campaign, but not openly. Andreas was a friend of Hubert Humphrey's but supported Nixon's position on the handling of the Vietnam War. He gave $25,000 to Dahlberg, who deposited the money in a Boca Raton bank in return for a cashier's check made out to himself. Dahlberg then gave the cashier's check to Maurice Stans, the treasurer of the Committee to Re-Elect the President. Gordon Liddy, whose official job at the CRP was general counsel to the finance committee, took the check and sent it back to Florida to Bernard Barker so Barker could run it through his bank account. Barker obliged and, after taking a commission for himself, sent the cash—in unmarked hundred-dollar bills—back to Liddy to store in a safe at the CRP, where it was intermingled with other cash. Some of these dollars by happenstance would eventually find their way to the pockets of the Watergate burglars.

Woodward and Bernstein wrote about the Dahlberg check and four other large checks that showed up in Barker's bank records. The other checks were made out to the order of Manuel Ogarrio, a prominent Mexico City lawyer, and they totaled $89,000. Woodward and Bernstein's first article about the strange checks appeared on August 1, 1972, in the *Washington Post*. (The checks would become the centerpiece for their book, *All the President's Men*, and the Robert Redford and Dustin Hoffman film of the same name. "Follow the money," the signature line of the film, was not a phrase that Woodward and Bernstein used in their book, but the origin of the money was one of the keys to unlocking the Watergate cover-up.) The Ogarrio checks were written on behalf of one of his clients, a Mexican subsidiary of a Texas company owned by Robert Allen. Allen was the president of Gulf Resources and Chemical Company, and he too wanted to contribute to the Nixon campaign without anyone knowing about it.[3]

All of this check laundering resulted from a change in campaign contribution disclosure laws in the spring of 1972. Prior to April 7, 1972, the law allowed anonymous contributions; afterward it did not. So huge sums of anonymous cash were collected before the deadline by the Republicans and the Democrats alike. Liddy routed the Dahlberg and Ogarrio checks through Barker's account as a precaution to avoid any argument that the money had come in after the date the law changed and to avoid suspicion about money that came in from a foreign country.[4] It would be one of his many blunders—Gordon Liddy had a reckless propensity for leaving tracks.

Prosecutor Earl Silbert told Sirica that he did expect to introduce evidence of the checks at trial, but it was not for the same reason that

Sirica wanted. Sirica hoped that someone would trace the money to higher-ups and expose the wider conspiracy he sensed had to be in place. Silbert, in contrast, merely wanted to show that the burglars were working for hire. He had no intention of showing *why* they had been given the money or necessarily the ultimate source of the funds. Silbert needed to prove only that the men were guilty of the crimes of conspiracy, burglary, illegal interception of oral and wire communications, and possession of illegal surveillance equipment.[5] He did not need to prove the reasons behind these illegal acts.

Sirica was displeased with Silbert's answer about the checks and probed further about the government's goal at trial. "Are you going to try and trace, I think there is an item of $89,000?" Sirica asked, referring to the checks from the Mexican lawyer.

"Not necessarily from the source," Silbert replied, "but we will trace it part of the way through the system."

Once again, Sirica was perturbed with Silbert. "Why don't you trace it from the source? Isn't that part of the case?"

It really wasn't, Silbert must have thought, but he needed to be diplomatic with this difficult judge. "If the court please," Silbert responded in his punctilious way, "first of all, part of it, the $89,000 check, would involve testimony of a person out of the country over whom we don't have subpoena power. So far as we are concerned, so far as materiality and relevancy, we can rely on the bank records of defendant Barker to show the checks were deposited in his account and we will produce other evidence to establish the link in its relevancy and materiality."

This dodge further aggravated the blunt Sirica. Not to be deterred, he stayed on point: "Now, on the question of motive and intent in this case, as you know, there has been a lot of talk about who hired whom to go into this place. Is the government going to offer any evidence on the question of motive and intent for entering the Democratic National Committee's headquarters?"

"There will be *some* evidence of it," Silbert equivocated.

"What do you mean by *some* evidence?" Sirica pressed.

"Well—" Silbert had to verbally pause to consider his response and measure his words. "There will be *some* evidence introduced. It is a question which the jury will make the proper inference, it is up to the jury to accept or reject the evidence that we propose to offer, but there will be evidence we will offer that will go—from which a jury may draw, we think, an appropriate inference as to perhaps a variety of interests."[6]

A variety of interests? Words were streaming from Silbert's mouth, but they were not connecting with John Sirica, the old boxer.[7]

Sirica later wrote that he knew the prosecutors did not have to prove motive, but that was beside the point: he wanted to know. "[I]t's true," he admitted in his memoirs, "that, technically, they didn't have to prove a motive, only that the seven men were guilty of the charges against them." From the standpoint of the law, it simply didn't matter *why* the men had broken into the Democratic headquarters; the only issue was whether they had committed the crimes. "But," Sirica wrote of his reason for continuing to prod Silbert, "the public was growing more and more suspicious. There had to be some reason these men had gone into the Watergate. Why not develop it? Why not get all the truth out and settle the question once and for all?"[8]

Earl Silbert was not a man to assume the burden of proof about something that made no difference to his ability to obtain a conviction, especially in such a high-profile case. He knew he was under a spotlight and that charges of "whitewash" were circulating in the press. Yet he did not think he had enough evidence of a conspiracy beyond the men arrested (including Hunt and Liddy), and he didn't want to start down that road. Silbert was meticulous, thorough, and scrupulous—verging on obsessive-compulsive. "His mother says that even the heels of his shoes must be lined up perfectly in the closet," one newspaper profile described him.[9] He was not a risk-taker.

John Sirica and Earl Silbert were a study in contrasts. Silbert was thirty-seven years old in 1973, a graduate of Harvard University and Harvard Law School, and had spent his entire twelve-year legal career working quietly but effectively as an attorney with the US Department of Justice. Owlish-looking with oversized glasses and thinning hair, he started as a matter-of-fact tax litigator at the Department of Justice before being elevated to an assistant US attorney for the District of Columbia in 1964, where he labored earnestly in the grand jury and criminal trial sections.

Brusque, domineering, and bullheaded, John Sirica, born in March 1904 (which made him almost sixty-nine years old in January 1973), wanted nothing more out of life than to become a professional boxer. Raised in relative poverty by parents who were both children of Italian immigrants, his family moved from city to city until finally landing in a tough neighborhood in Washington, DC, during the last year of the First World War, when Sirica was twelve years old. "We wound up in a little two-room flat on D Street, NW, between Ninth and Tenth streets, where the new FBI building is now," he remembered.

Young Sirica dropped out of school when he was fourteen to work as an auto mechanic but was persuaded later to return to private night schools to get his high school diploma. "In those days," he wrote, "it was possible to go directly from high school into law school without getting an undergraduate degree in college." So he applied to the George Washington University Law School and "amazingly," by his own estimation, was accepted. His lack of formal education, though, was evident, and he soon dropped out. He wrote, "I couldn't begin to understand what the professors were talking about; it was like being in a foreign country." He took up boxing at the YMCA and within a short time was sparring with "local professional welterweights and middleweights" in neighborhood boxing clubs.

Meanwhile he applied to Georgetown Law School, hoping to enjoy a "fresh start," and again to his astonishment was accepted. Academically, though, he was just as lost as before. His professors ridiculed him and he dejectedly left the study of law for a second time.

After an interlude, Sirica applied for a third try, was readmitted to Georgetown, and though he struggled with his studies, he at last graduated in 1926. While waiting for his bar examination results, he went to Florida, unsure of what he wanted to do with his life, and won his one and only professional fight. His parents convinced him to come back to Washington to practice law after, to his and everyone else's surprise, he passed the bar. (He had signed up to take the exam at the last minute, having spent no time studying for it.)

Sirica had an undistinguished career as a young lawyer in Washington. After a brief stint in private practice in small-time criminal courts, he became a federal prosecutor. It was during this time that he started working for the Republican Party on a local level. He left the government after three years to start his own practice, where he routinely stumbled through what he later called "starvation periods" from lack of business. Politics continued to be a hobby. He was elected as a member of the Republican state committee for the District of Columbia in 1940 and spent a stint as chief counsel to a congressional committee in 1944.

He kept up his boxing, eventually befriending the great Jack Dempsey. The two became constant associates. "The boxing arena turned out to be a failure," Sirica later wrote, "but my friendship with Dempsey developed steadily after our first meeting. I occasionally went to New York for weekends, and Dempsey took me into his circle of friends. He always introduced me as his Washington lawyer." Dempsey invited Sirica to travel the country with him in 1945 to sell government savings bonds. "It was the most exciting and interesting trip I ever made," Sirica recalled. Dempsey later served as Sirica's best man in 1952 when he married, for the first time, at age forty-eight.[10]

Over time, Sirica became more active on the national level in Republican politics, supporting the Eisenhower-Nixon ticket in 1952 and 1956. In a twist of fate, Sirica's labors on behalf of Eisenhower and Nixon led to his being appointed as a federal judge. "It was my work in the two Eisenhower elections that made me the friends who finally helped me get to the bench," he wrote. In April 1957, after a competition with several other candidates to take the seat of a retiring federal judge, John Sirica emerged the winner with the appointment and was sworn in as a federal district court judge, a position that carried with it lifetime tenure.[11]

By January 1973, Sirica had been on the bench for nearly sixteen years and was, by reason of his seniority, the chief judge of the district. As such, he had the power to appoint a judge to sit by special assignment in complicated or protracted cases, as the Watergate case promised to be. He decided to assign the case to himself. His self-appointment was controversial because he had presided over the very grand jury that had investigated the underlying Watergate crimes and returned the indictment against the Watergate Seven. "I thought that perhaps I should try the case myself," he blithely wrote of his provocative decision.[12]

At the December 4 pretrial conference with all the lawyers, Sirica didn't feel that his body punches were landing. "The point I was trying to make still didn't seem to be clear to the prosecutors," Sirica later wrote of his insistence at the pretrial that Silbert and his team concentrate on the motive underlying the crimes, though he knew of its legal irrelevance. "I returned to the question a few minutes later and was as direct as I could be," he wrote. Speaking to Bill Bittman's complaints that the government had not previously indicated it would rely on the Dahlberg and Ogarrio checks, Sirica interjected, making the case for Silbert's introduction of the checks. It was circumstantial evidence, he contended, that may help prove motive.

Sirica said the following to Bittman:

When you have a question of intent and motive involved, which I believe you have in this case, this jury is going to want to know somewhere along the line what did these men go into the Headquarters for? What was their purpose? Was it their sole purpose to go in there for so-called political espionage or were they paid to go in there? Did they go in there for financial gain? Who hired them to go in there? Who started this thing? There are a myriad of problems in this case that I can see coming up and so can you. They [meaning the jury] are going to want to know these things.[13]

Sirica did little to disguise his bias against the defendants and was even more direct in off-the-record encounters with Earl Silbert. As he retold it in his memoirs, a few days before trial was to start in January 1973, he spoke privately with Silbert about an administrative matter in another case. He took the occasion to deliver a pep talk to Silbert about the upcoming Watergate trial. "Earl, look," he said, "you've got a great opportunity in this case if you go right down the middle, let the chips fall where they may. Don't let anybody put any pressure on you." To underscore his meaning, Sirica presented Silbert with a bound copy of hearings before a congressional committee in which Sirica had acted as counsel in 1944. The proceeding was an investigation of activities of the Federal Communications Commission, and Sirica came to the conclusion that nothing was going to be done because the fix was in from the Roosevelt administration. Sirica resigned in protest. But his message to Silbert was intended to be, and likely was, plain: "I wanted the young prosecutor to know just how whitewashers were engineered," Sirica wrote. "And I wanted him to know that I had had direct experience with cover-ups as chief counsel to that commission."[14]

This highly improper ex parte communication between the judge and a lawyer representing only one of the parties was not only unethical under judicial and legal canons but also a patent violation of the basic concepts of fairness and due process for the defendants who were facing serious criminal charges. John Sirica didn't seem to think it mattered if his goal was to get to the truth as he saw it—and he sensed a "whitewasher" was in progress.

The Watergate Complex, Memorial Day Weekend, 1972
The problem was that Earl Silbert and the two lawyers working on his team had bought the cover story cooked up by the White House and

the CRP. Silbert, Glanzer, and Campbell, all experienced prosecutors, were not corrupt—far from it—but they were quite naive about the subtle lies that they were told, thereby enabling higher authorities to avoid indictment.

Things should have gone differently. The prosecutors had a quick start; their first big break came from telephone records that led them to Alfred Baldwin, an unmarried, thirty-six-year-old sometime college instructor from New Haven, Connecticut, who had been hired by Jim McCord in May 1972. Within mere days of the break-in the prosecutors knew who Baldwin was.

One aspect of Jim McCord's job as security consultant for the CRP was to identify and employ bodyguards for John and Martha Mitchell. John Mitchell, though the former attorney general of the United States, had no official security detail. Martha, whose no-holds-barred personality made her a popular campaigner, also needed protection. She, however, was mercurial and suspicious of her bodyguards, fearing they would tell the press about her heavy drinking and frequent behind-the-scenes antics and tantrums. McCord was having trouble keeping her security detail manned. In April he identified five ex-FBI agents from a list maintained by the New York City Society of Ex-FBI Agents. Several were interviewed but all declined the job, no doubt after hearing of Martha's irascibility.[15]

In desperation, McCord called another name on the list: Alfred Baldwin of New Haven, Connecticut. Baldwin was a former marine and ex–FBI agent who had gone to law school but not yet passed the bar. He was looking for work. McCord told Baldwin that he needed immediate help.

Baldwin flew from New Haven to Washington the night of McCord's call—May 1, 1972—and the next morning he met McCord, who took him over to be interviewed at the CRP by Fred LaRue, an old friend of the Mitchells. Baldwin was told that LaRue was John Mitchell's "right-hand man," and someone who knew how to handle Martha. The interview lasted all of five minutes. Baldwin remembered the day well because it was the morning that J. Edgar Hoover was found dead in his bedroom at his home in Washington.

Baldwin's initial assignment was to travel later that afternoon to Chicago with Martha Mitchell on Amtrak (she hated flying) for several campaign events. From Chicago, they journeyed to campaign stops in Michigan and then New York, completing the run back in Washington the following Monday, May 8.

Martha didn't like Baldwin. She took offense to a casual conversation she had witnessed him having with a couple at a luncheon at the Waldorf, though Baldwin swore to McCord that he had said nothing about her. It mattered little; Martha found Baldwin "pushy, vocal, and someone who would not stay in the background," according to her personal secretary, Kristen Forsberg. She told Forsberg, "That's it, I'm not taking any more recommendations from McCord."[16]

McCord decided to keep Baldwin on but reassigned him, shifting him to antiwar surveillance. And he told Baldwin to move out of the expensive Roger Smith Hotel, where he had been staying—a block from the White House and CRP headquarters—to the more economical, and surely less swanky, Howard Johnson's directly across the street from the Watergate complex. His room there, 419, was booked under the name of McCord Associates, Jim McCord's private security company. It is not clear if McCord had already formed a plan to have Baldwin monitor phone conversations at the Democratic National Committee headquarters in the Watergate. If he had, he did not tell Baldwin about it. Baldwin believed he was just moving into a cheaper hotel.

Baldwin's new job shadowing antiwar demonstration groups in the District of Columbia was a thrill for him. He was supposed to identify antiwar agitators who might represent a threat to the CRP or the Mitchells. And there was genuine reason for alarm in Washington, with rumors circulating that the CRP's offices might be bombed or stormed, or that the Mitchells could be kidnapped or physically attacked. In fact, just weeks after Baldwin's reassignment—on May 19—the Weather Underground organization planted and detonated a bomb in a fourth-floor women's restroom at the Pentagon, in retaliation for the Nixon administration's stepped-up bombings of North Vietnam. It was a shocking attack. The property damage was extensive; anyone in the restroom would have been killed.

On the following Monday, May 22, Baldwin, undercover, was among the protestors outside the Pentagon when police on horses descended, wielding clubs and breaking up the crowd.[17] Baldwin was gassed in the chaos. "I saw news people get it. I saw people get it that weren't even involved," he later said. "It kind of made you wonder."

But Baldwin was having the time of his life. He seemed to enjoy the young people he was spying on, infiltrating dissident groups and showing up at events that seemed like parties to him. "Sometimes I'd hang out at Lafayette Square [across from the White House], you know, sit in on the sing-ins and I was having a good time," he told reporters for the *Los Angeles Times.* "Don't get me wrong, it was a lot of fun. I met some pretty sensible people and I met some real crackpots."[18]

During the last week of May—on the very afternoon he was gassed at the Pentagon protest—Baldwin flew back to his home in Connecticut to get clean clothes. When he drove back to the Howard Johnson's at the end of the week (McCord asked him to drive his car so he could avoid the expense of air travel in future trips home), he found Jim McCord in Room 419, now brimming with high-tech and expensive electronics and recording equipment, which McCord was setting up and testing. McCord explained that there was a plan to wiretap the telephone conversations of Larry O'Brien, the chairman of the Democratic National Committee, from his office in the Democratic National Committee headquarters at the Watergate across the street.

Baldwin did not question the legality of what he was doing. He thought that his CRP superiors, including John Mitchell, the former attorney general of the United States, must have had good cause and legal justification for what he was being asked to do. He assumed what they were doing was authorized in some fashion.[19]

It was the beginning of the Memorial Day weekend, 1972. The afternoon he found McCord in his room (which may have been another day—Baldwin's later retelling of it to authorities would never be exactly the same about dates and details), Howard Hunt and Gordon Liddy showed up to inspect his room and survey its vantage point. McCord introduced both men to Baldwin using aliases (although McCord had to ask Hunt and Liddy to remind him of their aliases). Baldwin, however, was subsequently able to identify them in photographs he was shown by the FBI. Later that night Baldwin witnessed McCord crossing the street to enter the Watergate and saw him appear in the window of the DNC headquarters, where McCord and others— Baldwin could not say who—were busy planting listening devices in what they thought was Larry O'Brien's office.

Afterward McCord discovered that the office he had penetrated belonged to a man named Spencer Oliver, a Democratic Party official responsible for coordination with state party chairmen. To his annoyance, McCord also found that he had difficulty tuning in to one of the devices he had installed there. He instructed Baldwin to move up several floors in the Howard Johnson's, to Room 723, in the hopes of getting better reception.[20] The move didn't help; McCord continued to have trouble connecting to some of the bugs he planted.

Sometime over that same Memorial Day weekend, Baldwin went with McCord to case George McGovern's campaign headquarters near the Capitol. The operation was abandoned that night because of the presence of security officers at the headquarters and police patrol cars in the area. Baldwin, though, once again encountered Liddy, who got in the car with him and McCord, and Baldwin thought he saw Hunt sitting in the driver's seat of the car from which Liddy had emerged.

By his own calculation, Baldwin listened to more than two hundred phone conversations over the next three weeks from the devices installed at DNC headquarters. He kept detailed handwritten notes and then typed up logs of what he heard. He delivered the logs to McCord daily, and once, when McCord was out of town, he dropped off his work product directly with a security guard at the Committee to Re-Elect.

On June 6 McCord left town for Miami to work on setting up security operations for the upcoming political conventions (the Democrats and Republicans both held their conventions in Miami that year). He stayed a few days longer than anticipated and called Baldwin, ordering him to take his most recent notes over to the Committee to Re-Elect and leave them in care of a man whose name Baldwin later could not recall, even after scouring lists of the names of the people working for the CRP. It was apparent that there were some officials within the CRP—Jeb Magruder or perhaps even John Mitchell—who were anxiously reading what Baldwin was producing.

Because the listening devices McCord had planted at the DNC headquarters had been placed in the wrong office, and because at least one of the bugs appeared not to be working, McCord and Baldwin hatched a plan to have Baldwin gain access to the DNC headquarters under false pretenses to find out exactly where Larry O'Brien's office was located. On Monday, June 12, Baldwin walked into the Democratic National Committee headquarters and identified himself as Bill Johnson, the nephew of the state chairman of the Connecticut Democratic Party. He asked for Spencer Oliver, who he knew was out of town because of his wiretap on Oliver's phone.

Baldwin almost outsmarted himself. Unbeknownst to Baldwin, the chairman of the Connecticut Democratic Party, John Moran Bailey, had preceded O'Brien as national party chairman and had occupied the same office that O'Brien was then using. Thinking he was Bailey's nephew, the secretaries were thrilled to meet him and happily showed him around, but he privately fretted the entire time of his tour that he would be asked some question or detail about Bailey that he couldn't answer, thus blowing his cover. He didn't need to worry; helpful DNC secretaries even gave Baldwin Larry O'Brien's private phone number in Miami, where Democrats were already gathering for their convention. Despite the near-disaster, the experience emboldened Baldwin; it seemed that nothing could go wrong.

The second break-in was planned for later that weekend.

In the early hours of Saturday, June 17, Baldwin was the lookout as McCord and the four Miamians entered the DNC headquarters. Hunt and Liddy were in the Watergate Hotel, acting as the command center. Baldwin turned on the late show and kept one eye on the street below. Perhaps an hour later, he noticed a car drive up with plainclothesmen who jumped out and hustled inside the Watergate. He walked out onto his balcony to get a better look. Once the men were in the building, Baldwin could see them searching the upper floors of the Watergate with guns drawn. He tried to radio the burglars and Hunt and Liddy, but it was too late. "They got us," one of the burglars whispered into his walkie-talkie just before it went silent. The five men caught inside the DNC headquarters were arrested and led out in handcuffs. At almost the same time, Liddy and Hunt emerged from the nearby Watergate Hotel to make their getaway.

A panicked Howard Hunt burst into Baldwin's room minutes later and immediately dashed into Baldwin's bathroom. "He had to take a leak he was so upset," Baldwin later told Jack Nelson of the *Los Angeles Times*. When he emerged from the bathroom, Hunt dropped to the floor and crawled over to the window to peer down over the hectic scene below. Baldwin meanwhile stood in plain sight with electronic gadgetry glittering all around him. One of the officers who made the arrests at the DNC headquarters had noticed him standing on his balcony across the street when he was searching on the terrace of the sixth floor. He made a mental note of it because he was concerned that the man at the Howard Johnson's might mistake him for a burglar, given his old clothes and drawn service revolver, and report it.[21]

Hunt told Baldwin to get out immediately and to remove all of the electronic equipment and deliver it to McCord's wife at their home in Rockville, Maryland. Hunt then called a lawyer from Baldwin's room, threw his walkie-talkie on the bed, and left abruptly, telling him someone would be in touch.

"Does this mean I am out of a job?" Baldwin called to Hunt as he disappeared into the hallway.[22]

Baldwin drove the electronics equipment to McCord's home and delivered it to his wife and daughter in the middle of the night. He then got in his car and drove straight back to Connecticut, arriving around 10:00 AM.

The Federal Prosecutor's Office, July 5, 1972

It did not take long for the Washington Police and the FBI to identify and locate Baldwin. The arresting officer who noticed Baldwin told his fellow investigators, and they inquired at the Howard Johnson's. After getting a search warrant later that morning, they discovered that Baldwin had signed room service tickets and made a number of toll calls that were billed to his room, which had been booked under the name of McCord Associates. The FBI lost little time in calling the phone numbers the following week. Baldwin had phoned his mother, but she knew nothing about what he had been doing in Washington. Another number, though, belonged to Robert Mitro, a lawyer from West Haven, Connecticut, who was a law school classmate of Baldwin's and a good friend.

In fact, Baldwin had gone directly to see Mitro on the day he escaped from Washington. Mitro was distracted with another case, though, and told him to go away and come back later in the week.

Two days later Mitro, now frantic, called Baldwin. "Jesus Christ," he said over the phone. "Get over here right away." He told Baldwin that the FBI had just called him, asking questions about the Howard Johnson's and the Watergate break-in. "Holy Christ," Mitro blurted, "what did you do?"[23] It was Mitro who told the FBI on Monday, June 19, that he had received calls from Baldwin from the Howard Johnson's. The FBI had its suspect just two days after the break-in.

Mitro brought in his associate, John Cassidento, a former assistant US attorney, to help him interview Baldwin so he could respond to the inquiries from the FBI. On Wednesday, June 21, just five days after the arrests at the Watergate, Cassidento called the FBI to say he and Mitro were representing Baldwin and that Baldwin would not have anything to say at present but might later.[24] Mitro and Cassidento advised Baldwin to contact the CRP to find out what he should do. Baldwin did not know that Cassidento, a Connecticut Democratic state representative, would blatantly breach his attorney-client duty of confidentiality to Baldwin by calling the DNC and its attorneys, who had filed a civil case on June 20, to provide them with assistance.[25] Cassidento would be a critical backdoor source for the Democrats as the scandal unfolded, eventually allowing the lawyers for the Democrats to secretly interview Baldwin in early August.[26]

But before all this happened, Baldwin tried to work with the Committee to Re-Elect. As suggested by his lawyers, Baldwin spoke briefly with Fred LaRue from a pay phone later in the week, asking for some instructions. Baldwin complained that he was disturbed that no one from the CRP had reached out to him, and he was even hotter that he had not been paid. Immediately following this exchange, a lawyer for the CRP, a man named Paul O'Brien (no relation to Larry O'Brien), called Mitro and Cassidento. O'Brien eventually came to New Haven to talk to Baldwin's lawyers in person. "We were looking for guidance from him as to what was going to happen in Washington," Mitro later told the *Los Angeles Times*. "We gave him the whole story because at that point we were in this thing together."[27]

McCord, out on bail, told Baldwin to lie and testify before the grand jury that he worked for McCord Associates, not the Committee to Re-Elect. Baldwin's lawyers, sensing he was going to be abandoned by the CRP, started looking into immunity and decided to bargain with Earl Silbert for a promise not to prosecute. On July 5 Baldwin appeared before the grand jury investigating Watergate in Washington and was immediately dismissed to allow him to confer with his lawyers. His lawyers then met with the CRP's Paul O'Brien one last time to see if Baldwin would be supported if he did not talk, but O'Brien would give no such commitment.

Baldwin's lawyers returned to Silbert, Glanzer, and Campbell and, after some perfunctory sparring, cut a deal: Baldwin would not be a defendant in the Watergate case if he cooperated.

Baldwin would talk. That evening he identified photos of Hunt and Liddy for the FBI.[28]

The Federal Grand Jury, August 16, 1972

Critical as Baldwin's testimony was, he was a poor witness. He had trouble remembering dates and names and was often confused about details of the various break-ins. And in the end, even if he had had a better memory, he could not implicate anyone higher in the chain of command than McCord, Liddy, and Hunt. If Silbert and his team were going to prove a wider conspiracy, they would have to look elsewhere for the evidence.

The target became Jeb Magruder. On the same day that Baldwin appeared before the grand jury, July 5, Magruder showed up for what would turn out to be the first of his three appearances. Magruder was a youthful sales and marketing guru with an MBA from the University of Chicago who had worked at the White House for Bob Haldeman and Herb Klein, Nixon's communications director, before moving over to the CRP to become its first director, in 1971. Magruder slid into the deputy director role in March 1972 when John Mitchell resigned as attorney general and assumed the title of campaign chairman, as he had been in Nixon's successful 1968 run. Along with Mitchell and Fred LaRue, Magruder knew of and approved in advance Liddy's plans to eavesdrop on the DNC.

Magruder's problem with Silbert was that he had to explain how Liddy had access to so much money at the CRP.

Because the investigation was just getting started, Magruder's first trip to the grand jury was "brief and uneventful." He had not even yet been interviewed by the FBI. "I sat in a witness chair in a large room in the Federal Courthouse, with the prosecutors behind a table on my left and twenty-odd members of the grand jury on a raised platform on my right, some of them seemed bored by the proceedings," he wrote.[29] He explained organizational charts and administrative procedures of the CRP and left.

But as the grand jury heard from more witnesses and the FBI gathered more information, it became clear that Gordon Liddy, as counsel to the Finance Committee, had control of too much money—he had been given nearly $250,000 with no apparent strings attached. What was he doing with all that money? Who authorized it?

After an FBI interview of Magruder and his top assistant, Bart Porter, suspicion began to center on Magruder. The prosecutors informed lawyers for the CRP that Magruder was an official target of the grand jury investigation, meaning there was a good chance he could be indicted. Magruder was scheduled to testify before the grand jury for a second time on August 16. The prosecutors, as was their custom, asked Magruder to come in for a private session the day before he was to testify. Ominously they told him he could not bring his lawyer to the private interview. He could have declined the invitation, but that would have looked bad. Taking the Fifth Amendment or refusing to speak without his lawyer present would have likely resulted in Magruder being indicted. Going in was his only option, but he was making matters worse for himself by lying to the prosecutors. John Mitchell and John Dean both took turns practicing with Magruder to make sure he had his story down.

Earl Silbert made Magruder wait in the lobby of the courthouse for almost three hours prior to the interview, just to turn up the psychological pressure. "Saw him outside the grand jury," Silbert gleefully wrote in his diary. "He was very nervous—that struck me—very serious, and gloomy looking."[30] Magruder called it "an unsettling ploy" and admitted he was a "nervous wreck."[31]

There was good reason for the nerves. With the assistance of Porter, Magruder had concocted a cover story about Liddy that he intended to feed to the prosecutors. He and Porter would admit that Liddy had been given $250,000—this was an irrefutable fact—but they would claim that the money was for security and other legitimate intelligence-gathering purposes.

"Of this, we said, $100,000 was for a surrogate protection program wherein ten young people would be paid $1,000 a month for ten months to infiltrate radical groups that might endanger our thirty-odd surrogate speakers as they traveled around the country," Magruder wrote. "This was necessary, we said, because several of our headquarters had already been firebombed, our speakers had been heckled and threatened, and if we were going to send them around the country we had a responsibility to protect them."

The remaining $150,000, Magruder would claim, was "primarily to provide security for our convention." The difficulty with the story, Magruder recognized, was that the CRP "couldn't document a dime's worth of it." The excuse he and Porter would give: the CRP had "practiced shoddy bookkeeping." Because Liddy wasn't talking, they could lay the blame for the poor recordkeeping on him. "Talk to Liddy," they planned to say if Silbert pressed them to learn how the money was spent.[32]

Silbert's diary shows he bought Magruder's story hook, line, and sinker. At the least, he should have asked for the names of the "ten young people" who allegedly received $1,000 a month to protect surrogates.

To embellish the story and reinforce the lie that Liddy had left him out of the loop, Magruder went on at length about how he and Liddy had major personality clashes. A "big aspect" of Magruder's testimony, Silbert recorded in his diary, would be "his inability to get along with Liddy, who was dissatisfied with his work." Magruder told Silbert that Liddy "wanted to be doing projects for the White House, for Mr. Stans [the CRP finance director], and for other people in the committee." An intense jealousy had built up. Magruder described several arguments and public "blow-ups" between the two and said,

"Liddy felt he was older than I was and he should have been on the top of the ladder and not me, and we just didn't have a good relationship."[33] Knowing of Liddy's large and quirky persona, it all had the ring of truth. In fact, most of it was true: Gordon Liddy couldn't abide Jeb Magruder, and the feeling was mutual.

But this, of course, had nothing to do with Magruder's foreknowledge of the break-in.

Silbert decided that Magruder was on the up-and-up and should not be indicted. Silbert even recorded in his diary, closer to the time of the trial, that the prosecutors were encouraged by Magruder's cooperation. "We think [he] may be a pretty good witness," Silbert wrote.[34]

The trail, thus, would run cold with Hunt, Liddy, and McCord. No higher-ups were going to be held to account.

On September 15, 1972, when the grand jury returned an eight-count indictment, it included only the five men arrested, plus Hunt and Liddy—the Watergate Seven.[35] Speaking that same day with President Nixon in the White House, Chief of Staff Bob Haldeman observed that the indictment of Hunt and Liddy, who were identified as former presidential aides, was actually useful. "That's good," Haldeman said in a session the two had with John Dean. "That takes the edge off whitewash really." People around the country, he said, would think that two "big men" had been caught, and this would further the illusion that there had been a complete, no-holds-barred investigation by the FBI and the prosecutors.[36]

Nixon's prospects for reelection appeared all but certain.

Los Angeles, October 5, 1972

Meanwhile, as a result of his own lawyer's leaks to the Democrats, Al Baldwin's name began circulating among the Washington press corps as a person who might have been an eyewitness to the break-in.[37] Baldwin was distressed. He knew McCord and the other defendants would see him as a turncoat, and he did not want the national press bearing down on him.

Silbert recorded an entry in his diary on September 8 indicating that Larry O'Brien issued a press release asserting that there had been wiretaps of the DNC headquarters that had been planted three weeks before the actual arrests.[38] The aborted McGovern mission was also mentioned. It was obvious the Democrats had been talking to Baldwin.

Silbert didn't suspect the Democrats but instead worried that the leak came out of the Department of Justice itself. "This was very disturbing," Silbert wrote. He inquired of Henry Petersen, the chief of the criminal division at the Department of Justice, but Petersen "had no explanation for it, could not understand or imagine how the information was getting out."[39]

Silbert actually called the culprit, Baldwin's attorney John Cassidento, to see if Baldwin had been contacted by anyone. Cassidento told Silbert that Baldwin was "very upset about it" and had in fact received anonymous calls from Washington asking him about his cooperation with the authorities. Baldwin, Cassidento said, was going to get out of town and hide for ten days or so, with only his attorneys knowing his whereabouts.[40] He did not want to be played as "the heavy" in the case.

With all the heat, Baldwin and his attorneys decided he needed to get his side of the story out, lest he be cut to pieces by the slow leaks and innuendo. He and his lawyers met with journalists Jack Nelson and Ron Ostrow of the *Los Angeles Times* on the night of October 2 to lay it all out.[41] The session lasted until the small hours of October 3 and was taped by the reporters.

When Silbert got wind of the interview from Cassidento, he went ballistic. At that very time, he was working with Bittman and other counsel for defendants to hammer out an order for Sirica that would prohibit all extrajudicial statements about the case. Silbert threatened to revoke his agreement not to prosecute Baldwin if the story was issued.

It was too late. On October 5 the *Los Angeles Times* published Baldwin's first-person account of his story.[42] Silbert called Cassidento. "I really let him have it over the telephone," he wrote in his diary. "Just a devastating thing," Silbert lamented.[43]

By the time of the December 4 pretrial, the defendants advised the court that they would seek to subpoena the *L.A. Times* to obtain copies of the audiotapes Jack Nelson made of his interview with Baldwin. The *L.A. Times* resisted, citing the First Amendment, and Sirica threw its Washington bureau chief in jail.[44] But on December 21 the newspaper yielded after Baldwin consented, and it released the tapes to Judge Sirica "with the understanding that the voices on the tapes other than that of Mr. Baldwin will be excised by the court."[45] Baldwin's attorneys did not want their comments on the tape to become known.

Everything, however, changed four days after the December 4 pretrial conference, when Dorothy Hunt's plane crashed in Chicago. Howard Hunt instructed Bill Bittman to strike a deal with Earl Silbert, and to nail down a promise of clemency from the White House.

But even pleading guilty would prove problematic with this difficult and mistrustful judge. Bittman and Silbert worked out the broad strokes of a plea agreement in the waning days of December 1972, as American bombs pounded Hanoi. Hunt would plead guilty to three of the six counts against him: two counts of conspiracy—to bug and to commit burglary—and the burglary itself.

Silbert called Judge Sirica at his home on Sunday, January 7, 1973, to tell him of the deal. The news did not go down well with Sirica. According to Howard Hunt, Bittman called him that day to tell him Sirica had rejected the deal. "Bittman called," Hunt wrote in one of his memoirs, "his voice sounding like a doctor telling a patient that he has a fatal disease." Bittman told Hunt that "when Silbert told Sirica about your plea deal, he went crazy, saying, 'If Hunt wants to plead guilty, let him plead guilty to everything!' "[46]

The next day, January 8, in the ornate ceremonial courtroom for the District of Columbia, the burglars' trial began with the start of the jury selection process.

Executive Office Building, January 8, 1973

Down the street, Chuck Colson met with Richard Nixon in his office in the EOB late in the afternoon on January 8. The White House recording system was rolling as the two men discussed clemency for Hunt.

"Incidentally," Nixon said to Colson, "Haldeman was telling me that, apparently, Hunt is going to plead guilty now—very definitely. I do think that's the right thing for him to do, Chuck."[47]

"He's doing it at my urging," Colson lied.

Showing how closely he was following things, Nixon talked about a recent development in the case involving a student who worked undercover for Hunt and Liddy to infiltrate the McGovern campaign. The young man had been outside McGovern's headquarters in a Volkswagen the night Baldwin and McCord drove by during the aborted break-in attempt. Baldwin did not meet the student so knew little about him until he surfaced just before Christmas, when he was contacted by an agent from the FBI's office in Provo, Utah, where he was going to school at Brigham Young University.

The young man's name was Thomas Gregory, and he would become the lead witness in the trial, someone to set up and corroborate the unsteady Baldwin.[48]

Nixon turned back to the conversation of clemency for Hunt, which he and Colson had already discussed at least once over the weekend.

"Hunt's is a simple case," Nixon said to Colson. "I mean, after all, the man's wife is dead, was killed, he's got one child that has—"

"Brain damage from an automobile accident," Colson completed the president's sentence, referring to Hunt's daughter Lisa, who had been badly hurt in a car accident a few years earlier.

"That's right," Nixon said. "We'll build that son of a bitch up like nobody's business. We'll have Buckley write a column and say, you know, that he should have clemency, if you've given eighteen years of service [to your country]." Nixon knew that Hunt was close to William F. Buckley, the syndicated columnist, editor of the *National Review*, and television host of the PBS program *Firing Line*. Nixon had been reminded that Hunt was Bill Buckley's CIA case officer in Mexico City right after Buckley graduated from Yale. Buckley became the godfather of three of Hunt's children and the executor of his wife's estate.

The mercy shown Hunt would not be shared with the other burglars. Hunt's case for clemency, as Nixon saw it, "was on the merits" because of his wife's death and his long service to his country. "I would have difficulty with some of the others," Nixon told Colson.

"Oh yeah," Colson readily agreed.

"You know what I mean," Nixon said.

"Well, the others aren't going to get the same . . . aren't . . . the vulnerabilities are different with the others," Colson expounded.

"Are they?" Nixon inquired. "Why?"

Colson said, "Well, because Hunt and Liddy did the work. The others didn't know any direct information." Colson, it was clear, worried only about the men who could implicate him in the scandal—the Miamians had no direct knowledge of the involvement of higher-ups and so could be discarded.

Nixon responded, "Uh, well, I think I agree, but you know—"

Colson interrupted, "See, I don't give a damn if they [laughs] spend five years in jail in the interim."

Nixon agreed, "Oh, no." It was their own fault, they reassured themselves. These men had assumed the risk when they signed up for the dangerous assignment.

"I mean they can't hurt us," Colson said. "Hunt and Liddy were direct participants in the meetings, discussion [that was] very incriminating for us. More important than that they—"

"Liddy is pretty tough," Nixon interrupted, addressing the question of whether Liddy would hold firm even if he didn't get clemency.

"Yeah, he is," Colson replied. "He is apparently one of these guys who's a masochist—he enjoys punishing himself. That's as long as he remains stable. I think he's tough."[49]

John Sirica could not have imagined a better transcript to prove that a "whitewasher" was under way. Colson himself did not know he was being recorded; few did. It would not be until the summer of 1973 that the existence of the taping system would become known.

In the meantime, the next day, January 9, would be the president's sixtieth birthday. And on that day he would receive some very good news from Henry Kissinger in Paris. For a moment, he could ignore what was transpiring in the ceremonial courtroom a few blocks away. It was time to end a war.

10

"We Celebrated the President's Birthday Today by Making a Major Breakthrough in the Negotiations"

Gif-sur-Yvette, France, Southwestern Suburbs of Paris, Monday, January 8, 1973

In a one-story white stucco house in the bucolic commune town of Gif-sur-Yvette, Henry Kissinger and Le Duc Tho sat down to talk, each with a small delegation of advisors. Photographers and press from around the globe assembled outside on makeshift bleachers they had erected to record and document the comings and goings, hoping to catch any signal of progress in the peace negotiations. It was the first day of the renewed talks for both men, although a team of "technical experts" had met productively the week before to hammer out protocols for parts of the agreement.

The pastoral setting of Gif, as they called it in diplomatic cables, was a welcome relief from the more industrial Paris suburb of Choisy-le-Roi and the stone house at 11 Darthe Street. Negotiations had been conducted there from 1969 until September 1972, when the North Vietnamese inadvertently blew the cover of secrecy, requiring the parties to find a new location.

The house in Gif, selected by the North Vietnamese, was located at 108 Avenue de General Leclerc, a modest structure, though with a large garden, belonging to the French Communist Party. The house had been bequeathed to the party by French cubist painter and party member Fernard Léger, who kept it as his home and studio until his death in 1955. "Thus incongruously amid striking reproductions (and perhaps some originals) of Léger's abstract paintings and tapestries," Kissinger wrote, "we began a crucial round of increasingly concrete negotiations to end the war."[1] The secrecy of Gif was short-lived, lasting only a few months, so that when Tho and Kissinger met on January 8, the world's journalists lay in wait. People around the world hoped in earnest for an end to the war, and there was intense interest in gauging the reaction of the North Vietnamese to the brutal Christmas bombings.

The white-haired, usually genial Le Duc Tho sounded belligerent when he arrived at the Paris airport a few days earlier, announcing that "now the decisive moment had come either to settle the Vietnam problem quickly and sign the agreed accord or to continue the war."[2] He labeled the bombing attacks "demented war acts."

When Kissinger pulled up to the house in Gif in his limo, there were no handshakes or public greetings.[3] Instead, "in heavy and wet weather," the door to the home was opened from the inside as if "by some unseen factotum," Kissinger wrote, leaving the impression that he was being paid an especially chilly reception. "In fact," Kissinger remembered, "relations inside, out of the sight of the press, were rather warm. All the North Vietnamese were lined up to greet us."[4]

Kissinger knew that the pounding had taken its toll on North Vietnam. The Thursday before leaving for Paris, at an impromptu National Security Council meeting with the president and NSC members Melvin Laird, Bill Rogers, Admiral Moorer, and Richard Kennedy, Nixon and Kissinger had been briefed on the damage the bombing had inflicted. "We had 732 B-52 sorties over North Vietnam against forty targets," Admiral Tom Moorer, chairman of the Joint Chiefs of Staff, told the group. "We lost about two percent [of all the airplanes deployed in the attacks]." The North Vietnamese, he explained, had launched virtually all their Soviet-supplied SA-2 surface-to-air missiles, about nine hundred in total, he believed. "The reason they responded to us is we saturated their defenses—they ran out of missiles." The air force could have "gone on with relative impunity," Moorer claimed. "They use about fifty missiles for one aircraft they shoot down." The men at the NSC meeting assumed that Hanoi was essentially defenseless, at least for the next month or so, against another wave of bombings.[5]

Nixon and Kissinger, however, understood that they had to end the war. Both took pains to instruct subordinates not to "revel" in the bombing achievement. "For the reasons you will understand," Kissinger wrote in a back-channel message to Ambassador Ellsworth Bunker in Vietnam, "I cannot emphasize too strongly the importance of avoiding any implication of gloating over our success at getting the other side back to talks or the implication that our strong actions forced this result on them. The effect of such gloating on the upcoming negotiations could undo much of what we have accomplished. I hope you will impress this on all there." [6]

Kissinger even objected to Secretary of Defense Melvin Laird's plea that he be allowed to respond to the intense domestic or international reaction to the bombing by showing reconnaissance photos that demonstrated that the targets were military, heavy industry, or defense-oriented sites. "They know they got the shit kicked out of them," Kissinger observed; a detailed public defense of US actions would only alienate the North Vietnamese just as negotiations recommenced. [7]

For the same reasons, the Nixon administration steered clear of an open contest over claims that the bombing caused widespread civilian deaths and casualties, including those at Bach Mai Hospital, which they were certain had been exaggerated. The hospital, because it was about five hundred meters from the Bach Mai Airfield—the location of the headquarters of the North Vietnamese Air Defense Command—had been evacuated at the start of operations and, except for a skeletal staff, was empty when bombs directed at the airfield missed and leveled the hospital building. There were a few deaths as a result, and the United States knew it, but the hospital became a cause célèbre in the press. "Incidentally," Nixon said to the members of the NSC as they discussed the topic, "if anybody is punished for hitting any hospital, somebody will lose his ass."

Yet even with the administration's vow to hold its collective tongue, getting a deal done would be tricky. For one thing, Henry Kissinger simply did not trust the Communists. On January 3 he privately told the ambassador of the Republic of Vietnam (South Vietnam), Tran Kim Phuong, that he was under no illusions as he returned to the negotiating table. "They are a bunch of SOBs," he said. "They are the worst I have ever met. It was a pleasure to bomb them." [8] In another meeting two days later, he expressed similar sentiments. "We are not talking about nature's noblemen," he said. "They are the most miserable bastards. I have had a concentrated course for three years. I have never seen people who lie so much. They are totally treacherous." [9]

On the other hand, Kissinger continued to encounter major resistance from the South Vietnamese. He believed that their stubborn refusal to settle in October had delivered a serious setback to the chances for resolution (and resulted in his own personal humiliation following his "peace is at hand" comment). The South Vietnamese were obsessed primarily with one issue: the continued presence of North Vietnamese troops in the South once a cease-fire was declared. Kissinger was at his wits' end over the topic. He had told them a thousand times, he said, that the North would never agree to withdraw its troops—this had been long settled in the negotiations.[10]

Kissinger was frank with a legation of South Vietnamese officials who had come to Washington in the first week of January 1973 as part of a desperate effort to lobby Congress not to cut off military and other support. "I want to be honest," he told the group on the afternoon of Harry Truman's memorial service. "Our view is that your government should have stood next to us and thanked us for what we had done, even if it didn't mean it, so that for America, which had lost fifty thousand lives, it would be a Korean type situation. Who knows today about what the armistice was all about in Korea? If Korea is attacked, we would defend it. Why should we do this in Korea and not in Vietnam? There is no reason."[11]

The Korean analogy became the core argument. Kissinger had read in the press that the leaders in South Vietnam believed he was pushing for an agreement just to win the Nobel Peace Prize, or that he in fact wanted to see a united Communist Vietnam to block China in a balance-of-power setting. "Frankly," he said, "this is insane, totally insane."[12] The agreement Kissinger envisioned, while not perfect, would buy time, he argued; it would be just like the settlement of the Korean War. Kissinger told the delegation that there was no doubt that Congress was going to cut off funding. If an agreement could be reached before that happened, it would establish clear covenants that, if violated, would justify renewed bombing by the United States; just as violations of the peace accords in the Korean situation would give reason for an American military response. No one would question American action under these circumstances.

In fact, Kissinger told the South Vietnamese that he actually foresaw violations of the peace agreement that had yet to be finalized. "The Communists have no intention of keeping the major provisions," he predicted on January 5. "The agreement will never be fully implemented. With an army of over a million [South Vietnam's standing army] and controlling a large part of the territory, we think you can handle a ceasefire, at least for a long enough period until there are violations of the agreement. And there is no question about who will violate it. We thought that in the name of an agreement we would be better able to help than in the name of war. That is our cold-blooded appraisal." [13] Americans would no longer tolerate military action to support an ongoing war; but they would if the North violated agreements post-settlement.

On the first day of renewed negotiations back in Paris, Kissinger and Tho held a four-and-a-half-hour session, which Kissinger said was "totally inconclusive" in a memo to the president. "The atmosphere at the outset was frosty but thawed as we went along. Tho opened with a condemnation of our bombing and a summary of where the negotiations stood in December. The condemnation was relatively mild and brief, much milder than his airport statement."[14]

Several issues still divided the parties, and the United States was in the thorny position of representing not only its interests, but also those of the South Vietnamese, who were not participants in the meetings. The central definitional difficulty in drafting revolved around the concept of Vietnam as one nation. The North Vietnamese, or Democratic Republic of Vietnam (DRV), saw one nation following the settlement. This had been envisioned by the 1954 Geneva Conference at the end of the First Indochina War, when the country was partitioned into two zones, North and South, and separated by a military demarcation line (the Demilitarized Zone or DMZ), nominally at the seventeenth parallel, which was always meant to be "provisional." Reunification was supposed to follow free elections in July 1956. The elections never happened.[15]

The North Vietnamese argued that if Vietnam was one country, its forces in the South should be allowed to remain in place after a cease-fire; after all, they were not foreign troops. President Thieu correctly saw this as fatal to his bid for survival and independence. American ambassador Ellsworth Bunker reported that Thieu was telling anyone who would listen that, from his perspective, the decision of "whether to sign or not to sign the agreement in its present form is only a choice between sudden or lingering death for which he cannot take responsibility."[16]

Drafting off of the Geneva Conference of some two decades earlier, Kissinger and Tho proposed free elections to determine the political future of Vietnam. In the South, the contest would be between

Thieu's Saigon government, known as the Government of Vietnam, and the Communist National Liberation Front, which became known as the Provisional Revolutionary Government (PRG) or Vietcong. The cease-fire and American withdrawal would be monitored by joint military commissions, and complaints would be referred to an international monitoring group, known as the International Commission of Control and Supervision (ICCS). Meanwhile, elections in the South would take place under the National Council of National Reconciliation and Concord (NCRC), composed of three parties: South Vietnam, North Vietnam, and the Vietcong. The NCRC was supposed to pave the way for reunification and to organize free and democratic elections among the two South Vietnamese parties. It worked under the principle of unanimity—thus, any of the three parties had veto power over any act or proposal it did not like.

The entire structure seemed ambiguous and destined to failure. Even the signatories were the subject of dispute and obfuscation. South Vietnam did not want to recognize the Vietcong, let alone allow them to be a cosigner to the peace agreement. So the Vietcong were never mentioned by formal name; they were only referred to as one of "the Parties participating in the Paris Conference on Viet-Nam" or one of the "two South Vietnamese parties."

President Thieu, meanwhile, had two fundamental and immediate problems. He needed to be strong enough to contain and eventually run out the existing North Vietnamese troops that would be left in the South, and he needed to politically defeat the PRG in any general elections, thus establishing his claim to a separate government for South Vietnam. In both cases, he saw time as his primary ally. "I think that all these moves fit into Thieu's strategy of playing for time," Ambassador Bunker wrote Kissinger. "He prides himself on the fact that his maneuvering has secured him additional time and has made good use of it." Thieu's dilemma in the beginning of January 1973 was, as Bunker noted, "the fact that in other directions, time is running out."[17] In the United States, he was increasingly seen as an obstacle to peace, and the new US Congress was in the middle of a revolt against the continuation of the war. Thieu's stalling game was nearing its end.

Nixon issued a series of progressively more inflexible letters to Thieu, making it clear that if Thieu once again undercut negotiations, the United States was willing to go it alone. On January 5 a draft letter from Nixon was sent to Ambassador Bunker in Saigon to be hand-delivered to Thieu, unless Bunker believed it "too sharp." Nixon could not have been clearer about America's intentions. "Accordingly," the draft letter read, "if the North Vietnamese meet our concerns on the two outstanding substantive issues in the agreement, concerning the DMZ and methods of signing, we will proceed to conclude the settlement. The gravest consequences would then ensue if your government chose to reject the agreement and split with the United States."

Bunker, reading it, felt it needed softening, so he proposed a sentence that sounded supportive and positive to the starkly worded ultimatum, adding the following: "Should you decide, as I trust you will, to go with us you have my assurance of continued assistance in a post-settlement period and that we will respond with full force should the settlement be violated by North Viet-Nam." Kissinger approved Bunker's proposed insertion that same day.[18]

Saint-Nom-la-Bretèche, near Versailles, Tuesday, January 9, 1973

The venue for the peace negotiations alternated between the Communist Party home in Gif and the villa of an American businessman, who kept a residence on a golf course in the exclusive Paris suburb of Saint-Nom-la-Bretèche. On Tuesday, January 9, Tho and Kissinger arrived at the golf course residence around 10:00 AM for the second day of talks. Kissinger, to ensure the talks would not bog down, had announced before traveling to Europe that he could only stay three or four days at most on the trip, so Tho had to get down to his final bargaining position quickly—it was likely the last opportunity for a comprehensive settlement.

The two main issues left to hammer out were, as Nixon wrote in his letter to Thieu, the nature of the Demilitarized Zone and the signing procedures for the accords. The DMZ had been the source of intense debates. The Americans wanted the area to be respected as a provisional boundary, subject to future reunification negotiations. Only civilian traffic and goods could pass. The North Vietnamese continued to insist on language that, by its very ambiguity, would have permitted military vehicles and supplies to pass through, effectively emasculating the ban on infiltration. It was a straight-up dispute.

The signing question, on the other hand, was described by Kissinger as "a complex arrangement by which Saigon could sign without recognizing the Communist Provisional Revolutionary Government for South Vietnam."[19] Finesse would be required.

Both problems seemed intractable.

On a stroll through the tranquil surroundings near the golf course during one of the breaks, Tho finally gave Kissinger the signal that a leap forward was possible. "In order to prove our seriousness and good will to find a rapid solution," Tho said, "we should adequately take into account each other's attitudes." He said he was ready for "mutual concessions" and "reciprocity." "If one keeps one's own stand, then no settlement is possible," Tho said. "Do you agree?"

That afternoon, the North Vietnamese proceeded to compromise on the DMZ question—the final language would refer to "civilian movement" only. They also began discussions in earnest on a signing method that would "greatly lessen the problem of implied recognition for the PRG." This was the moment Kissinger had hoped for.[20]

It was Richard Nixon's sixtieth birthday and Kissinger, elated, sent word back to Washington. "We celebrated the President's birthday today by making a major breakthrough in the negotiations," he cabled. "In sum, we settled all the outstanding questions in the text of the agreement, made major progress on the method of signing the agreement, and made a constructive beginning on the associated understandings."

If things continued on that same pace, Kissinger projected, he could complete the negotiations by the end of the week. "The Vietnamese have broken our hearts several times," he cautioned, "and we cannot just assume success until everything is pinned down, but the mood and the businesslike approach was as close to October as we have seen since October."

Though he warned that it was premature to celebrate, Kissinger was careful to praise Nixon and give all credit to him. "What has brought us to this point," he wrote, "is the President's firmness and the North Vietnamese belief that he will not be affected by either Congressional or public pressures. Le Duc Tho has repeatedly made these points to me." He concluded his communiqué with a request for vigilance and care. "So it is essential that we keep our fierce posture during the coming days. The slightest hint of eagerness could prove suicidal."[21]

The Oval Office, January 9, 12:30 PM

Colonel Richard Kennedy, a quiet man, a veteran of the Second World War, and an experienced military advisor to the Kennedy and Johnson administrations, served as deputy assistant to Nixon and as a member of the National Security Council planning staff. He became the trusted point of contact between the White House and Kissinger in Paris. Colonel Kennedy came into the Oval Office and told Nixon just before 11:00 AM that the negotiations in Paris had concluded for the day, and that word was expected from Kissinger within the hour. Neither man ventured whether the news might be positive. Nixon kept up his busy schedule and tried to retain his equilibrium.[22]

Sometime around 12:15 PM, Bob Haldeman entered the Oval Office, just as a meeting on the economy was breaking up, and closed the door once everyone else had exited. Kissinger had called to send his birthday greetings, Haldeman said, and to "express his deepest personal gratitude to the president for letting him serve." This unusual outburst of emotion was a tip-off. Kissinger would not say more over the phone, Haldeman said, other than to ask him to tell the president "that some of what he's hoping for on his birthday may be coming to pass." [23]

With this lead-in, Haldeman handed over Kissinger's eyes-only cable. "That, I guess," he said, referring to the cable, "tells you what it is." Haldeman added a word of extra caution from Kissinger: "He urged, I'd say more than any other time that you and I, and nobody else, read that—that it not be seen by anybody or known by anybody at this point."

Nixon quickly scanned the top-secret wire. "He must have sounded very excited," he finally said.

"Nope," Haldeman said, "he was obviously playing it cool."

"Well he's playing it cool for the reason that he didn't want—he thought he might be overheard," the president surmised.

"That's right," Haldeman concurred.

Nixon started to read the message again. "This first paragraph is very interesting," he said in delight. He then began to speed-read the cable out loud. "We celebrated the President's birthday today," he said, zipping through the words. In this fashion, he read the entire message aloud, and when he completed the final lines about it being "essential that we keep our fierce posture" and that "the slightest hint of eagerness could prove suicidal," he declared, "I totally agree."

He was pleased, very pleased, but secrecy had to be the watchword. No one—not the secretary of state, the secretary of defense, or even his press secretary, Ron Ziegler—was to know about the breakthrough. They were at the absolute critical turning point, and any leak could unfasten it all.[24]

Nixon canceled an appointment at 12:30 PM and called for Colonel Kennedy to return to the Oval Office. When he arrived minutes later, Nixon went over his concern that only Kennedy and Al Haig should know about Kissinger's message. "Just say, it was tough going today," he told Kennedy to say if asked for a status update, even by his immediate superiors. He told Kennedy to say, "It's too early to tell whether they're going to make real progress. It was tough going." He even coached him on his demeanor: "You go in with a long face. You should play it absolutely cool."[25]

Nixon fretted about whether the negotiations would "go downhill" the next day. Could this all be ephemeral? "Sir, I don't think so," Kennedy responded. Nixon said he didn't have confidence in Kissinger's immediate reactions. "He is the perennial optimist," Nixon observed. "He is either up or down." Kennedy's clue that the North Vietnamese were serious was that they had accepted the offer to renew talks before the New Year. They could have waited a week, he said, for Congress to return and for pressure to build in Congress and in the media before giving in, but they did not do that. "I think they're there to finish it up. It's just my guess," Kennedy ventured. Nixon was skeptical but conceded, "Course that's sometimes the way things happen."

One item Nixon said he disagreed with in the cable was a line Kissinger inserted about probable difficulties with the South Vietnamese, predicting that the United States still faced "a massive problem in Saigon." Nixon did not want to hear of it.

"We have a problem," Kennedy said, gently agreeing with Kissinger. "But it isn't like it was," Nixon countered. "Don't you agree?"

Kennedy said he did, whether or not that was his true belief. "I think it is much more hopeful that we will be able to pull that off now," Kennedy allowed.

For the moment, Nixon was going to brook no more of Thieu's complaints or objections. "It may be tough, but it may not be that tough," Nixon said to Kennedy and Haldeman. "They can play that kind of a game, but if they do, it's going to be brutal. Thieu has got to expect it, because I can be brutal with the North, but you can be goddamn sure I will be brutal with him and the South Vietnamese people. Thieu screwed this up in October. He's not going to screw this up. Now that's just the way it's going to be."[26]

Nixon then dictated his response to Kissinger, which Kennedy dutifully took down. "I greatly appreciated your birthday greetings and your report. . . . If the other side stays on this track and doesn't go downhill tomorrow, what you have done today is the best birthday present I have had in sixty years." Haldeman approved the return message, especially "because he was quite sentimental about your birthday," he said of Kissinger.[27]

Executive Office Building, January 9, 2:30 PM
The hectic morning's work done just after the noon hour, the president escaped to his hideaway office in the EOB, probably taking a brief nap, as he frequently did on the couch in that office. At 2:30 PM he asked the White House operator to return the phone call left by entertainer Bob Hope.[28] The operator found him immediately, and Hope came on the line, singing, "Happy birthday, Mr. President. Happy birthday to you!"[29]

They talked briefly about Hope's Christmas specials in Vietnam and how they perennially had garnered the top Nielson ratings in the past number of years. The next special was scheduled to air in just more than a week. "We've had three or four number ones, you know," Hope said. He wanted to make sure that Nixon tuned in.

"Congratulations," Hope said, changing the subject to Nixon's birthday. "Welcome to the club."

"No, I don't ever celebrate anything," Nixon demurred. Then, catching on to his "Welcome to the club" line, Nixon asked, "Hell, are you sixty?" Hope said nothing. "I thought you were fifty-eight," Nixon joked.

"Thank you very much," Hope quickly rejoined. (Born in England in 1903, he was sixty-nine, about to turn seventy in 1973.)

"You can about shoot your age now, can't you?" Nixon mocked in reference to Hope's legendary love of the game of golf. Hope said he had just played a round with Arnold Palmer in the L.A. Open. "I hit the ball pretty good," he said.

Hope said he had a message for Nixon that he had brought back from his recent trip to Southeast Asia to film what would be his last Vietnam Christmas special. "I briefed the B-52 guys at Utapao [Thailand]," he said, speaking of one of the air force bases that was heavily involved in the Christmas bombings. "Oh boy," Nixon interjected. "They were all in tough shape," Hope said, "but I went into four rooms and told them some jokes, and how much we love them, and in Guam [another B-52 base], I went over with Roman Gabriel [the well-known quarterback of the Los Angeles Rams], and he talked to them and then I briefed them and told them about ten minutes of jokes." Hope commended to Nixon's attention General Jerry Johnson, the commander in Guam and asked the president to make a special note of something General Johnson had said. "Would you please tell the president if you talk to him," Hope recounted that Johnson had asked him to relay, "that we all admire him and work for him hard and believe in everything he's doing."

"Well, I tell you," Nixon said, "they've shown great courage and if this thing is settled—which it will be at one point—it will be because of what they did."

"Oh boy," Bob Hope said.

Nixon took a moment to justify the bombings, saying to Hope what he could not say to the American public. "You know, that's what you have to do," Nixon said. "It's the only language these guys understand, Bob."

He was preaching to the choir. Hope said he had just completed his own testy press conference in Los Angeles. "I said, I wish Congress would lay off all this antiwar legislation until we get the negotiations completed; then they can say anything they want."

Nixon could not have agreed more. "Sure," he responded, "because, after all, all they do is to encourage the other side." Then he caught himself—he was not going to let Hope know of the encouraging message he had just received from Henry Kissinger. "Well, just, I don't have to ask you to pray, but just ask Delores [Hope's wife] to pray a little. It'll all come out."

"Well, it's gotta happen," Hope said. "You know it's tough on those kids. I know you realize it more than anybody."

"Oh boy, I watch them every day, you know I see those . . . come back," Nixon could not verbalize the word *coffins*. "God it breaks your heart. But it's coming along."

"Well that's marvelous," Hope said somewhat incongruously, trying to keep it light. Neither of them wanted to descend too far into the darkness of the war.

"When I say it's coming along," Nixon was careful to add, "I don't mean to say I have any news to report, except to say that we're talking." He wanted to scrupulously avoid leaving any impression, even inadvertently, that something was afoot. Had Hope been with Nixon in person, he no doubt would have given him a long face and said, "It was tough going today. Tough going."[30]

Absolute secrecy was to be maintained at all costs.

The White House, January 9

It had been an emotional sixtieth for Richard Nixon. In his diary the night before, he had mused about how far he had come since January 9, 1963, a decade earlier. He was at his low point then, as his fiftieth year began, having melodramatically lost his bid for the governorship of California the previous November, just two years after losing the presidency to JFK in one of the tightest races in presidential history.

On November 7, 1962, Nixon delivered the famous meltdown line "You won't have Nixon to kick around anymore" at what he said was his "last press conference." While cameras rolled, he strode sullenly out of the Beverly Hilton, headed for political exile and the unglamorous grind of corporate law in New York City.

Then suddenly, as if fated, his archrival was assassinated and the war in Vietnam destroyed Lyndon Johnson's presidency, laying before him the opportunity to run again for president. No one, least of all Nixon, could have anticipated these dramatic turns of events.

"All in all," he wrote privately in his diary, "as the day is finished I look back over the past ten years and realize how life can seem to be at an end as it appeared to be on January 9, 1963, and then has turned completely around by January 9, 1973. It has to do with spirit, as I emphasized to Colson, who is only forty-one years of age. He was obviously depressed tonight, probably because of the Hunt matter, etc., but I think I lifted him a bit by what I said."[31]

The Oval Office, January 9

With all his mania for secrecy, however, the president and Bob Haldeman spoke on Nixon's birthday about, irony of ironies, concealed devices within the White House that would soon enough play a determinative role in sending him back into political oblivion.

About two hours before Henry Kissinger's "breakthrough" cable arrived, Nixon and Haldeman struck up a casual conversation about the secret White House taping system. Only a handful of people knew of its existence—Nixon, Haldeman, Alex Butterfield, and a few others. Kissinger, Ehrlichman, Dean, Colson, Haig, and many others had no clue.

The conversation about the tapes came about because Nixon was expressing his regret that he had not recorded an interview he gave a few days earlier to Helen Thomas and another wire reporter on the occasion of his birthday. The interview was not in the Oval Office, where it would have been recorded. Nixon thought he had made some particularly good points about age, youth, and perspective.

"Now tell me, where does this thing stand [referring to the Oval Office taping system]? You understand I want control of these things, I want nothing ever transcribed out of this," Nixon said.[32]

"You have total control," Haldeman responded with assurance. "Nobody knows it exists except Alex [Butterfield] and me and one technician."

"And this covers everything in the room—can they hear things over there too?" Nixon asked, pointing to a distant part of the Oval Office.

"It has pluses and minuses," Haldeman replied. "Some of it is better than others. It is not broadcast quality, but someone working on it can get the substance out of it." Haldeman ventured that Nixon certainly would not want to "have to sit and work on it"—which is exactly what Nixon would find himself doing six months later, after John Dean had broken rank and was about to testify before the Senate. On June 4, 1973, for example, Nixon would spend more than eight hours doing nothing but listening to tapes.

"We want it someday, if someone wants to write a history," Nixon said, revealing one of his main reasons for installing the system in the first place.

Then the two men said something that, in hindsight, was fairly amazing. Neither one seemed to know or remember that Nixon's office in the Executive Office Building had been bugged for as long as the Oval Office. Nor did they know that Camp David had a recording system installed.

"It covers here [the Oval Office]," Haldeman said, "and it covers the cabinet room," which adjoined the Oval Office.

"You should put it in the EOB too," Nixon said.

Haldeman agreed. "It should be in the EOB."

"I wouldn't put it in other places, like Camp David, because I make my own notes," Nixon said. But the EOB, they both agreed, was different. "It would save me having to recall some things," he said.[33]

Like speaking to Chuck Colson about clemency for Hunt.

The EOB is where Nixon had *all* of his conversations with Colson about Hunt and his request for executive clemency. And the location of these discussions may not have been an accident. Given this exchange so close in time to the clemency discussions, it seems probable that Nixon felt his EOB office was a safe place to talk of such things. He did not want to leave a record.

But because of the logs and systems put in place by the technicians who ran the taping system, the tapes of these criminal discussions would be easily located and recoverable when the prosecutors showed up with subpoenas later in the summer of 1973.

The obsession with secrecy within the Nixon White House was so profound that even Richard Nixon himself did not know the full reach of the taping system.[34]

The State Dining Room, Evening of January 9

There was a surprise birthday party that evening thrown for the president by his wife, Pat, and daughters Julie and Tricia. Cocktails were served in the Red Room of the White House, elegantly furnished in Empire style with richly carved woods. It was a small and private gathering, attended by Nixon's immediate family and his closest friends—aerosol king Robert Abplanalp and his wife, Bebe Rebozo, Rose Mary Woods, and a few select others.

After the reception in the Red Room, the group moved into the State Dining Room, where they dined at small tables under George Peter Alexander Healy's portrait of a sitting, listening Lincoln, painted in Paris in 1869, which occupied a place of honor above the fireplace. The pose for this isolated portrayal of Lincoln was lifted from an 1868 painting by Healy, known as *The Peacemakers*. It depicted a strategy meeting at the end of the Civil War among Lincoln, William Tecumseh Sherman, U. S. Grant, and Rear Admiral David Dixon Porter, aboard the steamboat *River Queen*.

At 8:00 PM the presidential party retired to the White House theater in the East Wing to watch Rowan and Martin's *Football Monologue* and the movie *The Maltese Falcon*.[35]

And as the president finally retired to the second-floor residence late that night, across the ocean in Paris things were just beginning to stir. Kissinger and his team woke up to another day of negotiations, with high hopes—and some foreboding.

Ten months later, in Oslo, Norway, in a surprising and controversial move, Henry Kissinger and Le Duc Tho would be jointly awarded the Nobel Peace Prize for 1973. Kissinger accepted and donated his share of the cash prize to a scholarship fund for children of American servicemen killed or missing in action in Indochina.[36]

Le Duc Tho refused to accept the prize and politely declined to attend the ceremony. He said the war was not over and peace was yet to be realized.

11

"He Can Renew It After the Opening Statement Is Made"

The Chambers of Honorable Chief Judge John Sirica, January 9, 1973, 10:30 AM

In a sealed proceeding held at almost the exact hour that President Nixon and Bob Haldeman were casually discussing the White House taping system in the Oval Office, and as Henry Kissinger was drafting his "breakthrough" cable in Paris, Judge John Sirica let Howard Hunt's lawyer make a statement for the record.

The building that housed the federal district court where Sirica sat was also the home of the US Court of Appeals for the District of Columbia. Located on Third Street and Constitution Avenue, facing the Mall and just blocks from the Capitol and the Supreme Court building, the courthouse was considered a 1950s example of "stripped classicism," an institutional style of government architecture that was a nonrepresentational abstraction of the classical style—a fancy way of saying it was a nondescript gray building.[1]

President Harry S. Truman laid the cornerstone for the building on June 27, 1950. With the chief justice of the United States, Fred Vinson, and the chief judge of the DC District Court, Bolitha J. Laws, in attendance, Truman took the opportunity of the stone-laying to attack totalitarianism, which he said "had made a mockery of the forms of justice." In totalitarian governments, Truman observed, "Their judges are prosecutors; their prosecutors are hangmen; their defense attorneys are puppets."

The *New York Times* also noted that President Truman delivered these remarks "only a few hours after his historic announcement that the United States would resist the spread of communism in the Pacific area."[2]

That referenced announcement represented the start of the Korean War. Over the weekend before the ceremonial event for the new federal courthouse, "the Republic of Korea had been invaded by communist forces from the north of the 38th parallel." In Tokyo, General MacArthur, in accordance with a prearranged plan, began to evacuate American personnel and moved naval and air units into the area to protect evacuees and to offer the "fullest possible support to South Korean forces." In urgent, top-secret military cables, Truman was advised by his top command in Asia that the surging North Korean troops had the capability of taking Seoul within twenty-four hours if not stopped and that "a complete collapse [was] possible."[3]

The United States, through an emergency resolution passed in the Security Council of the United Nations, had to make a stand, Truman concluded.[4] The minutes from his meeting with congressional leaders in the Cabinet Room in the White House on the morning of June 27, 1950, show that his concern was not just for Korea but for that entire region of the world. "It was equally necessary," he told leaders, "for us to draw the line at Indo-China, the Philippines, and Formosa."[5]

Intense historical synchronicity and connectivity were at work here. Korea was the beginning and the end of Vietnam, given Henry Kissinger's argument that the peace accords in Vietnam would mimic the armistice in Korea. Thus the very timing of Harry Truman's death took on added symbolic meaning. His policy of containment, begun in the throes of an international emergency, led to the nightmare of Vietnam; his death a quarter of a century later coincided with the death knell of America's efforts in Vietnam, and across all Indochina. And now all of it somehow had strange ties to the Watergate drama unfolding in the very courthouse Truman christened at the start of the Korean conflict.

Judge Sirica turned to Bill Bittman and asked: "You want to make a statement?"

Bittman replied: "Yes, Your Honor, extemporaneously." The judge and lawyers had interrupted jury selection that morning to go into private session. "Right after the death of Mr. Hunt's wife, Your Honor, Mr. Mittler [Bittman's associate] and I had no communication with Mr. Hunt concerning this case," Bittman began. "There were other personal reasons—revising his will and things of that nature we had to discuss, but we did not discuss this case. So it was only approximately a week and a half ago that we again began discussing the government's case and the case against him. And it was at that time stated by Mr. Hunt that he did not want to go to trial, that he wished to plead guilty."[6]

Sirica let him go on but was clearly unmoved.

Bittman then detailed his meetings with the government to work out a deal. The negotiations boiled down to Hunt pleading guilty to three of the six counts against him, with the government making no promises about sentencing. Bittman said the plea carried with it "a $20,000 fine and/or 25 years in prison." Hunt, he said, understood the "ramifications." Bittman thought the deal fair because it basically covered all the crimes Hunt was accused of—conspiracy, burglary and wiretapping. "The other counts are nothing but accumulative," he argued.

Bittman encouraged the judge to recall from his years of experience on the bench that "there is a lot of psychology in dealing with clients, [and] pleading guilty to less than the totality of the charges is something that seems palatable to them and I just think in the interest of justice, interests of the case, that it would be in my client's best interest, hopefully the government's best interest, and the Court's to accept that kind of pleading." He was pulling out all the stops.

Then to address what he knew was the big issue bothering Sirica, Bittman provided what he thought would be a critical and dispositive representation. "And I might also add," he said, "that during the course of discussions with the government I have made a statement to the government on behalf of my client, which is something they requested, and part of our discussions, and that is to Mr. Hunt's personal knowledge that there are no so-called higher-ups involved in the so-called Watergate episode." In a move that is always dangerous for a lawyer, Bittman took the unusual step of actually vouching for his client's statement, saying, "I believe that statement to be truthful and accurate."[7]

One can imagine Sirica's reaction. But for the moment, he merely called on prosecutor Earl Silbert to respond. Silbert identified three points in support of the plea deal. The first was, as Bittman had said, that the prosecutors had made no commitments on sentencing. "Second," Silbert added, "it was understood also at the time of these negotiations that no plea would be accepted by us without making a detailed statement of the facts that we had intended to prove before

Your Honor with respect to the charges in the indictment." And third, after sentencing, the government intended to immunize Hunt and put him back in front of the grand jury "to explore with him what knowledge, if any, he had with respect to the involvement of others in this case."[8]

Silbert, however, quickly added that he understood "that Mr. Hunt would be willing to state to you under oath as the presiding judge, or in the grand jury under oath, that [he, Hunt,] had no knowledge of—no personal knowledge of any higher-ups involved in the so-called Watergate case."[9]

This was a strange posture for the prosecutor to take, and Sirica did not like it. Silbert himself was in effect also vouching for Hunt.

Sirica was frosted: "The only statement I have to make is at this time I am going to deny his request without prejudice. That is all I have to say—period."[10]

Stone-cold silence.

Bittman panicked. He was not prepared to go to trial, and Hunt wanted out under any circumstances, believing that executive clemency was in the offing no matter what happened in Judge Sirica's courtroom. "I gather from that short statement, Your Honor, either Mr. Hunt pleads guilty to the entire indictment or he and his counsel have to go through a very protracted trial and at the close of the government's case enter, or attempt to enter, a plea of guilty to three counts?" Bittman asked, probing for the court's outer limits.

"Well," Sirica responded, "I am not going to say anything more." But then he did say more. "I might say that if he does plead guilty to the entire indictment, to every count, I have the question of commitment to consider after conviction so I am not going to decide that now. I don't want to go into it." Sirica was rejecting a deal the prosecutors found acceptable and then impliedly threatening Bittman with severe sentencing and immediate commitment to jail if Hunt did not plead to the entire case. Sirica was acting as prosecutor, judge, and executioner. He didn't really care about Hunt's scalp per se; he wanted to assert maximum pressure to cause Hunt to spill what he knew about who was behind the Watergate break-in.

Bittman's bluff had been called. He totally dissolved into defense jelly. "I appreciate that, Your Honor," he said, likely with a tinge of sarcasm. "I also discussed this with Mr. Silbert, I believe, and I made my position clear to him that I believe there are some strong compelling reasons why Mr. Hunt should not be committed at the time of entering a plea of guilty until such time as Your Honor feels appropriate after the pre-sentence report and disposition of the case, and I gather Your Honor does not want me to make that statement at this time?"[11]

> Sirica: All I am going to decide now is I denied the request [for a plea deal] at this time without prejudice.

> Bittman: Your Honor, in view of that, because of my client's desire not to go through the trial, his tremendous family responsibility, as Your Honor knows he has [here even the unsealed record is still redacted]. I make this statement because I know this record is going to be sealed. [Further redaction] and I believe that Mr. Hunt will then wish to plead guilty to the entire indictment. I don't think it is completely palatable but I believe under the circumstances I will recommend he do this and he will.

Bittman had given all he could give. It was total capitulation, unconditional surrender. Sirica was unyielding. "I said I am denying the request at this time without prejudice. He can renew it after the opening statement is made or after the evidence is offered by the government. The record is clear."[12] Here was the trump card that Sirica had undoubtedly intended to play all along. Sirica would require Hunt to sit through Earl Silbert's opening statement, in which Silbert would detail all the evidence arrayed against Hunt and the others, and only then would the judge consider taking a plea. The prejudice to the remaining defendants was obvious. The jury would have to conclude that Hunt and his lawyer, after hearing the evidence the government had garnered, were so devastated that they felt they had no choice but to cave and throw themselves on the mercy of the court. It would be impossible for the jury not to notice Hunt's sudden disappearance from the case.

And this, Sirica must have known, would add a powerful, perhaps insurmountable, boost to the prosecutor's case from the very outset of the trial. The atmosphere would reek of conspiracy and guilt.

Bittman could only exclaim "Good God!" in his response to Sirica. He was given no choice; he would renew his request to change Hunt's plea from not guilty to guilty following the opening statements. Everyone was reeling, including the prosecutors.[13]

Jury Selection, January 8 and 9, 1973

Eight women and four men were selected and impaneled as the jury after two days of questioning by Judge Sirica in the cavernous, ceremonial courtroom on the sixth floor of the federal courthouse. They were sworn in on Richard Nixon's sixtieth birthday. Six alternates were also chosen.

The courtroom was imposing. Carved, stark-white statutes of Hammurabi, Moses, Solon, and Justinian—historically significant lawgivers—were mounted on corbels behind the judge's bench, lending an air of authority and majesty to the proceeding. Painted portraits of judges from the past adorned the walls. Judge Sirica conducted the *voir dire* examinations (a term meaning "to speak the truth") of nearly one hundred prospective jurors to determine bias or prejudice using his own questions and those provided by the lawyers. Once individual questioning began, it was done out of the hearing of everyone in the courtroom save the lawyers. Some of the juror candidates were taken to an adjoining anteroom for private questioning; others were summoned to the bench.

Remarkably, given concerns about jury tampering in public cases, the identities of the jurors made it into the papers. "Ten members of the regular panel are black," the newspapers found it necessary to point out. "The jury is predominantly middle-class in appearance. It ranges from an 81-year-old white housewife, Mary W. Goldman, to a 26-year-old black nurse's aid, Marion E. Duncan." Even the identity, age, race, and occupation of each juror were sketched out in the newspapers. After much debate, Judge Sirica decided he would sequester the jury for the entire trial. "Judge Sirica's decision to sequester the panel came despite defense objections," it was noted. "The jurors will be escorted from their quarters for church services on Sundays."[14]

The three lawyers for the prosecution were typecast by the newsmen who followed the trial. "Seymour Glanzer plays the bad guy, grilling witnesses relentlessly. Donald Campbell plays the good guy, gently coaxing the witness. Earl Silbert, the chief, moderates."

Don Campbell, invariably described as "the deceptively mild one," was thirty-five and balding, with a freckled face and red mustache. He was the team's expert in wiretapping, having "learned about bugging when he was a member of the board that reviewed all the requests for wiretaps." In an era before computers, he also devised a system for keeping track of the events and potential witnesses in the case. "I keep calendars in front of me," he told a reporter. "Whenever a witness gives us a date I mark it down. It's the only way to keep track of what went on," he said.[15]

In his methodical preparations for trial, Campbell had noticed a couple of telephone toll calls to area code 801 in Hunt's phone records from his time at Robert R. Mullen & Company that had yet to be checked out. In December, with just weeks to go before trial started, Campbell instructed Angie Lano of the FBI to have someone in the FBI field office in Salt Lake City call the number in Utah. "They struck gold," Earl Silbert wrote in his diary around December 21. A student from Brigham Young University in Provo answered the phone and agreed to be interviewed. An FBI agent showed up at his apartment on December 19 and 20. The student's name was Thomas James Gregory.[16]

Tom Gregory was a close friend of the nephew of Robert Bennett, who had been Howard Hunt's boss at the public relations firm of Robert R. Mullen & Company, where Hunt landed after "retiring" from the CIA. Bennett, a conservative with ties to Howard Hughes, would later become a three-term senator from Utah. It was widely believed at the time that Mullen & Company acted at times as a CIA front.[17] Hunt worked there, often using the pseudonym Edward Warren.

Tom Gregory had been identified by Robert Bennett's nephew as a student and friend who might be interested in working undercover for the Republicans by infiltrating Edmund Muskie's campaign. In February 1972 Gregory was flown to Washington from Utah to discuss the job. He met with Hunt at Mullen & Company. He agreed to take the job, though he needed to return to Brigham Young University to secure credit for "off-campus study" (which he did). Paid $175 a week, Gregory ended up working as a faux volunteer for the Muskie and later McGovern campaigns, reporting back to Hunt on matters such as scheduling, bank records, dissension in the ranks, and speeches.

Then in late May, Gregory told the FBI, he attended a meeting in a room at the Manger Hamilton Hotel at 14th and K Streets with Hunt, McCord, Liddy, and the Cubans. The group discussed bugging McGovern's campaign headquarters. Gregory grew increasingly concerned with what he was doing and, with the help of Bob Bennett, who drafted a letter for him to give to Howard Hunt, quit around June 15, several days before the second Watergate break-in.[18]

Nevertheless, there was a critical link, placing McCord, Liddy, Hunt, and the Cubans in a meeting discussing a plan to wiretap McGovern's headquarters around the time of the first break-in at the Watergate. And unlike the screwy and absentminded Baldwin, Gregory was clear and consistent in his account. Silbert met with Gregory, who had returned home to New Jersey for Christmas break, in Washington at his office on Tuesday, December 26, the day Harry Truman died. Gregory, Silbert discovered, would make a superb witness; he could fill out the facts of the attempts on the McGovern headquarters and provide vital corroborative testimony to bolster Baldwin in his testimony. Silbert and his team agreed to place Gregory at the head of their list of witnesses, following a few preliminary witnesses who would identify aerial photos of the Watergate complex and floor plans of the DNC headquarters. Thomas Gregory shot to the top of the government's case as a star witness.

With witnesses set and the jury selected, it was time for the trial of the seven burglars to begin in earnest. A packed gallery showed up the next day, Wednesday, January 10, for opening statements.

The Ceremonial Courtroom, Opening Statements, Wednesday, January 10, 1973

After some preliminaries over the need for Spanish interpreters for the Cubans (the request was denied), Judge Sirica asked Earl Silbert if he was prepared to proceed with his opening statement. "Yes, Your Honor," Silbert responded. The jurors rose up in their seats. Howard Hunt, looking ashen faced, and his lawyer, Bill Bittman, sat conspicuously and dejectedly at defense counsel table. Liddy, appearing chipper as always, was represented by Peter Maroulis of Poughkeepsie, New York, where Liddy had once been the prosecuting attorney. McCord, stolid and stone-faced, was next to his lawyer, Gerald Alch, F. Lee Bailey's associate. And the four Miamians were all represented by the pencil-mustachioed and bow-tie-wearing Henry Rothblatt, a lawyer from New York who spoke fluent Spanish.

"May it please the Court, ladies and gentlemen of the jury," Silbert began, but what he was about to do would turn out to be anything but pleasing to the court.[19] This was Silbert's chance to lay out the entire case for the jury—provide the "road map," as trial lawyers call it—but it became instantly clear that he was going to build his case around the lies Jeb Magruder and his associate Bart Porter had spun. The cover story was going to become the prosecution's story. Liddy and Hunt would be painted as rogues working outside their scope of authority; the clear implication was that the buck stopped with them—no higher authorities were mixed up with the affair.

After reviewing the counts in the indictment and briefly introducing the cast of characters, Silbert jumped straight into Magruder's sham "surrogates" explanation for why Liddy had so much money at his disposal, and Silbert adopted it as his own. Liddy, Silbert said, had been hired by the Committee to Re-Elect in December 1971. "He was to report to Jeb Magruder, who will be a witness in this case. Mr. Magruder was then deputy campaign manager for the Committee for the Re-Election of the President," he said to the jurors. Bart Porter, Magruder's top assistant, was also introduced. "And as will be explained to you at that time the president was not planning on doing much campaigning in the primaries. In his place there was going to be used what they call surrogate candidates. They were going to be stand-ins for the president at the open primaries being held in such states as New Hampshire, Florida, and Wisconsin."

Silbert reminded the jurors of "demonstrations" and "extremist groups" that threatened political campaign events, images that dominated television and news reports at the time. Naturally the CRP, Magruder, and Porter would fear for the safety of their surrogates. "Mr. Magruder and Mr. Porter turned to Mr. Liddy and gave him an assignment," Silbert explained. Liddy was given $100,000—$1,000 per month for ten people for ten months—to buy intelligence and protection for the surrogates. Silbert, like Magruder, could not explain why no one could identify any of these ten people around the country who were to be paid this money.

Mr. Magruder gave Liddy a second assignment: to protect the Republican convention. To make it seem real, Silbert, buying Magruder's line, said, "They had in mind the unfortunate experiences of the Democratic Party in Chicago in 1968 that some of you might recall." This was a reference to the infamous bloody riot outside the 1968 Democratic National Convention in Chicago, where antiwar students and activists were brutally beaten by Mayor Richard Daley's police forces. It all seemed plausible.

For this second assignment, Silbert said, Liddy was allocated an additional $150,000. Silbert conceded that of the total $250,000 that Liddy was given, the government could only document spending for about $50,000. This massive hole in the proofs did not trouble Earl Silbert. He would let Magruder explain that the CRP was simply poor at record keeping and that Mr. Liddy was the only one who really knew where the money went—an improbable explanation given normal campaign record-keeping practices. "We cannot account for the rest," Silbert simply asserted.

Silbert spent the balance of his opening focusing mainly on the twin stories of Tom Gregory and Alfred Baldwin. Gregory would tie McCord, Hunt, Liddy, and the Cubans to the failed attempt at planting devices at McGovern's headquarters. Baldwin would tell his story of the operations at the Howard Johnson listening post and the multiple Watergate break-ins. Silbert had more than enough from these two witnesses to hang the two men he worried most about—Hunt and Liddy—neither of whom had been arrested at the scene, although Hunt left behind a good deal of circumstantial evidence pointing to his involvement.

Silbert did not need Magruder or Porter or even Hugh Sloan and the tangential and convoluted story of the flow of money to prove the burglary, conspiracy, and wiretapping charges against Liddy and Hunt. He had the direct testimony of two different insiders, both working independently of each other, who were participants in, and eyewitness to, the conspiracies and other crimes at issue.

Silbert obviously felt he needed to do more. And rather than discounting and then discarding the questionable and unverifiable stories of Magruder and Porter, Silbert embraced them and chose to present them as the truth.

Silbert did all this as a powerless Howard Hunt sat stoically and took his lumps. Deliberately or not, Silbert emphasized Hunt's involvement and role in the crimes, knowing all the while that Hunt was going to plead guilty immediately after openings. No detail was too small. For example, Silbert relayed that when Tom Gregory finally decided to quit the conspiracy, Hunt told him that he should "not tell anyone about the different people he had met during his work in Washington." Gregory complied with Hunt's demand, and Gregory's role only came to light, Silbert stressed, when he was confronted by the FBI in mid-December. (Hunt in later writings would refer to Gregory bitterly as "the Gutless Wonder."[20])

Hunt was portrayed darkly as one of the two free-spending, high-living masterminds of the espionage schemes, with Gordon Liddy, his boon friend and travel companion, as the ultimate boss. Silbert pointed out that Hunt and Liddy stayed at only the fanciest and priciest of hotels, including the Playboy Plaza Hotel in Miami and the Beverly Wilshire in Los Angeles (although Silbert neglected to tell them that he himself had visited the Playboy Plaza Hotel in December as part of a last-minute fact-finding mission to Florida to prepare for trial).[21]

Silbert concluded his opening remarks by doing two things that were guaranteed to anger Judge Sirica. He went to lengths to distance Jeb Magruder from Gordon Liddy. "Mr. Magruder and Mr. Liddy did not get along," he said. "Mr. Magruder was younger and in charge and Mr. Liddy did not like taking orders from him. Mr. Magruder never knew who Mr. Liddy was, didn't like the kind of reports he made either. They had a blow-up, and at the end of March or early April, Mr. Liddy left and went downstairs to work for the Finance Committee." Jeb Magruder, Earl Silbert was emphasizing, had no idea what Gordon Liddy was up to. He was a black box to Magruder.

And the coup de grâce had to be Silbert's discussion of Sirica's favorite hobbyhorse: motive. Though perhaps Silbert was trying to respond to Sirica's repeated prodding on the topic, he did nothing but muddy the waters and sow confusion. "[T]he question may have arisen in your minds during this opening statement as I described events and the facts the government will produce before you during the course of this trial: What were the motives behind this conduct? What are the reasons for their activities?" Here is where Sirica had to have perked up.

Silbert seemed to be headed in the right direction when he said, "Obviously it was a political motive." The operation, he said, "was directed against the Democratic Party, particularly Senator McGovern, because of his alleged left-wing views." Sirica would have thought, *So far, so good.* But then Silbert began veering off course, badly. "The interests of the persons, the defendants in this case, may vary, that is, the motivation of defendant Hunt and defendant Liddy may have been different from the motivations of the four defendants from Miami, and they in turn may have had a different motivation than defendant McCord." What did Silbert mean?

"Certainly the facts will suggest . . . based on the information we produce . . . it was a financial motive," he said. Financial motive! Sirica had to have privately growled.

Silbert spent the final minutes of his remarks outlining in great detail how desperate the financial straits were for the Cubans and Jim McCord. They were in this because of money, plain and simple. That was their motive: money. It was a complete sideshow. It drew attention away from the CRP and the White House, and it made the trial about personal crimes of individuals who were nothing but common thieves engaged in crime sprees because they were hard up for money.

If Nixon had been present in the courtroom, he could not have been more pleased with this recitation of the facts.[22]

★ ★ ★

Then it was the defense counsel's turn to, deliver opening statements, if they so chose. Because it is the government's burden to prove the criminal charges beyond a reasonable doubt, and because of a defendant's Fifth Amendment privilege against self-incrimination, defense lawyers sometimes skip opening, or defer it until after the government has put on its case in chief. It was a given that Bill Bittman would make no statement on behalf of Howard Hunt, but McCord's lawyer and the lawyer for the Miamians decided to give it a go.

First up was McCord's lawyer, Gerald Alch, who gave a very short opening—one that started inauspiciously and then fizzled entirely. Repeating the mantra that "a defendant need prove nothing," he turned to some lines that must have tied Jim McCord's stomach in knots. "Now, ladies and gentlemen, no lawyer is a magician," Alch said. "Mr. McCord does not intend to refute the irrefutable. We are not going to bang our heads against stone walls. We are here to search for the truth." He then mumbled something about McCord having no criminal intent. "He had no evil-doing hand," he said, and sat down. Alch was no F. Lee Bailey.

Henry Rothblatt was not going to let Alch's downer infect the rest of the defense. Rothblatt had flair. "May it please Your Honor," he boomed grandiosely, "colleagues on the prosecution side, and my brothers on the defense side. Ladies and gentlemen of the jury! I proudly represent that I speak for all four of the accused in this case: Mr. Virgilio Gonzalez, Mr. Rolando Martinez, Mr. Frank Fiorini Sturgis, and Mr. Bernard Barker." He practically took a bow.

Based on a letter that would be delivered by the Miami defendants to Judge Sirica before the week was out, it would become clear that none of these defendants wanted Rothblatt to make the arguments he was about to make.

"I am sure that all of you were moved as I was when we heard the prosecution story-presentation, the outline of proof presented by the prosecution, by Mr. Silbert," Rothblatt said to the jury. "It was thorough. It was dramatic. And it was moving." One could almost feel the Miamians telling him to sit down under their breath.

Rothblatt said he labored under an immense burden. Silbert not only presented a good story (Rothblatt made sure to call it a "story" several times) but also was aided by "the most thorough investigation undertaken by the Federal Bureau of Investigation, Department of Justice, since the death of President Kennedy."

Judge Sirica finally intervened. He told Rothblatt to save his argument for the end of the case. He insisted he stick to what he believed the evidence would show.

Like Alch, Rothblatt conceded that his clients were caught red-handed in the Watergate. "We might as well close that chapter as far as they are concerned," he said. He also wanted the jury to pay close attention, as Alch did, to "criminal intent, evil mind, and motives."

Rothblatt then launched into a rambling monologue about the character of the defendants. "A man's character does not change," he said. Take Mr. Barker, for example. "A Cuban citizen of mixed heritage, when our country was involved in the Second World War, on Pearl Harbor Day, even though he had Cuban citizenship, the evidence will show that he was the first to go to the American Embassy to enlist in our army, to serve our country. He went on to become an officer in our air force. He was shot down over Germany and kept in a Nazi prison camp for over a year. And later, he was discharged as a captain. Honorably discharged as a captain in the United States Army and returned to civilian life."

"Excuse me," Mr. Glanzer interrupted, "may we approach the bench?"

"I don't think it is necessary," Sirica quickly responded. "Mr. Rothblatt," he said, "you are an experienced attorney. You've tried many, many cases throughout the country. You are speaking about character testimony. I want to ask you a direct question: how are you going to introduce character testimony?" Sirica knew the defendants were not likely to testify, and besides, this all sounded like argument, not what the evidence would show. Sirica told Rothblatt to move on. "Try to control your emotions," he admonished him in front of the jury. "That is the important thing. Just keep it on an even keel and don't let your blood pressure go up."

"That is most important," Rothblatt responded. "We will try to keep that under control. I will try to keep my voice up and blood pressure down."

He then continued to talk about the impeccable character of his clients. Sturgis also was a veteran of World War Two, he said, and "since then, the evidence will show, he has led a life devoted to making himself available to people who want to see democratic systems of justice prevail. Particularly in this part of the hemisphere."

Sirica had heard enough. "Now let's get down to the reason why he went into the Watergate," he stormed. "Let's get down to the motive you have been talking about. Let's find out what the facts are."

Rothblatt responded by saying that all his clients were part of "our government" and served in planned operations such as the Bay of Pigs. "They were men who took orders in military fashion and never questioned orders." Rothblatt sounded strangely like he was arguing the My Lai court-martial all over again. "Those were men who were used to serving their government loyally and following orders."

Sirica saw an opening. "Let me ask you a question," he said. "Is it your defense that they were taking orders from somebody, were ordered to go into the Watergate? Is that what you are going to show?"

Though the Cubans wanted to sack Rothblatt at that very moment, he was no longer under their control. He thoughtlessly agreed with Sirica. "I think the evidence even as outlined by Mr. Silbert shows that in part, Your Honor." Rothblatt's remarks had become a circus and a disaster for the defendants.

"Tell the jury what you think the evidence is going to be," Sirica again demanded.

Rothblatt had made some laudatory remarks about the power of juries and the court being a "temple of justice" when Sirica finally put his foot down. "Just a minute, counsel," he interjected. "I think you have gone about far enough. If you want to argue these things later and get dramatic about it, that is your business, but I don't want you to do it in opening statement."

Mercifully, Rothblatt finally sat down. Sirica said, "Thank you. Anybody else?" Bittman rose to say that he needed to bring up a matter outside the presence of the jury. It was time for Howard Hunt to plead guilty.

The jury was dismissed.

Bittman, repeating many of the arguments made in private the day before, asked the court to accept the plea deal in which Hunt would plead guilty to three of the six counts against him. Silbert strongly urged that the court approve the deal. Sirica took a fifteen-minute break, and when he came back he asked why Hunt would not just plead to the entire case. After a back-and-forth, Sirica said he had not made up his mind about whether to accept the plea, but he warned Hunt and any other defendant who might be thinking about changing his plea that he would put him in jail immediately if he pled guilty. That was Sirica's policy.

John Sirica clearly wanted to have a trial. He did not want everyone suddenly running for the hills and pleading guilty.[23] Howard Hunt would have to wait another sleepless night, perhaps his last as a free man with his children, to learn of his fate.

The Oval Office, Thursday, January 11, 1973

President Nixon met with his press secretary, Ron Ziegler, the next morning in the Oval Office to go over topics for the morning press briefing. They discussed congressional spending, the negotiations in Paris on Vietnam, and ever so briefly what Ziegler was to say about the court proceedings before Judge Sirica. Nixon noted that Hunt's determination to plead guilty was on the front pages of the *New York Times* and the *Washington Post*.

"How about Hunt?" Nixon asked. "Watergate?"

Ziegler said it might come up. Nixon told him to say, "I will not comment on a case that's currently before the courts and is going to be for some time. One or two may go to trial."

"We don't need to comment on it," Ziegler added. "It's not our problem, not a White House problem."

"But Hunt pleaded guilty and both the *Times* and *Post* had big stories about it," Nixon said. "What the hell is here?" he asked. This was a nonstory.

"Everybody knows they're guilty," Nixon said.[24]

12

"Only Kings, Monarchs, Dictators, and United States Federal Judges"

The Oval Office, January 10, 1973

As opening statements in the Watergate Seven trial were being delivered in the federal courthouse, Richard Nixon, Bob Haldeman, and Rose Mary Woods huddled in the Oval Office and talked for hours about plans for the upcoming inaugural festivities: invitation lists, second-term White House personnel decisions, and Washington parties in general.

It was a lively conversation, lacking in any sense of the menace that what was taking shape in Judge Sirica's courtroom. Rose Woods in particular was feeling her oats, at one point suggesting that former chief justice Earl Warren not be invited to church services on the day of the inauguration, referring to him as "that old goat."[1]

The subject drifted into the question of lifetime tenure for federal judges, a guarantee of Article III of the Constitution.[2] Haldeman noted that the day before, Virginia senator Harry Flood Byrd Jr. introduced a bill for a proposed constitutional amendment that would require Senate reconfirmation of all federal judges every eight years. Byrd wanted federal judges to be appointed to an initial eight-year term, after which they would be automatically renominated for another eight-year term but would be subject to "reconfirmation" by the Senate. Byrd had first announced the plan in 1971, saying that "too many of them [federal judges] had assumed powers reserved to other branches of government."[3]

"Harry Byrd introduced the reconfirmation of judges [bill] yesterday," Haldeman said to Nixon. "Oh he did?" Nixon asked. "Yes, so we've got that one in the mill and rolling," Haldeman said.

"Good for him," Nixon responded.

"He made a strong speech," Haldeman added. "He said only kings, monarchs, dictators, and United States federal judges have lifetime appointments." They all chuckled. Nixon said, "The Supreme Court you can't mess with, but we should be able to."

Rose chimed in: "You know there ought to be an age when they have to retire."

"Oh absolutely," Nixon agreed, "absolutely."[4]

Harry Byrd's proposed amendment, most liberal newspapers recognized, grew "out of his disagreement with the actions of certain federal judges in the South in relation to integration, or school busing, or both."[5] Byrd challenged the notion first expressed by Alexander Hamilton that the judiciary was the "weakest" of the three branches of government because it had, Hamilton wrote, "neither force nor will but merely judgment." Byrd contended the opposite was true, especially in the modern context of the busing of schoolchildren to promote integration. "I submit," he wrote a few years after busing programs began, "that there is a well-founded sentiment in this nation today that some members of the federal judiciary are exercising a considerable amount of will, armed with too much force, and given to less than a full measure of judgment. There is widespread dissatisfaction with the existing system, under which some judges are exercising dictatorial powers."[6]

No one had in mind the subject of abortion when questions about the limits of judicial power were being kicked around in January 1973. No one, that is, except the nine justices who were still trying to figure out how to deal with *Roe v. Wade* and *Doe v. Bolton*.

The Chambers of Justice Lewis F. Powell, US Supreme Court, June 1972

When Lewis Powell came to the court in January 1972, he had to decide whether to keep the law clerks who had been hired by the man he was replacing—the deceased Hugo Lafayette Black. On the Supreme Court, law clerks are the confidants of the justices and frequently produce the original drafts of opinions, which are the stock and trade of the court. Powell inherited Justice Black's law clerks because of a court tradition that allows clerks to stay on for the remainder of the term when the justice who engaged them retired or died in office. It is then up to the new justice to elect whether to keep the clerks for

Justice Lewis F. Powell.
Collection of the Supreme Court of the United States

the new term. In Black's case, his latest clerks were hired through the October 1971 term, which had expired in December.[7]

One of Hugo Black's law clerks was a young man named Larry Hammond.

Hammond was from El Paso, Texas, "the son of a wholesale druggist, a strongly religious Episcopalian who took Hammond with him on the road through small towns in West Texas and New Mexico to visit independent drugstores."[8] Hammond suffered from a major speech impediment as a child: he had a pronounced stuttering problem. He found relief in foreign languages. When he was a boy he developed a keen interest in Russia and the Cold War—Sputnik in 1957 and the Bay of Pigs in 1962 captured his imagination. So he signed up to study the Russian language in high school and to his amazement found that his stammer disappeared entirely when he spoke in a foreign language. This led him to the University of New Mexico for college, which had just started a program in Russian. When he exhausted all of the Russian courses offered at New Mexico, he transferred to the University of Texas in Austin and, after graduation, stayed there for law school.

Two students at the University of Texas School of Law at the same time Hammond studied there (though not in his class) were Sarah Weddington and Linda Coffee, the young women who would later represent Norma McCorvey in *Roe v. Wade.* Hammond knew Weddington, but not well.

Hammond flourished in law school. He was editor in chief of the law review and became a chancellor, a member of the law school's prestigious honor society that recognizes the sixteen students who achieved the highest grade point averages in their class through the second year. Hammond, because he stood fourth in his class, automatically became an officer of the chancellors: he was the so-called Keeper of the Peregrinus. The Peregrinus was the school's mascot, a mythical bird/mammal made up as a joke in 1902 and named for Praetor Peregrinus, a traveling Roman law official. Carved in wood and set on a platform, the bizarre statue was to be protected by the Keeper from defacement or theft (mainly from marauding University of Texas engineering students). His assignment was to maintain tabs on the bird at all times.[9] Hammond remembers carrying the beast around with him during his third year in law school. Though he found the "stupid bird tradition" somewhat embarrassing and humiliating, he accepted it with good humor.[10]

His sterling academic performance caught the attention of several of his professors. Charles Alan Wright, an eccentric but nationally recognized constitutional law expert—and later one of Nixon's lead defense lawyers in his Watergate battles with Congress and the special prosecutor Archibald Cox—and Leon Green, notable in his time as the "King of Torts," recommended Hammond for a federal clerkship following graduation. Hammond sent an application to Judge Carl McGowan, among others, who sat on the Court of Appeals for the District of Columbia in the same building, one floor down, from the ceremonial courtroom where Judge Sirica would hold the Watergate burglars' trial. McGowan had been counsel to Governor Adlai Stevenson of Illinois, a faculty member at Northwestern Law School, and general counsel to a railroad. He was nominated to the DC Court of Appeals in 1963 by President John F. Kennedy.[11]

Judge McGowan hired Larry Hammond as a law clerk sight unseen in 1970. Hammond at the time did not have the money to travel from Texas to Washington for an in-person interview, but his distinguished faculty recommendations and strong record were sufficient for McGowan. Judge McGowan would eventually take part in two opinions that helped determine the fate of Richard Nixon's White House tapes, both cases being decided after Hammond had finished his clerkships and gone into practice. In September 1973

Judge McGowan voted in the majority in *Nixon v. Sirica,* the case
where Nixon was first ordered to turn over tapes to Judge Sirica for
in camera review. The decision led directly to the momentous Saturday Night Massacre, which saw Archibald Cox fired by Robert
Bork at Nixon's direction.[12] Charles Alan Wright argued the *Sirica*
case on behalf of President Nixon. Almost a decade later, McGowan
authored the opinion that rejected Nixon's attempt to keep portions
of six thousand hours of the White House tapes from being released
to the public.[13]

Clerks have always had a symbiotic relationship with the judges
for whom they work. Much has been written of the substantial influence Supreme Court law clerks quietly exert over their justices
and the development of the law. According to Hammond, one of
the Supreme Court justices whom Judge McGowan admired most
was Justice Louis Brandeis, the first Jew appointed to the Supreme
Court. (Brandeis served from 1916 to 1939, having been nominated
by Woodrow Wilson.) Brandeis was known for his progressive philosophy on the court and his development and molding of law clerks,
inculcating in them his vision that the law was not stagnant but constantly in flux, responding to society. "Law, for Brandeis, was not a
derivative of eternal principles, but instead a pragmatic response to
societal needs,"[14] a scholar has written.

As this scholar further explained, Brandeis's judicial philosophy came down to this: "Just as anyone seeking to understand what
law was at any point in time first had to understand society, so too,
Brandeis thought, a lawyer seeking to argue what the law ought to be
first needed to grasp what society was becoming."[15]

The so-called "Brandeis brief" was a document identified by its
heavy reliance on societal data, as opposed to the more traditional
citation of dry legal authorities. Under the Brandeis model for law
clerks, young lawyers were selected and trained to assist the justices in
promoting sociological jurisprudence, mainly by paying close attention to nonlegal factual data in support of an opinion. Brandeis then
encouraged his clerks to join academia after their clerkships to spread
the Brandeis gospel to the next generations of lawyers.

Larry Hammond, in important ways, would fit this mold, though
he did not become a member of the academy.

When his year with Judge McGowan was coming to an end,
Hammond decided to inquire about a position as a Supreme Court
clerk and was encouraged by McGowan to apply to the chambers of

Justice Hugo Black. Black phoned McGowan to find out his views on Hammond. Unbeknownst to Hammond, Black was most intrigued with McGowan's report of Hammond's stuttering problem. What Larry Hammond later learned was that Justice Black liked to play the role of a modern-day "Alabama-born Pygmalion to a generation of young clerks."[16] Black's selection process was weighted in favor of a candidate who could use some help or personal guidance. "I don't pick my law clerks for what they can do for me, I pick my law clerks for what I can do for them," Black once said.[17]

Though Black's method could seem intrusive and meddling, his goal was to try to change lives. His interest ran from deficiencies in a clerk's social skills to issues with his or her appearance, habits, weight, attitude, or temperament. If one suffered from too much arrogance, Black tried to work on humility. Slobs were encouraged to become neater. A clerk tending toward obesity was advised to lose weight. With Larry Hammond it was his stammer. One scholar who has made a career of studying Supreme Court law clerks recently documented Larry Hammond's first interaction with Justice Black. "When interviewing future law clerk Larry Hammond (October Term 1971)," Professor Todd Peppers wrote in the *Journal of Supreme Court History*, "Justice Black startled the young applicant by announcing that he had decided to meet with Hammond because he knew the young man stuttered. Black proceeded to show Hammond several books on stuttering and hypothesized it was a psychological condition."[18] Hammond was told later that no book made it to Black's bookshelf in his office unless he had thoroughly read and digested it. Hammond counted at least four books on stuttering.

Three months after Larry Hammond was hired as a clerk, Hugo Black resigned due to illness. He died a week later on September 25, 1971. Richard Nixon and John Mitchell attended his funeral service in Francis Sayre's National Cathedral, the one in which Nixon thought he had been bushwhacked from the pulpit.

Hammond remained an employee of the court but found himself writing condolence-acknowledgment notes for Elizabeth Black, the justice's widow; playing basketball in the Supreme Court's gym (located directly above the main courtroom and of course nicknamed "the Highest Court in the Land"), and escorting schoolchildren on court tours. He even had a few extraordinary occasions to sit in with the loquacious Justice Thurgood Marshall, enjoying long afternoon conversations and in the process offering a much-needed respite for Marshall's overworked clerks. "I had the time of my life," he remembered.[19]

On January 7, 1972, Lewis Powell was sworn in as an associate justice of the United States Supreme Court. He brought one clerk with him but kept Hammond and another black law clerk.[20] Because the October term had expired, Hammond had no expectation of a continuing job. He was not sure how he made the grade; there was no interview process. Once again Larry Hammond had been chosen sight unseen. He recalled his first meeting with Powell. It was a "lovely meeting," with Powell explaining his thoughts about how things would work. Powell came from an old-line law firm in Richmond, Hunton & Williams, and he treated his clerks as junior associates, favoring a back-and-forth process, a dialogue-driven mode of reasoning and writing, rather than pronouncements from on high.

He told Hammond and the other clerks that they were to assume he had no set opinions on criminal law questions, despite his fairly high-profile speeches and writings on law and order while he was the president of the American Bar Association (ABA). He wanted a fresh look. To Hammond's great relief, Powell also said that, because of his long experience in the practice of law, he would need little help in the areas of antitrust and tax law—two esoteric areas of the law for a clerk—but he would be looking for major assistance in other areas of constitutional law—mainly in the area of individual rights. Hammond felt as if he had "died and gone to heaven."

Over time, Hammond and Powell developed a deep personal relationship. Larry Hammond ended up being one of Powell's only law clerks who was asked to stay on a second year. Lewis Powell was an easy man to like. His courtly Southern manners, soft accent, and attention to a clerk as a person, including his or her family and well-being, were legendary. Hammond remembers Powell being especially attentive to children at extended-family events, which often included clerks and their families.

But this did not mean that Powell and his clerks didn't work hard. At sixty-four and with eyesight problems, Powell initially was over-whelmed with the job of being a justice. He and his clerks kept at it seven days a week, taking papers home most nights. At one point, Powell even considered resigning because of the crush of the work.[21] He was at the nadir in the spring of 1972. But then, mysteriously, Powell began to recover from his personal crisis, and it was at this

exact point that he ran into the question of whether to vote to reargue
Roe v. Wade and *Doe v. Bolton.*

The Chambers of Justice Lewis F. Powell, October 11, 1972

Lewis Powell was in no hurry to jump into the debate that had broken out within the court over the abortion cases. But on June 1—
the Thursday following the first Watergate break-in and the casing
of George McGovern's headquarters—Powell wrote a Memorandum
to the conference (the formal manner to internally address all of the
justices) indicating that he was prepared to take part in the abortion cases. "I have been on the Court for more than half a term,"
he wrote. "It may be that I now have a duty to participate in the
decision, although from a purely personal viewpoint I would be more
than happy to leave this one to others." Powell said he had not read
the first drafts that Blackmun had circulated at the end of May and
had no idea how he would vote. Powell's decision to step in was based
"primarily on the fact that Harry Blackmun, the author of the opinions, [thought] the cases should be carried over and reargued [the]
next fall. His position, based on months of study, [suggested] enough
doubt on the issue of large national importance to justify the few
months delay."[22]

After the firestorm over reargument—stoked by Justice Douglas's
blistering dissent that was never filed—finally subsided (coincident,
naturally, with the second break-in at the Watergate), the justices disbanded for the long summer recess, and Lewis Powell asked Larry
Hammond to study up on all the briefs filed in *Roe* and *Doe.* Though
the actual evidentiary record in each case was scant, Hammond took
home stacks of amicus briefs (so-called "friend of the court" briefs)
loaded with the kinds of sociological and medical arguments and statistics that would have pleased Justice Brandeis.[23] Powell told Hammond
that Justice Douglas's opinion in *Griswold* would be important, and
he asked him to do his own independent factual and legal research.
These cases became Hammond's priority.

As Harry Blackmun worked in a corner of the medical library at
the Mayo Clinic in Minnesota, Larry Hammond spent the summer
studying the abortion briefs and writing a thirty-page memo for Justice Powell.[24] Sometime after Labor Day, when Powell finally returned
from his summer away, he and Hammond had lunch at the Monocle
Restaurant, a white-tablecloth steak and seafood establishment a few

blocks from the Supreme Court on Capitol Hill. Powell told Hammond that he had pondered the problem during the break and had come down on the side of a woman's right to an abortion. Hammond remembered being quite surprised but pleased. He agreed with Powell.

On Monday, October 2, Powell pulled all of Blackmun's memos and his first drafts of *Roe* and *Doe* from the previous May, carefully underlining the text and making marginal "off the cuff" notes as he went. He did not agree that the Texas statute was vague. Next to Blackmun's lines in *Doe* that "somewhere, either forthwith at conception, or at 'quickening,' or at birth, or at some other point in between, another being becomes involved and the privacy of woman possessed has become dual rather than sole," Powell scribbled telling marginalia: "'another being' becomes involved." He added double lines of emphasis next to the sentence that followed: "It is not for us of the judiciary, especially at this point in the development of man's knowledge, to speculate or to specify when life begins."[25]

Then a critical turning point happened. At the end of that first week of October—Friday, October 6—Powell sent a memo to Hammond about a "cert note" that Hammond had prepared on a Connecticut case known as *Abele v. Markle*. First decided by a three-judge panel in April 1972, *Abele* declared Connecticut's 1860 abortion statute unconstitutional. Hammond's "cert note" was his evaluation of the certiorari briefs requesting a review of the case in the Supreme Court. Hammond thought the opinion especially well reasoned and that it might be of interest when deciding *Roe* and *Doe*.

The importance of this relatively obscure Connecticut proceeding in the ultimate outcome of the abortion cases cannot be overstated. Powell was intrigued. "I have just read your cert note in 72-56 *Abele v. Markle*, in which Judges Lumbard and Newman, Clarke dissenting, struck down Connecticut's 1860 abortion law," he wrote to Hammond. "When we come to decision time in the pending abortion cases, keep in mind that we may wish to look at the Lumbard/Newman opinions."[26]

Hammond prepared a "bench memo" over the weekend of October 7 and 8 for Powell's use in the upcoming oral arguments in *Roe* and *Doe* and delivered it to Powell on Monday morning, October 9. Hammond took the opportunity to expound on *Abele* and recent developments in the litigation. In an odd procedural twist, the case had gone to a second round—a second opinion had been generated since the first one in April. The new opinion, *Abele II*, was written by Jon O. Newman, a Nixon appointee on the US District Court for the

District of Connecticut. *Abele II* was handed down on September 20, 1972, two weeks before Hammond put his thoughts down on paper.

Abele II, it turned out, would become the Rosetta Stone for unlocking the secret of *Roe.*

Judge Newman had written a concurring opinion as part of the three-judge panel in *Abele I.* In it Newman expressed his agreement to strike down the 1860 Connecticut law because he had been unable to discern any legislative intent from 1860 to support the state's argument that the law was enacted, in part, to protect fetal life.[27]

In direct response to this judicial challenge, the governor and state legislature of Connecticut quickly passed a new abortion statute in May 1972 that left no doubt about the state's purpose. The new law expressed "the intent of the legislature to protect and preserve human life from the moment of conception."[28]

Judge Newman and his fellow judges would squarely face the ultimate constitutional question: did Connecticut's interest in protecting fetal life, clearly articulated by its legislature, support the abridgment of a woman's fundamental right to choose whether to continue a pregnancy?

This presented a more difficult question to resolve than *Abele I.* Newman's effort in navigating this minefield produced an analysis that strongly resonated with Hammond and then Powell.

As it happened, Judge Newman's law clerk, a 1972 Yale Law graduate named Andrew Hurwitz, had applied for a Supreme Court clerkship that fall, and his résumé was floating around the court. Judge Newman's letter of reference touted the young man's assistance in the drafting of *Abele.* Larry Hammond knew about this when he wrote his bench memo to Powell, possibly from reviewing Hurwitz's recommendations.[29] In his memo, he noted parenthetically: "This was drafted in part by Andy Hurwitz, so you may gain some feeling for his writing ability."[30] Hurwitz wrote that Powell spent over an hour discussing *Abele* with him when he interviewed.[31]

The opinion that Andy Hurwitz helped fashion followed a certain logic.

First, for Judge Newman and his clerk Hurwitz, it was a given that a woman had a fundamental, constitutionally protected right of privacy with respect to intimate family decisions, including the right to terminate an unwanted pregnancy. The Supreme Court decisions in *Griswold* and *Eisenstadt v. Baird* allowing family planning through the use of contraceptives, they reasoned, could by simple extension support a woman's private right to choose whether to keep a pregnancy.[32] Little discussion was needed on this point, from their perspective.

So the question became, did the state ever have a sufficiently important interest in protecting the fetus to justify an invasion of the woman's fundamental right? If it did, the interest had to be "compelling," that is, clear, established, and without argument. Newman and Hurwitz thought the interest of the fetus was far from clear or well established. People—theologians, scientists, doctors, ethicists—disagreed on what it was, when life began, or when there was "ensoulment," and consequently judges varied on its legal status.

A fetus had never been recognized as a "person" under the due process clause of the Fourteenth Amendment; from the Constitution's perspective, a fetus was not a "person" entitled to protection against the state's deprivation of "life, liberty or property."

But on a more elementary level, there was in our modern, pluralistic society wide disagreement over the nature of a fetus. "Some believe the fetus is in every respect a human being from the moment of conception," Newman wrote. "Others believe there is a point during the pregnancy when it becomes in many respects a human being. Still others believe that until it is born, a fetus is a mass of protoplasm, which, though it may have some attributes of a human being such as hunger and a nervous system, is not a human being in any sense."

Compared to the recognized right of the woman to choose, the fetus's rights were "a matter of diverse personal judgment."

Therefore, such a disputed interest could not be used by the government to invade a clear, constitutionally protected right of a woman to choose. A person may believe that abortion is the deliberate killing of a human being and may hold that belief with profound sincerity. "But under the Constitution," Newman opined, "their judgment must remain a personal judgment, one that they may follow in their personal lives and seek to persuade others to follow, but a judgment they may not impose upon others by force of law."

It was casting the debate about the nature of a fetus much like a dispute over the existence of God—it was a matter of conscience, one in which the state couldn't and shouldn't take sides. No one knew for sure. And science and medicine couldn't definitively answer the question of when a fetus became human life.

Here, though, is where Newman expanded the opinion in *Abele II*, using what lawyers call *dicta*. He had come to his conclusion; he did not need to say more—the law would be struck down. But to buttress and further explain his reasoning, he decided to address a gruesome question posed by the attorneys for the State of Connecticut. The only purpose of addressing this question was, he said, "to highlight the invalidity of the statute before" the court. In other words, the discussion that followed was entirely unnecessary and extraneous. It was what Hurwitz himself later characterized as "sweeping dictum."[33]

"The state earnestly urges upon us consideration of the situation where an abortion performed late in a pregnancy results in a 'live birth,'" Newman wrote. "Evidence was offered to show that an aborted fetus had on occasion remained alive for several hours after an abortion operation." Would this present a situation where there was a "compelling interest" to support a ban on abortion? Newman thought perhaps, in this instance, it would. Newman seemed to be issuing advice to the Connecticut legislature on how to narrowly fashion an abortion law that could survive judicial scrutiny. "If a statute sought to protect the lives of fetuses which could survive outside the uterus," he wrote, "such a statute would be a legislative acceptance of the concept of viability."

Viability! Here was mention in a judicial decision of the idea that would become the cornerstone of *Roe*.

"While authorities may differ on the precise time, there is no doubt that at some point during pregnancy a fetus is capable, with proper medical attention, of surviving outside the uterus," Newman wrote. "And it is equally clear that there is a minimum point before which survival outside the uterus is not possible."

Why would viability establish a "compelling" interest in the context of a properly structured abortion statute? Because, Newman explained, "protecting the life of a fetus capable of living outside the uterus could be shown *to be more generally accepted* and, therefore, of more weight in a constitutional sense than the interest in preventing the abortion of a fetus that is not viable."[34]

What he was saying was that this dividing line—viability—would find broader public acceptance, thus making it "compelling." Few if any would argue, he was postulating, that a live birth, or a fetus that could survive outside the womb, could not be protected by the state. The very indisputability of the proposition made for a "compelling state interest" that could counter a woman's constitutional right to choose.

Larry Hammond told Justice Powell that the "thesis of the Newman opinion is similar to the one I would find most supportable based on existing precedent." He encouraged Powell to suggest that the court follow Judge Newman's reasoning "that the state's interest becomes more dominant when the fetus is capable of independent existence (or becomes 'viable')." Hammond expounded on his understanding of Newman's thinking: "The closer to term the unborn fetus is the greater the state's concern. And, since the state would not be imposing an absolute bar to abortional freedom but only a time restriction a balance might be permissible that would allow a state to sustain a statute saying that abortion may be prohibited after the 6th month."[35]

The next day, October 10, 1972, Powell reviewed and annotated a copy of the Newman opinion in *Abele II*.[36] It was the day before the second round of oral arguments in both *Roe* and *Doe*. Larry Hammond's fellow law students from his days at the University of Texas School of Law, Sarah Weddington and Linda Coffee, would appear once again in the court chamber, with its forty-four-foot ceiling and raised bench. The arguments took place on Wednesday, October 11, 1972. Powell would ask no questions in the *Roe* arguments.[37]

No one would even mention the term "viability."[38]

The Chambers of Justice Harry Blackmun, November 21, 1972

In between the time of the second oral argument and Harry Blackmun's next drafts in *Roe* and *Doe*, Henry Kissinger declared "peace is at hand," Richard Nixon won his landslide victory, and Chuck Colson tape-recorded Howard Hunt's demand for more money so that "things did not fall apart." Eight days after the Hunt-Colson phone call and two days before the Thanksgiving holiday—on November 21, 1972—Blackmun sent a note to the other justices with his revised drafts of *Roe* and *Doe*. He had struggled again to come up with his opinions. "This has proved for me to be both difficult and elusive," Blackmun conceded.[39]

Justice Blackmun continued to cling to a physician-centered bias in his drafts. He went on at length about the medical and legal history of abortion, including a rambling discussion of the ancient Hippocratic oath, considered, he said, the ethical guide of the medical profession.[40] Most of the material in this section had been gathered from his research at the Mayo Clinic.[41] And he still couched his argument in the context of a physician's broad discretion to make a medical judgment for his patient about an abortion; a woman's right to choose was of secondary importance at best. But two critical things changed from his May draft. He gave up his void-for-vagueness position on the

Texas statute in *Roe*, as Powell had suggested. So *Roe*, not *Doe*, would become the lead case on the merits of the right to an abortion. Blackmun also jettisoned his reluctance to draw lines as to when a fetus could be protected by the state. He chose, for reasons not evident in the draft, the end of the first trimester as the "cut off point."

"You will observe," he wrote in his pre-Thanksgiving memorandum to the conference, "that I have concluded that the end of the first trimester is critical. This is arbitrary, but perhaps any other selected point, such as quickening or viability, is equally arbitrary." Blackmun left the decision of whether a woman could have an abortion entirely in the hands of the responsible physician during the first three months of pregnancy: "If during the first trimester, the attending physician decides in consultation with his patient that in his best medical judgment her pregnancy should be terminated that judgment is sufficient."[42]

The justices all reacted to the new drafts with various degrees of approval and nonapproval, but Powell's response would prove decisive. As before, Powell would look to his law clerk to assist him in thinking through his next move.

The Chambers of Justice Lewis F. Powell, December 11, 1972

On the Monday after Thanksgiving, November 27, Larry Hammond wrote a six-page memo on Justice Blackmun's second drafts in the abortion cases. He said his "most important reservation" with the *Roe* opinion was Blackmun's line-drawing at the end of the first trimester. "Nowhere does he state the basis for that 'fixing,'" Hammond observed. He worried that if there was no reasoning to explain "how that decision [was] arrived at," it would hardly command public support. The first-trimester line seemed to have been pulled from thin air.

Hammond continued to believe that if a line was going to be drawn, viability was a better answer. "In this case, since the statutory prohibition was total, it is unnecessary to the result that we draw the line," he cautioned. But "if a line ultimately must be drawn, it seems that viability provided the better point. This is where Judge Newman would have drawn the line." Hammond found viability "consistent with the common law history," and he said it addressed the core problem that no one seemed to be able to resolve: the great controversy over when life begins. "At some point the controversy does not appear to be so great," Hammond continued. "Most people would probably agree that the state has a much greater interest in protecting a viable entity than it does at some earlier point."[43]

Two days later, on November 29, Lewis Powell wrote a personal letter to Harry Blackmun. He started with flattery. He said he was impressed with the scholarship and analysis of Blackmun's drafts and added, "I have no doubt that they will command a court." Then he went to work, in his own very polite way, to try to convince Blackmun to adopt the position that Larry Hammond had recommended. "I write at this time to inquire whether you view your choice of 'the first trimester' as essential to your decision," he inquired. "I wondered," Powell wrote, "whether drawing the line at 'viability'—if we conclude to designate a particular point of time—would not be more defensible in logic and biologically than perhaps any other single time." He then pointed to Judge Newman's opinion in *Abele II*, quoting from it and saying he agreed that the interest of the state in protecting a fetus after viability was more likely to be "generally understood." He wrote, "At any point in time prior thereto, it is more difficult to justify a cutoff date."

Powell decided he would keep his lobbying with Blackmun private. "I am not sending a copy of this letter to other members of the Court," he ended his letter. "No doubt we will discuss your opinion in Conference, and I thought it might be helpful—to you and certainly to me—if you had the opportunity in advance to consider my reservation as above expressed."[44]

One of Blackmun's clerks, after being shown the Powell letter, told Blackmun to stand his ground. He thought the state could regulate abortions after the first trimester in some narrow ways before viability.[45] Accordingly, Blackmun responded to Powell on December 4. "Dear Lewis," he wrote, "I appreciate your letter of November 29 with its suggestions." He said he had "no particular commitment to the point marking the end of the first trimester as contrasted with some other point, such as quickening or viability." He chose the end of the first trimester because "medical statistics and statistical writings seemed to focus on it and draw their contrasts between the first three months and the remainder of the pregnancy." But Blackmun was willing to bargain. "I could go along with viability if it could command a court," he wrote Powell. For the moment, though, he was going to stick to his first-trimester line.[46]

A week later, on December 11—a Monday (it is striking how many major events in *Roe* took place on a Monday)—Powell wrote a deferential but gently nudging note to Blackmun, which he passed down to him as they sat on the bench while listening to oral arguments in another case. "Harry," Powell scribbled, "I will join your opinion and so I leave entirely to you whether to address the 'viability' issue." Powell, as usual, was courteous to a fault, but it is clear that he wanted to take one more run at convincing Blackmun. He had apparently seen a draft of a memo that Blackmun had proposed to circulate to the other justices to raise the issue. "It does seem to me that viability is a more logical and supportable time," Powell continued, "but this is not a critical issue with me. If you decide to raise the issue, your memo is fine."[47]

That afternoon, Blackmun, sensitive to Powell's persistence and appreciating his discreet politicking, sent a memorandum to the conference. "One of the members of the Conference [he maintained Powell's anonymity] has asked whether my choice of the end of the first trimester, as the point beyond which a state may appropriately regulate abortion practices, is critical," Blackmun wrote. "He asked whether the point of viability might not be a better choice." Blackmun pointed out one practical benefit to viability versus a first trimester cutoff: "[I] am sure that there are many pregnant women, particularly young girls, who may refuse to face the fact of pregnancy and who, for one reason or another, do not get around to medical consultation until the end of the first trimester is upon them or, indeed, has passed."

Blackmun said he was prepared to "recast the opinions at the later date" but did not want to risk alienating the other justices. He concluded by pointing to Judge Newman's *Abele II* opinion.[48]

Reactions were fast. That day, William O. Douglas, surprisingly, shot back a curt note: "I favor the first trimester, rather than viability."[49] Others wrote back over the next few days. Marshall was "inclined to agree" on viability. "Given the difficulties which many woman may have in believing that they are pregnant and in deciding to seek an abortion," he wrote, "I fear that an earlier date may not in practice serve the interests of those women, which your opinion does seek to serve." The mother's health could be considered in regulating the period in between the end of the first trimester and viability, Marshall added. But he did not want to let a state prohibit an abortion on the basis of the "potential life of the unborn child" prior to viability.[50]

Justice Brennan had a more complicated response, but he too favored multiple markers—regulation for the sake of the mother's health only after the first trimester and consideration of the potential life of the fetus only after viability. The hard outlines of *Roe* were start-ing to form.[51] And yet no lawyer argued for these divisions—viability was an invention of the Supreme Court.

Behind the scenes in Justice Powell's chambers, Larry Hammond was vexed by Blackmun's lack of leadership. When Blackmun's December 11 memo was issued, Hammond wrote a three-page note to Powell with his thoughts. He observed that Blackmun seemed pliable—he appeared to be "willing to sacrifice his personal views for the benefit of getting a full Court." Nonetheless, he was pleased that Blackmun had expressed what Hammond thought was the bedrock rationale for viability. "For many poor, or frightened, or uneducated, or unsophisticated girls," Hammond wrote, "the decision to seek help may not occur during the first 12 weeks." As he put it: "The girl might be hoping against hope that she is not pregnant but is just missing periods. Or she might know perfectly well that she is preg-nant but be unwilling to make the decision—unwilling to tell her parents or her boyfriend." To this paragraph Powell penciled in the margin, "Yes."

Like Marshall and Brennan, Hammond thought that the viability standard could be used without interfering with some earlier regula-tion on behalf of the woman's health, such as the need for all abor-tions after the first trimester to be performed in a hospital. "In the same opinion," he argued, "the Ct could well say that where the inter-est asserted by the State is protection of fetal life or 'potential life' no point earlier than viability is permissible (for the reasons stated in Judge Newman's opinion)."[52]

Justice Douglas's brief note opposing viability surprised Hammond. "I am shocked at Justice Douglas' note," he wrote to Powell on December 12. "The Justice, who more than anyone else on this Court stakes his judicial reputation on protecting the poor and the black . . . cannot fail to recognize that a first trimester rule falls most heavily on those classes." Hammond committed to finding "empirical research" on "the question of how long it takes women—especially the young, the poor, and the minorities—to recognize their predicament."[53]

Blackmun would give it one more shot. Thanking all for the com-ments, he asked for permission "to revise the proposed opinions in light of these suggestions." He had come to a synthesis of the various positions. "I have in mind associating the end of the first trimester with an emphasis on health, and associating viability with an emphasis on the State's interest in potential life. The period between the two points would be treated with flexibility."[54]

Roe v. Wade and its tripartite structure had found its genesis. No abortion could be prohibited prior to the end of the first trimester. During the second trimester the state could regulate abortions, but only on behalf of the mother's health. During the third trimester, the life of the fetus could be considered in regulations.

One justice who was still undecided was the chief. Burger wrote to Blackmun on December 13 that he still had more "ploughing" to do with Blackmun's drafts. Among other things, he wondered about the "possible need to deal with the husbands as such or parents of minors." They too had rights in this area, he wrote.[55]

Blackmun expressed his hope that the opinions would be finalized by January 15, 1973, when most state legislatures would reconvene after the holiday break. He wanted to give them ample time to adjust their abortion laws.

His next draft, the third, appeared on December 21, three days after the start of the Christmas bombing in Vietnam.[56] The draft inspired general agreement among those justices in the majority, including William O. Douglas.

But more drafting was to come. When Chief Justice Burger spoke with President Nixon on the second day of January 1973, he was still trying to decide what to do. A few weeks later, at the conference on January 12, the justices had lost patience with Burger's stalling. They suspected that he was determined to block the abortion cases from coming down until after he swore Nixon in for a second term. They believed he wanted to spare Nixon, and perhaps himself, embarrassment.[57] In frustration, Justice Potter Stewart suggested in conference that Burger allow the decisions to be released without his participation.

The Chambers of Justice Lewis F. Powell, January 3, 1972

On the same day that Bill Bittman visited Chuck Colson in the Executive Office Building to demand a promise of clemency for Howard Hunt, Lewis Powell wrote a short note to Larry Hammond. The note, dated January 3, 1973, was Powell's internal communication that he was ready to formally join in Blackmun's abortion opinions. "I have read more carefully the third draft, and I am prepared to join—unless you have some last minute advice," he wrote.

But Powell felt the need to say more about Hammond's crucial role in the decisions. "It seems to me," he wrote, "that Justice Blackmun has reached a constitutionally sound result and stated it clearly." And though Blackmun gave credit to others, Powell wrote, "I suggest that you [Hammond] are entitled—particularly in view of your education of me on the viability issue—to credit that is nonetheless substantial because it will never be recognized. I think I was perhaps the first to press for [the] viability change."[58]

When Larry Hammond completed his clerkship under Lewis Powell in the summer of 1973, he joined the Watergate Special Prosecution Task Force, working for Archibald Cox on the burgeoning scandal and listening to segments of tapes that Nixon had been forced to turn over.

After finishing his stint with the Watergate prosecutors in the summer of 1974, as Richard Nixon headed for political exile in California following his resignation, Hammond also headed west to join a law firm in Phoenix—Osborn Maledon—where he would become one of Phoenix's premier criminal defense attorneys and devote himself to community service and Arizona's version of the National Innocence Project.

Hammond was joined in Phoenix by Andy Hurwitz, Judge Jon Newman's law clerk in *Abele*, in a firm that also included Justice Brennan's law clerk, Bill Maledon, who likewise worked on *Roe*. "In one of the many coincidences that seem to occur throughout the story of the abortion cases," Hurwitz wrote in 2002, "Larry Hammond and I joined the same law firm in Phoenix during the summer of 1974, and we have been colleagues in the practice of law in that firm and its successors ever since."[59]

Andy Hurwitz became a Supreme Court Justice on Arizona's highest court and was nominated to the Ninth Circuit Court of Appeals by President Barack Obama in 2012. He was confirmed after a long and messy fight in the Senate over Hurwitz's role in *Abele*.

He obtained lifetime tenure.[60]

13

"We May Be Doomed to Come to an Agreement Today"

Forces began to gather, stir, swirl, and snarl around the date of January 22, 1973. Events were quietly but inexorably shifting in that direction. On its face, the day hardly stood out as potentially epic. It looked to be an ordinary Monday following the inaugural weekend, a time when Washington could catch its breath and recover from the parties and balls and festivities that accompanied the swearing in of a president. But January 22 seemed to develop its own cyclonic power, sweeping events into its vortex and spitting out a new political world order on the other side.

Paris, France, January 10, 1973

The day after Richard Nixon's sixtieth birthday, Henry Kissinger and his team met with the North Vietnamese for a four-hour session. The question on everyone's mind was whether the breakthrough they had reached the day before was real, or whether the North Vietnamese would go back to their old ways, as they had done so often in these maddening negotiations.

Kissinger had received a long cable from Ambassador Ellsworth Bunker in Saigon earlier that morning. Bunker was in regular contact with President Thieu of South Vietnam, trying to measure his reactions to what was transpiring in Paris. Bunker was also reviewing drafts of the agreements and protocols to provide Kissinger with his input from what he thought was the South Vietnamese perspective.

Bunker pointed out that Thieu had all manner of complicated political concerns to work out: "Thieu's problem with the signing procedure, I think, will be that it publicly assigns a major role to the U.S. and DRV (North Vietnam), leaving the Republic of Vietnam in a subsidiary position." The South Vietnamese weren't at the table, as it were, and the difficulty for Thieu was that he could not appear to have been force-fed a bad agreement that he had no part in negotiating.

Under no circumstances could Thieu recognize the legitimacy of the Vietcong, though they would be a signatory to the four-party agreement and would be part of the joint military commission that would oversee the cease-fire, the withdrawal of US forces, and the return of prisoners. They also would be a party to the National Council of National Reconciliation and Concord (NCRC) that would organize elections after the cease-fire. Yet the official name of the Vietcong, the Provisional Revolutionary Government (PRG), sometimes called the National Liberation Front (NLF), would appear nowhere in the text of the four-party agreement that would be signed by the North Vietnamese, the South Vietnamese, the United States, and the PRC.[1]

And Thieu would have to deal with the so-called "leopard spot" aspect of the agreement—leaving North Vietnamese (NVN) and Vietcong forces in place in the South in enclaves that would be monitored by the joint military commission.

Bunker saw Thieu's options as coming down to four possibilities. First, he could submit the treaty to the National Assembly to approve and ratify his signing. Second, he could sign the agreement, "adding a demurrer indicating the points in the agreement on which the GVN has reservations, i.e., that it does not accept the principle that NVN troops have a right to remain in South Viet-Nam; that the NCRC has any governmental functions; or that Viet-Nam is one in the absence of agreement between the two sides." Third, he could refrain from signing but agree formally in a separate writing to abide by its conditions. Fourth, he could resign along with his vice president, leaving it to the president of the Senate to sign the accords.[2] Bunker thought the second and third options were the most likely.

An especially delicate issue for Kissinger in Paris was the where and when to sign. The North Vietnamese had insisted that the agreement be signed in Hanoi, and Kissinger had tentatively agreed. This obviously was unacceptable to the South Vietnamese, and Nixon told Haldeman that going to the enemy capital to sign a peace agreement "smacked of surrender."[3] During Kissinger's session on January 10, he gingerly suggested that the initialing and signing of the agreements take place in Paris, with a post-agreement visit by Kissinger to Hanoi a week or so later to begin the process of postwar reconciliation (read: the United States would set up the machinery to pay billions to help reconstruct North Vietnam). The language circulating in the drafts read: "In pursuance of its traditional policy, the United States will contribute to healing the wounds of war and to postwar reconstruction of the Democratic Republic of Viet-Nam and throughout Indochina."

To Kissinger's surprise, Le Duc Tho, North Vietnam's "Special Advisor" to the peace talks, agreed to consider the Paris signing option.

A series of issues were hitting all at once. The inauguration was set for Saturday, January 20, ten days away. If Kissinger returned from Paris the weekend before, having successfully completed negotiations, time would have to be set aside for him to brief Al Haig on the details, as Haig was the official who would formally present the agreement to President Thieu in Saigon, on a "take-it-or-leave-it" basis. Haig could not depart before Kissinger completed his negotiations, because that might signal to the North Vietnamese a certain eagerness on the part of the Americans. The Communists might then stiffen their final positions, knowing the United States was keen to complete things before the Inauguration. Kissinger cautioned patience.

Once Haig was in the air, the briefing memos prepared for the president predicted that his trip would be at the least a "sixty-hour tactical detail," a brutal, body-bending trip, with Haig crossing the international date line twice, once over and then back. He would present Thieu with a letter from Nixon and return with Thieu's answer.

If Thieu agreed to the peace accords as negotiated, one scenario could be followed; if he balked, things became more complicated.

The general approach was to start with an announcement that the United States had halted its bombing in Vietnam because of "progress" in the talks. With Haig dispatched to Saigon, it was going to be natural for the press to speculate that an agreement was nigh, and a peace euphoria would begin to build in the country and around the world. Expectations and information would be difficult to control or manage.

But Nixon, as usual, started to fret about Henry Kissinger as his rival for historical notice. This obsession seemed to capture more of his attention in the second week of January 1973 than the actual details of the agreements being negotiated in Paris.

The Oval Office, January 10, 1973

Before Kissinger's cable could arrive announcing that Le Duc Tho might be amenable to the Paris initialing and signing, Nixon and

Haldeman went over the various scenarios for concluding the peace agreements. Nixon observed that he thought Kissinger wanted to arrange things so he could be back in Washington to attend the inauguration parties. Haldeman was not so sure.

Then the two men began to discuss Nixon's worries about how things would play out. They talked about Kissinger's arrangement to go to Hanoi to sign the agreements and his intention to meet with America's allies in the region to explain the settlement. "He wants the publicity," Nixon said. "He wants to be a peacemaker." It was for the same reason, Nixon conjectured, that Kissinger had gone behind his back and disingenuously told journalists Joseph Kraft and James "Scotty" Reston that he had opposed the bombing. He wanted everyone to believe "that he was the dove, and I was the hawk," Nixon said. But, he added, "it just isn't going to make him look very good historically" to have equivocated about his role in the bombing. Nixon thought that when the peace agreement came to fruition, the bombing would be seen as not only necessary but the correct strategic move.

"That silly overreaction to the bombing is starting to fade in the light of dawn—into a recognition that maybe there was some reason for it," Haldeman asserted.

"Well the overreaction to the bombing was stimulated by the goddamn Congress," Nixon said.

"Absolutely," Haldeman agreed, "and the country didn't react until the press whipped them up, along with those idiots on the Hill."

"But the country, even then, didn't react, Bob, as it had done previously," Nixon said. "Are the campuses burning?" he asked. "I haven't seen any of that. I mean, I don't follow it that closely, but I would think it would be on the front pages of the papers if it were."

Minutes later, Nixon circled back to Kissinger: "Bob, we've got to realize Henry's mixed up—he's terribly mixed up." Haldeman agreed. Nixon explained, "I don't really think that he ever wanted to draw any open space between the president and himself, but on the other hand, he was looking at his historical place, and he just wanted to look good, he just couldn't stand the heat." Nixon said that Kissinger recoiled when journalists and antiwar activists said, "Good God, look at all this bombing! And who did it?" Kissinger withered in the censure, even though, Nixon said, "he put me in a position of doing it."

Haldeman tried to show some fairness toward Kissinger. "But I don't think he intended to draw public attention to it," he said. "I think he wanted just to get the word around—you know, 'Henry wouldn't have done this.' He never quite judges how the press stuff and public stuff is going to go. I think he was playing this—if he was playing it at all—on the assumption that it wasn't going to snap him in the rear end, and then all of the sudden it did. It scared the hell out of him. He's worried about it."

Nixon wondered whether he should make sure to take Kissinger with him to Florida for the week before the inauguration. Nixon wanted to get out of town to write his second inaugural address, and his plan had been to withdraw to Key Biscayne. But he was starting to reconsider whether it was the right time to leave Washington. Would Congress take offense that he was in Florida, not reporting to them about what was going on in the peace negotiations? And as important, could he leave Kissinger alone with the press in Washington while he was away? He knew that Kissinger would be under fantastic pressure to say something about the negotiations. Haldeman was fairly agnostic about it, recognizing that Kissinger would have access to phones in Florida. On balance, though, Haldeman thought it might be best to take Kissinger to Florida.

This discussion about access to telephones pricked Nixon, causing him to bring up one of his favorite ideas: he wanted Haldeman to arrange for Henry's calls—on both his private and work lines—to be logged once he returned from Paris. Haldeman, knowing that as they spoke the Watergate trial was under way across town, was somewhat taken aback. He would not be as compliant as Colson, who two weeks earlier thought a similar idea was splendid.

"You mean you want his phones bugged?" Haldeman asked, with a degree of incredulity in his voice. "Oh, God no," Nixon shot back. "I don't care what he said, I just want to know who he talks to." Nixon gave this example: "It was very valuable for me to know that he talked to Kraft two days before [Kraft] came out for peace."

Haldeman explained that he thought the log of phone calls would be of minimal use. Though the White House switchboard could monitor outgoing calls, it was unusual for the operators to ask who was calling in—they usually just transferred the caller to the appropriate office. "OK," Nixon reluctantly conceded, "don't do anything that's not legal or looks like we are spying on him."

"If he ever finds out we were spying on him . . ." Haldeman began to warn. "He thinks we are anyway. He's convinced that I've bugged him."

Nixon said, "Really?"

"He really does," Haldeman said. "He's come in a couple of times on a very serious basis. He said someone's told him his phone is being tapped. He said, 'If you're tapping my phone, I can understand why you would.'"

"Sheesh," Nixon hissed, as if the comment was on its face ludicrous.

"And then he says," Haldeman continued, "'I just want you to know I know you are doing it.'"

"Oh Christ," Nixon moaned.

Haldeman said he responded, "Henry, I can't conceive of anything I would find less interesting than tapping your phone."[4]

Paris, End of Day, January 10

"Today's four-hour session continued the momentum of yesterday," Kissinger cheerily cabled a few hours later. It was evening in Paris but mid-afternoon in Washington—there was a six-hour time difference. "Whatever the press and other observers may say about our military actions, they certainly seem to have contributed to this result," he wrote. It was as if he somehow knew what Haldeman and Nixon had been discussing that very afternoon in the Oval Office.

Kissinger thought that, given the accelerated pace of discussions, he might wrap things up in time to return to the United States on Saturday, January 13, one week before the inauguration.

In light of Le Duc Tho's willingness to entertain a signing ceremony in Paris, Kissinger sketched out a proposed new schedule for Nixon to consider. He would return to the United States on January 13. Haig would be briefed and leave for Saigon with the president's ultimatum the next day, Sunday, January 14. On Monday, an announcement would be made that the United States had halted bombing due to progress in Paris. Haig would return to Washington by Wednesday or Thursday at the latest. On Friday, the day before the inauguration, the White House would announce Kissinger's return to Paris on Monday, January 22, to conclude negotiations.

The initialing in Paris would be followed by a more formal signing ceremony at the end of the week, on Saturday, January 27. Kissinger would then travel to Hanoi sometime around February 1.[5]

Kissinger's cable, received in Washington around 3:00 PM, set off a new round of Nixonian mania over the prospect that Kissinger would overshadow the president. Nixon's anxiety was that Kissinger would initial the agreement before he had a chance to announce it to the American people. A presidential announcement after the initialing "would then be sort of an anticlimactic nothing" Nixon said to Haldeman in a phone call. "I mean, what the hell am I announcing? The word would go out from there—an agreement has been reached. So the president goes on for what purpose?" Haldeman, this time, shared the president's concern. "You can't go on TV to explain Henry's agreement." Nixon said it was vitally important that he be in a position to speak first.[6]

Haig joined a meeting with Haldeman and the president and was assigned the task of responding to Kissinger's cable. With his return message to Kissinger, Haig appended his own private note. "Attached is a message from the President," Haig began, "which was dictated in substance following a lengthy and tortuous meeting between the President, Haldeman, and myself addressing Hakto 14 [Henry Kissinger's cable to the president earlier that day]." Haig said that Nixon was "very concerned that his public statement following the initialing in Paris would be a total flop. It would occur after all the peace euphoria had peaked off. He is also adamant about making the announcement if we succeed prior to the inaugural."

Haig then assured Kissinger that he had gone out of his way in the meeting to make certain that Kissinger would be back in Washington for the inaugural. "My efforts throughout the discussions were to insure that you could participate in inaugural events here," Haig wrote. "This took some doing as repeated alternative schedules were discussed."[7]

Nixon's message to Kissinger focused on the two alternative scenarios: one in which Thieu went along, and the other in which Thieu refused to sign. Contingency planning was needed. If Thieu agreed, Nixon could possibly announce on Thursday night, January 18, that Kissinger would be returning to Paris, either the next day, the Friday before the inaugural, or, "if you prefer," the following Monday, January 22, with the view to initialing the document.

If Thieu hesitated or refused to agree, Nixon wanted to say nothing before the inaugural. His plan was to have Haig delay leaving Southeast Asia, letting the pressure build on Thieu. Haig would then return to Washington the day after the inaugural, and Nixon would go on television to announce "that we had arrived at an acceptable settlement with Hanoi but that President Thieu [had] refused to accept." The president would publicly urge Thieu to reconsider and say that Kissinger was "continuing discussions with Hanoi in Paris in light of these circumstances."[8] This, as Haldeman wrote in his diary, would be a "massive bluff" to force Thieu to go along.[9]

Paris, Thursday Morning, January 11, 1973

To say that Nixon's message caused a major panic within Henry Kissinger's delegation the next morning would be an understatement. It was "peace is at hand" all over again. The president's message seemed to suggest that President Thieu could once more hold up an agreement with the North Vietnamese. But Kissinger and his staff knew that no further delay was possible. This was it. Everything could fall apart if the North Vietnamese thought they had been misled yet again about America's intention to end the war.

Kissinger whipped back an urgent message. "It must be clearly understood," he cabled, "that when we conclude here we must proceed to an initialing whatever Thieu's answer is. Under no circumstances will Hanoi hold still for a repetition of October or for a renegotiation without blowing the whole agreement." He emphasized that the United States "[could not] get any more concessions." If Nixon truly intended to renegotiate if Thieu balked, Kissinger wrote, "I should know immediately by return cable. But I strongly urge against that."[10]

The Oval Office, January 11, 9:04 AM

Colonel Richard Kennedy walked in with Kissinger's cable. "It's a very short reply," he said. Nixon read it and saw immediately that Kissinger was right.

Nixon told Colonel Kennedy that there had been a misunderstanding. He had no intention of allowing Thieu veto power over the agreement. "The only thing we were trying to get across is: what the hell do you tell Al [Haig] to do?" Nixon said. "Absolutely, we're just going to tell Thieu to go to hell. I will tell Haig to go out there and say, 'This is it, this is the best we can get, we're going to go forward, now what do you want to do, Mr. Thieu?'" Nixon understood the necessity of sending an immediate clarification to Kissinger. "Say, I totally agree we go forward with the agreement with Hanoi, regardless of whether Thieu goes along," he dictated to Kennedy. "However, if we cannot deliver Thieu, we have a problem."

Nixon thought that perhaps Kissinger didn't get the nuance of his message. The point was that he did not want to say anything before the inauguration if Thieu was resisting. Instead, he wanted to let Haig "mosey around" Indochina, consulting, for example, with the leaders of Thailand, and not returning for several days, giving President Thieu time to confer with his leaders in order to come to the right decision. Such a delay would not expose a public rift between the US and South Vietnam prior to or during the inaugural weekend. After Nixon was sworn in, and only after the United States and North Vietnam had initialed the agreement, he would call Congress together, potentially on January 22, and say that Thieu was not going along, letting further public pressure build for him to join the agreement. He told Kennedy that he understood that Kissinger had to set a firm timetable for initialing and signing the agreements with the North Vietnamese, "come hell or high water."[11] He did not mean to suggest the agreement could be put on hold.

Events were moving at a rapid pace. Nixon knew things were going to unfold in quick succession, so he began to spell out his plans for Kennedy. Congressional leadership had to be informed once Haig took off for Saigon and before Ron Ziegler announced the bombing halt. He instructed Colonel Kennedy to inform Kissinger that, when he returned on Saturday, January 13, he was to call the top leaders on Sunday night to tell them that, due to progress in the talks, a bombing halt was about to be announced and that General Haig was on his way to inform President Thieu of the progress. The message had to be carefully scripted. No substantive discussions were to be revealed other than to confirm that the three goals of the United States, as previously announced, were being pursued: a cease-fire, the return of prisoners, and a political process in which all South Vietnamese people could determine their own future.

Characteristic of Nixon's response to an impending victory, he then turned malevolent. "Get me a list," he told Colonel Kennedy, "of the heads of state who raised hell about the bombing." He ticked off names that came to mind: Pierre Trudeau of Canada, Kakuei Tanaka, prime minister of Japan, and Olaf Palme of Sweden. He had a clear directive for Kennedy, to be conveyed to the appropriate officials within the administration: for a period of sixty days following the announcement of a peace agreement, the countries who protested the Christmas bombing were to be frozen out from any presidential communications or acknowledgments. If Trudeau, for example, sent a note congratulating the United States on the peace accords, his message was to be ignored. "We say absolutely nothing," Nixon said. None of the ambassadors from these countries were to be allowed in or near the White House. There would be no exceptions, not even for friendly ambassadors. "No man can separate himself from his government," Nixon said. The State Department was to issue no courtesy notes, such as "The President appreciated . . ."

"This is not being vindictive," he explained to Kennedy. "What I am trying to do is build a little respect for a future time. You just can't have this sort of thing." Nixon said that Kissinger was right when he said these nations treated their allies like their enemies. The only exception, he said, was the Italians. They had, Nixon said, "a terrible left-wing problem," and risked the downfall of their government if they had not criticized the bombing. They could be treated "a little differently," whatever that meant.[12]

Kennedy's cable went out immediately to Kissinger and his team in Paris.[13]

Kissinger wrote back that night. "We had another very productive day, as Tho and I met for six hours and the experts continued work simultaneously on the protocols." The two men privately discussed the schedule, and Tho insisted that the initialing be set for January 23. The details of how to announce everything would depend on Thieu. But two things emerged as certain: Kissinger would be in Washington for the inaugural and he would fly back out to initial the agreements in Paris on Monday, January 22.[14]

The American-Owned Villa, La Fontaine au Blanc, in the Paris Suburb of Saint-Nom-la-Bretèche, Saturday, January 13, 1973

Henry Kissinger was in a giddy mood. Perhaps he was punch-drunk. The negotiations had been long and hard, with fourteen- and fifteen-hour days, but when he and his advisors met with Le Duc Tho and his team on Saturday morning, January 13, Kissinger knew he was going to be on a plane back to the United States at 7:00 PM that night, no matter what. They were in the final stretch and he sounded at times more like a stand-up comedian than a negotiator who was ending a long, bloody war.

"Ambassador Sullivan said to me last night that we are running into a terrible dilemma for negotiators," Kissinger started the meeting. "Even with our cantankerous nature we are running out of issues. And we may be doomed to come to an agreement today."[15]

Later in explaining a proposed change to some language, Kissinger said, "I have one other clause, which we agreed to yesterday but of which we are extremely proud because it turns a very simple idea into unbelievably complex language."

Still at another point: "But will the Special Advisor read the article?" Kissinger asked Tho. "We are very proud of it. I want to assign it to my students. It is drawn from the German Constitution of 1871."[16]

There were some picayune issues to iron out, but one major topic had been held for this final meeting: the American commitment to pay for war damage. It was a touchy subject, filled with political, symbolic, and historical overtones. The payments could not be called "reparations." Nor could they be seen as extortion payments demanded by the North Vietnamese. The payments were to be couched in terms of "healing of war wounds" and "America's traditional policy of benevolence." But none of it could be written in detail in the accords. Kissinger said, "We cannot sign a protocol and cannot even exchange messages before this agreement is complete."[17]

What the Americans proposed was a diplomatic message, to be delivered several weeks after the accords were signed. So there would be no surprises, Kissinger read the text of the note he planned to bring to Hanoi after the agreements had been executed. Most of it was uncontroversial, but two parts of the draft note abruptly turned the cordial atmosphere deadly serious. The first was a provision that the availability of the necessary funds would be subject to annual appropriations by the US Congress. The second was a paragraph that promised that the funds would "fall in the range of $3 billion over five years." Neither of these stipulations was acceptable to Le Duc Tho.

He did not care about Congress or its appropriation process—that, he said, was an internal affair for the United States. "How to get the money is up to you," he said, "and we need not have it in this writing." Kissinger patiently explained that when it came to the appropriation of money, congressional approval was a matter of the US Constitution. Moreover, as a practical matter, if the note ever became public, Congress would oppose it if its prerogative had not been clearly delineated and respected.

Tho still opposed it.

And he found $3 billion over five years to be insufficient. "The amount is smaller than the amount we proposed to you," Tho said. He also insisted on a clause that said "without repayment."

"No one else has ever repaid us," Kissinger cracked, trying to break the mounting tension in the room. "I don't know why you should be the first."

Tho, the dedicated revolutionary, walked right past the attempt at humor. "The words 'without repayment' imply your obligation to heal our war wounds," he came right back.

Kissinger turned grim. It was time to lecture Tho with a jab at his lack of understanding of the basics of the American political structure.

"After the Special Advisor has taught his course at Harvard and studied the American political system, he will understand the following: In the conduct of foreign policy the power of the Congress to influence the day-to-day operation is different than what it is when the expenditure of money is involved." Congress held the power of the purse, and no commitment could be made about aid or postwar assistance without recognizing its prerogative in the area.[18]

The lecture fell on deaf ears. Tho freely admitted his ignorance of the American political system and remained unyielding. Moreover, he argued, Kissinger had twice promised the language "without repayment."

Kissinger started to respond but decided it was best to table further debate. "It doesn't really make any difference," he said. "The question is, what can we say in a note to you? Let me reflect about your point and I will transmit a proposal through Ambassador Sullivan."

Tho wasn't yet ready to relent and insisted on summing up his position. "The points that we are concerned about is, first, the amount of money that should have been greater because the recent bombing caused a great deal of loss. Two, the point on no repayment. Three, the question of the Congress."

Kissinger held his fire. "I will say this," Kissinger said drolly, "it is harder to give away $3 billion to you than anyone we have ever dealt with."[19]

The quip seemed to neutralize things. For the first time since the negotiations began, Kissinger and Tho, along with their advisors, sat down to a luncheon together. No one could miss the symbolism.

By day's end, Kissinger and Tho exchanged solemn remarks as it neared 5:00 PM, Paris time, and Kissinger had to leave for the airport. "We are parting now in a very successful moment," Tho said. "What I have been telling you today, I will honor it." Kissinger said. "There have been many agreements in Indochina that have only been interludes in warfare. This should be an agreement that marks the beginning of genuine peace."[20]

It would be peace with honor after all.

Key Biscayne, Florida, January 13 to 14, 1973

Kissinger took off from Paris at the scheduled time, but his ultimate destination was no longer Washington. He would stop there only briefly to pick up Al Haig and then would head for Florida. Nixon had insisted that the two join him in Key Biscayne, where he had flown on Friday afternoon, January 12. The morning before he left for Florida, Nixon fussed with Haldeman that they had to keep Kissinger in Florida for the entire week; he could hold his business meetings there and engage in "his social stuff" in Miami. As Haldeman noted in his diary, "We have to keep the focus on Florida and with the P through the week, so he's got to stay there this time."[21]

Kissinger was not pleased about it. He cabled Colonel Kennedy that he had to be back in Washington for necessary meetings the first part of the week after reporting to the president in Florida. But recognizing that his desires may not matter much in the circumstance, Kissinger wrote dejectedly to Kennedy: "For Key Biscayne, I will need the proper clothes." He asked the colonel to "arrange to have sent down [to Key Biscayne] some sport clothes which are in the right hand closet [of Kissinger's West Wing office], the one closest to the window, and my bathing suit in the lower left hand drawer of my bureau. . . . Also there is a wide belt in the upper right hand drawer."[22]

One needed proper attire to end a war.

Nixon stayed up late Saturday into the wee hours of Sunday, January 14, to greet Kissinger and Haig when they arrived. He and Bebe Rebozo waited in the tropical breezes at the Key Biscayne compound helipad for two men. The helicopter carrying Kissinger and Haig from the nearby Homestead Air Force Base finally touched down at 1:15 AM. Back at the president's residence, they talked until 2:30 in the morning, going over the negotiations. Kissinger had been up for more than twenty-four hours.

In his diary, Nixon wrote that he walked Kissinger out to his car after the debriefing and "told him that the country was indebted to him for what he had done." This almost intimate interaction was highly unusual for Nixon, by his own admission. He wrote that "it was not really a comfortable feeling for me to praise people so openly," but he thought Kissinger expected it, "and it was good that I did so." According to Nixon, Kissinger in turn warmly responded that "without my having, as he put it, the courage to make the difficult decision of December 18, we would not be where we are today."[23]

Kissinger remembered the encounter in a similar vein. "That strange man," he wrote in *White House Years*, "who could be so ruthless, fierce and devious in defending his turf was capable of considerable gentleness in his personal dealings." Kissinger saw this side of Nixon on this night. "Though I was unhappy with some of Nixon's actions toward me," he wrote, "though I objected to some of his tactics, I felt that night an odd tenderness toward him." Kissinger thought that Nixon was "entitled in an hour of triumph to the limelight." He wrote, "We spoke to each other in nearly affectionate terms, like veterans of bitter battles at a last reunion, even though we both sensed somehow that too much had happened between us to make the rest of the journey together."[24]

Later that day, Haig would fly out for Saigon with a letter from the president.

Nixon spent Sunday afternoon watching Super Bowl VII on television (it was played in Los Angeles) with his friend Bebe Rebozo.[25] The Miami Dolphins defeated Nixon's beloved Washington Redskins, 14–7, to complete the only perfect, undefeated season ever in the NFL, a mark of distinction that still stands today. It was a defensive struggle, with a safety, Jake Scott, winning the most valuable player award in recognition of his two interceptions of Billy Kilmer passes, including a clincher in the fourth quarter.

The game's most memorable moment came with less than three minutes to play in the fourth quarter. The Dolphins had dominated the game and led 14–0. A drive by the Dolphins stalled in the Redskins' territory and rather than punt the ball, Coach Don Shula decided to go for a forty-two-yard field goal to make it 17–0, a symbolic score for a team that would end the season with seventeen wins and no losses.

Things, however, went terribly wrong. Kicker Garo Yepremian, the former soccer player from Cyprus, kicked a low ball and it was blocked right back to him. Panicked, Yepremian scooped up the ball and started to run, but with an angry Redskins lineman bearing down on him, he decided it was a good time to attempt a forward pass. The ball slipped out of his tiny grip; it was batted and floated straight up in the air. It landed in the hands of Mike Bass of the Redskins, who ran it back for a touchdown, making the score 14–7 with just two minutes and seven seconds left to play.

Fortunately for Yepremian, the Dolphins' defense held and they won the game.

Because of the widening Watergate scandal, the Dolphins did not make the traditional celebratory visit to the White House later that summer. It wasn't until August 2013, forty years later, that they finally made the trip, at the request of President Barack Obama.[26]

14

"LBJ Got Very Hot"

The Oval Office, Week of January 8, 1973

He kept coming back to it. During the week that Henry Kissinger wrapped up negotiations in Paris, Richard Nixon grappled with the mushrooming Watergate scandal. With Hunt's guilty plea, Nixon knew that the burglars' trial was going to run its course, whatever that might be. There was little he could do to control it, beyond what he had already done with his clandestine and roundabout promises of executive clemency. His only hope in the court was that the remaining defendants would keep their mouths shut.

But the problem was becoming multiheaded. Nixon also had to be concerned about congressional investigations that Senators Mike Mansfield and Sam Ervin, among others, had fired up, largely in reaction to the Christmas bombings and the worry that too much unfettered power had been amassed in the executive. Nixon needed to find a way to turn off the Congress when it came to Watergate. But to do so—it was becoming increasingly clear—he would need to mount a frontal attack on his predecessor, Lyndon Johnson. This was a dicey business, especially since Nixon was simultaneously zeroing in on a peace agreement in Vietnam that would bring an end to what, in many respects, had been Mr. Johnson's ruinous war. The last thing he desired, as he moved toward his victory in Paris, was for former president Johnson to become alienated, or worse, furious and perhaps even pressed into a nasty counteroffensive.

But a certain desperation was starting to creep into the Oval Office, and desperate times called for desperate measures.

The strategy de jure to neutralize Congress on Watergate found its origin in Nixon's longstanding belief that his campaign plane had been bugged by LBJ during the 1968 election. Nixon said he had been so informed by J. Edgar Hoover himself, but Hoover was dead and Nixon could not be the source of the story. John Mitchell, too, had been told of the plane bugging by Hoover, but he also suffered from a credibility problem given the allegations that he played a central role in authorizing the Watergate break-in.

John Dean suggested to Bob Haldeman on Monday, January 8, that if some corroborating proof could be dredged up of the plane bugging, they could use it to force "Congress to investigate hanky-panky both in '68 and '72, rather than just letting them go to an investigation of '72 activities." The pressure created by the expanded inquiry, Dean reasoned, might cause Congress to back away from digging into Watergate, because it potentially could open Pandora's box for the Democrats.[1]

There were three people who might provide confirmation of the 1968 activities: LBJ himself, but that would never happen; George Christian, Johnson's press secretary, who replaced Bill Moyers in 1967;[2] and Cartha DeLoach of the FBI. George Christian was a conservative Texan who was sympathetic to the Nixon administration. Haldeman was friendly with Christian and asked him about the allegation of the plane bugging. According to Haldeman, Christian inquired of Johnson, who admitted it to him.

And then there was Cartha "Deke" DeLoach, the longtime assistant to J. Edgar Hoover, number three in the FBI (behind Hoover and Clyde Tolson). DeLoach was known to have been close to LBJ. Indeed, because of their personal relationship from Johnson's Senate days, LBJ asked Hoover to assign DeLoach as liaison to the White House in November 1963, immediately after the Kennedy assassination. To his credit, DeLoach oversaw vigorous FBI investigations into civil rights murders in the Deep South. But he also got caught up in Johnson's political intelligence investigations, which included domestic wiretappings of people like Martin Luther King Jr.[3]

Haldeman, Ehrlichman, and Nixon believed that DeLoach, at the request of LBJ, was the FBI official who actually oversaw the operation to bug Nixon's plane.

Nixon was greatly uncertain about what to do, so the topic kept popping up like a midsummer afternoon thunderstorm in the Texas hill country. If true, the revelation would hurt the FBI and Johnson, two things Nixon was loathe to do. "It's a hellava reflection on Johnson," he said to Haldeman and Ehrlichman. "It's a messy business."

But first things first. Mitchell needed to be consulted to see if he had any hard proof of the bugging and to see what DeLoach may have told him about it. DeLoach retired from the FBI in 1970, so he had served for a short time under Mitchell as attorney general, and the two men had developed a decent rapport. If some solid proof emerged, Nixon thought that maybe entreaties could be made to Hubert Humphrey or even Johnson himself to intervene behind the scenes to try to get the congressional Democrats to stand down on Watergate.[4]

Mitchell's response would come toward the end of the week.

Ceremonial Courtroom, US District Court for the District of Columbia, January 11 and 12, 1973

Judge Sirica took the bench on Thursday morning, January 11, the day after opening statements and Hunt's request to change his plea from not guilty to guilty. Sirica was in his glory. He read a prepared statement, going over the rules and cases that gave him the discretion to accept or not accept a plea. He quickly came to his ruling: "Mr. Hunt's request for leave to plead guilty, to Counts One, Two, and Eight only, is denied."[5]

Bittman was stunned. Hunt sat in disbelief.

"Will you file the opinion, Mr. Clerk?" Sirica blithely requested of his bailiff. "Anything further?" Sirica then asked, staring directly at Bittman.

Bittman had prepared for the worst, though he had hoped it wouldn't come to this. "Yes, Your Honor," he said in resignation. "In view of Your Honor's ruling, Mr. Hunt at this time respectfully asks leave of the Court to withdraw his plea of not guilty and plead guilty to Counts One, Two, Three, Four, Five, and Eight." As if to rub it in, Sirica inquired, "Those are *all* the counts he is charged in?" Bittman, probably biting his tongue, meekly replied, "Yes sir."

Sirica asked for Howard Hunt to come forward so he could question him. Hunt complied. Sirica began to walk through a series of standard questions, structured to ensure that a defendant like Hunt understood his constitutional rights, the waiver of those rights, and the potential consequences of the plea. Hunt would need to also affirm that he knowingly, voluntarily, and freely entered into the plea agreement without any side promises or inducements.

It was a long, tedious process, going over every count he had been charged with, reciting the elements of each, and pointing out the government's burden of proving each of these elements beyond a reasonable doubt. Hunt or Bittman, alternatively, responded in the affirmative to all of the questions.

Then Sirica, the old fox, surprised everyone when he tried to get Hunt to confess publicly to what had happened. "Now," Sirica said, "in your own words, I would like you to tell me from the beginning just how you got into this conspiracy, what you did, various things that you did, so I can decide whether or not you are knowingly and intentionally entering this plea voluntarily with full knowledge of the consequences." The inquiry was way out of bounds.

Bittman stepped in. He said Hunt was going to be called back before the grand jury after sentencing, given immunity by the prosecutors, and asked to tell what he knew. His statement now could prejudice that testimony. It could also prejudice the remaining defendants' right to a fair trial before Sirica.

Sirica saw the peril to Hunt's future grand jury testimony and to the remainder of the case, so he backed off.

Once the plea was accepted, Sirica decided to make an example of Hunt, lest the others entertain thoughts of changing their pleas. Hunt, he said, would be subject to $40,000 in fines and thirty years in prison. He was going to jail that day, where he would await sentencing. Only if he could come up with $100,000 for bond would he be freed. Bittman began to beg piteously. He spoke of Hunt's four children, the youngest nine years old, and of his humble financial situation as a long-serving government employee, and of the need to wind up his wife's affairs following her tragic death. Sirica responded, "I don't want to hear argument. You can argue until doomsday, but that is my decision. If you don't like it, you can go to the Court of Appeals."[6]

After Hunt was led away, counsel for the remaining defendants all moved for a mistrial. The court, they argued, knew prior to the start of proceedings that Hunt wanted to plead guilty and that he was willing to plead to all of the counts if necessary. If the court insisted on hearing an outline of the evidence the government intended to introduce against Hunt before taking the plea, Sirica could have severed Hunt's case, listened to the opening argument, and then taken the plea. This way, Hunt would not have been sitting through the opening for the jury to see.

Instead, as it transpired, the jury was left to speculate that Hunt pled guilty after hearing the evidence the government had collected against him. Since conspiracy charges were pending, the prejudice to the remaining defendants was obvious and magnified.

Sirica perfunctorily denied the motions.[7]

The trial started in earnest. Witnesses were finally called to the stand. Silbert and his team began with the arresting officers and some government technicians who authenticated photos of the Watergate and floor plans of the DNC. Things did not start hopping until the afternoon session, when Thomas Gregory, the Brigham Young University (BYU) student who infiltrated the Muskie and McGovern campaigns, was called by the government. Aside from coming off looking a bit too slick and like something of a snake—infiltrating a political campaign for money and seeking and receiving sixteen credit hours from BYU for the "off-campus experience"—Gregory was a meticulous and polite witness. He convincingly and positively identified Hunt, Liddy, McCord, and the Miamians as all being involved in the attempts to bug the McGovern headquarters.[8]

The big surprise came the next morning—a bolt from the blue.

Court convened as usual on Friday morning, January 12. Outside the hearing of the jury, Judge Sirica attended to some spillover questions from the day before and noted that the jury would have to be recessed for the morning so that the lawyers could argue discreet issues in the court of appeals on whether the government could introduce and use Alfred Baldwin's notes taken of private conversations overheard through wiretaps placed in the offices of the DNC headquarters.

And then, unexpectedly, the always-dapper Henry Rothblatt, who represented the four Miamians, stood up, interrupted everyone, and said, "Your Honor, may we approach the bench?" Sirica motioned the lawyers to come forward.

Rothblatt announced, "Your Honor, I just received a communication from my clients that apparently indicates there are some strong differences of opinion and that I probably am being discharged. I need a recess to confer with them."[9] Just prior to Rothblatt's revelation, one of his clients, Bernard Barker, a veteran from the Bay of Pigs and a man who told the press he would follow Howard Hunt "to hell and back," had walked up to prosecutor Earl Silbert and handed him a typewritten message, which Silbert refused to read.

The press was kept at a distance. "There were several conferences at the bench between the judge and the attorneys for both sides," a curious reporter for the *New York Times* wrote. "None of these could be heard. There was scarcely a word of public proceeding throughout a six-hour period."[10]

"What do you mean discharged?" Sirica asked in private. It was Earl Silbert's turn to interrupt. "May I make a representation?" he whispered. "Just thirty seconds ago I was handed a communication by Mr. Barker and I wish to have it marked as an exhibit of the Court and show it to Your Honor. I haven't read it myself but I do want to provide it to Your Honor." He handed it up.[11]

Sirica sealed the proceedings and told the court reporter to so mark the record that was about to be made. Sirica then quietly read aloud the letter. It was addressed to Henry Rothblatt, Attorney at Law, and it was from all four of his clients:

> Dear Mr. Rothblatt:
>
> We have been asking you since Sunday, January 7, 1973, to change our plea from not guilty to guilty. You have not complied with our request. We have made it clear from the beginning that the defense which you presented in your opening statement to the press is not acceptable to us.
>
> We respectfully inform you as of this date, January 12, 1973, you will no longer represent us. We intend to pay any reasonable fees presented by you. Please accept our sincere gratitude for your past services.
>
> /s/ Bernard L. Barker, Eugenio Martinez, Frank A. Sturgis, Virgilio R. Gonzalez[12]

Rothblatt had been sacked! One of the prosecutors, Seymour Glanzer, jumped in. "Your Honor, I think this problem has been faced before," he said. Glanzer contended that the defendants couldn't simply discharge their attorney and change horses "midstream." They could proceed pro se, that is, representing themselves, but, Glanzer continued, "I think they cannot dismiss Mr. Rothblatt. They can say they dismiss him but the Court can insist Mr. Rothblatt stay."[13]

Henry Rothblatt was crestfallen. He stumbled on what to say. He said that if his clients wanted to change their plea, they had the right to do so and didn't need him. "I don't know if I agree with you," Sirica replied. Sirica's reaction was that they could have discharged Rothblatt before trial began, but they couldn't now that trial was under way—and in any event, Sirica was not going to continue the trial for them to get a new lawyer.

Rothblatt said he couldn't, as a member of the bar, represent the men if they wanted to plead guilty—he simply didn't agree with the change in the plea. "If they want to get somebody else, do it," he said. "That is all right with me, but I cannot in good conscience get up before Your Honor and tell you my clients have met all constitutional requirements when they entered a plea of guilty." He practically whimpered: "I cannot do it; that is my position, and that is where the differences of opinion exist."

Glanzer probed, "Are you implying there is coercion?"

"I cannot comment," Rothblatt melodramatically responded. "I feel if I say anything beyond that I might be breaching a confidential communication."[14]

Sirica asked Rothblatt whether he thought that another lawyer could be appointed simply to advise the Miamians on changing their pleas. Rothblatt, continuing to insinuate his clients might be under duress, said, "I agree, Your Honor, as long as other counsel are satisfied that the plea is free and voluntary and meets all tests, but I cannot, knowing what I do, stand before Your Honor and do that, it would be a violation of my conscience and professional opinion."[15]

Sirica sent Rothblatt to talk with the Miamians while Silbert went down one floor in the courthouse to argue in the court of appeals. Sirica said he would think about replacement counsel for Mr. Rothblatt, if it came to that. Silbert did not fare well in his arguments. "A three-judge panel held, 2–1, that the Government could not disclose details of the information obtained in the alleged eavesdropping on the Democrats without the approval of the party officials who had been overheard," the newspapers reported.[16] Earl Silbert lost.

After the lunch break, they were back in the ceremonial courtroom. Once again, they approached the bench for a private talk with Judge Sirica. Rothblatt reported that he had come to a parting of the ways with the Miamians; there was no reconciling their positions. Sirica was flummoxed. He kept saying, "Wait just a minute," as if he needed things to slow down so he could get his hands around what to do next. He decided he wanted to question the Miamians himself, to "hear it from their lips." But no press would be allowed. He would recess to his regular courtroom on the second floor and hold proceedings in camera, with only lawyers and parties present. An interpreter was brought in.[17]

Once on the second floor, Frank Sturgis was the first of the Miamians to speak up. He asked for the court to appoint another attorney with whom he could discuss his plea. The others all agreed. Sirica began to call lawyers by phone from his courtroom. His first two selections were not available. On the third try he got his man: Alvin Newmyer Sr., an old acquaintance of Sirica's. "He said he could come down as soon as he can get a cab," Sirica reported. Ominously Sirica added about Newmyer, "At one time he was one of our outstanding trial lawyers, but he is more or less in the civil field." Whoever he was, he apparently had little experience as a criminal lawyer and perhaps was nearing retirement.[18]

When Alvin Newmyer arrived, it must have shocked the Miamians. He was nearly ninety years old. Sirica proudly introduced him. "Now, for the record," he said, "and because some of the counsel present may not know you and know of your reputation like I do, I want to say that your are one of our most respected and outstanding lawyers."

As an aside to Newmyer, Sirica said, "I don't know where we will get your fee from. We are going to have to work that out."

Sirica pulled out his copy of the lawyer directory and reference book, *Martindale-Hubbell*, and began to read the entry for Alvin Newmyer. Born in 1884 (on January 9, exactly twenty-nine years before Richard Nixon's birthday in 1913), he served on a special legal committee for the draft in World War I. Most of his awards and distinctions dated back to the 1930s and trailed off during the 1950s, when he was nearing seventy years of age. Sirica didn't seem the least fazed by Newmyer's advanced age. "You can tell your clients," he cheerily said to Rothblatt after reading the *Martindale-Hubbell* bio, "they are getting a very fine, experienced, and excellent lawyer."[19]

Mr. Newmyer was given a crash course by Judge Sirica in what had transpired in the trial to date and the Hunt plea. Sirica made it clear he would be equally tough on the Miamians—they had to plead to all the counts, and they would be sent immediately to jail. Earl Silbert graciously offered to brief Mr. Newmyer on the evidence, if he was interested. Rothblatt said that he didn't think the consultation between Mr. Newmyer and the Miamians would be all that involved. "I think they only have one request," Rothblatt predicted, "that after they confer with Mr. Newmyer that they be given at least until Monday to enter the plea. In other words, they would like to have the weekend to clean up their affairs."

Alvin Newmyer would have the weekend to study up and decide what to do with all four of his new clients. The case would be continued until 11:00 AM Monday, because Mr. Newmyer told the court he could not make it in before 10:00 AM. Rothblatt, relieved of his duties, advised the court that he needed to scoot back to his home in New York City for the weekend to be with his wife and family. "Otherwise," he said, "I may have a divorce proceeding on my hands or some similar proceeding." He would of course be available by phone to consult with Mr. Newmyer.

At the end of the day on Friday, January 12, the jury was brought back into the courtroom. "I am sorry we were unable to make any headway to amount to anything today," Judge Sirica told them. "This case will be continued until 11:00 Monday morning, at which time we hope to get started and I hope you have a nice weekend."[20]

The Oval Office, Thursday, January 11

The president met with his chief of staff at around 10:30 in the Oval Office, and the tapes were rolling. Nixon wanted to follow up on the question of the 1968 bugging of his campaign plane by the FBI at President Lyndon Johnson's request.

> Nixon: "Have you had any further development, Bob, with regard to the bugging at the—I mean, with regard to Mitchell and his talks with DeLoach? Did he have them? Do you know?"
>
> Haldeman: "Yes, he talked to DeLoach."
>
> Nixon: "Did DeLoach deny it?"
>
> Haldeman: "No, DeLoach says it's true, and that he has hard evidence, or some specifics that will lock the thing up."
>
> Nixon: "Will he say so?"
>
> Haldeman: "I don't know whether he'll say so, but he'll give us the information so that we can say so, and that's all we need."

Nixon disagreed. He didn't want this to become a game of hearsay. "Bob, I want it from DeLoach," he said. "We know he knows, he was in charge of that, you know. Probably still is in the Bureau; a bugger." He proposed to have Pat Gray, the acting director of the FBI since Hoover's death, administer a lie detector test to DeLoach or whoever was involved in installing the taps. "I'd like to do it so that it's nailed down in terms of evidence," Nixon said, "rather than that DeLoach told Mitchell, or that Hoover, [now] a dead man, told Mitchell, because Johnson will lie about this if necessary."[21]

Haldeman said that John Dean had another idea of how to take advantage of DeLoach's admission. He suggested using the information on Johnson himself in the hope that LBJ would bring in people like Joseph Califano, a Johnson administration cabinet member and one of the lawyers in the civil suit brought by the Democrats against the Committee to Re-Elect the President, who could encourage members on the Hill to kill the Watergate inquiry before it began.

"Why doesn't someone go down and tell Johnson?" Nixon asked bluntly.

Haldeman, who enjoyed thinking out loud with Nixon, suggested a more subtle way to handle it. Because a rumor was circulating that the *Washington Star* was back on the trail of this story—the newspaper had first reported it during the 1972 campaign, to little note—it made sense to let the *Star* article come out first. "That'll stir Johnson up," Haldeman predicted, "and that gives us a little way to get back to Johnson on that basis that, you know, we've got to get this [the Watergate investigation] turned off, because it's going to bounce back to the other story [the 1968 plane bugging], and we can't hold them."[22]

But by the next morning, Friday, January 12, Nixon was starting to worry that his ploy might boomerang. "Could he come after me?" he asked Haldeman about Johnson.[23] The risk was that Johnson might reveal his strong suspicion that the Nixon campaign in 1968 had submarined his peace initiative through a "subterranean" maneuver with Anna Chen Chennault, the China lobbyist and widow of famed US Army Air Force Major General Claire Lee Chennault of the Flying Tigers. Madame Chennault (who lived at the Watergate) purportedly got word to President Thieu through Bui Diem, Thieu's ambassador in Washington, to resist President Johnson's October 1968 attempts in Paris to get the South Vietnamese to join the talks already under way with the North Vietnamese to end the war.[24]

The question was, did the Nixon camp send the message through Madame Chennault?

LBJ believed so. In Haldeman's diary for January 12, 1973, he noted that he called John Mitchell that day to talk further about the DeLoach matter. It appears Johnson had already been contacted by the *Washington Star* about the story. "I talked to Mitchell on the phone on this subject," Haldeman wrote, "and he said DeLoach had told him that he was up to date on the thing because he had a call from Texas. A *Star* reporter was making an inquiry in the last week or so, and LBJ got very hot and called Deke, and said to him that if the Nixon people are going to play with this, that he would release [*deleted material—national security*], saying that our side was asking for certain things to be done. By our side, I assume he means the Nixon campaign organization."

Haldeman continued, "DeLoach took this as a direct threat from Johnson. He says he'll bring his file in on Monday for Mitchell to review. As he recalls it, bugging was requested on the planes, but was turned down, and all they did was check the phone calls, and put a tap on the Dragon Lady (Mrs. Anna Chennault)."[25]

What Nixon and Haldeman didn't know was that "hard evidence" of Johnson's wiretaps and surveillance did exist, in the form of taped telephone conversations between LBJ and several people, including Deke DeLoach, during October and November 1968.[26] These conversations were recorded on Dictabelts that LBJ had put away in the Federal Records Center at the National Archives after he left the White House. Johnson intended for the tapes to remain secret for fifty years following his death, which should have been until 2023.[27]

The boxes containing the tapes were quietly turned over to the LBJ Library a week after Johnson's death and only came to light decades later, after Oliver Stone's 1991 film *JFK* resulted in congressional legislation mandating the release of all government files related to the assassination.[28] Once the seal of secrecy was broken, the LBJ Library eventually decided to release transcripts of the remaining tapes over time.[29]

Two tapes, recorded a week after Nixon's election, on November 12 and 13, 1968, provide the "hard evidence" of the 1968 campaign plane activity that Nixon was searching for, though it was not his plane that was bugged. On the tapes, Johnson and DeLoach discuss the Johnson administration's surveillance of Spiro Agnew's chartered campaign plane while it idled at the airport in Albuquerque, New Mexico, on November 2, 1968, three days before the election.

The backstory of the DeLoach tapes starts with the Johnson administration's wiretapping of the South Vietnamese Embassy in Washington during October 1968. LBJ was monitoring the communications between Saigon and its embassy in Washington.[30] On November 2, the government intercepted a call that indicated that Madame

Chennault had told the South Vietnamese ambassador that she had "just heard from [her] boss in Albuquerque who [said] his boss [said] [they were] going to win." According to the transcript, she added, "And tell your boss to hold on a while longer."[31]

At first, the Johnson administration suspected that Chennault's call was the result of a direct communication between Chennault and Nixon, but it turned out he was not in Albuquerque on that day. Spiro Agnew, though, was in Albuquerque for a brief campaign stop on November 2.

After the election, LBJ asked DeLoach to check on calls made from Agnew's plane that day.

A day later, DeLoach responded that the FBI had information that one of the phones on the Agnew plane was used to make five calls from the Albuquerque airport. It appears that the FBI did not record the conversations, but monitored to whom the calls were placed using the telephone company records of the calls that were made.[32]

The records showed that around noon on November 2, Agnew called then–secretary of state Dean Rusk, who filled him in on the most recent negotiations in Paris and progress in getting the South Vietnamese to Paris. Rusk noted the call back in Washington and later told LBJ about it.[33] An hour later, a call was placed from Agnew's plane to the Nixon/Agnew campaign headquarters at the Willard Hotel in Washington. Johnson and DeLoach both believed that either Anna Chennault took the call from Agnew at Nixon's campaign headquarters or someone else did and then reported it to her. Later that day, she passed on the message to the South Vietnamese ambassador in his Washington embassy to tell Thieu to "hold on a while longer."[34] As Johnson told DeLoach, "She got the message from Albuquerque. That's logical that he [Agnew] was the one [who] gave it, because he called Rusk, that's what we thought, because that's the only way he could get information to give her, from Rusk."[35]

If true—and it seems likely, given all the circumstantial evidence—this activity by the Nixon camp completely undercut the Johnson administration's negotiations in Paris, which after long, hard months had resulted in an agreement by Le Duc Tho and the North Vietnamese to accept South Vietnam's direct participation in the Paris talks, provided the United States stopped all bombing in Vietnam. When Thieu would not go to Paris, LBJ halted the bombing nonetheless, because he felt he had made a deal. The failure of these talks ensured that the appalling conflict and loss of life would go on for an indefinite period of time. Johnson told Everett Dirksen on the evening of November 2 that he considered the actions of Nixon's campaign to be "treason."[36]

Ironically, four years later, Nixon was trying to find ways to use the Johnson wiretaps and surveillance to obstruct the growing Watergate investigation at the very moment Nixon was finally bringing the bloody war to its ambiguous conclusion. The prospect of revisiting this damaging past caused Nixon to develop cold feet on the whole topic. Upon reflection, Nixon determined that he was the one who had too much to lose by revealing what he thought were Johnson's nefarious activities in 1968.

Andrews Air Force Base, Friday, January 12, 1973

After attending a reception for a Chinese acrobatic troupe in the State Dining Room, the president and the First Lady went to the South Grounds of the White House at 3:30 PM to step aboard a helicopter to take them to Andrews Air Force Base. After a seven-minute flight, Nixon and his party, including Ray Price, his speechwriter, transferred onto the *Spirit of '76*, the name given Air Force One, to take off for Florida.[37]

Nixon was withdrawing to write his second inaugural address.

That same afternoon, Walter Cronkite of CBS News sat down with Lyndon Johnson at his ranch in Texas to talk about civil rights and Johnson's legacy.

With exactly ten days to live, Johnson gave what would become known as "the Last Interview."

15

"And We Shall Overcome"

LBJ Ranch, Johnson City, Texas, Friday, January 12, 1973

Dressed in casual clothes, including a rust-colored open shirt, with his hair brushed straight back and hanging in long curls over his collar, Lyndon B. Johnson looked more like an old Texas ranch hand than a former President of the United States. He stared through thick eyeglasses at Walter Cronkite, who was there to talk about Johnson's record on civil rights. Johnson shifted back and forth in his chair as the two-hour interview progressed. His breathing was slightly labored and he intermittently grunted and snorted, sounding as if he was getting over a nasty cold. Walter Cronkite, in coat and tie, thought the former president appeared ill.

"He looked like he was not in the best of health," Cronkite later said.[1]

LBJ had agreed to a series of television interviews with CBS shortly after he left the presidency. The first was filmed in July 1969, eleven days before Apollo 11 took off for the moon. This interview covered Johnson's contributions to the space program and was scheduled to air on the day that Neil Armstrong and Buzz Aldrin landed on the moon, which turned out to be the same weekend of Teddy Kennedy's car accident at Chappaquiddick. Though financial terms for the TV series were not disclosed, it had been reported that Johnson had signed a whopping $1.5 million deal with a CBS-owned publishing house for his memoirs.[2]

The interview on January 12, 1973, was the fifth and final in the series. The topic of civil rights had always been on the agenda, but Cronkite found that it fit nicely with a civil rights symposium that the Johnson Library and the University of Texas had convened a month earlier in Austin.

Too many things had gone wrong for LBJ as president, but civil rights was one of his major, though controversial, areas of accomplishment. This interview promised to be a cakewalk compared to interviews on Vietnam and his decision not to run in 1968. Yet it proved to be physically exhausting.

His presidency had been born out of violence—the unthinkable assassination of a popular and youthful president, a "cruel and shocking act," as Chief Justice Warren's commission labeled it. The grief and trauma for the nation proved nearly unbearable. The deep psychic injury never mended. One scholar, Max Holland, has posited that Johnson was driven from office as much by the shadow cast by Kennedy's assassination as by Vietnam. He carried with him a lingering sense that the nation never truly accepted the legitimacy of his presidency. He also feared that he was vulnerable within his own party, increasingly so as 1968 drew near, especially to a challenge from Robert Kennedy, who, Johnson knew, saw him as a pretender to the office. "The assassination was a wound in the body politic that had never healed, and was not being allowed to," Holland wrote.[3]

President Johnson, Walter Cronkite, Bud Benjamin, and Jewell Malechek while filming a CBS special, December 1971.

LBJ Library photo by Frank Wolfe

In his second interview with Walter Cronkite—this one in September 1969—LBJ spoke of the Kennedy assassination and in an unguarded moment said, "I can't honestly say that I had ever been completely relieved of the fact that there might have been international connections." Johnson had become convinced over time—based on briefings by the CIA and the FBI—that the Kennedy-backed CIA plans to assassinate Castro, with mafia help, after the failed Bay of Pigs, had provoked a retaliatory move by Castro against JFK. He remained reluctant, however, to go public with his doubts. After the Cronkite interview, and under pressure from advisors, LBJ asked CBS to remove the part of the interview in which he spoke of his suspicions of international involvement in the assassination, and CBS reluctantly complied. According to LBJ friend and legal advisor Arthur Krim, Walter Cronkite "blew his stack but deleted it."[4] Johnson later told Leo Janos, a Houston journalist who worked for *Time* magazine, that he "never believed that Oswald acted alone, although I can accept that he pulled the trigger." Johnson said to Janos that when he took office, "we had been operating a damned Murder, Inc. in the Caribbean." Janos did not print Johnson's remark until after he was dead.[5]

The same sense of drama did not accompany Johnson's final interview with Cronkite in January 1973.

The interview began with a look back at the recent civil rights symposium in Austin. The conclave had been organized to mark the opening of Johnson's civil rights papers and was held in the auditorium of the Lyndon Baines Johnson Library on the campus of the University of Texas in Austin (where Larry Hammond and Sarah Weddington had gone to law school). "What is left of the civil rights establishment of the nineteen-sixties gathered here today to celebrate the opening of former President Johnson's rights papers and to urge President Nixon to assume in his second term the leadership of a renewed movement for minority rights," the *New York Times* described the opening day of the event in an article datelined December 12, 1972.[6]

Despite a doctor's orders and a severe ice storm that hit central Texas, LBJ and Lady Bird Johnson drove over from their ranch to attend both days of the conference. Former chief justice of the United States Earl Warren, "ruddy-faced and in high spirits," was also on hand. Vice President Hubert Humphrey; Vernon Jordan, executive director of the National Urban League; an aging Roy Wilkins of the NAACP; newly elected Texas congresswoman Barbara Jordan (who would later serve on the House Judiciary Committee's impeachment investigation of Watergate); and other civil rights luminaries all came to Austin. "It's been more years than I care to count," Hubert Humphrey said on the first day, "since such a group of national leaders have come together in something called a civil rights symposium."[7]

Humphrey called on Nixon to "confound his critics," as he had done with his China initiative and dramatic trips to the Soviet Union, by seizing the initiative on the civil rights front. "A second-term president must begin to think seriously about the historical judgments of his Administration," Humphrey said. "And I can imagine no more harsh indictment than his having failed to lead the United States in the most critical and urgent area of domestic concern."

Earl Warren issued a sideways knock of the Nixon administration with a reference to the term "benign neglect," an allusion to a strategy urged upon Nixon by advisor Daniel Patrick Moynihan at the beginning of his first term. But Warren was not all downbeat. Pointing to the ice storm that necessitated the busing of most of the guests to the Johnson Library, the former chief justice joked, "My wife and I did not object to being bussed, and I hope we never will if it is in the interests of civil rights."[8]

Buried beneath the plaudits for LBJ on this day was the painful history of his break with so many of the top civil rights leaders, including Dr. Martin Luther King Jr., over the war in Vietnam. Nixon's Christmas bombing campaign was still a week away, and Vietnam didn't even register a ripple at the conference. "It was not unlike a college reunion," the *Times* writer observed, "and no one mentioned the sourness and disappointment that crept into the rights movement after Mr. Johnson stepped up American participation in Vietnam with the resources that rights leaders contended should go to domestic causes."[9]

On the second day, Tuesday, December 12, it was Lyndon Johnson's time to speak, and he slowly rose and shuffled up the six steps to the stage to deliver what were supposed to be the closing remarks of the symposium. He plainly struggled to get to the rostrum and once there spoke in a labored, muted voice. "All is not lost," he started, leaning heavily on the podium. "All has not been in vain. All we have to do is kinda reorganize and reevaluate; and Rome wasn't built in a day; and we can't overcome all the injustices or make this a perfect world overnight." Then, looking up and squinting his eyes, he smiled and said to his audience in his intimate way, "But we are on our way, and we are going to do just that before it's over." The crowd applauded loudly.[10]

"I don't speak very often, nor very long," he continued rather weakly. "My doctor admonished me not to speak at all this morning, but I am going to do that because I have some things I want to say to you."

He didn't need to verbalize it; it was obvious that at sixty-four he was spent.

Eight months earlier, on a trip to visit his daughter Lynda and son-in-law Charles Robb in Charlottesville, Virginia, where Robb was attending law school, Johnson had suffered a major heart attack.[11] Seventeen years before that, in July 1955, when he was forty-six, Johnson had his first heart attack, only a year after becoming the Senate majority leader.[12] He was hospitalized in 1955 for a month and then recuperated for the balance of the year "on his rocking chair" at his ranch in Texas. At the time, Johnson had smoked sixty cigarettes a day, but he gave them up, more or less, until his retirement from the presidency. Lady Bird Johnson acknowledged to the press the day after his heart attack in Virginia that her husband had indeed resumed his smoking habit in the fall of 1971. Dr. John Willis Hurst, LBJ's heart specialist in 1955 and 1972, was asked in April 1972 whether he would try to make Johnson quit smoking permanently. Hurst's response: "Just say we're negotiating at this point." He gave Johnson "an 80 percent chance of recovery."[13]

His advanced congestive heart failure was unmistakable at the December symposium. During the middle of one of his sentences, Johnson reached into his pocket, which held a stash of nitroglycerin pills, and deftly popped one into his mouth so discreetly that most in the audience probably didn't notice it. He was in great distress, but he persevered, slowly and steadfastly.

He said, "Of all the records that are housed in this library—thirty-one million papers over a forty-year period of public life—it is the record of this work that we've been discussing for the last two days which holds the most of myself within it, and holds for me the most intimate meanings." Johnson had spent some of his formative years as a young man teaching at a segregated school for Mexican American children in rural Texas. This experience and that of having Mexican American playmates when he was a child were pivotal. He gradually came to understand, he said, that the special plight of the "black" man included the "brown" and "yellow" and "red" and "all other people who suffer discrimination because of their color or their heritage." His awakening, he admitted, came slowly over an extended period of time, but it advanced to its full luminosity during his presidency.

He added, "I believe that the essence of government lies with the unceasing concern for the welfare and dignity and decency and innate integrity of life for every individual."

LBJ told the audience that upstairs from where they were sitting, in a special exhibit designed especially for that occasion, lay the original Emancipation Proclamation, signed by Abraham Lincoln. Johnson recalled that ten years prior to the symposium, on Memorial Day 1963, he had been asked to speak at the Gettysburg cemetery to commemorate the hundredth anniversary of the great battle and the Emancipation Proclamation. At the time he was the vice president and almost passed on the opportunity, so depressed and disinterested was he with what he saw as his otherwise useless job. But with his staff's urging, he went and gave a speech that many now believe to be one of the more important speeches in the civil rights movement, because it caused LBJ to think long and hard about a seething issue that he would soon enough have to deal with as President of the United States.[14]

He reminded the participants of the conference of his words a decade earlier at Gettysburg, before all the changes of the 1960s. "Until justice is blind to color," he had said in 1963 while standing near where Lincoln once stood, "until education is unaware of race, until opportunity is unconcerned with the color of men's skin, emancipation will be a proclamation, but not a fact. To the extent that the proclamation of emancipation is not fulfilled in fact, to that extent, we have fallen short of assuring freedom to the free."

He specifically took the opportunity in 1963 to respond to Martin Luther King's open "Letter from Birmingham Jail," written a few months earlier on April 16, 1963. From jail, King questioned the pace of change and the advice of some of his fellow clergymen who counseled "Wait!" "The Negro today asks justice," Johnson said at Gettysburg. "We do not answer him—we do not answer those who lie beneath this soil—when we reply to the Negro by asking, 'Patience.' It is empty to plead that the solution to the dilemmas of the present rests on the hands of the clock."

He said that when he spoke those words, he "could not know that the future would present [him] shortly with the opportunity and the responsibility to contribute more toward fulfilling *the fact* of emancipation."

Even if he could have known what lay ahead, he said, he would never have dreamed of the progress that would be won. In 1964, after a lengthy filibuster by some of LBJ's closest friends in the Senate, he orchestrated the passage of the Civil Rights Act of 1964, a towering milestone outlawing voter literacy tests and discrimination in public accommodations and in employment practices, and encouraging the desegregation of public schools through the filing of suits by the attorney general of the United States. A year later, after several voter registration marches in Alabama turned violent, with "Bloody Sunday" and the attempt to cross the Edmund Pettus Bridge in Selma, Alabama, Congress passed the Voting Rights Act of 1965. And in 1968 Johnson urged, and Congress passed, the Civil Rights Act of 1968, which dealt with equal housing opportunities.

For many Americans the progress was too fast and too disruptive, paving the way for Richard Nixon to exploit the anger and fear that resulted from the intense backlash. But Johnson thought it had not been enough. "I'm kind of ashamed of myself that I had six years and couldn't do more than I did," he said to the people gathered in Austin.

What Johnson recognized was that African Americans were fighting history. "We cannot obscure the blunt fact," he said, that "the black problem remains what it has always been: the simple problem of being black in a white society." The history of the nation left a staggering imbalance of power between the races. "To be black in a white society is not to stand on equal ground. While the races may stand side by side, whites stand on history's mountain and blacks stand in history's hollow. Until we overcome unequal history, we cannot overcome unequal opportunity."

A huge college football fan, Johnson crafted a football analogy to try to illustrate his point. "Not a white American in all this land would fail to be outraged if an opposing team tried to insert a twelfth man in their football line-up to stop a black fullback on the football field," he said. "Yet off the field, away from the stadium, outside the reach of the television cameras and the watching eyes of millions of their fellow men, every black American in this land—man or woman—plays out life running against the twelfth man of a history that they did not make and a fate that they did not choose."

It is not hard to imagine that Lyndon Johnson understood that this might be his last great public address and a final opportunity to talk about the one issue that he said held "the most of myself within it." Those closest to him at the LBJ Ranch knew that he was keenly aware

Lyndon B. Johnson speaking at the Civil Rights Symposium at the LBJ Library on December 12, 1972.

LBJ Library photo by Frank Wolfe

of the history of Johnson men dropping dead before they reached their sixties. "I think that was his biggest worry," Jewell Malechek Scott told a historian at the LBJ Library in 1978. "I think he knew he was going to have to make his days count." Scott, her late husband Dale Malechek, and their children had lived on the LBJ Ranch with the Johnsons from the time he was vice president. Dale tended to the cattle and Jewell became LBJ's principal secretary in retirement. "I think he was worried about Mrs. Johnson," she said. "He wanted her to be able to take care of herself, and his children." Jewell saw his increasing infirmity and his planning for those he would leave behind. "I think basically he was trying to get everybody aware of the fact that there were a lot of things they were going to have to do for themselves."[15]

His final remarks at the Austin symposium echoed what was probably his greatest speech as president. Delivered on March 15, 1965, to a joint session of Congress a week following the Selma uprisings, Johnson said, "I speak tonight for the dignity of man and the destiny of democracy." He called to mind the American Revolution and the Civil War, as if to emphasize his plea for a new rights revolution, a second reconstruction: "At times history and fate meet at a single time in a single place to shape a turning point in man's unending search for freedom. So it was at Lexington and Concord. So it was a century ago at Appomattox. So it was last week in Selma, Alabama."

His speechwriter, Richard Goodwin (who later married Doris Kearns Goodwin), said he had less than twelve hours to work up his draft. He inserted a line from the spiritual anthem of the civil rights movement, resulting in the speech's emotional signature. "Their cause must be our cause too," Johnson said. "Because it is not just Negroes, but really it is all of us, who must overcome the heritage of bigotry and injustice. *And we shall overcome.*" The reaction in the House chamber was overwhelming. The speech was interrupted more than thirty times with torrents of applause and several times with standing ovations. Martin Luther King Jr. reportedly broke down and wept while watching the speech on television.[16]

At Austin, Johnson finished his talk with the same flourish. "We know how much still remains to be done," he said. "And if our efforts continue, and if our will is strong, and if our hearts are right, and if courage remains our constant companion, then, my fellow Americans, I am confident, we shall overcome."[17]

Lyndon B. Johnson and Richard Goodwin, April 1965.
LBJ Library

It should have been fade to black, but there were some unexpected fireworks to come. Two activists, Reverend A. Kendall Smith of the New York City Task Force on Racism, and Roy C. Innis of Texas, demanded the right to speak, mainly over anger at the Nixon administration's hostility toward the Great Society's programs and the gains of the civil rights movement. "The former President had delivered a prepared speech at the close of the two-day meeting and had taken his seat in the audience when a dispute broke out on the floor between separatists and integrationists," the *Times* reported.

Johnson immediately reacted, assuming the role he knew so well in public life: that of mediator. He let the men speak and then came to Nixon's defense. He encouraged the group to reason together and come up with a set of goals to present to President Nixon. Nixon would listen, he told them. In the Cronkite interview, Johnson explained why he thought reasoned debate was the better alternative to confrontational politics.[18] "Now I don't think you're going to be very effective," he said, "if you say the Congress is no good and antiquated and ought to get it out of the way, and the cabinet officer is dishonest and won't do anything about it, and the president can't read and write and he's no good." Johnson said such tactics were bound to fail. "Because none of those people—you can't sell them that argument. They don't believe that. They think they are good and are doing the best they can and they want to do what's right."[19]

The crisis avoided, the symposium came to a peaceful conclusion and, according to the *Times*, "adjourned in harmony." An exhausted LBJ headed for his ranch.[20] But a mood of pessimism, and "a sense of sadness for what might have been," was the takeaway for many who attended.[21]

Exactly a month to the day later, when LBJ sat down with Walter Cronkite, he was again smoking heavily—two to three packs a day. "Apparently doctors had said he was so nervous without cigarettes that it would probably be better for his heart to go ahead and smoke them than to be as cantankerous as he was without them," Cronkite later told reporters. Johnson had several "angina seizures" during the interview, Cronkite noted, and actually had to interrupt filming at one point to take a nitroglycerin pill. Cronkite did not understand the import of Johnson's off-camera comments about selling off cattle and land.[22]

Jewell Malechek Scott described LBJ's decision to keep smoking. "I think at that point," she said, "he decided that you could have quality or quantity in your life and he decided to live and do whatever he wanted to do because he didn't think he had that much time left."[23]

Air Force One, En Route to Florida, Friday, January 12, 1973

As the Cronkite interview wrapped up in Texas and the cameramen and sound men packed up their equipment, Bob Haldeman took notes aboard the flight to Homestead Air Force Base in Florida. He was writing about Richard Nixon's plans now that Henry Kissinger would be returning from Paris with what at last seemed to be an agreement to end the war. "On the plane to Key Biscayne," Haldeman wrote in his diary, "the P made the point that if we get a settlement, we should get every commentator, columnist, and so on that has hit us and really badger them on an all-out basis."[24]

Presidents, after all, do want to do what is right.

16

"I Want to Do This Job That Lincoln Started"

Justice Rehnquist's Chambers, January 11, 1973
Anyone paying attention to simultaneity and the five great stories of January 1973, if in possession of sufficient inside information, would have noticed how closely the *Roe* and *Doe* opinions were tracking with the LBJ story in particular. These two narratives seemed to be running in parallel as events merged into January 22, the day *Roe* would issue and LBJ would die.

On December 11, 1972, the morning that the Austin civil rights symposium was kicking off, Lewis Powell handed Harry Blackmun his handwritten note on the bench during oral argument of another case, politely nudging Blackmun to address the "viability" issue. That same day, Blackmun circulated his fateful memorandum to the conference, asking if "viability might not be a better choice" than a cutoff point after the first trimester.[1]

It was the same day that day that Justice William O. Douglas wrote tersely, "I favor the first trimester, rather than viability."[2]

The next day, December 12, the second day of the rights symposium when LBJ would deliver his last public address, Justice Thurgood Marshall wrote to Blackmun that he was "inclined to agree that drawing the line at viability accommodates the interests at stake better than drawing it at the end of the first trimester."[3]

Marshall, the crusading civil rights lawyer who argued *Brown v. Board of Education*, had been appointed to the Supreme Court by Lyndon Johnson through a series of political maneuvers that made Machiavelli look like a piker. First, Johnson had to convince Marshall to resign from his seat on the US Court of Appeals for the Second Circuit, a lifetime appointment (made by JFK), to become his solicitor general, an at-the-pleasure-of-the-president position, to replace Archibald Cox (future Watergate special prosecutor), who wanted to return to Harvard to teach law. The solicitor general acts as the government's lawyer before the Supreme Court. LBJ's purpose, he made understandable to Marshall in a phone call on July 7, 1965, was to groom him for the next move—"something better," Johnson called it, a pointed reference to the Supreme Court.

"I want to do this job that Lincoln started and I want to do it the right way," Johnson said to Marshall. "I want to be the first president that really goes all the way."[4]Lyndon Johnson sought to be the first president to appoint an African American—the grandson of a slave—to the US Supreme Court.

But before Marshall could be appointed, Johnson had to persuade a sitting justice to step down from the court to create a spot for him.[5] Lyndon Johnson was not one to wait for someone to fortuitously resign or die in office.

Perhaps with this in mind, Johnson appointed Ramsey Clark to be his attorney general in 1967, triggering his father, Tom C. Clark, an associate justice of the Supreme Court since the Truman era, to resign. Tom Clark was from Texas and a longtime friend and supporter of LBJ's. In an oral history with the LBJ Library, the elder Clark said the Johnson and Clark families had been "thrown together" over the years.[6] They lived in the same neighborhoods in Washington, and the two wives christened navy ships and submarines together; they went to New York for weekend trips; and the children were friends. "So there's a thread of affection and of admiration that has been all through our lives," Clark said. Although he denied that he had spoken with Johnson about his son's appointment, the fact is that Johnson must have known that Ramsey Clark's elevation to attorney general would create pressure on his father to resign.

The two moves, at the least, seemed to be orchestrated. "President Johnson named Acting Attorney General Ramsey Clark today to become Attorney General," the newspapers reported on February 28, 1967. "Two hours after the announcement, Mr. Clark's father, Justice Tom C. Clark of the Supreme Court, disclosed that he would retire from the bench no later than the end of the present session of the Court, in June to avoid any suspicion of a conflict of interest."[7]

President Johnson nominated Thurgood Marshall to fill Clark's seat the day after Clark's formal resignation at the end of the Supreme Court term, on June 13, 1967. Marshall was confirmed by the Senate on August 30, 1967. But Southerners, like Sam Ervin and James O. Eastland, opposed Marshall as a "judicial activist." Ervin, a former Supreme Court justice of North Carolina and the senator who would become known as the leading constitutional scholar during his Watergate hearings in the summer of 1973, argued in 1967 that "Judge Marshall is by practice and philosophy a constitutional iconoclast, and his elevation to the Supreme Court at this juncture in our history would make it virtually certain that for years to come, if not forever, the American people will be ruled by the arbitrary notions of Supreme Court Justices rather than by the precepts of the Constitution."[8]

Clark, in his retirement, would author an influential law review article entitled "Religion, Morality, and Abortion: A Constitutional Appraisal," which Harry Blackmun would cite in his *Roe* and *Doe* opinions.[9] As a former justice writing in the law review of a law school that was part of a private Catholic university in the Jesuit and Marymount traditions, the article received considerable attention. "To say that life is present at conception is to give recognition to the potential, rather than the actual," Clark wrote and Blackmun quoted in *Doe*. "The unfertilized egg has life, and if fertilized, it takes on human proportions. But the law deals in reality, not obscurity—the known, rather than the unknown. When sperm meets egg, life may eventually form, but quite often it does not. The law does not deal in speculation. The phenomenon of life takes time to develop, and, until it is actually present, it cannot be destroyed."[10]

Lyndon Johnson took some credit—paternalistic though it might have been—for the progress of women, which he saw as part and parcel of the civil rights movement. Early in his speech at Austin he singled out the women in the audience for special note. "I have a touch of sentimentality about me, which has cost me a great deal in my forty years in public life," he said. "I'll say to all you women who are here," he began, looking out at the women seated in front of him. He began listing off the names of the Democratic Party's new up-and-comers— like Barbara Jordan of Texas and Yvonne Burke of California—"it's natural for me to get a certain amount of glory by seeing the advances you are making."[11]

Thurgood Marshall for one saw the right to an abortion as especially important for the poor and underprivileged, and this was his main reason for signing on to the viability notion. "Given the difficulties which many women may have in believing that they are pregnant and in deciding to seek an abortion, I fear that the earlier date may not in practice serve the interests of those women, which your opinion does seek to serve," he wrote to Blackmun.[12]

So Justice Blackmun fashioned his three-stage test in *Roe*, as outlined by his clerk, Randy Bezanson, in a memo two days after Marshall's letter, on December 14:

> As I have stated in earlier memos on this issue, I do not read your opinions to say that after the first trimester the state can enact a Texas-style statute. Rather, in the manner described by Justices Brennan and Marshall, state regulation can be "staged-in," so to speak. While I am in agreement with the Marshall letter, I think it would still be appropriate, as Justice Brennan suggests, to define some sort of threshold cutoff— "quickening," the end of the 1st trimester, or "somewhere between 16 and 24 weeks"—before which the state must leave the matter entirely within the medical judgment of the physician (with some exceptions as permitted in your Doe opinion). Thereafter, it might be useful, as part of the opinion, to articulate the two state interests and the point at which they assume increasing significance. With respect to the state's interest in preserving the safety of the operation and the conditions surrounding it, regulation might be permissible somewhere between the end of the 1st trimester (if that cut-off is selected) and "viability" or beyond. But with respect to the state's interest in preserving fetal life, the opinion might, for example, indicate that only after "viability" does this interest become sufficiently compelling to support regulation in furtherance of this interest.[13]

A month later, the day before LBJ's interview with Cronkite and Nixon's flight to Florida, Justices Byron White and William Rehnquist circulated their dissents. "The decision here to break the term of pregnancy into three distinct terms and to outline the permissible restrictions the State may impose in each one, for example, partakes more of judicial legislation than it does of a determination of the intent of the drafters of the Fourteenth Amendment," Rehnquist charged in an otherwise esoteric and dry dissent.[14]

Byron White, appointed to the bench by John F. Kennedy, expressed the only direct concern for the fetal life: "The Court, for the most part, sustains this position: during the period prior to the time the fetus becomes viable, the Constitution of the United States values the convenience, whim, or caprice of the putative mother more than the life or potential life of the fetus. . . . With all due respect, I dissent." White thought that such a sensitive area "should be left with the people and to the political processes the people have devised to govern their affairs."[15]

Neither of these short dissents by White or Rehnquist changed anyone's view. There was nothing of the fire or vitriol that would mark opinions in later abortion decisions that were to come before the court.

The only justice yet to make a firm commitment was Chief Justice Warren Burger, but even if he turned on Blackmun at the last minute, it would make no difference at that point. The decisions were final, and firm majorities were in place—it remained only for some final edits and the selection of the date for the announcement.

The die was cast for both *Roe* and Lyndon Baines Johnson. Time was growing short.

Key Biscayne, Florida, the Weekend of January 13 to 14, 1973

Back in the Florida warmth, Nixon spent the morning of Saturday, January 13, nervously rambling around in his modest but heavily guarded waterfront compound with his chief of staff. "The P had me over this morning for three or four hours going over lots of miscellaneous things," Haldeman wrote in his diary.

The topics bounced from inaugural planning—making sure Frank Sinatra and Sammy Davis Jr. both were extended offers to stay for an evening at the White House—to media relations, to Kissinger's return that night from Paris, to what books he wanted to read. Nixon was talking in disjointed free association. "Wanted to check out burial opportunities at Yorba Linda, as well as Rose Hills," Haldeman wrote in bewilderment. "I don't know how that came in from left field."[16]

John Dean called Haldeman that afternoon to report a disturbing new development in the Watergate matter. Seymour Hersh of the *New York Times* was going to write that weekend that "the Cubans told [the *Times*] that they're all on salary, that there's a $900,000 fund at

The *Roe* Court: Justices Stewart, Powell, Douglas, Marshal, Burger, Blackmun, Brennan, Rehnquist, and White.

Collection of the Supreme Court of the United States

the Reelection Committee for them, and that they dropped bugs all over town."[17] The payment of hush money to the defendants had been a carefully guarded secret by the White House. No one was sure how the news got out, though a person of interest was certainly the lawyer the Cubans had discarded, the embittered Henry Rothblatt.

Dean thought the situation could be managed. His coolness under fire is what so impressed Haldeman and Nixon about the young lawyer. Dean assured Haldeman that flat denials would be issued by the reelection committee and John Mitchell. And even though James McCord was again showing signs that he might break, Dean thought McCord could only go so high in the organizational chart with any firsthand knowledge of who was in the know at the committee or the White House. "McCord is off the reservation now," Haldeman noted. "Apparently McCord was distressed at the judge's severity. The Cubans plead on Monday."[18]

Dean communicated with McCord through Jack Caulfield, the former New York City cop who had worked for Dean in the White House but had been moved to drug enforcement duties at the Treasury Department.[19] Caulfield had received McCord's "every tree in the forest will fall" letter in December 1972. At Dean's request, Caulfield met surreptitiously with McCord during the course of the trial at the second overlook on the George Washington Parkway. He encouraged McCord to plead guilty and promised he would be granted clemency after he served eleven or twelve months in prison. "A year is a long time; your wife and family will be taken care of; and you will be rehabilitated with employment when this is all over," was the message Caulfield was instructed to deliver. McCord responded that he was "different from all the others," that he was going to follow his own "independent course." He thought that if one person involved went to jail, all involved should go to jail. He was particularly inflamed that people like Jeb Magruder and John Dean walked free while he faced a long prison sentence. McCord didn't want to go to jail at all. "I can take care of my family," he told Caulfield. "I don't need any jobs; I want my freedom."[20]

McCord continued to espouse his wacky idea that if he threatened to disclose secret government wiretaps of foreign embassies he would be freed. He was not going to hear of executive clemency.[21]

The *Times* on Sunday morning carried the provocative headline: 4 WATERGATE DEFENDANTS REPORTED STILL BEING PAID.[22] Seymour Hersh broke the story. Rothblatt's fingerprints seemed to be all over it. "At least four of the five men arrested last June in the Watergate raid are still being paid by persons as yet unnamed, according to sources close to the case." Hersh had a source who reportedly had been told by burglar Frank Fiorini (aka Frank Sturgis) that his funds had been sharply reduced in the months leading up to the trial. But Rothblatt may have been the crucial confirming source. "Mr. Sturgis's statements on the financial arrangements of the arrested group were corroborated by a source close to the defense."

Hersh's article, which had scooped the *Washington Post* and had surprisingly exposed some core facts about the cover-up, had little impact because the story fell of its own internal weight. Parts of it were plainly wrong. And Hersh himself questioned the credibility of his source: a freelance author named Andrew St. George. St. George, then living in upstate New York, had been a famed correspondent and photographer in Cuba during Fidel Castro's revolution. He remained in contact with the anti-Castro group in Miami and was known to be hawking the outline for a book on the burglars to New York publishers. The book was purportedly based on his free-flowing discussions St.

George had with Sturgis, who at the time was free on bail in Miami. St. George was also lining up an exclusive TV interview of Sturgis with NBC in return for a significant finder's fee.

Hersh felt constrained to acknowledge that "both Mr. St. George and Mr. Sturgis are controversial figures in their own circles and have mixed reputations." Some in Miami found Mr. St. George intelligent and resourceful; others described him as sensationalist, a man who had trouble distinguishing between "fact and fantasy."[23]

Further deflecting attention, as Dean had predicted, the public affairs officer for the Committee to Re-Elect told the *New York Times* that the allegations in the Hersh article were "outrageous, false, and preposterous." John Mitchell added his own obligatory denial.[24]

Another bullet dodged by the White House. John Dean seemed to be holding the line.

On Sunday morning, January 14, Haldeman was again summoned to the president's home. He found him in his living room, having breakfast, with a fire going in the fireplace even though the day outside was already warm and inviting. Kissinger and Haig showed up a little after 10:00 AM, having caught a few hours of sleep. The men retired to the president's office to talk for several hours over the schedule for handling the various announcements on the bombing halt and Haig's trip to Southeast Asia.

The president spent the afternoon watching the Super Bowl with Bebe Rebozo at Rebozo's residence at the Ocean Reef Club in Key Largo. They went swimming at halftime and had dinner at the club, and Nixon returned to his compound in Key Biscayne by helicopter around 7:30 PM. He tried to call both coaches from the Super Bowl teams—George Allen of the Redskins and Don Shula of the Dolphins—but he was only able to speak to a dejected Allen that night. He went to bed for the evening after talking to his daughter Julie by phone in Washington.[25]

Haldeman made it his business to have a long dinner with Henry Kissinger that night. He wanted to keep an eye on him. "After I dictated the report for Sunday," Haldeman wrote in his diary, "I had dinner with K, which I scheduled in order to keep him from going out to dinner and getting caught in the public down here." They ate at Henry's villa and talked for three hours. Haldeman tried to get Kissinger to tell him the whole story of the peace negotiations, but Kissinger kept asking him about whether Nixon still had confidence in him. "He's concerned that the stories that he keeps reading may be partly or totally true," Kissinger confided to Haldeman. Haldeman took pains to reassure Kissinger, but warned him about talking to the press. "I told him that there wasn't any problem with the P having confidence in him substantively, but the P does get concerned about the whole business of Henry's talking to the left-wing set, and the campuses and the media, etc."

Kissinger conceded his problem. "He basically understands," Haldeman wrote, "and is compulsively unable to do anything about it."[26]

Meanwhile, Al Haig, aboard a presidential Boeing 707, was on his way to Saigon with a chilling letter from Nixon to President Thieu. There would be no further negotiation. It was time for Thieu to get on board.

17

"We Should Wait for His Formal Reply Before Popping Corks"

Ceremonial Courtroom, US Federal Court, Monday, January 15, 1973
Judge John Sirica looked at the four defendants standing in front of him—Barker, Martinez, Sturgis, and Gonzalez—and he then said, "Will the four defendants stand up before the court, please." The four men stepped forward.[1]

He was about to take their pleas of guilty and he was going to run them through the same set of questions he had put to Howard Hunt the week before.

The morning had not started well. With the *New York Times* article over the weekend suggesting that the defendants were being paid to remain silent and with the appearance of the aged Alvin Newmyer as their new lawyer, even the government lawyers had reason to be nervous about the record that was being created.

Sirica advised counsel that he was going to take away all newspapers from the jury, because so much was being written about Watergate and the trial. Previously, he had relied on the US marshals to clip out any stories about Watergate from juror newspapers. But he had seen four or five mentions of the case in the Sunday paper, including one in the sports pages, in the caption under a photo of Edward Bennett Williams at the Super Bowl. The famous lawyer, a part-owner of the Redskins, was representing the Democrats in their civil suit against the Committee to Re-Elect the President. Sirica would take no more chances; henceforth, all newspapers were banned from the jury room.[2]

Alvin Newmyer finally showed up just before 11:00 AM. Though Henry Rothblatt had been discharged, he was present in the courtroom.

It turned out he was needed. Newmyer cut to the chase and told Judge Sirica that his clients would plead guilty to all counts. Rothblatt had to gently reprove him. "Let me, Mr. Newmyer, if I may, correct it, just to be [of] assistance to you," Rothblatt interrupted, with his trademark politeness. What Newmyer had meant to say, Rothblatt told the court, was that the defendants wanted to plead guilty to three of the counts. He was only supposed to agree to pleas on all counts if the court rejected this offer. But the cat was out of the bag. Sirica said no, he would only accept pleas to all the charges.[3]

Sirica then began to ask Newmyer if he had spoken with the defendants about bail. Newmyer said that he had. Rothblatt again corrected him. "I think Mr. Newmyer sort of jumped the gun," he said. "That request [on bail] was to be made to you when and if you should accept their plea and not at this time." Sirica looked quizzically to Mr. Newmyer. "Mr. Newmyer," he said, "would you go down with him [Rothblatt] and confirm it?" Both men left to consult with the defendants, who were in a waiting room downstairs.

The two lawyers returned sometime later, and Rothblatt confirmed that Mr. Newmyer had "conveyed to the defendants Your Honor's position." Sirica then asked Mr. Newmyer if he had explained to each of the defendants that he would be "asking them many questions in connection with the question of voluntariness and that [he expected] truthful answers to the questions and [would] be going over the questions with them." Mr. Newmyer responded, "Yes, I think I better tell them that now." For a second time he scurried off to consult with the defendants. He came back and said everything was set.[4]

The scene that was emerging on the record was an embarrassment. From a due process standpoint, it was anything but clear that the defendants were receiving the effective assistance of counsel. Attorney Newmyer was plainly lacking in criminal defense expertise, and worse, he appeared to be more than a bit addled. Seymour Glanzer, one of the prosecutors, was so worried that he felt it necessary to interject that Rothblatt, though formally discharged by the defendants, was still on the job, sort of.

"I want the record to be perfectly clear about one matter," Glanzer interjected without being asked to speak by the court. "The Defendants Martinez, Gonzalez, Sturgis, and Barker have not lost their trust in Mr. Rothblatt and Mr. Rothblatt will tell you they have not lost confidence in him." Rothblatt said he was in agreement with the sentiment Glanzer was expressing. Glanzer continued, "Mr. Rothblatt, simply stated, opposes the decision to enter a plea and therefore did not want to be a party to it; however, he has still made himself available to advise them at every juncture."[5]

Sirica seemed puzzled by Glanzer's sudden effusiveness in support of Rothblatt. "I know that," he said dismissively. Glanzer, however, was not done; he wanted to further embellish the record, addressing Sy Hersh's article without mentioning him or the *New York Times* by name. "I also want to say this," he added. "The Government was concerned about certain articles that appeared in the paper about certain innuendos and insinuations, so the Government asked the defendants, with leave of counsel, whether in any manner, shape or form, directly or indirectly, or suggestively, they were coerced in any manner to enter this plea and they stated they were not, in the presence of their counsel."

Sirica said, "Very well. I think the record is clear."[6] He either had not read the Hersh article or had other ideas of what he wanted to accomplish with the pleas and was anxious to get to it.

Sirica opened court and read a lengthy statement for the benefit of the press as to what had taken place behind closed doors since Friday. He asked Mr. Newmyer to formally make a statement. Newmyer kept it brief: his clients would plead to every count.[7]

Sirica once again asked the defendants to come forward. He went over the charges, the government's burden of proof, and the constitutional rights that the defendants would be waiving if they pled guilty. He admonished the four men that they had to be candid with him, had to "pull no punches," and had to be truthful with him no matter whom it might "hurt or help." He reminded them that he had the power to set their sentences but that he was going to wait until he heard more. "I am not threatening or coercing you, or anything like that," he said, though this was precisely what he was doing.[8]

He came back to his obsession: motive. The jury would want to know why they committed the crimes. Were higher-ups involved? Where did the money come from? Who was the money man?

He started with Eugenio Martinez, the native Cuban who had defected in 1959 after the Castro revolution, had worked for the CIA, and now had a job as a real estate broker in the Miami real estate company owned by Bernard Barker. "I want you to start from the beginning and I want you to tell me how you got involved in this conspiracy," Sirica said. "How did it happen that you got involved?" With Bill Bittman gone, Rothblatt sacked, and Newmyer clueless, no one stood up to stop Sirica's questioning, as had been done in Hunt's case. The problem for Sirica was that none of these Miamians knew much about the involvement of anyone above Hunt and Liddy. As John Dean had coolly assessed it, there was not much danger in these men speaking.

But even better, the men turned out to be the steadfast soldiers Hunt and Liddy had said they would be. Martinez, who went first, was evasive, sparring with Sirica. He would not give up any secrets that he knew. "I believe the facts that you have read in the charges are true and are just to the truth," he said in broken English.

"That was a blanket answer," Sirica replied. "I want specifics."

Martinez responded, "I'm sorry?"

"I want specific answers to my questions," Sirica said again. "I am not satisfied."

"Your Honor, asked me questions," Martinez replied, stalling.

Sirica started peppering him with questions about details, but Martinez kept up his cat-and-mouse game. Rather than answer Sirica's inquiry of who provided the money for the operation, he went on a long digression. "Money doesn't mean a thing to us, Your Honor," Martinez said. "I own a hospital in Cuba, one of the best hospitals. I own a factory of furniture in Cuba. I was the owner of a hotel in Cuba. I left everything in the hands of the Communists there. So money, really, I lose everything and really money is not a great deal in my decisions, so I never worry about money."[9]

He was running Sirica around in circles.

Finally, Gerald Alch, F. Lee Bailey's associate and McCord's attorney, stepped in. "Your Honor, Mr. McCord has pled not guilty to this indictment," Alch said. "He is in the midst of a trial which is already commenced. Although strictly speaking, Your Honor is not a trier of the facts; nevertheless, should Mr. McCord take the stand, and Your Honor well knows you will be able to ask him questions, you will be called upon during the course of the trial to rule on objections made by me in his behalf."

What he was saying was that the continued questioning of the Miamians could prejudice McCord's right to a fair trial. "I most respectfully submit," Alch said, "any questions pertaining to alleged activities of Mr. McCord are not relevant to this proceeding— wherein the purpose is to ascertain whether or not the plea of guilty is voluntary—and may inure to the prejudice of my client. I would respectfully ask the court to refrain from attempting to elicit details regarding my client who is presumed to be innocent."

Sirica surprisingly relented. "Well, you may have something there," he said. He would not ask questions about McCord, but he wasn't going to stop asking about other details.[10]

"Before you went into the Democratic Headquarters on the morning of June 17th, where did you four men meet in Washington?" Sirica continued with Martinez. The Cuban again responded with a non-answer, concluding after an obfuscating statement: "This I want you to believe, it is not a way out or anything." Sirica was getting nowhere with Martinez.[11]

He turned to the defendant who seemed most vulnerable: Virgilio Gonzalez, the young Miami locksmith and the one who also seemed to struggle the most with his English. "I understand 95 percent of what you say," he told the judge when asked if he needed an interpreter. But even Gonzalez held the line. He said he barely knew Howard Hunt and that he wasn't being paid for his work. "I do it because I believe what I did was the right thing to do," he said.

"Who did you do it for?" Sirica asked, hoping to pry from him whether higher-ups were involved. Gonzalez nimbly deflected the question. "Because of my idea," he said. "I figured that this is the political scene representing Cuba and I am an American citizen and I keep feeling about my country and the way people suffer over there," Gonzalez replied. "That is the only reason I did my cooperation in that situation."

"What did Cuba have to do with breaking in and entering the Democratic Headquarters?" Sirica asked. "I don't know," Gonzalez responded. "That is what they told me and I believed him."

"Who told you that?" Sirica requested.

"Mr. Barker and Mr. Hunt," Gonzalez said.[12]

Sirica's exercise was useless. He was not going to get the information he wanted. These men were going to give the appearance of cooperation, but they had obviously hashed out a party line and were not going to stray from the script. They were freedom fighters, soldiers following orders. In the process, though, they lied, dissembled, and denied the obvious. Martinez and Barker both said they had not worked for the CIA, though they clearly had during the Bay of Pigs operation and thereafter (Martinez was still on the CIA payroll at the time of the break-in). "Not that I know of," Martinez and Barker both responded when Sirica asked them if they had ever worked for the CIA. Barker refused to say where the money for expenses came from. "The money came to me in a closed envelope by mail," he asserted. He could only guess who had sent it.[13]

The four defendants all in chorus denied that they were being paid for their services, beyond being reimbursed for expenses (planes, hotels, meals). They claimed that they had not been promised that their families would be taken care of if they went to jail. They said there were no undertakings of executive clemency.

It was all mush. "Even I want to forget all the things," Martinez said. "I don't want to remember anymore." Sirica finally threw up his hands. "I am sorry," he said to Barker, "I don't believe you."[14]

Though they put up a united front, privately Frank Sturgis (born Frank Fiorini), the only Miamian who was not a Cuban, was contemptuous of their leader, Bernard Barker. "Hey listen," he told journalist Andrew St. George (Sy Hersh's source for his *Times* article), "our bunch was a good team—all except that faking, brown-nosing [Bernard] Barker." Sturgis said that Liddy was the commanding officer of the operations but that he was a "nut about guns and silencers and so on." Liddy fancied himself the leader of a "special-ops unit," though Sturgis said he more resembled "an Eagle Scout who finds he's passed the exams and become a CIA chief." Howard Hunt, Sturgis said, was different: "He was a professional. He'd been a clandestine services officer his whole life."

But Barker was a nobody, according to Sturgis. "Bernard Barker was Hunt's right-hand man, his confidential clerk—his body servant, really; that's how I met Barker," he told St. George. "I wish I had never met that dumbhead," he continued, his language no doubt cleaned up by St. Andrews for publication. "You know, Barker tells everybody to call him 'Macho.' That's supposed to be his nickname. A man who is macho is supposed to be some kind of virile hard-charger," Sturgis said. "Calling Barker 'Macho' is like calling Liberace 'Slugger.' "[15]

"Commit the defendants," Sirica said, as he wrapped up his plea-taking, directing the marshal to take all four men back to jail to await sentencing.[16] The case was down to just two defendants: McCord and Liddy.

Key Biscayne, Florida, January 15, 1973

At roughly the same time that Judge Sirica recessed for lunch in Washington, the administration announced in Key Biscayne that the

United States was suspending offensive actions throughout North Vietnam.[17] The reason: "progress" was being made in the cease-fire negotiations in Paris.

"Ronald L. Ziegler, the White House press secretary, announced the suspension this morning after several hours of consultations between the president and his chief negotiator, Henry A. Kissinger," the *New York Times* reported.[18]

As Nixon anticipated, "peace euphoria" began to build around the world. "By halting the bombing, mining, and shelling of North Vietnam today," the *Times* wrote, "President Nixon has raised new expectations here that an end to the Vietnam war may again be near." Observers noted that a script previously announced was being followed: once the United States achieved an acceptable agreement with Hanoi, there would be the unilateral cessation of hostilities in the North by the United States, and General Haig would return to South Vietnam for consultation with President Thieu.[19]

The only other news that Ron Ziegler had to share with the hungry reporters in Florida was that Henry Kissinger would be returning to Washington that night. Somehow, Kissinger had convinced Nixon to let him go. "I should tell you that Dr. Kissinger plans as of now to return to Washington sometime later today, probably this evening, for meetings and so forth, which he will be having in Washington as part of his ongoing schedule," Ziegler told the assembled press.[20]

Kissinger barely had time to make good use of the bathing suit that had been so meticulously packed and shipped by Colonel Kennedy.

Saigon, South Vietnam, January 15 to 16, 1973

Nixon sent Al Haig back to Saigon with an angry message. There would be no negotiation with Saigon; Nixon would not meet with Thieu; Haig was merely a messenger. And the president would look very darkly upon Thieu's "shooting his mouth off before the Inaugural," Haldeman wrote in his diary the day Haig flew out. If Thieu criticized Henry Kissinger, which he was wont to do, Nixon told Haig to tell Thieu that he would consider it a personal attack on himself. In short, Haig was told to "take a very hard line with Thieu."[21]

The letter Haig carried with him was, by Kissinger's lights, brutal.[22] The letter listed all of the "improvements" to the agreement since October, when Thieu last undermined the negotiations. The additional three months had "served to strengthen your position in preparation for a ceasefire," Nixon wrote. The Communist military plans had been disrupted, and the United States had accelerated the completion of "Vietnamization," through the provision of more than $1 billion in military equipment. "And your government has further solidified its popular support and made preparations for the coming political competition."

But further delay by Thieu, Nixon warned, would be "disastrous." Nixon wrote that he had "irrevocably decided to proceed to initial the agreement on January 23, 1973, and to sign it on January 27, 1973, in Paris." He was prepared to do so alone, if necessary. If Thieu obstructed, Nixon foretold of "an inevitable and immediate termination of US economic and military assistance which cannot be forestalled by a change of personnel in your government."

He reiterated that the United States would continue to recognize Thieu's government as the only legal government of South Vietnam, and that the American government would not "recognize the right of any foreign troops to be present on South Vietnamese territory." And he reaffirmed his ultimate commitment. "We will react strongly," Nixon wrote, "in the event the Agreement is violated." He gave his personal pledge to come to the aid of South Vietnam if the North did not keep its word.[23]

Haig arrived in Saigon on Tuesday morning, January 16 (as he had crossed the dateline, it was still January 15 in Washington). He sent a back-channel message to Kissinger to describe his meeting, also attended by US ambassador Ellsworth Bunker, with President Thieu at the Presidential Palace. "I told Thieu that we are now at the final decision point in what had been a prolonged and difficult period for all parties," Haig wrote. He could not come up with enough clichés to describe the stark state of affairs, advising Thieu: "[W]e had arrived at a point of no return."

Thieu, according to Haig, read Nixon's letter slowly and carefully. He complained that the protocols he had seen were far from complete. He still found the presence of three hundred thousand North Vietnamese troops in the South to be the core problem. Though he could handle the North Vietnamese militarily, he said, their presence created a "psychological" hurdle that his people could not surmount. He said the agreements lacked "balance and equilibrium." As long as the North maintained military forces, it remained impossible to "implement the political formula." This was only a cease-fire in place, Thieu again protested, not a prescription of a durable peace.

The scene was somber. Thieu told Haig that he faced the most difficult decision of his public life and that he would be judged harshly by
the "court of history" if he got it wrong. He recognized the incorrect
move could result in his ouster from office, or even his death. He said
that he alone would make the final decision. "He referred to Bunker
as an old friend who had shared many travails with him and [Hoang
Duc] Nha [Thieu's private secretary, press spokesman, nephew, and
confidant] was silent and dejected," Haig wrote.

Haig demanded a response by the next evening, January 17. He
told Thieu that he was leaving that day for stops in Cambodia, Laos,
and Bangkok. He wanted an answer when he returned. Haig wrote to
Kissinger that his assessment was that Thieu would "reluctantly join
[them]."

But, he cautioned, "we have been fooled before." He said, "I think
we should wait for his formal reply before popping corks."[24]

The next morning, January 16, Kissinger called Nixon from
Washington about Haig's cable. He said Thieu basically had two
choices: "I can be an immediate hero and ruin my country [by rejecting the agreements] or I can be a statesman." He advised Nixon to
stand strong. "One more day of toughness and then he is going to
cave," Kissinger said.[25]

Senators Goldwater and Stennis, right-wing hawks, both appeared
on television to encourage Thieu to bring an end to the war. Goldwater
said, "If everyone will just shut up and back the president, progress
will be made."[26]

Key Biscayne, Tuesday, January 16, 1973

Richard Nixon turned his attention to drafting his second inaugural
address, which he would deliver at the end of the week, on Saturday, January 20. After talking to Kissinger long-distance on Tuesday
morning, Nixon called for his speechwriter, Raymond Price, whom
he had brought with him to Florida. Price had been the chief editorial writer of the *New York Herald Tribune* before joining the Nixon
team in 1967. He was considered a liberal among Nixon's advisors.
Pat Buchanan, another top speechwriter, was, by contrast, the ultra-
conservative, hard-nosed street fighter. Price tended to write in broad
abstractions, using lofty phrases.[27]

Nixon's twin themes for his inaugural would be the creation of an
enduring peace in the world and a shift in the way people saw the role
of government at home. Government, he asserted, was not the solution

to every problem. He wanted a government, he said, that would "take less from the people so that people can do more for themselves."

None of it would be especially memorable, but his words did represent the start of a new political order.

Haldeman noticed the quiet in Florida following the announcement of the bombing halt. "For the first time since we've been here," he wrote on Wednesday, January 17, "I didn't have to go over at all today." When Nixon called him by phone, it was "mainly to be sure the staff mood is up and that we're doing everything to keep everyone cranked up and upbeat, especially as people are starting to come into town for the Inaugural."[28]

The silence that had descended was truly the quiet before the storm of January 22.

18

"I'm Going to Be
with the Rich Cats Tonight"

On January 16, the same day that Al Haig presented President Thieu with Nixon's blistering letter, the chief justice of the United States, Warren Burger, sent a note on *Roe* and *Doe* to his boyhood friend Harry Blackmun. Up to that point, Burger had been coy about how he would vote.

"Dear Harry," he wrote, "I am working on some concurrences in the above cases and will try to have them in your hands and circulated sometime tomorrow." Blackmun had hoped to issue the opinions by January 15, giving returning state legislatures time to consider immediate revisions to their abortion laws that would be required by the holdings of the decisions. Almost all state abortion laws would fall or need to be fine-tuned as a result of *Roe* and *Doe*.[1]

"I do not believe they will involve any significant change in what you have written," Burger wrote about his expected concurrences. Confirmation that he would join in the opinions was followed by Burger's assessment of the timing of the announcement: it would be after the inaugural. "I see no reason we cannot schedule these cases for Monday," he wrote. January 22 would be the date.[2]

Later that day, Blackmun circulated a memorandum to the conference with a typed statement that he expected to read the day the decisions were announced. "I anticipate the headlines that will be produced over the country when the abortion decisions are announced," he wrote. Blackmun was so worried about the public reaction that he suggested something that had never been done before—to give his eight-page summary to the press on the morning the opinions were announced. "I suggest," he wrote to the conference, "that copies be given to Mr. Wittington for distribution to the press if any reporters desire it. It will in effect be a transcript of what I shall say, and there should be at least some reason for the press not going all the way off the deep end."[3]

In his explanatory statement, Blackmun conceded that the "abortion issue, of course, is a most sensitive, emotional, and controversial one, perhaps one of the most emotional that has reached the Court for some time." He was well aware of the fact that "attitudes were firmly rooted and firmly held." Yet those attitudes, he had to admit, were not uniformly held. "We are aware of this, and we are fully aware that, however the Court decides these cases, the controversy will continue."[4]

During this week, Larry Hammond innocently bought himself a boatload of trouble. A trusted acquaintance who had gone to the University of Texas Law School with him, David Beckwith, now worked for *Time* magazine as a staff reporter.[5] He spoke with Hammond "on background" to get a jump on what the opinions would be. Hammond thought at the time that the opinions were going to issue on January 17. Because of Burger's delay, Beckwith's editors had a scoop and decided to run with it. Hammond was double-crossed by his friend. A two-page story was drafted for release on Monday, January 22, entitled "Abortion on Demand." The issue of the magazine would hit the newsstands a few hours before Blackmun read his announcement.

Larry Hammond would hear about it from Warren Burger.[6]

Ceremonial Courtroom, US Federal Courthouse of the District of Columbia, January 15 to 18, 1973

The arguments started right after the lunch break on January 15, hours after the four Miamians had entered their guilty pleas. The remaining attorneys for McCord and Liddy once again asked for mistrials based on the obvious prejudice to their clients, as five of the defendants had suddenly vanished from the courtroom. Judge Sirica thought no more of this argument for mistrial than he had when it was made after Hunt exited. The trial would continue.[7] People plead guilty all the time after a trial starts, Sirica observed.

Thomas Gregory, the Mormon student from Brigham Young, resumed the stand to complete his testimony. He continued to cause damage and wasn't touched on cross-examination, except for an embarrassing moment when it was pointed out that he received sixteen credit hours for what BYU had labeled "paraprofessional experience" while he engaged in political espionage in return for a large salary. (Gregory never did repay the money.)[8]

The case was taking on an air of inevitability. The jury had to have been influenced by the disappearance of five of the seven defendants. Sirica gave only the most cursory instruction about the absence of the four Miamians. "Ladies and gentlemen of the jury, the cases of [Barker, Martinez, Sturgis, and Gonzalez] are no longer before you," he told the jury when they returned. "You need no longer be concerned with these cases and these four men." With that, he turned to Earl Silbert and said, "Alright, you can proceed."[9]

Gerald Alch, attorney for James McCord, continue to hammer on the defense of "duress" or "necessity." Alch claimed that McCord had been so worked up by antiwar protests and bombings—which he felt were incited by the Democratic Party and resulted in a physical danger to Republican campaign officials—that he was compelled to take action, even though he knew his acts were illegal. Alch's analogy was that of someone holding a gun to another's head and insisting that the person drive the getaway car in a bank robbery. The person driving with the gun to his head was acting "under duress." And so McCord, Alch contended. Sirica found the argument less than persuasive and would not let him present any such evidence.[10]

Gregory's time on the stand carried over to Tuesday, January 16. After him, Earl Silbert called a series of quick witnesses, including Frank Wills, the security officer who famously discovered the tape and re-tape over the door locks in the Watergate basement garage and called police. The officers who arrived at the Watergate in casual clothes were next. One of them said that while he was on the terrace of the Watergate, he noticed a man standing on the balcony of one of the upper rooms in the Howard Johnson's across the street—the man who would turn out to be the lookout, Alfred Baldwin. He remembered it because "we were in plainclothes and I had my weapon drawn, [and] I was concerned that he might call the police and report a man with a gun."[11]

Wednesday and Thursday were filled with fairly mundane evidence taking—identifying and listing the items found on the men and in their hotel rooms. But a trial tactic used by Liddy's lawyer, Peter Maroulis, got under Sirica's skin. Maroulis, a Poughkeepsie, New York, lawyer and former law partner of Gordon Liddy's, kept asking each testifying officer if he was armed as part of his routine cross-examination. Sirica finally asked the purpose of the question. Maroulis replied that it made him feel uncomfortable to cross someone who had a loaded gun on his person. "Are you afraid they are going to shoot you?" Sirica asked sarcastically. Maroulis agreed to refrain from asking the question again, and the moment seemed to pass.[12]

The next morning, Wednesday, January 17, Sirica had had a night to stew about it. In his private chambers with all the lawyers present, he demanded that Maroulis rise. He asked Earl Silbert to bring in every police officer he intended to call as a witness that day. He had each officer dramatically hand over his gun to his US marshal. "Mr. Maroulis," he then said, "I am going to permit you to cross-examine any of these witnesses you didn't have the opportunity to yesterday. Which one do you want to cross-examine now?"

Maroulis was dumbfounded. "Your Honor," he replied, "I find myself in a most uncomfortable position. I don't have any of my notes from yesterday with me."[13]

Saigon, South Vietnam, January 17, 1973

Though a bombing halt went into effect in North Vietnam on January 15, the South Vietnamese and Americans intensified military operations in South Vietnam, Laos, and Cambodia to solidify positions in anticipation of the cease-fire. The US air forces that had been used against targets in the North were diverted for support operations along the Ho Chi Minh Trail and elsewhere.[14] The North Vietnamese likewise stepped up their hostilities and resupply activities.

When General Haig returned to Saigon on January 17 to meet with President Thieu, he was in for a surprise. Thieu was not going to go along. "He was emotional and extremely despondent," Haig cabled Kissinger. Thieu handed Haig a sealed reply to the president's January 14 letter and asked that Haig read it after their meeting. He went on a "lengthy exposition to the effect that the agreement would be viewed by the people of South Vietnam as a defeat but constantly repeated the theme that nevertheless he understood he had to maintain US support." When Haig read Thieu's letter following the meeting, he found it to be much more strident than his remarks in person—the letter, Haig wrote, was "brittle and uncompromising." Thieu insisted on major changes to the documents. He wanted some commitment that after demobilization the North Vietnamese forces would "return to their native places." His letter had a list of other demands.[15]

Haig had intelligence (apparently through wiretaps) that Thieu was posturing.[16] Thieu had told his own National Security Council that day that he was prepared to go along with the agreement despite its shortcomings. His reason was simple: "to ensure a continuation of American aid." He knew that Nixon was a "minority president," and that if he bucked the Democratic Congress and charged on alone with his Vietnam position, he would be "finished politically." Better to accept the current agreement, Thieu argued, and hope that Nixon's successes in Russia and China would result in the election of a Republican in 1976. Anyone, Thieu said, but Senator Ted Kennedy. According to Haig's intelligence sources, "Thieu asked the other participants rhetorically what would be the South Vietnamese position now if McGovern had won?"[17]

Haig was convinced that Thieu believed he could "get further improvements in the agreement or at a minimum . . . buy more time." He recommended a "prompt, unemotional, but nevertheless steely, matter of fact response." Haig and Ambassador Bunker remained convinced that Thieu would yield.

Nixon, however, got nervous. He spoke to Kissinger in Washington from Key Biscayne at 4:30 PM on Wednesday, January 17. He was having trouble seeing what Thieu thought he was accomplishing with his reply. He wanted Kissinger to map out a contingency plan in the event they needed to initial the agreement without South Vietnam's participation. Kissinger was less concerned. As Haig had suggested, a tough response from Nixon was already on its way. There would be an announcement the next day, Thursday, January 18, that Henry Kissinger was going to return to Paris on January 22 "in order to complete the text of the agreements."[18]

Nixon the politician worried most about dashing the hopes of the nation and the world. His second inaugural address, all but completed, would hit hard on the theme of world peace. If just three days later Nixon had to go on television to say the South Vietnamese would not go along, the expectations that had been "raised beyond belief" would suddenly be "shattered." It would be, per Nixon, "one hell of a thing."[19]

Kissinger flatly said, "Mr. President, the fact is that we are now doomed to settle."[20]

Nixon's letter in response to Thieu's reply, delivered by Ambassador Ellsworth Bunker, simply stated that the president intended to proceed to initialing on January 23 and signing on January 27.[21] The letter reiterated the strengths of the new agreement since October.

Nixon wrote that he was prepared to send Vice President Agnew to South Vietnam following the peace accords to emphasize America's continuing support of Thieu and to reiterate that the United States did not recognize the right of foreign troops to remain on South Vietnamese soil. Agnew would state unequivocally that America would react vigorously to violations of the agreement by the North. Nixon also suggested that he would meet with Thieu in the United States at some point in the late winter or early spring as a show of solidarity.

Thieu was told by Bunker that he had to give General Haig his final position on Saturday morning, January 20. "This is the latest possible occasion for us to have your final position so that I will know whether we will be proceeding alone or together with you," Nixon wrote. "The schedule is final and cannot be changed in any way."[22]

Things were getting dicey. The following day, Thursday, January 18, at noon Ron Ziegler read to reporters in Key Biscayne an agreed joint statement issued by the United States and North Vietnam: "Dr. Henry Kissinger will resume private meetings with Special Advisor Le Duc Tho and Minister Xuan Thuy on January 23, 1973 for the purpose of completing the text of an agreement."[23] Dr. Kissinger, it was noted, was expected to depart for Paris sometime on Monday.[24]

In Florida on Thursday, after a day of meetings and more work on his second inaugural speech, Richard Nixon helicoptered to Homestead Air Force Base and climbed aboard Air Force One to fly back to Washington, arriving at 10:16 PM. Because air space was always cleared for his flight, he made the trip from Miami to Washington in less than two hours.[25]

Station KQED, San Francisco, California, January 18, 1973

Howard Hunt needed to post a $100,000 bond to get out of jail pending his sentencing. Bill Bittman, his lawyer, figured out the way to get the bond. He would use the checks Hunt received from his wife's $250,000 life insurance policy—the one she purchased just before getting on the plane to fly to Chicago. Hunt endorsed the checks and the funds were placed in a joint account with the surety company as collateral for the bond. Hunt would go free temporarily.

As he was released from jail, Hunt stood squinting in front of a gaggle of reporters under bright lights, Bittman by his side, and said, "Anything I may have done, I did for what I believed to be in the best interests of my country."[26]

He flew to California to film an episode with journalist William F. Buckley on his popular PBS show *Firing Line* on Thursday, January 18. The program was videotaped at KQED, a public broadcasting station in San Francisco. It was scheduled to air on Sunday night, January 21, in prime time.

Hunt's appearance seemed to be following the exact script outlined by Nixon to Colson in the Executive Office Building on January 8, when Nixon approved of a plan to grant Hunt clemency after he served some period of time in prison.

"Hunt's is a simple case," Nixon told Colson. "I mean, after all, the man's wife is dead, was killed, he's got a child that has—"

"Brain damage from an automobile accident," Colson finished the sentence.

"That's right," Nixon said. "We'll build that son of a bitch up like nobody's business. We'll have Buckley write a column and say, you know, that he should have clemency, if you've given 18 years of service [to your country]."[27]

Ten days after this conversation, Hunt was taping a program with Buckley. Buckley found a good hook to add Hunt to the program without it looking like an obvious public relations stunt. Senator Ted Kennedy, on Sunday, January 14, had written a lengthy article in the *New York Times* calling for the reestablishment of normal relations with Cuba. Citing President Nixon's bold initiatives in Communist China and Russia, Kennedy thought it was time to take a similar tack toward Cuba. Isolation was not working. "Now is the time," Kennedy wrote, "to lift the veil once more and begin the process of normalizing relations with Cuba."[28]

Buckley used this article as the pretext to have Hunt on his program. Hunt appeared with a Cuban expatriate, a well-known lawyer named Mario Lazo, who had fled Havana after the Castro revolution. The announced topic was "The CIA and Foreign Policy." Although Buckley made a big point that Hunt had been instructed by his lawyer not to talk about Watergate, that is precisely what they talked about for the first ten minutes of the program. And, on cue, Buckley "built up" Hunt's long service to his country. In the process, he also made it appear that Hunt was working for the CIA during the Watergate operation, or that he could at least be forgiven if he crossed the line in service of his country.

First came the build-up. "Howard Hunt was intimately involved as an official in the Bay of Pigs," Buckley said by way of introduction.

"The *New York Times* named him as the principal CIA official directly involved in that venture." He was "a graduate of Brown University who was a war correspondent for *Life* magazine, a freelance writer who [had] published 42 books, most of them spy novels."

Next came the long service: "On retiring from the CIA after 20 years of duty, he did freelance work as a White House consultant, and last June was arrested in connection with the Watergate case."

Hunt corrected Buckley. "I was never arrested," he said. "I surrendered to the US authorities at the appropriate time."

The preliminaries accomplished, Buckley inquired whether Hunt felt free to talk about his activities for the CIA. Hunt said he did, especially since his involvement with the agency had been widely publicized by the government itself. "And I consider [the breach of secrecy] then and I consider it now," Hunt complained, "a unilateral abrogation by the government of its commitment that we entered into upon my retirement from the Central Intelligence Agency." Hunt was serving notice to the agency that he felt free to talk.

Buckley then steered the conversation to the potential involvement of the CIA in Watergate. Because the CIA under its charter had no jurisdiction to conduct operations within the territorial United States, didn't that necessarily mean that the CIA had no involvement in Watergate? Not so, Hunt replied. He gave a recently publicized example of the CIA supporting the National Security Agency in recruiting American students on US campuses "for work in this country which led eventually to work abroad." Buckley had his opening—Hunt, he would contend, lived in a rough-and-tumble world and played by a different set of rules, all in service to his country. In classic Buckley-speak, he argued:

Well, what about the suspicion that has been widely ventilated that experience, especially lifelong experience, with the CIA teaches a person to forget about the legal impediments that lie between him and the accomplishment of a mission that he seeks to achieve? In the grown-up world, as I understand it, everybody recognizes that it is illegal for a CIA operative to work in Cuba and it's illegal for a Cuban operative to work in the United States, but they both do it.

Hunt agreed. Buckley continued to pound on the theme. "I guess the question I'm asking," he said, "is if one spends 20 years working for the CIA, it is likely that on returning to one's own country one has so much absorbed the ethos of the CIA that one tends to go after what it is that one wants and consider local legislation that stands in the way as sort of irrelevant?" Hunt again agreed, pointing out that a burglary in Canada by the CIA would not be a crime, whereas it would be if conducted in "Florida or Texas or Southern California."

To wrap it up in a bow, Buckley asked the final question, all the while disclaiming his intention to "try any sneak punches" with respect to the ground rules of not talking about Watergate:

> MR. BUCKLEY: But I guess what I'm asking is: Is it fair to say, without violating our understanding, that in approaching the Watergate business, you and your associates approached it in the *spirit* of a CIA operation?
>
> MR. HUNT: Yes.[29]

Mario Lazo, the Cuban expatriate attorney who was Buckley's other guest, joined in the conversation to build up the burglars. He interrupted Buckley questions of Hunt to personally vouch for Bernard Barker, the chief of the Miamians. "I hope you won't think that this is a digression," he said, "but may I go back a little bit and tell you how I met Bernard Barker, who is one of the Watergate group."

"Sure, sure," Buckley accommodated.

Lazo went on to describe how Barker had been one of the first in Cuba to sign up for service in the Second World War, how he had secretly led the security detail for the visit of Mrs. Truman and her daughter to Cuba, and how his best friend had been kidnapped, tortured, and brutally executed by the Castro regime. Barker, according to Lazo, turned violently anti-Castro. "Then he came to my office and he said, 'I want you to tell me what I can do to help bring down the monster who murdered my best friend,'" Lazo said. "And I took him over to the American embassy and introduced him to the CIA agent there, and that's the way he started working for the CIA."

According to Lazo, Barker became involved in the Bay of Pigs operations and witnessed how the Kennedy administration had "betrayed" the freedom fighters during the early hours of the operation by withdrawing promised US air support at the last second.

In 1972, Lazo said, Barker feared that the antiwar Democrats—Kennedy, Fulbright, McGovern—were going to move to recognize the Castro regime, just as Castro was, by Lazo's calculations, failing.

Thus Bernard Barker needed to find any way he could to support the Republicans. The implication was that Barker's participation in Watergate was the natural result of his anti-Castro activities.[30]

Chuck Colson could not have come up with a tighter script. The message had to resonate with the Miamians, who could deduce that this was an outward sign of support from the Nixon administration. Perhaps they weren't going to be abandoned after all.

The White House, Friday, January 19, 1973

Nixon was up for breakfast by 8:30 on Friday morning. The weather was beautiful in Washington—near 60 degrees. The day promised to be hectic, full of inaugural preparations all around the White House. But Nixon would closet himself away for most of it. He met Ray Price several times, going over edit after edit of his inaugural address. At 12:30 PM, he went to the White House barbershop for a haircut.

Of all the members of his immediate family, he seemed to be most engaged that afternoon with his daughter Julie in making final plans for the inaugural festivities. She called him around midday to ask if the family wanted to invite the Marriotts to sit in the presidential box at the inaugural concerts that night. "Frankly, I think it should just be the family, and everybody will understand," he replied.

Julie had some disturbing news: Alice Roosevelt Longworth, now eighty-eight, was not going to make it to the inaugural. "She's spitting up blood," Julie reported.

"She's really that sick, is she?" a concerned Nixon asked. Julie thought it might be a nice gesture for the family to leave one of the seats in the front row on the inaugural platform empty for her, with a rose symbolically placed on it showing the deepest respect for the Washington icon. "Very nice thought," Nixon said.

"Alrighty," a perky Julie responded. "It would be a nice touch; people would like the idea that she's been loyal and all that."[31]

"We'll have a good time tonight, sweetie," Nixon said to his daughter. He looked forward to the multiple concerts planned at the John F. Kennedy Center for the Performing Arts that night.

At 6:40 PM Nixon returned to the second-floor residence and had dinner by himself in the Lincoln Sitting Room. At some point he switched into his tux. He kept working over his speech until 8:30 PM, when he joined the First Lady and went to the South Grounds of the White House to motor over to the Kennedy Center. Sirens screamed across Washington as he made his way. White House security noted his every move was choreographed and watched: "The President's activities during the Inaugural concerts were televised nationwide and recorded by White House photographers."[32]

When the president arrived at the Kennedy Center, he and Pat Nixon hooked up with Ed and Tricia Cox, Julie Eisenhower, and Mamie Eisenhower, the ex-president's widow. They were taken to a holding room in the Eisenhower Theater, the smallest of the theaters on the Kennedy Center's main level (seating eleven hundred).[33] There they were greeted by J. Willard Marriott, chairman of the 1973 Inaugural Committee, and his wife, but the Nixon party entered the presidential box with just the family members and the chairwoman of the inaugural concerts, Pam Powell, a friend of Julie's and daughter of actress June Allyson.

There were three different concerts running simultaneously at the Kennedy Center. A youth concert, featuring Miss America 1972 (Laurie Lea Schaefer—her predecessor had been Phyllis George), was held in the Eisenhower Theater. After watching this concert for twenty minutes, the president and his group moved next door to the opera house in the Kennedy Center (which seats twenty-three hundred), where they witnessed the second half of the American Music Concert, featuring Bob Hope, Vicki Carr, and Roger Williams. Forty-five minutes later, they took their leave and entered the concert hall in the Kennedy Center (which seats twenty-four hundred and had just opened a few years earlier) to attend the 1973 Symphonic Concert, performed by the Philadelphia Symphony Orchestra, conducted by the acclaimed Eugene Ormandy. Charlton Heston was the master of ceremonies; Billy Graham and his wife joined the president as his guests in the presidential box.

Of the three events, Nixon was most taken by the Ormandy concert. He had asked the conductor to play Tchaikovsky's triumphant *1812 Overture*, with its climactic cannonade volley, and several other favorites. But it was a piano concerto, composed by Edvard Grieg and selected by the orchestra's piano soloist, Van Cliburn, that set Nixon afire. "Although that Opera House is the ugliest goddamned room I've ever seen," he later said to Haldeman, "—Jesus, I mean, when you compare it to the Bolshoi or to the Philadelphia place, it's something; but my God, that Ormandy is a showman, isn't he?" Haldeman, who also attended, agreed. "He takes these numbers—and I must say that Grieg was a hellava good choice, [and] nobody has ever played it better. See, most orchestras override piano. Ormandy *fits it in*. It was the most graceful, beautiful thing," Nixon effused. "I mean most of those clowns in there didn't know what the hell was going on," he said of his supporters who turned out to celebrate his inauguration, "but *that* was one of the great performances."[34]

The Ormandy concert was marred by some controversy because sixteen of the orchestra's members had asked to be excused in protest of the Christmas bombings. Ormandy wouldn't hear of it. He told Nixon that he warned the musicians, "Hell, no, we'll throw you out of the symphony." According to Nixon, Ormandy went on to say, "If the president decides to come back [stage], I hope he does, and I want him to put his arm around me in front of those goddamn left-wingers."[35]

One thing Nixon could not have failed to observe was that there were many open seats at the concerts at the Kennedy Center. Despite his overwhelming landslide in November, the *New York Times* took note of what it called "a heaving sprinkling of empty seats" that dotted the concert halls. Perhaps it was the elitist tone or the cost of these lavish events. "The concert at the Kennedy center," the *Times* wrote of the orchestra performance, "one of three presented tonight at the center by the Inaugural Committee, was open to formally dressed ticket-holders only, with a bonus of a candlelight dinner—Long Island duckling with wild rice and California wine—for those who spent $250 or more for their seats."[36]

These celebratory concerts were heavily contrasted in the press with a solemn counter-concert performed across town at the National Cathedral and overseen by none other than Dean Francis Sayre. "The concert at the Washington Cathedral, unofficial and free on a first-come, first-served basis, was called 'a plea for peace,' rather than a protest, but the choice of music alone made clear the counterpoint," the *Times* wrote. Tchaikovsky's *1812 Overture*, which celebrated the rout of Napoleon's army in Russia in the winter of 1812, was juxtaposed by the peace group with Joseph Haydn's gentle, meditative *Mass in the Time of War*, written in 1796, the year Napoleon defeated the Austrians in Italy. "It is sometimes called the 'Kettledrum' mass," the *Times* wrote, "because of the urgent drumrolls that underscore the final plea, 'Dona nobis pacem'—'Give us peace.'"

Unlike the Kennedy Center events, the peace concert was mobbed. More than ten thousand people began lining up at 4:30 PM for the 9:00 PM event, waiting in the rain for a chance to get into the cathedral. Senator Edward Kennedy appeared with his wife, Joan, around the same time that the Nixons left the White House for the inaugural events. Eunice and Sergeant Shriver and former senator Eugene McCarthy followed closely behind. The church was filled to capacity and an estimated twelve to fifteen thousand people stood outside in the damp night listening to the concert through a public address system. Leonard Bernstein conducted. He and several prominent soloists and locally recruited orchestra members all donated their time or were paid scale wages and dressed in ordinary business clothes to contrast with the formal attire at the inaugural events.

Dean Sayre said that a longing for peace had brought everyone together that night.

At the exclusive F Street Club in a fashionable part of downtown Washington, Henry Ford II and his wife hosted their traditional inaugural party.[37] Henry Kissinger showed up and by coincidence so did John and Martha Mitchell. "Henry!" Martha exclaimed. "Martha!" he responded, and they both hugged and kissed. "I'm going to be with the rich cats tonight," Martha unabashedly told a reporter. "For a minute," the reporter wrote, "as gawking Congressmen nudged their wives surreptitiously, it was the rich, elegant, and powerful playing old home week."[38]

Nixon returned to the White House at 11:54 PM. He and his family withdrew to the second-floor residence. Everyone went to bed except Nixon. Though he would be inaugurated at precisely noon the next day, he was wired. He went to the Lincoln Sitting Room, where he called Bob Haldeman and talked for half an hour, burning logs crackling in the fireplace in the background.

And then, at a little past 1:00 in the morning, he ordered another drink and asked the White House operator to get Chuck Colson on the line.

The night was still young.

19

"In Our Own Lives, Let Each of Us Ask—Not Just What Government Will Do for Me, But What I Can Do for Myself"

The Lincoln Sitting Room, Early Hours of January 20, 1973

Nixon was tipsy, slurring his words, trying his best to unwind. In less than eleven hours, he would stand on the pavilion that had been erected on the East Front of the Capitol building and take the solemn oath of office before millions watching on television in the United States and around the world. He needed to rest, yet there in the Lincoln Sitting Room at 1:00 in the morning, Richard Nixon's desire was to spend time communing and ruminating with his dark angel, Chuck Colson.

"Hello?" he said, once the White House operator had located the ever-available Colson.[1]

"Yes sir, Mr. President," Colson chirped back, fully alert and sober despite the late hour and number of parties he had attended that evening. Colson was aware of the extraordinary access he had to the most powerful man in the world, who at that moment in time was at the peak of his authority, crowned in his ultimate moment of triumph.

"Well, how'd you like the evening?" Nixon asked, his words slow and deliberate. Colson said he enjoyed it. He had gone to the American Music Concert. Nixon said he had missed the best program by not attending the symphony, going on about Ormandy and Grieg as he had just done with Haldeman. "Well I wanted the symphony and my wife wanted the American Music, so we compromised and went to the American Music," Colson joked, but his attempt at lightness walked right past Nixon. With few exceptions, Nixon appeared to find humor a waste of time.

"Don't you think the idea of having three concerts was great?" Nixon said. "Sticking it to Washington, having Ormandy, the great [Philadelphia] symphony, rather than that goddamn Washington Symphony, even with [Music Director Antal] Dorati, who's a great composer."[2]

Nixon and Colson paid little heed to the Leonard Bernstein concert that night at the National Cathedral, or to the scattering of protests that were breaking out across Washington. Nixon saw the young performers at the inaugural concerts at the Kennedy Center as the true representatives of America's youth: warm, friendly, and enthusiastic. "You know, with all these, you know, few assholes who say they want to demonstrate against the war," Nixon remarked acidly, "most of the kids are all for us."

Colson agreed. "Sure they are," he said, "Oh, hell yes." Colson said even his children agreed. "No, my kids were there, and they said it was a great crowd," he added. "Those kids were marvelous."

They spoke of the bombings and the peace negotiations and the connection between the two. Nixon thought that anyone "who had his damn head screwed on tight" would recognize that the bombings had led to the recent breakthrough in the negotiations. "You mustn't say it too soon," he cautioned, " 'til we sign the agreement. And we still have this problem with that son of a bitch Thieu. We'll get the word on him tomorrow," he said. "But he'll go—he'll go [along] before committing suicide." Nixon wondered how his political opponents now felt about the bombing since it seemed to have worked in bringing peace negotiations to completion. "But put yourself in the position of [our] opposition," he said to Colson, "how in the hell do [they] think we got it? When Henry after ten days—you remember the cables—he gave up. We would have been in the war for three of four more months and hundreds of Americans would've been killed. What do they want?"[3]

Nixon took solace from the cheering and shouting that followed an extemporaneous remark made that night by a musician named Mike Curb, whose group, Mike Curb and the Congregation, had recorded the upbeat 1972 campaign song "Nixon Now." Curb's group performed during one of the inaugural concerts, and he stood up after a song about bringing people together and said, "President Nixon has done more for peace than any president in our history!" The crowd erupted.

Nixon loved it—the applause, to his surprise, was sustained and deafening. In his memoirs he wrote that he thought the remark would provoke "a few boos." The opposite proved to be true. "Interestingly enough," he wrote, "he got a pretty good cheer out of it."[4] To Colson in this late-night phone call he was more blunt: "Shit, they all took the roof off."[5]

Darkness, though, returned to Nixon's mood. If and when peace finally did come, he reminded Colson, he wanted to get even with his war critics: "But listen, Chuck, as I told Haldeman, your job is to see, by God, we put it to them, I mean, assuming it works out." Once "peace with honor" became a reality, he said, "then we just pour it right to 'em."

Then, curiously, fifteen minutes into the conversation, instead of signing off and going to bed, Nixon decided he wanted to read long passages from his inaugural address to Colson.

"You want to hear a little of the acceptance speech?" Nixon asked. Colson was more than obliging. "Yeah, I'd love to, sir," he responded.

Nixon's theme was peace, but as the accords were yet to be inked, he could only speak of the anticipation of peace—one, he said, that would not be "a flimsy peace which is merely an interlude between wars, but a peace that can endure for generations to come."

His main thrust was not about American power but its limitations. Though the United States would continue to play a key role in the world, Nixon saw a new era, forged by his innovative policies. "The time is passed," he read to Colson, "when America will make every other nation's conflict our own, or make every other nation's future our responsibility, or presume to tell the people of other nations how to manage their own affairs." The United States would no longer be the world's policeman. This was not the "bear any burden, oppose any foe" philosophy that John Kennedy had spoken of in his inaugural twelve years earlier.

This was the Nixon Doctrine. The United States would do its share in defending peace and freedom around the world, but other nations needed to do their part, too, and take responsibility, like in South Vietnam, for their own futures. Ultimately, the message was one of self-determination and self-reliance. There was nothing particularly novel about this declaration—it was a reaffirmation of a policy he first articulated in 1969.[6]

This message of self-sufficiency, though, was to be expanded by Nixon to the domestic sphere.[7] This is what Nixon wanted to preview for Colson. The "key point" of his inaugural address, he said, was applying the Nixon Doctrine to domestic policies. "And this, I think you're going to like," he predicted.

Then he started reading: "Just as building a structure of peace abroad has required turning away from old policies that failed, so building a new era of progress at home requires turning away from old policies that have failed." Colson was pleased. "Beautiful," he said quietly.

A few lines later, Colson was brought figuratively to his feet when Nixon read this sentence: "Abroad and at home, the time has come to turn away from the condescending policies of paternalism—of 'Washington knows best.'" Colson chortled: "Ah-ha! Great! Love that."

Nixon knew he had his one-man audience. "Listen to this," he continued. "A person can be expected to act responsibly only if he has responsibility. This is human nature. So let us encourage individuals at home and nations abroad to do more for themselves, to decide more for themselves. Let us locate responsibility in more places." Colson was aglow.

"And this is a key line," Nixon said. "Let us measure what we will do for others by what they will do for themselves." Colson muttered, "Mmm, beautiful."

"Listen to this," Nixon went on, gathering steam as he read. "Government must learn to take less from people so that people can do more for themselves." Colson sounded practically orgasmic: "Oh, magnificent!"

Nixon read, "Let each of us remember that America was built not by government, but by people—not by welfare, but by work—not by shirking responsibility, but by seeking responsibility." Colson was like a man experiencing the rapture. "Oh Jesus" was all he could say.

Nixon was the anti-Kennedy. He even purposely appropriated John Kennedy's line, "Ask not what your country can do for you, ask what you can do for your country," and twisted it to his own. "In our own lives," Nixon wrote, "let each of us ask—not just, 'What will government do for me?' but 'What can I do for myself?'"

"Magnificent!" Colson exclaimed. "Just magnificent, Mr. President."

Nixon was starting a revolution, one that would be co-opted by Ronald Reagan seven years later. The "me generation" had found its voice, full throttle. "That is the Nixon legacy, in my humble judgment," Colson said. "Because what you are really saying is you believe in self-reliance— self-reliance in nations around the world, self-reliance of people."

"That's right," Nixon agreed. "We will help those that help themselves."[8]

It was quarter to 2:00 in the morning when they finally wrapped up the call.[9] Nixon made one more brief phone call to Haldeman, and sometime around 2:00 AM he finally went to bed.[10]

The White House Residence, Morning of January 20, 1973

At 8:30 AM, Nixon was up having breakfast.[11] Before eating, though, he ran five hundred steps in place. "It left me breathless," he wrote in his memoirs, "but I thought it was a good idea to be in as good a shape as I could for the ceremonies to take place later that day."[12]

For some reason—strange given the underlying bitterness toward poor black Americans and civil rights in his inaugural speech—Nixon wanted to connect with Lincoln on the morning of his second inaugural. "Before going downstairs," he wrote, "I stepped into the Lincoln Bedroom in the spot where the Emancipation Proclamation was and where I understood Lincoln's desk was located and bowed my head for a moment, and prayed that I might be able to give the country some lift, some inspiration, and some leadership in the rather brief inaugural that I had prepared."[13]

This statement in Nixon's memoirs stands in odd juxtaposition to Colson's report a few hours earlier. "I'm convinced of what the mood of the country is," Colson said to Nixon in their nighttime call. He said he had been speaking with Dick Scammon, an elections analyst and the coauthor of the highly influential 1970 book *The Real Majority: An Extraordinary Examination of the American Electorate*.[14] "I am convinced from talking with Scammon," Colson said. "What'd Scammon say?" Nixon interrupted, always interested in the views of this political forecaster, who had assumed almost guru status within the Nixon White House, especially with Colson. "Well, of course," Colson said, "he just thinks we are absolutely on the right course, that people are fed up with a lot of government, that they don't want a charismatic, exciting call to higher purpose."[15]

At 9:32 AM Nixon asked White House operators to get Henry Kissinger on the line.

"Hello," Nixon said, taking the call in the Lincoln Sitting Room.[16]

"Mr. President," Kissinger replied.

"Did you enjoy the evening?"

"I think it was really very nice," Kissinger said.

"Which one did you go to?" Nixon asked.

"I went to the symphony concert," Kissinger said.

Nixon liked this. "Yeah, I saw the last part of it—came in at the intermission. Boy that Ormandy certainly knows how to play up to a piano, doesn't he?"

Kissinger said, "Beautiful. That is really hard to do." He didn't realize how much he had hit it on the head.

Nixon, "The Grieg [piece] of course is famous, every pianist loves to play it. But orchestras usually overwhelm it. Of course, this Cliburn was never better, and so was Ormandy. They're both great actors. They were just fantastic."

"It was done with great delicacy, very beautiful," Kissinger agreed.

Then they moved to the peace negotiations. "What is the word from Haig?" Nixon asked.

"Well, he's had a session and Thieu has written you another letter," Kissinger responded.

Nixon turned black and anxious—this news was unexpected and bad. His breathing became heavier. "Oh God!" Nixon said, deep concern in his voice. Kissinger said it was important to be patient. Nixon heavily sighed.

"What the guy is doing, he's obviously posturing himself, step-by-step," Kissinger said. "He's now reduced—in his last letter he made four conditions, he's now reduced them to two. He's also sending his foreign minister to Paris to meet with me."

Nixon again exclaimed, "Oh God!" He sounded almost desperate.

Kissinger saw he had to talk him off the ledge. "Well, Mr. President, it has this advantage," he quickly followed up. "My first reaction was like yours; I've been in now for two hours analyzing it, together with my staff. And we all have come to this conclusion: the problem with him is that if we initial an agreement on Tuesday, without visible participation by them, it is a great loss of face."

Nixon: "Yeah."

Kissinger: "If he has his foreign minister there . . ."

Nixon: "Yeah."

Kissinger: "Then he can claim he participated."

Nixon: "Yeah." Another heavy sigh by Nixon. "The foreign minister is his nephew?" Nixon asked.

Kissinger chuckled. "No, no, the nephew is that little bastard, that kid who is the Minister of Information," referring to Thieu's nephew, Hoang Duc Nha. "The foreign minister is an ass," Kissinger said of Tran Van Lam, "and he won't be able to do anything."

Kissinger had a plan. Of Thieu's two remaining conditions, one could be addressed and the other was impossible. The one that was negotiable was Thieu's objection to a provision in the protocols that allowed South Vietnamese police to carry only pistols or sidearms. The police had routinely armed themselves with carbines and M16 rifles. Kissinger thought this was just an oversight by his people in Paris, who had, as he put it, "goofed." Kissinger thought this could be changed or at least a request could be made. The other condition— that all North Vietnamese troops leave the South—was not negotiable.

Haig had wired Kissinger that it was his conclusion from CIA intelligence on the ground in South Vietnam that Thieu was going to go along, but that "he is going to play every card until the last minute so that he can tell his constituents he had made every effort to improve the agreement."[17] He further explained that it was important to "view Thieu's response in the context of Oriental pride and face."[18] Kissinger thus suggested that Nixon respond to Thieu's letter by welcoming the trip of the foreign minister to Paris, but that Nixon should reiterate that the United States was going to initial on Tuesday, and he needed an answer by the next day, before Kissinger returned to Paris. If Thieu had not agreed by then, Nixon would call in selected congressional leaders on Sunday night and say that Thieu was not cooperating. Thieu risked a total cutoff of all aid from the United States under such circumstances. Kissinger said that they should not allow Thieu to string this out until Tuesday—that would be too late.

"I'll do any damn thing it is, or cut off his head if necessary," Nixon said in complete exasperation.[19]

Kissinger reassured Nixon that all the signals coming out of South Vietnam confirmed that Thieu had already told his commanders that there would be a cease-fire on January 28, the day after the formal signing of the accords. Nixon knew that this intelligence came mainly from CIA wiretaps and bugs installed in Thieu's offices and else-where. In his fitful attempts to sleep the night before, Nixon started to wonder if the intelligence was wrong.

"One thing that sort of got into my mind last night which perhaps occurred to you," he said to Kissinger, "I'm not sure how much we can rely on these intercepts. After all, these people are not stupid and I remember when I was in Moscow and Peking, knowing the rooms were bugged, I used to say outlandish things sometimes just for the purpose of putting them on the wrong trail. These characters may be doing this in order to set us up for a fall, has that occurred to you?"

Kissinger said that if they had only bugged one room he might agree, but because the intelligence was coming from so many sources, he thought it was reliable. Besides, he said, such a course by Thieu would be "totally suicidal."

The bottom line was that the peace accords would be initialed on Tuesday next, and Thieu would either go along or face an end to all support from the United States. The decision of the president was "irreversible." Kissinger would draft the president's response. Given Nixon's schedule that day, Kissinger was provided the president's proxy to send the letter without Nixon's review. Thieu was to have until noon Washington time the next day to get on board.

"Any other wars in the world you've started?" Nixon asked Kissinger as they signed off.

"No," Kissinger laughed, "I thought we should get the Inauguration behind us before starting another."[20]

The Inaugural Platform, Noon, January 20, 1973

At 11:03 AM Nixon and the First Lady hosted a coffee for select guests in the Map Room at the White House. Seven minutes later, they exited to a waiting limousine and motored from the South Grounds of the White House to the East Front of the Capitol, where they were taken to a holding room. At 11:41, to the tune of "Hail to the Chief," Nixon was escorted to the inaugural platform. The temperatures were in the low 40s, with a stiff wind. All flags still flew at half-staff in memory of Harry Truman. At noon the chief justice of the United States, Warren E. Burger, administered the oath of office. Nixon appeared drawn and tired as he read quickly, "almost methodically," his inaugural address, his first public speech since election night in early November.[21] The huge crowd seemed mostly uninspired and distracted, interrupting with applause only sparingly.

"We shall answer to God, to history, and to our conscience for the way in which we use these years," Nixon concluded.

After attending a luncheon hosted by the Congress at the Capitol, the president and First Lady traveled by motorcade from the Capitol to the White House, standing up in the car through an open sunroof, waving to the crowd. Along the way, war protestors made themselves known, hurling eggs, apples, oranges, and expletives as the president's car passed by. One demonstrator broke free and charged the limousine before being tackled by Secret Service. All the while, Pat Nixon refused to sit back down, despite Secret Service warnings, much to her husband's pride and satisfaction.

In a receiving line back at the White House, John Dean recalled Nixon grabbing him by the hand and leading him away from everyone to very sternly admonish him to make sure the protestor who rushed the car was arrested and prosecuted.[22] Later, after the inaugural parade ended, Nixon called Robert Taylor, special agent in charge of the White House Secret Service detail, to make sure that a charge had been filed against the young man.[23]

Saigon, Saturday Evening, January 20, 1973

"No point is served in reviewing the record of our exchanges regarding the agreement and the protocols," Nixon's letter to President Thieu, written by Kissinger, started.[24] The letter had been hand-delivered to Thieu by Ambassador Ellsworth Bunker because Haig was already in South Korea, consulting with President Park Chung-hee on his way back to Washington. Nixon, through Kissinger's writing, continued to argue that the North Vietnamese troops left in the South really had no legal right to remain, given all the provisions of the agreement that spoke to the independence and sovereignty of South Vietnam, including the fact that reunification could only be achieved by peaceful means; that the introduction of war materials into the South was prohibited; and that the Demilitarized Zone was to be respected by all parties. A unilateral note, summing up these arguments, was to be delivered to President Thieu on the day the peace accords were signed.

It was all a lawyer's argument, aggregating various provisions from the agreement with a logical argument to reach a predetermined conclusion.[25] It had little to do with reality. Thieu knew it and so did Kissinger. "We have now reached a decisive point," Nixon's letter read. "I can no longer hold up my decision pending the outcome of further exchanges." The threat to call in congressional leaders was delivered. Nixon demanded Thieu's response by noon, January 21.[26]

The White House, Sunday, January 21, 1973

After staying up late attending five inaugural balls, Nixon slept in on Sunday, taking breakfast at 10:00 AM. He called Kissinger at 10:30 AM to get the latest report.[27] Nothing yet had been received from Thieu. Noon came and went. Nixon was buried in worship services and receptions for the remainder of the day.

Shortly after noon, Thieu's letter arrived. It was all but an unconditional surrender. On the most problematic point—the one over which he had fought with such tenacity—he finally caved. He accepted, "for the sake of unity," the refusal by Hanoi to withdraw its troops, so long as Nixon continued to give "strong assurances for the continuation of aid and support to the GVN [South Vietnam] after the cease-fire." As part of his face-saving actions, Thieu continued to insist he would wait for the results of further negotiations in Paris on the protocols involving the handgun-only restrictions on his police force. "It is for these important negotiations that I am sending today Foreign Minister Tran Van Lam."[28] He wanted it to appear that he had participated in the final negotiations in some meaningful way before signing the agreements. Haig and Kissinger saw this as Thieu's final capitulation. They were convinced they could obtain this minor change from the North Vietnamese. The letters Thieu had written, Haig guaranteed Nixon by midafternoon, were merely "for history and his constituency."[29]

Kissinger would meet with Thieu's foreign minister in Paris— South Vietnamese face would be saved. Nixon directed Kissinger to meet with him at 8:00 AM the following morning in his Executive Office Building office before Kissinger made his way to Andrews Air Force Base to fly to Paris.

It had been a nerve-wracking weekend for the president. He was still edgy on Sunday night about whether Thieu would finally be persuaded to go along. His schedule does not reflect whether he turned on the television on Sunday night to watch Howard Hunt on William F. Buckley's program, *Firing Line*. It is doubtful he did. He had a private dinner in the Yellow Oval Room in the residence with the First Lady, Julie Eisenhower, and Bebe Rebozo that started at 8:10 PM.[30]

But one thing he should have noticed on Inauguration Day was a harbinger. More than half of Congress did not show for the swearing-in ceremony, including all but one of the fifteen black House members.[31] George McGovern was conspicuously out of the country, delivering a scathing speech in Oxford, England. He warned that liberals needed to resurrect Congress if the country was to escape "one-man rule" by the current occupant of the White House.[32] But it was the absence of North Carolina senator Sam Ervin, future chair of the Senate Watergate Committee, that should have caused Nixon and his advisors to pause.

"Senator Sam J. Ervin Jr., whose chairmanship of two Senate subcommittees and one committee has placed him at the center of the gathering Congressional demand for a restoration of legislative authority, stayed in his home state of North Carolina to make a series of speeches," the *New York Times* reported.[33]

The storm had gathered. January 22, 1973, was finally at hand.

20

January 22, 1973

It was a day no one had marked down for significance. In the flinty Hill Country of central Texas, as morning's first light brought life to the scenic area surrounding the Pedernales River, Secret Service agent James "Mike" Howard awoke for what he thought would be another routine day at the LBJ Ranch. In Washington, Harry Blackmun and Lewis Powell arrived at the Supreme Court building for the start of a busy week. The indefatigable Henry Kissinger packed his bags for Paris and appeared early at the White House for one final meeting with the president before flying off to initial the Vietnam peace accords. Judge John Sirica prepared for the start of the third week of the Watergate burglars' trial after having given his staff and the jury the afternoon off the previous Friday in recognition of the inaugural events and the president's declaration of a half-day holiday for most government employees.

On the streets in Washington, New York, Austin, and other cities around the country, bundles of *Time* magazines were dropped off at newsstands. On the cover was a caricature of Nixon, hand on Bible, at his swearing-in, with the leaders of China and the Soviet Union, the chief participants in the Vietnam peace negotiations, a soldier, an American POW, and an antiwar movement protester all looking on as symbolic spectators. The banner across the front of the magazine read NIXON II: BEYOND VIET NAM. Inside, there was an article titled "The Sexes: Abortion on Demand." It broke the big story: "Last week *Time* learned that the Supreme Court has decided to strike down nearly every anti-abortion law in the land."[1] It was a scoop for *Time*.

Nixon arrived at his Executive Office Building hideaway office at
7:56 AM. He dictated a letter to Billy Graham, commending his participation at the White House Sunday worship services the day before
and his inspirational remarks about the Lord's Prayer.[2] At 8:15 AM
Henry Kissinger walked into the president's office. "You all set for
your trip?" Nixon greeted him. Kissinger warned that it may take an
extra day to wrap up all the paperwork in Paris, but he would do all he
could to cause the initialing to take place the next day, Tuesday, January 23. Nixon agreed to the delay so long as the formal signing date of
January 27 did not slip and so long as the one-day delay didn't spook
the North Vietnamese.[3]

Kissinger slipped away at 9:10 AM. He was flown by helicopter to
Andrews Air Force Base to board a plane that was already fired up
and waiting to take him to Paris.

In Texas, LBJ's secretary, Jewell Malechek, ate her breakfast and
started getting ready for the customary morning drive around the
360-acre ranch, which was located about fifteen miles from Johnson
City. Things had not been right with her boss since he returned from
Virginia the year before, when he had had a serious heart attack while

Henry Kissinger on his way to Paris to initial the peace accords, January
22, 1973.

White House Photo Office, Nixon Library

visiting his daughter and son-in-law, Lynda and Chuck Robb. He had changed so much. He walked slower and he didn't do the driving anymore. Jewell drove him everywhere he went. He didn't climb stairs. He had to watch his diet. And he had started chain-smoking again. She later said, "You don't really think that a man that's that dynamic—that anything could ever happen to them."[4]

Lyndon Johnson appeared at the backdoor of the ranch house that morning, as he did every morning, for his walk. Secret Service agent Mike Howard came out from the nearby security shack, and the two met on the back driveway for his constitutional. Something seemed drastically wrong. "This particular day," Howard later remembered, "we were walking down the drive and he was shuffling *real* slow, and I said, 'Mr. President, you sure you're alright?' "

Johnson replied, "Oh, I'm fine."

Howard asked the former president if he had completed his arrangements to go to Acapulco, Mexico, where Johnson expected to spend six weeks on vacation at a home owned by Miguel Aleman, the former president of Mexico. Acapulco had been a favorite getaway destination for LBJ since his Senate days.[5] Mike Howard didn't think LBJ was physically up to the trip this year but did not feel it was his place to say anything about it.

As they moved further down the drive, Howard became alarmed. "So we were walking along and I said, 'Mr. President, I really think you ought to go sit down someplace.' " Howard's pestering did not sit well with Johnson. "He said, 'Sweetheart,'—that's what he called you when he wanted to get a point over—'Sweetheart, don't worry about me. None of the men in my family live past sixty-five, and I'm not worried about it. I'm ready to go.' " Howard responded, "Yeah, but I'm not ready for you to go."[6]

The two men turned around and walked back up the drive, where Johnson got into his big, white Lincoln convertible to be driven over to pick up Jewell Malechek at her home on the ranch grounds. Howard, as usual, followed in his car. "He hadn't been feeling good," Malechek remembered. That day, she said, he was having a cattle guard installed near a house Mrs. Johnson called her "sunset house," in the northwest part of the property. "We drove up there to look at the cattle guard," Malechek said, "and Lyle, my youngest son, was working with a field hand putting that cattle guard in and also put up a lot of deer-proof fencing. So he was kidding Lyle about being a fence builder and all that."[7]

Seventy-five miles away in Austin, Sarah Weddington thought about whether this might be the day that the Supreme Court would finally announce its opinion in *Roe v. Wade*. She had run for and won a seat in the Texas House of Representatives the previous November—a month after the second oral argument in *Roe* in the Supreme Court—and had begun working on legislation to repeal the Texas abortion statute in the event the court upheld the Texas law in *Roe*. "I'd always heard that where there is a will there is a way," she wrote. "If so, somehow, someday—whether in the courts or through legislative action, whether this coming year or the next—we would free women from the horrors of illegal abortion." Weddington had gone to the state capitol early on January 22 to get organized for the week and catch up on correspondence. She remembers the morning as "wet and wintry, the kind of day I wished I could stay in bed and read a book."[8]

Nixon called Al Haig at 9:47 AM, after Kissinger left for the airport, to talk more about the statement about the initialing of the agreements that were being drafted for Nixon to deliver Tuesday evening on national television, assuming Kissinger could pull it all together.

The talk turned to Nixon's enemies and their likely reaction to the announcement of peace. "You know, it's an interesting thing," he mused. "I've been sitting here thinking after talking to Henry this morning of how our whole opposition in this country and so forth—how they must be gnashing their goddamn teeth, you know?"[9]

Haig, always more partisan politician than neutral army general, could not have agreed more. "Oh, it's killing them," he said.

"They of course will come back and say we didn't get anything out of it," Nixon predicted. "We didn't get anything out of waiting since October; we could have gotten it then; it wasn't worth fighting for four years; and it isn't going to last; and it's a bad peace, and so forth. I don't think that's going to wash with most people, what do you think, I don't know?"

"I don't think it washes at all," Haig said. This all brought up the image of McGovern's speaking in England over the weekend, which had been particularly nauseating to Haig. "This guy, he's just an out-and-out revolutionary," he declared. "There is another revulsion building to this crap," he added.

"They were really a pitiful bunch during the inauguration, squealing around," Nixon said of the war protesters. "They all know it's coming [peace], and yet they still have to have something to squeal about. They're going to commit suicide, some of these bastards, you know," he said. "Really, physically—when they don't have something to hate about. Isn't that it?" Haig agreed. "They're really so frustrated—they hate the country, they hate themselves," Nixon said. "And that's what it's really about. It isn't just about the war." The call ended at 9:53 AM.[10]

Seven minutes later, at 10:00 AM, with the nine justices gathered behind the slightly concave bench of the US Supreme Court, Justice Harry Blackmun started reading from his eight-page prepared statement on *Roe* and *Doe*. The Supreme Court had its usual assortment of court watchers and media present. Dottie Blackmun, Justice Blackmun's spouse, was among them. She had come down to the court to witness her husband deliver his statement on the opinions. Lewis Powell noticed her in the audience and scribbled a handwritten note from the bench to be delivered to her by a court messenger. "Dottie," he wrote, "Harry has written an historic opinion, which I was proud to join. His statement from the bench this morning also was excellent. I am glad you were here."[11]

The phone at Sarah Weddington's home law office in Austin began to ring. She was eventually located at her office at the state capitol and told of her victory. "Pandemonium broke out," she wrote. "The phones erupted with press calls, congratulatory calls, calls requesting information about the decision."[12] She and Linda Coffee both were surprised by the scope and breadth of the opinions. They could not have imagined the rulings as ultimately fashioned.[13] They had never argued for viability or the trimester analysis. "Never in any of our briefs had we suggested anything about a trimester approach to pregnancy," Weddington wrote. "Almost never do attorneys find a concept for the first time in the opinion in their own case. But here exactly that had happened. I wondered where the concept had come from."[14]

Warren Burger, whose three-paragraph concurring opinion ended by declaring, "Plainly, the Court today rejects any claim that the Constitution requires abortion on demand," was "absolutely livid" when he found out about the *Time* leak and story.[15] It probably didn't help that the article was titled "The Sexes: Abortion on Demand." According to Powell biographer John Jeffries, "Burger sent a confidential letter demanding that the Justices question their clerks and [threaten] lie detector tests to uncover the culprit."[16]

In Judge Sirica's courtroom, the morning started off with a delay. The week before, the issue of the personal privacy of those who had been wiretapped at the Democratic National Convention had been taken up to the court of appeals in anticipation of the testimony of

Alfred Baldwin, the monitor and lookout in the Howard Johnson hotel across the street from the Watergate. Baldwin's examination started on Wednesday and continued on Friday, but he had not yet finished his testimony on the stand. The court of appeals ruled that the content of the overheard conversations could not be divulged.[17]

On Monday morning, January 22, Baldwin's plane was delayed in New Haven because of bad weather. He chartered a plane to get to New York, where he planned to catch the shuttle to Washington, but when he had still not arrived by 10:30 AM, Judge Sirica decided to have the prosecutors proceed with other witnesses. Baldwin had been unable to find a hotel in Washington over the weekend because of the influx of visitors for the inaugural events.[18]

In Key Biscayne, Florida, sometime after returning from a trip to the bank, Bebe Rebozo opened his mailbox to find a "beautiful letter" from Lyndon Johnson, inviting him to visit his ranch in Texas.[19]

At noon at the LBJ Ranch, Jewell Malechek and Lyndon Johnson had lunch. Johnson asked Secret Service agent Mike Howard to check in on his favorite mare, Lady B, in one of the ranch barns. He told Howard that they would take another ride in the evening, but he was going to take a nap. Howard went to check on the horse and made sure she was fed and watered. He was about a quarter of a mile from the ranch house.

And then, several hours later, he heard the anguished call over his walkie-talkie radio. LBJ was on his phone from his bedroom calling the ranch switchboard operator, saying, "Get me Mike. Mike where are you? Get me Mike." Johnson had put on an oxygen mask from a hookup to an oxygen tank he kept next to his bed. Howard radioed the two agents in the security shack to get to the former president right away. The two, Ed Nowland and Harry Harris, were first on the scene; Howard was not far behind. They found Johnson lying next to his bed. He was already blue. His oxygen mask had been torn off. "He's spit up in it," Howard said. It was 3:55 PM Central Standard Time. The agents immediately began to administer CPR, including mouth-to-mouth resuscitation. Lyndon Johnson was totally unresponsive and appeared to be already dead.

They got the former president on a stretcher to take him to the family's twin-engine Beach King Air plane in the ranch hangar. Doctors were called, and one arrived just as the plane was taxiing to take off from the ranch's 6,300-foot asphalt airstrip. The destination was the Brooke Army Medical Center in San Antonio. The doctor on board,

Dr. David Abbott from Johnson City, worked on LBJ the entire eighty-mile trip but said to the Secret Service agents, "It's no use, he's gone."

When the plane got to San Antonio International Airport at 4:33 PM, Johnson was pronounced dead by Dr. Abbott, and Mike Howard called the Secret Service in Washington to say he was with "Old Texas," a code signifying that the former president had expired. He then called Mrs. Johnson. When she arrived by helicopter, Howard went out to meet her and said, "Mrs. Johnson, he just didn't make it this time."[20]

This was the second time in just more than a decade that Howard had a front row seat to a presidential death. He had been part of the Secret Service detail in Texas on the day John Kennedy was assassinated and was one of two Secret Service agents assigned to keep Oswald's family—his wife, Marina, his mother, Marguerite, and his brother, Robert—in protective custody.[21] Johnson himself called Howard. Johnson worried, he told him, about rumors that mobs might kill Oswald's family. Johnson said, "Mike, I don't care what you do, you don't let anything happen to these people."[22]

In Washington, Richard Nixon was on the warpath. For the second time in one day, that morning's issue of *Time* magazine was causing a crisis at the topmost echelons of the federal government. And both articles could be traced back to one young reporter: David Beckwith, Larry Hammond's former University of Texas Law School acquaintance–turned-journalist. Beckwith was behind the *Roe* scoop that so infuriated the chief justice and another article that caught Nixon's attention, titled "Trials: The Spy in the Cold." Beckwith had scored an interview with Howard Hunt. The resulting article claimed that Hunt had convinced the Miamians to plead guilty, promising each defendant up to $1,000 for every month spent in prison. In addition, the article explosively asserted that Hunt had told the Miamians that the Watergate bugging had been approved by the White House, "specifically two presidential advisors: former Attorney General John Mitchell, then head of the Committee for the Re-Election of the President, and Charles W. Colson, who at the time was on the White House staff as special counsel to the President."[23]

Hunt told Beckwith that he was taking care of his people. "Nobody above or below me was ever sold out. I protect the people I deal with."

Although the article had many of the overtones of the staged Buckley interview—Hunt as long-serving patriot, Bay of Pigs commander, Castro fighter, beset by adversaries and abandoned by the

CIA—Nixon was in a white fury when he read the names of Mitchell and Colson as the responsible actors in the commissioning of the Watergate break-in.[24]

At virtually the same time that LBJ was suffering his fatal heart attack in Texas, Nixon called his press secretary, Ron Ziegler, to order a complete embargo on *Time* as a result of the Beckwith article. Chuck Colson was meeting with Nixon at the time.[25] "In view of *Time's* using that story on Mitchell and Colson," Nixon said to Ziegler, "anybody, *anybody* in the White House who talks to anybody from *Time*, his resignation must be on my desk within one minute. Is that clear?"

Ziegler said, "Yes sir."

Nixon: "You get that order around as fast as you can."

Ziegler: "Alright."

Nixon: "And you are to enforce it. And that means [Jerry] Schecter [*Time's* White House correspondent], everybody else. You tell the NSC crowd: no calls at all are to be taken or returned from *Time* magazine unless I approve them in the future. Is that clear?"

Ziegler: "Yes sir."[26]

A few minutes later Nixon, even more worked up, called Ziegler again. He said he had found out that *Time* had run the article with malice aforethought. "You are to hit [John] Ehrlichman hard on it. He is to take that whole goddamn domestic council—all the left-wingers in there—and they are to shut their damn mouths."[27]

Colson wanted to bring a libel suit against *Time*.

Ten minutes after Johnson's plane touched down at the San Antonio International Airport, the president's assistant, Steve Bull, entered the EOB office where Nixon was going over the draft of his Vietnam speech for Tuesday night with Bob Haldeman and Ray Price. Bull told them that Johnson had been taken by plane to San Antonio and that he might have died.

Haldeman picked up the phone in the EOB to call Dr. Walter Tkach, the president's personal physician, to check on LBJ's condition. Nixon can be heard in the background talking about how Eisenhower and Johnson were both hypochondriacs. "I guess anyone who's had a heart attack maybe always [becomes] one."[28]

"Walter, Bob," Haldeman said to Tkach once he was on the line. "Yes Bob," Tkach responded. Haldeman asked, "Have you talked to a doctor down there?" Tkach said, "Yeah, I talked to a doctor. He was waiting at the International Airport in San Antonio. But he hadn't seen him yet. But we got word directly from the Secret Service who found him, they thought he was dead already before they even put him on the plane to go to San Antonio."

Haldeman was incredulous: "You mean there's no doctor there at the ranch?"

Tkach replied, "No, there's no doctor at the ranch, there's like a corpsman."

Haldeman: "Well, for Christ sakes. Does the corpsman think he's dead?"

Tkach: "Yep. But I will verify, Bob, as soon as I can. They don't want to let it out, is what it really is, before the family knows."

Haldeman grew stern: "Well that's fine, but the president needs to know, 'cause he's got to call Mrs. Johnson."[29]

Moments later, Tkach called back. He could still not confirm. Mrs. Johnson was already at the hospital and Johnson was in an ambulance still in transit from the airport.[30] Then on a third call, Tkach finally had definitive news. "OK, here's the story," he said to Haldeman. "He's dead alright. They tried to revive him on the plane and it didn't work, but they did take him up to a suite at the Brooke Army Hospital. There was a doctor who came down with him [on the plane]. He is dead, but they aren't going to say anything until Mrs. Johnson gives the OK."[31] As they were hanging up, Haldeman can be heard saying to Nixon, "He's dead."

Lady Bird Johnson called the family spokesman, Tom Johnson (no relation), the man who would become the publisher of the *Los Angeles Times* and the president of CNN, but who at the time was the executive vice president of the Johnson family television and radio station, KTBC in Austin. Mrs. Johnson said to him in a solemn, steady voice: "Tom, we didn't make it this time. Lyndon is dead." She asked him to make the public announcement and to take charge of the arrangements.[32] LBJ and Lady Bird had already dictated the detailed plans for his funeral.

Tom Johnson reached out to the three major networks, and Walter Cronkite of CBS insisted that he take the call on the air. "I am talking to Tom Johnson, the press secretary for Lyndon Johnson's family," Cronkite told a live audience as he held a phone to his ear, "who has reported that the thirty-sixth president of the United States died this afternoon in an ambulance plane on the way to San Antonio where he was being taken after being stricken at his ranch, the LBJ ranch in Johnson City, Texas." It was the first live interruption of Cronkite's evening news program in history.

After completing the breaking news with Tom Johnson, Cronkite hung up and returned to the story on the peace negotiations in Paris, reporting that when presidential aide Henry Kissinger arrived in Paris that day he went directly to the residence of the foreign minister of South Vietnam. "The subject of their conference was not immediately revealed," Cronkite said.[33]

Nixon called Al Haig. "Al, Johnson died," he said. "Oh my," Haig responded. He wondered if the news of Johnson's death could provide Kissinger with an excuse for letting the initialing ceremony slip a day, if necessary. In the meantime, Nixon had to return to the residence, he said, to call Mrs. Johnson.[34] Their discussion was brief. Nixon told her there was going to be an announcement in the next couple of days that LBJ would like. A stoic woman, Lady Bird said she appreciated the president's call.

After dinner, Nixon called Haldeman to lay down the law: he would not attend a Johnson memorial service at the National Cathedral.[35] Haldeman had just talked to Tom Johnson about possible arrangements. "Now you told him that I would not attend anything at the cathedral, flatly, didn't you?" Nixon asked. Haldeman was already ahead of Nixon. He had suggested to Tom Johnson that he didn't think the cathedral would be a suitable venue for a Johnson memorial, given Francis Sayre's antiwar antics. "Because I am not going," Nixon said again, "regardless of what all these babbling idiots like [advisor] Dick Moore say. There is to be nothing at that cathedral. I will not go, even if it's the only thing. Is that clear?" Haldeman understood but said he thought Tom Johnson got the message.

"Goddamit, have it up at the Capitol, in the rotunda," Nixon insisted. "Draw the line, goddamit."

Johnson's death meant that Nixon would have to postpone a nationally televised speech he planned for that coming Sunday night to attack the Great Society. "I just can't go on with that Sunday night thing now, Ehrlichman's [advice] to the contrary notwithstanding," he said to Haldeman. "Because as [Ray] Price says, if you go on and attack the Great Society and all the rest on Sunday night, that isn't in very goddamn good taste, as you well realize. I am just not in the mood, after doing another funeral on Thursday or Friday, to go on national television and kick the hell out of the Great Society and while we're scuttling all of these programs."[36]

He thought that instead the Johnson funeral might be a good opportunity for him to get away to Florida for some rest afterward. He instructed Haldeman to have Ehrlichman see if they could reschedule the anti–Great Society speech for a week later.[37]

That evening Chuck Colson called Nixon. "Well, how's your lawsuit coming?" Nixon asked, referring to Colson's expressed intention to sue *Time*. "I think I have a hellava case," Colson said. They talked briefly about Johnson's death and the irony that he did not live to see peace. "It's the first time in forty years there hasn't been a former president," Nixon observed. "My God, I hadn't thought of that," Colson said.[38]

And at day's end—this hectic, drama-filled day of such profound significance—Harry Blackmun wrote in his diary, simply, "Abortion decisions down. LBJ dies."[39]

21

"The Sun Is Shining in Paris This Afternoon"

The Oval Office, January 23, 1973

It was 8:30 AM on the day after January 22. Nixon phoned United Feature Syndicate journalist William Smith White from the Oval Office.

White, a Texan by birth, had been a *New York Times* correspondent before becoming a respected nationally syndicated columnist. He had known LBJ since 1933, when the two first came to Washington.[1] White wrote a flattering biography of LBJ in 1964, titled *The Professional: Lyndon B. Johnson*, and had won the Pulitzer for his 1955 biography of Robert Taft, the Ohio senator who ran for president in 1952.

"Bill, I knew how close you were to President Johnson," Nixon said to White, "and I wanted you to know that we all feel the deepest sympathy not only for his family but for his close friends."[2] Nixon was speaking not just to White but to history itself, expecting the gifted journalist to record in some manner what Nixon wanted to convey to him.

Nixon recounted for White, fairly accurately as far as it went, his last conversation with Johnson the day after New Year's. He implied that he had let Johnson know with some certainty that the war was coming to an end, and in a way that would do honor to LBJ's legacy. Nixon lamented that the Democratic Party had abandoned Johnson. Nixon said, "The people in his own party—the people *he made*—who didn't go down to see him before and after that [1972] Democratic convention, that cut him to the quick." But, he forecast, over time Johnson's stature would recover. "You take Herbert Hoover," Nixon gave as his example. "He went down to a smashing defeat [in 1932], but people went on pilgrimages—Republicans and Democrats, but mostly Republicans—for years to New York to the Waldorf to see Herbert Hoover [where he lived]."

White penned a column a few days later after peace was announced, relaying that "by an immensely fortunate circumstance, as it turned out, President Nixon telephoned to former President Johnson after the current negotiations had reached a point where the end, however improbable, was at last truly in sight."

William White was one of the holdouts, an old-school, WWII-era reporter who had supported Johnson and Nixon in their handling of the war. Over the course of his extended relationship with Lyndon Johnson, White became one of his most intimate confidants. "More than once," he wrote in his farewell to LBJ column, "I saw Lyndon Johnson weep surreptitiously in the nighttime in his darkened White House office as the aide brought in the daily casualty figures." Echoing Nixon's comments from their phone call, he wrote, "Pity Lyndon Johnson had for others, in the fullest measure. From him pity was withheld—especially by those liberals for whom he had done the most—as from no other President in our time."[3]

White did not write—because Nixon left this part out—that the real reason for Nixon's last call to Johnson was to find cover for his not attending President Truman's memorial service at the National Cathedral.

The country meanwhile, knowing of Kissinger's trip to Paris, held its breath to see if peace was finally in hand.

William Sullivan in Paris—the deputy assistant secretary of state for East Asian and Pacific affairs, and Kissinger's top negotiator—reported to Kissinger about the final, long day of haggling with the North Vietnamese. Most of it had been spent bickering over the protocol on the question of the South Vietnamese police being allowed to carry more than pistols. The North Vietnamese were, Sullivan reported, "as stubborn as yesterday." But after much debate, a new sentence was hammered out. It read, "As required by their responsibilities, normally [the police] shall be authorized to be armed with pistols, but, when required by unusual circumstances, with other individual small arms."

Sullivan frankly admitted to Kissinger that he took no particular pride in the new sentence but cheerfully observed that "it can be read with a slightly different emphasis to our darlings [the South

Vietnamese] to persuade them that significance is somehow lurking in the syntax, and at least they will have the satisfaction of knowing they made Thach [the North Vietnamese deputy foreign minister] and me sweat blood for 6 hours on their *amour-propre*."[4] The South Vietnamese had their face-saving concession.

Everything was a go. "As of this very moment," Sullivan wrote, "the language experts are proofreading comparative texts, binding them into four monumental piles of documents, attaching them with ribbons and affixing seals." Sullivan was ecstatic it was nearly over. "The sun is shining in Paris this afternoon," he wrote at the end of his message.[5]

Kissinger spent his final hours with Le Duc Tho on Tuesday, January 23, at the Hotel Majestic on the Avenue Kléber in Paris proper. "Everything went smoothly in my meeting with Le Duc Tho and we initialed the agreement and protocols at about one o'clock," Kissinger cabled Ambassador Ellsworth Bunker in Saigon. What Kissinger did not put in the official record was that he and Tho had wrangled for most of their four-hour meeting in a contest over the nature of America's future commitment to fund the economic reconstruction of North Vietnam. "Le Duc Tho managed even on this solemn occasion to make himself obnoxious by insisting on ironclad assurances of American economic aid to North Vietnam," Kissinger wrote years later in his memoirs.[6]

Yet it was all radiant smiles and hearty handshakes when Kissinger and Tho emerged to mug for the cameras. Neither said a word. Kissinger and his team went straight to lunch at Tran Van Lam's residence, making it three appearances with South Vietnam's foreign minister in less than twenty-four hours. "I took every occasion to publicly associate myself with Lam and the South Vietnamese while I was in Paris," Kissinger wrote to Bunker.[7] Following lunch Kissinger bolted, rushing out to Orly Airport to jet back to Washington.[8]

LBJ's passing was much on Kissinger's mind as he flew back to the United States. "It was symbolic," he wrote, "that this hulking, imperious, vulnerable, expansive, aspiring man, so full of life, should die with the war that had broken his heart."[9]

In Washington, Nixon huddled with Haldeman, Ray Price, Al Haig, and Ron Ziegler to pore over and edit the statement about peace that he would read that night on television while simultaneously trying to juggle all the logistics for a major presidential funeral—the second in less than a month. Nixon fretted about whether he should appear

Henry Kissinger and Le Duc
Tho after initialing the peace
accords, January 23, 1973.
White House Photo Office, Nixon Library

in person before Congress to make the historic announcement of the
cease-fire agreement but decided that it would be inappropriate in the
time of mourning for Lyndon Johnson.[10]

At the LBJ Library in Austin, Texas, thousands lined up to walk
past the flag-draped coffin of the dead president, which was positioned
on a catafalque at the top of a stairway "in front of a long metal wall
etched with scenes representing various stages of his life." Lady Bird,
in a dark-blue suit, and her two daughters and sons-in-law gathered
near the coffin, receiving every person who walked by. "Oh, but didn't
he live well!" Mrs. Johnson was overheard saying through tears to old
friend and reporter Norma Milligan of *Newsweek*. The doors to the
library stayed open all evening to accommodate the mourners who
waited in the chill of a Texas winter night to file past the casket.[11]

The response to *Roe v. Wade* was comparatively muted, given all
the noise of the great events that had transpired on the day it was
handed down. In Rome the Vatican radio "harshly criticized" the
opinion, issuing a statement calling the ruling "a decision of extreme
gravity that deeply affects the concepts of human life and the dignity

of the human person."[12] In the United States, Terence Cardinal Cooke of New York called the decision "a tragic utilitarian decision regarding who shall live and who shall die," while Cardinal Krol of Philadelphia, the president of the National Conference of Catholic Bishops, branded it "an unspeakable tragedy for the nation."[13] Krol, a favored guest at the Nixon White House, went on to say, "This is not a question of sectarian morality but instead concerns the law of God and the basis of civilized society."

Others lavished praise. A representative from the Planned Parenthood Federation of America called *Roe* "wise and courageous," the American Civil Liberties Union said it was a "step in the right direction," and even a top leader of the United Church of Christ labeled *Roe* "historic not only in terms of women's individual rights but also in terms of the relationships of church and state."[14] The clergyman's reasoning: "Although religious principles often form the basis of secular

Military officers carry President Lyndon B. Johnson's casket up the steps of the Great Hall in the LBJ Library where it will lie in state, January 23, 1973.

LBJ Library photo by Frank Wolfe

law, we hold that where religious beliefs vary, American law traditionally establishes the neutrality of the state. The doctrine of one religious group is not imposed by legal fiat or enforced by criminal sanction on the rest of American society."[15]

The woman who was the president of an early Right to Life chapter in the Bronx thought the decision was incongruous in an age when liberals were arguing for expanded human rights. "It is ironic," Barbara Meara said, "that at a time when this country is trying to improve the lot of so many people and is so opposed to violence the Court should sanction the destruction of life."[16]

Larry Hammond remembers that, within the court, there was the hope and belief that this agonizing and contentious issue was being solved, once and for all, with Blackmun's decision.[17] So argued the editorial board of the *New York Times*: "The Court's seven-to-two ruling could bring to an end the emotional and divisive public argument over what always should have been an intensely private and personal matter," the paper's editors wrote the day after the decision was issued. "It will end that argument if those who are now inveighing against the decision as a threat to civilization's survival will pause long enough to recognize the limits of what the Court has done."[18]

The media took note that three of the four Nixon appointees to the Supreme Court had voted in favor of the majority decision in *Roe*, Justice Rehnquist being the lone dissenter. "The Court's decision was at odds with the expressed views of President Nixon," the *Times* wrote. "Last May, in a letter to Cardinal Cooke, he opposed 'liberalized abortion policies,' and spoke out for 'the right to life of literally hundreds of thousands of unborn children.'"[19]

In a strange way, the abortion decision matched Nixon's political manifesto of self-reliance and his new "ask what can I do for myself" philosophy. The choice of whether to abort was now to be left to each person's individual conscience. *Time* commented on this paradox: "In fact, as legal restraints are removed, the ethical issues become more urgent; every woman must then rely entirely on herself in deciding whether or not to end an unwelcome pregnancy."[20]

As Tuesday, January 23, wore on, the planning within the White House for the peace announcement intensified. Nixon decided he would meet with his cabinet at 8:30 PM and then with the "Big Five," the bipartisan leaders in Congress—Speaker Carl Albert, Senate Majority Leader Mike Mansfield, Senate Minority Leader Hugh Scott, House Majority Leader Tip O'Neill, and House Minority

Leader Gerald R. Ford—just before appearing on national television at 10:00 PM.

One of the first persons outside the inner circle to know about the timing of events was the First Lady, Thelma "Pat" Nixon. In a surprisingly personal moment for a couple who studiously avoided any public display of affection or even connectedness, Nixon took the time to share his achievement.[21] Nixon called her from his EOB office just after 1:30 PM. "Hello," he said.

"Hi Dick," Pat Nixon responded in a matter-of-fact tone.

"Oh I thought you'd like to know—and tell the girls—that Kissinger is on his way back, and we got the agreement, and I'm going to announce it at 10:00 tonight on television."

The First Lady, known for her subdued public persona, reacted with true enthusiasm and joy. "Oh great!" she exclaimed. "Isn't that marvelous!"[22]

Nixon then called in Chuck Colson and things turned particularly vicious.[23] Nixon wanted Colson to launch a "savage attack" on his antiwar foes. "Kick them right in the balls," he said. Nothing was to be held back. "We must go after our enemies with savage brutality," he frothed. The bombing and his policy of toughness in Vietnam had been fully vindicated, he said, and it was payback time. He even encouraged Colson to sue *Time* for libel over the Watergate story. By the time Colson left the president's EOB office just a half hour later, Nixon was in a complete lather over *Time*. Press Secretary Ziegler received another verbal wallop. "Ron," Nixon said in a recorded phone call, "just wanted you to be totally sure that my order on [Jerrold] Schecter and [Hugh] Sidey and all the bastards at *Time* is totally understood and totally enforced for the next four years I am in office. Under no circumstances whatever is any call to be returned to *Time* magazine and no one is to see them." As Ziegler was attempting to respond, Nixon abruptly hung up on him.[24]

Nixon worked some more on his speech with Ray Price and Al Haig.

Then at 6:22 PM Nixon called for Colson to join him in his office in the Executive Office Building. The two continued their diatribe against the leaders of the peace movement and again talked about Colson's potential libel suit against *Time*. This led to a discussion about the caricature of Marlon Brando on the cover of *Time* in the issue that came out on the Monday before the inauguration.[25] Brando had starred in a controversial erotic-drama film, *Last Tango in Paris*, which had created a worldwide sensation because of its raw portrayal of sex and violence. When it was first released, the Motion Picture Arts Association gave it an *X* rating. Nixon was as angry about not being on the cover on the week of his inauguration as he was about the glorification of what he thought was an immoral film.[26]

In was in this context that Nixon raised the *Roe* decision from the day before. "What's the situation incidentally with regard to the Supreme Court decision on abortion?" he asked Colson. "Who were the dissenters?" Colson didn't know. "It doesn't matter," Nixon said. "There were only two."[27]

Nixon and Colson consulted press reports of the decision and its impact on the constitutionality of state abortion laws. Then Nixon said, "A girl doesn't have to worry about taking the pill anymore. She can go down to the doctor and have an abortion for five dollars."[28]

Colson said, "The weird thing about it, Mr. President, I'm not a Catholic, but I'm . . ." Nixon interrupted, saying, "There are times when abortions are necessary, I know that—let's suppose there is a black and a white."

"Or a rape," Colson added.

"A rape," Nixon agreed. "They're all the same, as a matter of fact. You know what I mean. There are times."

Colson worried about the opinion: "It encourages permissiveness."

Nixon followed, "It breaks the family."[29]

In the middle of this unstructured discussion, Henry Kissinger entered the office, freshly back from Paris. The subject abruptly changed. "Congratulations!" Nixon greeted him. "Congratulations," Kissinger returned the compliment to the president. "You were right and I was wrong," Nixon said. "You kept saying Thieu would cave."[30]

Colson left. Kissinger and Nixon took some time to study the peace statement that Nixon was going to deliver in just a few hours on national television.[31] Nixon returned to the residence for a change of clothes.

Meanwhile, cabinet members were assembled in the Cabinet Room, just off the Oval Office, and Nixon joined them as scheduled at precisely 8:30 PM. They were told this meeting was merely pro forma to make it appear "to the eyes of the world and to the nation" that the president had consulted with them, but he could not talk specifics because the texts of the agreements were not going to be released until the next day.[32] Then he met with the congressional leadership in his EOB office at 9:00 PM and briefed them.

He walked back to the White House, went to Alexander Butterfield's office, had his makeup consultant apply his powder, and stepped into the Oval Office to address the nation at 10:00 PM.[33] He was relaxed and joked with the newsmen present about how a fly had once interrupted the taping of one of his campaign commercials, causing him to redo the filming multiple times until the crew finally gave up and left the fly in the final version. "Is there a fly in the room?" he asked the cameramen in mock seriousness. "I will not do this over. [laughter]"[34]

Once the TV cameras blinked to life, he sounded magnanimous in his time of triumph. A huge audience—ninety-four million—anxiously tuned in.[35] Nixon apologized for his isolation during the past weeks but said it had been necessary to achieve the agreements. "With our secret negotiations at the sensitive stage they were during the recent period, for me to have discussed publicly our efforts to secure peace would not only have violated our understanding with North Vietnam, it would have seriously harmed and possibly destroyed the chances for peace."

The key assurances for Thieu and South Vietnam were duly included. "The United States will continue to recognize the Government of the Republic of Vietnam as the sole legitimate government of South Vietnam," he read. "We shall continue to aid South Vietnam within the terms of the agreement, and we shall support efforts for the people of South Vietnam to settle their problems peacefully among themselves."

He spoke directly to certain groups who had been parties to the conflict: the people of South Vietnam, the leaders of North Vietnam, the other major powers that had been involved directly and indirectly, and the American people and the families of POWs, who "had the courage to stand for the right kind of peace."[36]

Finally, he said a brief word about Lyndon Johnson. "Just yesterday," he said, "a great American who once occupied this office died. In his life, President Johnson endured the vilification of those who sought to portray him as a man of war, but there was nothing he cared about more deeply than achieving a lasting peace in the world. . . . No one would have welcomed this peace more than he."[37]

"Thank you and good evening," he signed off. It had been a ten-minute speech. The press was shown in and clicked away with photos once he finished. Nixon entertained no questions and disappeared immediately to the second-floor residence.

He went to the third-floor solarium to talk briefly with his family (Pat was allowed to hug him) and then he wandered off by himself. "I went to the Lincoln Sitting Room and had a light dinner there by myself," he wrote in his memoirs. "I played several records and sat watching the fire. I had specifically asked that all telephone calls be shut off."[38]

Some picked up on Nixon's snub of antiwar Americans in his speech. Senator Harold Hughes, a Democrat from Iowa, said that the president "left out the need for reconciliation here at home." Hughes was disappointed, he said, that "there were no healing words from the President" for those, like him, who had opposed the war.[39] Notwithstanding the silent presence of Leo Cherne's bronze bust of Abraham Lincoln on Nixon's credenza behind him in the Oval Office, this presidential address contained not a hint of "with malice toward none, with charity for all."[40]

Nixon's slight in his speech had been intentional.

At 10:45 PM Nixon broke his own self-imposed embargo on telephone traffic and started making phone calls. He talked first to his speechwriter, Ray Price. "I thought you'd be interested to know that my daughter Julie gave me an indication that we must have been successful," he said. "She said she had never seen the CBS crew—Dan Rather, Eric Sevareid, Marvin Kalb—they were just *dying*," Nixon chortled. "They thought it was a horrible thing that peace had come; they were so sick about it." He said that the problem for these newsmen was that they just couldn't stand having been proved wrong. "It pleased her," Nixon said of Julie, "because she realized with the line they had taken [against the bombing], we had really stuck 'em in the groin."[41]

Colson was next. "God bless, Mr. President," Colson said as he came on the line.[42] Nixon repeated his Julie story. "I hope to Christ," he said, "that this will cause some of our bomb throwers to get off their asses." Not to worry, Colson responded, his "boys" were on it. Colson was especially pleased that Nixon did not embrace "those who fought us" in the speech. Nixon said a staffer had given him a memo that day suggesting he initiate an "era of good feeling," but he had responded by saying that if he ever was shown another such memo, he would "flush it down the goddamn john."

The one thing that did gain Nixon universal approbation was his mention of Johnson in his speech.[43] Colson said it was a brilliant move, "a stroke of genius." Colson had just hung up from a call with George Christian, Johnson's last press secretary, and he was, according to

Colson, choked up. "Well, he must have been," Nixon said, "because that was a pretty damn good thing for me to do, 'cause LBJ hadn't done a goddamn thing for me, as you know."

Nixon went further: "Well, this makes Johnson's place in history, you know."

"Of course it does," Colson agreed. "You made it. You made it tonight, it was a beautiful touch, Mr. President, because really what you did was bring credit to yourself by giving him credit, because he stood against the same critics."

All this was fine and good, but Nixon's immediate concern remained that Colson understand the urgency of stepping up the attack on the doves. He said, "the Silent Majority must rise now." It was time to fight. This, to Nixon, was like a disputed election in its last hours—his team had to pull out all the stops to win the public relations battle that he knew would break out over the meaning of peace. "It's like November 3rd," he kept saying to Colson, "only bigger." He was near frantic with him. "If there was ever any time for you to kick ass, you do it tonight."[44]

A call to Kissinger followed. Nixon repeated the same stories about the newsmen on CBS being "green." Kissinger later wrote that he found Nixon's behavior odd. "What extraordinary vehicles destiny selects to accomplish its design," he observed of Nixon. "This man, so lonely in his hour of triumph, so ungenerous in some of his motivations, had navigated our nation through one of the most anguishing periods in its history."[45] The tape of the phone conversation, however, shows Kissinger agreeing with everything Nixon said that night. "It just kills the bloody liberals," Kissinger parroted.[46]

In Saigon, President Thieu was openly skeptical in his speech to his countrymen. "Let me say frankly of the peace accord to be signed in three days, that it is only a ceasefire agreement. As to whether or not we will have real peace, we must wait and see." Nobody in the United States paid much attention to, or even seemed to care about, Thieu or his reaction.[47] People were exhausted with the war.

It was the end of a nightmare.[48] But was it the beginning of another?

Austin, Texas, January 24, 1973

At 9:00 the next morning, the doors to the LBJ Library were closed and Lyndon Johnson's casket was transported to nearby Bergstrom Air Force Base, where Air Force One awaited, sent by President Nixon. It was the same aircraft that carried John Kennedy's body back to Washington from Dallas on November 22, 1963, and the plane in which federal judge Sarah Hughes administered the oath of office to LBJ.[49] Mike Howard was among those who flew back with the body.

The plane touched down at Andrews Air Force Base at 1:00 PM and was met by a military honor guard. A hearse carried Johnson's casket the sixteen miles into Washington in a long motorcade. Once in Washington the hearse stopped on Constitution Avenue, and the coffin was placed on a four-wheeled caisson with six white horses to be driven to the Capitol. Nixon joined there in the presidential limousine that followed the family and the coffin.

The scene evoked the Kennedy funeral procession from a decade earlier, the cortege moving slowly to the tempo set by the muffled drums of the Marine Band, with the same riderless horse, a twenty-six-year-old gelding named Black Jack, boots placed backward in the stirrups to signify a fallen leader.[50] Johnson's coffin was carried up the steps of the Capitol and placed on a catafalque in the Rotunda, where Nixon participated in a brief wreath-laying ceremony with the family, leaders, and official mourners. Nixon did not speak. In the audience, William P. Rogers, secretary of state and the man who would fly to Paris to sign the accords, collapsed. His fainting spell was attributed to fatigue.[51] Johnson's body lay in state for the rest of the day and evening. By midnight the line of mourners stretched beyond the Capitol grounds all the way back to the Supreme Court Building.[52] More than forty thousand people came to pay respects.

A funeral service was planned for the National City Christian Church the next day. The National Cathedral and Francis Sayre, to Nixon's great relief, were shut out. He would attend the memorial service after all.

Kissinger gave an hourlong press briefing at the Executive Office Building as Johnson's body was being flown back to Washington. Had Nixon heard Kissinger's concluding remarks, he would have snarled. Kissinger advocated for reconciliation at home. Just before opening it up for questions, Kissinger said, "And together with healing the wounds in Indochina, we can begin to heal the wounds in America."[53] This attitude would place him in hot water two days later, when he would present privately to the members of Congress. The editors at the *New York Times* found Kissinger's remarks fitting. "This is what America needs to hear," they wrote. "Although the United States has hardly experienced the hatred and bitterness of a magnitude

President Nixon laying a wreath before President Johnson's casket in the
Capitol Rotunda, January 24, 1973.

LBJ Library photo by Frank Wolfe

comparable to that which divides the Vietnamese after a generation of
fratricidal strife, the emotional wounds of war cut deeply here too."[54]

Back from the wreath-laying ceremony, Nixon briefly met with
Haldeman and Ziegler and reminded Ziegler to emphasize to Kissinger
that he must not speak to anyone from *Time*.[55] Nixon opened a cabinet
meeting to discuss the budget but took a moment to comment on how
so many of the occupants of his office died in their early sixties: Teddy
Roosevelt, Coolidge, FDR, and now LBJ. He didn't worry about himself—"whatever happens, happens," he said. But the important point
was to "approach each day as if it might be our last day here." He had
Haldeman distribute leather table binders, each with a large desk cal-
endar. Inside, Nixon had had inscribed the dates for what he thought
would be his next four years in office—January 20, 1973, to January 20, 1977. He also included a special message with the calendars.
"Every moment of history is a fleeting time, precious and unique," he
wrote. "The Presidential term which begins today consists of 1461
days—no more and no less. Each day can be a day of strengthening
and renewal for America; each can add depth and dimension to the
American experience."[56]

National City Christian Church, Washington, January 25, 1973

The next morning, January 25, the First Lady and president did indeed show up for the Johnson funeral at the National City Christian Church. LBJ's eulogist, W. Marvin Watson, former postmaster general, said of him: "In victory he taught us to be magnanimous; in defeat he taught us not to hate, for hate was never in this man's heart." Leontyne Price of the Metropolitan Opera sang two solos, reducing many, including those in a huge crowd outside the church listening via outdoor loudspeakers, to tears.[57]

Johnson's body was flown back to Texas immediately following the services, where the weather had turned blustery, cold, and rainy. Bebe Rebozo came from Miami as Nixon's representative, with singer and former Miss America Anita Bryant.[58] Billy Graham and John Connally spoke at the gravesite in the Johnson family plot in Stonewall, Texas. Graham said, "A great leader is dead, a great nation must move on. Yesterday is not ours to recover, but tomorrow is ours to win or to lose."[59] Johnson was buried beneath aged oaks next to the graves of his mother and father.

In Washington, Nixon met with Yitzhak Rabin, Israeli ambassador to the United States, and then recorded an audio message that afternoon on the 1974 budget that was intended to eviscerate the Great Society.[60] Vietnam was over, but so was the war on poverty. "Thus, the Great Society programs and the Vietnam War—after growing up side by side during 1965–1968 and creating an inflationary environment that is still with us, after deeply impacting the economic and social fabric of the country since the mid-nineteen-sixties—are now fading away side by side," the *New York Times* observed.[61]

Nixon insisted that the message not be broadcast until January 29. He wanted to keep the Vietnam settlement front and center in the news for the next week.[62]

On Friday, January 26, after an emotional meeting with the relatives of American prisoners of war and a testy conference with congressional leaders on the budget, Nixon flew off to Florida for a long weekend vacation.[63] That same day Kissinger appeared in two closed-door sessions with members of the House and the Senate to report on the settlement agreements. He promised to consult with Congress on any postwar aid programs to North Vietnam.[64] Kissinger, now an immensely popular figure, was warmly received, with prolonged standing ovations in each meeting.[65]

Haldeman, per Nixon's instructions, had given a written memo to Kissinger prior to the briefing, directing him to "give no quarter whatever to the doves."[66] Kissinger did not follow the script. Told of this in Key Biscayne, Nixon was bitter. Kissinger didn't "hit our critics at all," Haldeman reported, and there was "no criticism of congress for their resolutions [calling for an end to funding of the war]." Nixon was mainly sore, Haldeman wrote, that Kissinger hadn't built up the president, extolling "the character of the man and how he toughed it through."[67]

Nixon was supposed to be the hero of this story, not Kissinger. "The P alone held on and pulled it out," Haldeman wrote in his diary.[68]

Paris, France, January 27, 1973

Across the ocean, preparations for the official signing ceremony in Paris were under way. Le Duc Tho headed for home. "My mission is accomplished," he told reporters. It was a strong signal that Kissinger himself would not be in Paris for the official signing ceremony. The accords would be signed by the Vietnamese foreign ministers and US Secretary of State William Rogers. The Vietcong's Provisional Revolutionary Government's foreign minister was a woman, Nguyen Thi Binh. She said that Nixon had violated the spirit of the agreement in his January 23 speech by recognizing President Thieu's government as the "sole legitimate Government of South Vietnam."[69] Trouble lay ahead.

On Saturday, January 27, 1973, the accords were signed in the great ballroom of the Hotel Majestic, with its gigantic round table, crystal and gilt chandeliers, and lush tapestries. Because the South Vietnamese refused to recognize the Vietcong Provisional Revolutionary Government, the agreements were signed in two separate ceremonies. In the morning, an agreement that did not refer to the PRG by name was signed by the United States, North Vietnam, South Vietnam, and the Vietcong. In the afternoon, an agreement that did mention the PRG was signed by only the United States and North Vietnam.

There were unmistakable portents of the accords' stillbirth. "The Vietnam ceasefire agreement was signed here today in eerie silence," the *New York Times* reported, "without a word or a gesture to express the world's relief that the years of war were officially ending." The parties engaged in no public clinking of champagne glasses or toasts to peace. Reportedly, such gestures took place behind the scenes in a curtained foyer, but to the eyes of the world press, the rite of peace seemed "strangely emotionless" and "oddly muted."[70]

With little fanfare, Secretary Rogers and his team headed straight for the airport following the ceremony, where Rogers finally spoke. "It's a great day," he said.[71] Having been a mere spectator to the negotiations, he truly had nothing else to add.

South Vietnam's foreign minister, Tran Van Lam—the man Henry Kissinger called "an ass"—flew back to Washington with Rogers. He was, according to reports, an uninvited and unexpected passenger on the plane.[72]

In Texas, Lady Bird Johnson, her two daughters and their husbands, and Jewell Malechek visited the grave of LBJ to thank the honor guard and military police who had been posted to stand watch. After the family left, "the grave was leveled and covered with the turf that had been there before the grave was dug."[73]

Lyndon Baines Johnson, the thirty-sixth president of the United States, returned to the Hill Country whence he had come, his body and his Great Society two of the last casualties of the Vietnam War.[74]

"Along this stream and under these trees he loved, he will now rest," John Connally had said a few days earlier at the gravesite service. "He first saw light here. He last felt life here. May he now find peace here."[75]

Luci Johnson Nugent, son Patrick, Lady Bird Johnson, Lynda Johnson Robb, and Chuck Robb holding daughter Lucinda, pay their last respects in the Johnson Family Cemetery, LBJ Ranch, January 25, 1973.
White House Photo Office, Nixon Library

22

"Now Your Client Is Smiling"

Ceremonial Courtroom, January 22 to 26, 1973

The final full week of the Watergate burglars' trial was anticlimactic. Judge Sirica believed the witnesses who were lying and questioned those who actually were telling the truth.

On the day that Kissinger flew back to Paris, *Roe* was issued, and Lyndon Johnson drew his last breath, lookout and monitor Alfred Baldwin returned to the stand, late because of weather interference with his flight that morning. After a round of cross-examination, Sirica excused the jury and told the lawyers that he wanted to ask questions directly of Baldwin. Sirica said that he very seldom interfered in a trial with his own questioning but that he did so from time to time if he felt, as he did here, "that all the facts have not been developed by either side." His questions, he said, were in the "interest of justice and of seeing that all of the facts are developed, whether it hurts anybody or helps anybody."[1]

His concerns about Baldwin were twofold. Baldwin had testified that he thought what he was doing was legal. Sirica found this puzzling. "Weren't you suspicious that something was wrong when you were told to use an assumed name?" Sirica asked Baldwin (imaginatively enough the assumed name was Bill Johnson, staying at the Howard Johnson hotel). "Did that indicate to you some hanky-panky was going on, to use an old expression?" Baldwin wasn't permitted to answer before Sirica launched into his second point. Baldwin testified that once, when McCord was out of town, he asked Baldwin to drop off his notes of the conversations he was monitoring to the Committee to Re-Elect. Baldwin did so but could not remember the name of the official to whom the notes were to be delivered. Worse, from Sirica's perspective, Baldwin said he left the envelope containing the notes with a security guard at the CRP whom he did not know.

"You have been an FBI agent for how many years?" Sirica inquired. Baldwin responded, "Two years, Your Honor."

"But you can't remember the name of the party to whom you delivered this particular log?" Sirica asked. Baldwin said he had tried to remember the name and even consulted a list of employees that had been produced by the CRP for the FBI. "Here you are, a former FBI agent, you knew this log was very important," Sirica said, "and you want this jury to believe that you gave it to a guard, is that your testimony?"

"I did give it to the guard," a perplexed Baldwin mildly protested.

"That is all," Sirica harrumphed, clearly incredulous.[2]

The next day, January 23, Jeb Magruder was called by prosecutor Earl Silbert to the stand. His examination, filled with perjury, went swimmingly. The good-looking, thirty-eight-year-old deputy campaign director came off as a model citizen, with a beautiful wife in the audience and four children at home. Under the practiced guidance of Silbert, Magruder spun his tale of how substantial money had been allocated to Liddy to protect surrogates who campaigned for the president in states where there was a threat of disruption or physical violence at rallies. Additional money was needed for convention protection, especially in light of the tumult that had broken out in Chicago outside the 1968 Democratic National Convention. The same people—"I guess we would call them the radical elements in the society," Magruder said— threatened massive protests at the Republican National Convention, according to CRP intelligence. Liddy got this money, too. All told, $250,000 had been allotted to Liddy, Magruder confirmed.

Magruder pointed out that he could hardly have been expected to fuss over such amounts in a campaign that had expended $48 million, an astounding amount in 1973. Besides, Magruder said, he and Liddy didn't get along personally, so it was all the more understandable that Magruder was clueless as to what Liddy was actually doing with all that money.[3]

"Mr. Magruder, did you ever give Mr. Liddy any assignment concerning the Democratic National Committee?" Silbert asked. "No," Magruder responded.

"Did you ever receive any report of any kind from Mr. Liddy concerning the Democratic National Committee offices and headquarters at 2600 Virginia Avenue, Northwest here in the District?" Silbert followed up. "No," Magruder responded.

Jeb Magruder was on and off the witness stand in less than forty-five minutes.

His story held together in one neat package. It was all an unexamined lie. Sirica later wrote that "Magruder was smooth as silk."[4] Though he claims he was skeptical of his testimony, Judge Sirica made no comments and asked no questions. Magruder wrote in his autobiography that the "most memorable moment in my appearance at trial came when I left the witness stand and Gordon Liddy, sitting at the defense table, smiled at me and winked."[5] He was amazed. "Neither the prosecutors (and I was their witness) nor the defense lawyers challenged my story."[6] His assistant, Bart Porter, followed, corroborating Magruder's lies, again without any significant pushback.[7]

The same was not true of another witness who was telling the truth: Hugh Sloan, the treasurer of the Finance Committee to Reelect the President. Sloan would later be immortalized as a hero in Alan Pakula's 1976 film *All the President's Men*, but in Judge Sirica's courtroom in January 1973, he became a target of the judge's suspicion.[8] "For the second consecutive day, Chief Judge John J. Sirica indicated dissatisfaction with the prosecution's examination of a witness, excused the jury, and posed a series of questions himself," the *Times* reported.[9] This time, Sirica actually stumbled onto something when he questioned Sloan's testimony that he did not know why Liddy had received the money. Sloan clarified that, though he didn't know the purpose, he did verify with both Maurice Stans, the finance chairman, and John Mitchell, the campaign chairman, that Jeb Magruder had sufficient authority to direct him to give up to $199,000 to Liddy. Sloan was careful to qualify what he was saying. "Not the specific amount," he said of his conversations with Stans and Mitchell, "but Mr. Magruder, his authorization was authorization enough to turn over the sums in question."[10]

Sloan never said that Stans or Mitchell knew what Liddy was doing, only that they confirmed that Jeb Magruder had enough spending authority to provide Liddy with, as Sirica characterized it, "a pretty sizable piece of money."[11] Nevertheless Mitchell's name made headlines the next day.[12] It was as close as the trial would come to linking John Mitchell to the Watergate break-in. Earl Silbert did not subpoena Mitchell or Stans to appear as witnesses. For the time being, John Mitchell would skate.[13]

On Wednesday morning, January 24, as LBJ's body was being flown to Washington, Sirica consulted privately with the lawyers. The case was moving faster than anticipated. Defense counsel for McCord and Liddy were asking fewer and fewer questions on cross-examination, and many of the minor witnesses were being presented to the jury through stipulations—summaries of their testimony read by the prosecutors with the consent of the defendants. The remaining witnesses in the prosecution's case were "mop up" witnesses—miscellaneous bank employees who touched some of the money in the case, electronics technicians and experts, and a smattering of employees of the Democratic Party who worked at the Watergate over the weekend of the break-in.[14]

As a consequence, and because President Nixon had declared a national day of mourning, Sirica decided that he would suspend the proceedings on Thursday, January 25, in honor of President Johnson's funeral.[15]

McCord's lawyer, Gerald Alch, again asked the court to reconsider his request that he be permitted to put on a defense that McCord was acting under "duress" when he participated in the eavesdropping and break-in. McCord, Alch repeated, felt threatened by all the radical violence and demonstrations, causing him to "have an apprehension of bodily harm or serious bodily injury to himself, the President [and others]." Sirica was steadfast. He would let Alch argue his theory to the jury as part of the question of whether McCord had "criminal intent," but he would not allow him to put on evidence of duress. He found the argument, he said, "ridiculous, frankly, to put it bluntly." McCord, he said, had no right to take the law into his own hands. He was a former FBI agent and CIA employee—he could have brought in the authorities if he perceived a threat.

"I happen to be a Republican," Sirica said, "and I used to be very active in the [presidential] campaign, but decent Americans, whether they are Republican or Democrat, deplore this and so does everybody else."[16]

By Friday, January 26, the case had all but petered out. The only fireworks came when Sirica decided to read to the jury his questioning of Hugh Sloan that had been conducted outside their presence. Liddy's lawyer objected, observing that having the judge read one witness's testimony would "place unusual emphasis and importance on that testimony." Sirica felt challenged and responded, "Let me tell you one thing: I exercise my judgment as a Federal Judge and Chief Judge of this Court and I have done it on many occasions and in the presence of the jury examined witnesses where I thought all the fact [*sic*] were not brought out by counsel on either side. . . . I could care less what happens to this case on appeal."

Liddy made the mistake of smirking as the judge was defending himself. "Now your client is smiling," Sirica said to Mr. Maroulis. "He is probably not impressed with what I am saying," Sirica seethed. "I don't care what he thinks either. Is that clear to you? You made your record." It was one of the most intense moments of the trial.

Maroulis stood his ground. "Your Honor," he said after Sirica's outburst, "I then respectfully move for a mistrial."

Sirica shot back, "Your motion will be respectfully denied."[17] He then read all of Sloan's testimony, including the bench conferences with counsel, to the jury. It was the coup de grâce for Liddy. In addition to his remarks about Stans and Mitchell, Sloan had told the story of his encounter with Liddy at the Committee to Re-Elect on the morning after the break-in. A flustered Liddy had said to Sloan, "My boys got caught last night; I made a mistake; I used somebody from here [meaning McCord], which I said I would never do. I am afraid I am going to lose my job."[18] The jury would hear this testimony repeated several times as Sirica read the transcript. Under Sirica's questioning, Sloan had slightly restated the dialogue, adding the words "which I *told them* I would never do." The implication was that Liddy had spoken with higher-ups about the operation, promising "them" he would not use someone who could be traceable back to the Committee to Re-Elect.[19]

By the end of the day on Friday, January 26, it was becoming clear that the case would wrap up on Monday, with closing arguments on Tuesday, January 30.[20]

January 1973 was fast approaching its terminus.

Justice Powell's Chambers, January 24 to 26, 1973

Not far from Sirica's courtroom—just on the other side of the Capitol building—Larry Hammond in the Supreme Court opened the mail for Justice Powell, as was his custom when his boss was out of town, and discovered the "eyes only" letter from the chief justice demanding to know who had leaked the *Roe* decision to *Time*. According to Powell biographer John Jeffries, "a shaken Larry Hammond repaired to the upstairs office to call Powell, who was visiting [his Army Air Corps friend] General Pete Quesada in Florida. After several frantic hours, Hammond found Powell and told him the story."[21]

Hammond offered to resign immediately. Powell would not hear of it. Powell called Burger to tell him what happened and, a few minutes later, Hammond received a call from Burger's secretary. His presence was requested by the chief. With great trepidation, he trudged to Burger's chambers, expecting the worst. "To Hammond's surprise, Burger was all grace and generosity. Powell had praised Hammond's ability and character," Jeffries reported. "The Chief ruminated about the terrible things [David] Beckwith had done, congratulated Hammond on his candor, shook his hand, and sent him on his way." Burger later met with the editors of *Time* and told them that what their reporter had done was the moral equivalent of wiretapping.[22]

Washington, January 26, 1973
Chuck Colson, of course, had his own score to settle with *Time*. He wrote a letter to the editor, no doubt having had second thoughts of how a libel suit might turn ugly for him. "Sir," Colson wrote, "The Jan. 29 *Time* report on the Watergate affair draws upon the rankest form of unsubstantiated hearsay to attempt to connect Mr. Mitchell and me to the incident. That connection is totally false." The letter appeared in the issue of the magazine that hit the streets on January 29, 1973. Beckwith did not correct the story, and *Time* did not apologize.

Key Biscayne, Florida, January 27 to 29, 1973
In Florida over the last weekend of January 1973, Nixon walked along the beach, swam in the Key Biscayne compound pool, and attended peace worship services with the First Lady at the Key Biscayne Presbyterian Church on Saturday evening. Nixon had proclaimed that on Saturday at 7:00 PM, as the cease-fire went into effect in Vietnam, there would be "a national moment of prayer and thanksgiving." After the services, he, Bebe Rebozo, Pat Nixon, and Julie Nixon Eisenhower went to dinner at the Key Biscayne Hotel, where Nixon surprised everyone by dancing with his daughter Julie.[23]

On Sunday, January 28, the president and Bebe Rebozo traveled by helicopter to Grand Cay, Bahamas, to stay with their friend, industrialist Robert Abplanalp. While there, the three men swam in the ocean, had dinner at the Abplanalp residence, and watched Rowan and Martin's *Football Monologue*, a film made for Nixon's sixtieth birthday.

That evening, as he relaxed in the Bahamas, Nixon's eleven-minute radio address on the federal budget, which he had recorded just after attending LBJ's funeral, was broadcast nationally. "It is time to get big government off your back," Nixon said, "and out of your pocket."[24]

He would fly back to Miami and then to Washington on the following day, Monday, January 29.[25] The trip and its timing had a powerful echo to one he had taken seven months earlier, in June 1972. On the weekend of the Watergate break-in, Nixon was in the Bahamas with Abplanalp and Rebozo. He returned to the White House late on Monday night, June 19, 1972. The next morning, he spoke with Haldeman in his Executive Office Building hideaway office about the break-in, the tape of which was found later to contain a mysterious eighteen-and-a-half-minute gap.

On the final Sunday of January 1973, the *New York Times* ran a probing and prescient editorial that uncannily anticipated what would be Nixon's final crisis. Entitled "Now It's in a Mood for a Real Fight," the piece focused on the puzzle of the continuing hostilities between the White House and Congress, even though the war had ended. "There was an almost audible sigh of relief on Capitol Hill last week when the declaration of a Vietnam accord wiped out the chief stimulus of the congressional movement to recapture power from the White House," the *Times* observed. "Yet curiously enough, by halting combat in Indochina, President Nixon may have increased the prospects for an all-out battle with congress."[26] Peace had left him vulnerable.

In Washington, Vice President Spiro Agnew flew out of Andrews Air Force Base on Sunday night to travel to Saigon and six other Asian nations, keeping a promise Nixon made in letters to President Thieu during the final negotiations of the peace accords. Agnew's press secretary said the trip was intended to assure America's allies in the region that "we're not abandoning our friends."[27]

With just three days left, January 1973 prepared for its final shocks.

23

"It Is a Rule of Life"

Washington, DC, January 29 to 31, 1973

Something was stuck in John Sirica's craw. He was in a nasty and imperious mood when the lawyers showed up for court on Monday, January 29. "Now we are going to move right along this morning," Sirica said. "How long will your witnesses take?" he asked Earl Silbert. "No more than an hour," Silbert responded. The defendants, who had not even started their cases, indicated they would have four to seven witnesses each. Sirica responded, "We should conclude all the evidence in this case by lunchtime and the arguments will start at 1:45. You gentlemen have had plenty of time. I am not going to delay this case any longer."[1]

The lawyers were shocked. They assumed it would be at least until Tuesday, if not later, before arguments would begin. Alch, McCord's attorney, mildly protested, saying that after consultation with Mr. Silbert over the weekend about the number and timing of witnesses, he had concluded that final arguments would commence first thing on Tuesday at the earliest.

"Unfortunately, Mr. Silbert does not run my courtroom and neither does any other party," Sirica growled back.

Liddy's lawyer, Maroulis, joined the fray: "I would like to point out my weekend was consumed with preparation of my case. I fully anticipated that today would be consumed and that I would have this evening to marshal the facts and make my argument to the jury, and I am unprepared to do that."

"You had no right to presume anything," Sirica said. "This court has had a jury sequestered for over three weeks and they have a right to be considered also. It is costing the government a lot of money to keep this jury sequestered. You gentlemen have been in this case for months and months and you will know just as much to argue this afternoon as you will tomorrow. This case will be argued starting at 1:45."[2]

Sirica's reaction was a complete turnabout from the week before, when he reminded counsel that he had told the jury this would be a six-week trial and the court was happily ahead of schedule. Something, perhaps newspaper articles and editorials he read over the weekend, had darkened his mood considerably. One letter writer to the Sunday editors of the *New York Times* smelled a rat in all the guilty pleas and the round denials at the trial by everyone with any knowledge regarding who sponsored and authorized the affair. This feigned ignorance, the writer guessed, "may, conjecturally, be ascribed to a 'deal.' If they stay mum and thus play ball with the Administration, their sentences, which may be to many years' imprisonment, will be ended shortly by a Presidential pardon after serving a few months in jail."[3]

Or maybe it was just Liddy's smart-ass demeanor from the Friday before.

In any event, the defendants were in trouble. They were forced to sprint through fifteen witness examinations in a little more than half a day. Several were simple reputation witnesses on behalf of McCord and Liddy, but it was nevertheless a feverish merry-go-round, especially considering that during this time Maroulis delivered his brief opening statement to the jury, as was his right, after the state rested its case and the defense began its own.[4]

Sirica was mad at everyone and even showed some antagonism toward the reputation witnesses. For example, one of McCord's reputation witnesses was Sister Mary Riley, the director of the Kennedy Institute, "which is a program for retarded children in Washington."[5] Sister Riley said she knew McCord because one of his daughters was a special-needs child. Sirica, perturbed, interrupted her examination to say to Alch: "I am not accusing you of any wrongdoing but it seems to me you are trying to develop a little sympathy by getting into this retarded child business. It seems to me that if she is going to be a character witness you don't have to go into the fact that his wife had a child that was mentally defective or anything like that, which might create sympathy with the jury."[6]

Sensing the futility of argument, Alch tried to quickly wrap up, but not before Sister Riley inadvertently stepped in it with another reference to disabled children, at which point Sirica quickly interjected,

"Now, he asked you Sister, if you know other people who know him, and the answer is yes or no."[7]

After all sides rested, the lawyers and judge raced through a conference on jury instructions and Silbert then began his closing remarks at 3:45 PM. In a statement filled with invective and sarcasm, Silbert tore into Liddy and McCord, frequently raising his voice. But he did the one thing that drove Sirica crazy—he made out the entire affair as a lark, a frolic, and a detour by Liddy and his coconspirators. McCord, whose financial condition was shaky, was in it for the money, Silbert contended, and Liddy misused the money issued by Hugh Sloan so he could live the high life with Howard Hunt. He and Hunt traveled only in first class, Silbert pointed out, their hotels were the most expensive and extravagant, and their food bills were astronomical. Silbert emphasized that Liddy was not conducting the "legitimate intelligence gathering activities" that Magruder and Porter thought he was engaged in. "He wasn't content to follow out what he was supposed to do," Silbert argued. Instead, he and McCord were "off on an enterprise of their own, diverting that money for their own uses."[8]

Silbert had been consistent about this since the first day of the trial. The entire enterprise stopped at Gordon Liddy's level. No higher-ups were implicated; none were involved.

Sirica, exhausted from the marathon session, yielded and called it a day following Silbert's closing. The next morning, January 30, Alch and Maroulis gave their summations, followed by a brief rebuttal from Silbert, who had the burden of proving the crimes beyond a reasonable doubt. The defense closings were rambling and disjointed. Maroulis spent a fair amount of time arguing about why Liddy had grown a mustache, and the color of his hair.[9]

The jury was then instructed by Sirica. It was a strange mix of confounding statements of the law and Sirica's own anecdotal experiences from prior cases. At one point even Sirica recognized he was veering bizarrely off course and said, "So much for that. I better stop adlibbing."[10]

At 4:32 PM the jury retired to deliberate.

They returned with their verdicts ninety minutes later. Both McCord and Liddy were found guilty on all counts.[11] Sirica bounded out of the courtroom, refusing to hear arguments about bail. McCord and Liddy were both taken to jail that night.[12]

The beat went on at the White House. As he had done after his return to the White House following the Watergate break-in, Nixon met with Haldeman for a lengthy meeting. Despite his commands and edicts that no one speak with Jerrold Schecter or anyone from *Time*, an article titled "Henry Kissinger Riding High" had appeared in the previous day's edition. Its author: Jerrold Schecter. "Henry Kissinger is back on top now," Schecter wrote. "His darkest days are behind him." Schecter praised Kissinger as dogged, "carrying on what Washington pundits called 'threeway negotiations—with Hanoi, Saigon, and Nixon.'"[13]

The cycle began afresh: Kissinger would be confronted by Haldeman; Kissinger would disclaim any contact with the journalist; Nixon would express his fear that Kissinger's star was outshining his; and Nixon and Haldeman would both agree that Kissinger needed to be restrained. Nixon said, "You can't have a situation, Bob, where a [magazine] staff member gets up and says, 'Look he's doing great, it's that poor, darn president who is holding him back.'"[14]

At 9:41 AM Kissinger entered the Oval Office, interrupting the conversation. Haldeman exited minutes later. Kissinger complained about how unfair the press was being with the president. Nixon hardly reacted. Kissinger and Nixon then met with Tran Van Lam, the South Vietnamese foreign minister, who had been a stowaway on Secretary of State Rogers's plane back from Paris. After a photo session with the press, Nixon told Lam, "We are your friends." He thanked Lam for the way he handled the situation in Paris—whatever that meant.[15]

That evening, Nixon called Colson. The two talked about their continuing war with the press. Colson cackled about an op-ed he had placed in the *New York Times* entitled "The Georgetown Blacking Factory." His point: the press had been all wrong about a fissure between Nixon and Kissinger. The rumors had all been born in the Georgetown cocktail circuit, Colson declared. "One thing is clear," he wrote. "There was no Nixon Kissinger rift and through all of the torrent of gossip-column reports, President Nixon and his chief negotiator persevered to achieve that which many thought the President would never achieve—an honorable and successful peace in Vietnam."[16]

Privately, though, Colson took the opportunity to again stab Kissinger in the back—Kissinger was talking to the press, Colson told Nixon. The two men harkened back to the first days of January 1973, when Colson had uncovered Kissinger's contacts with James Reston and Joe Kraft. Colson said he hoped his op-ed in the *Times* would serve as a warning to Kissinger.[17]

Neither said a word about the guilty verdicts that had been handed out in Sirica's courtroom just hours earlier.

Minutes after Nixon hung up with Colson, he received a startling call. It was Henry Kissinger. Senator John Stennis of Mississippi, seventy-one, had just been shot. "My God, shot!? By whom?" Nixon asked. "They think it was a burglar," Kissinger replied. "A holdup just outside his home. He's in Walter Reed. He got it in the stomach and the leg."

Nixon wondered about the race of the assailant. "If it's a holdup, it's a black," he said. "If it's something else, it's a white. That's my view." Kissinger agreed with Nixon's appraisal. Nixon said, "That's the way it always works. Might be some damn stupid black out to get his pocketbook; but if it's some peacenik, it'll be a damn white, some college kid."

Both worried that the reliable Stennis, who was the chairman of the Senate Armed Services Committee, would be replaced by Stuart Symington from Missouri, someone Nixon considered senile.[18]

Nixon immediately called Mrs. Stennis at the hospital. She told him it had been two young boys who had shot him, just as he got home from work. Stennis managed to walk into his house, where Mrs. Stennis made him lie down on the couch.[19] It would later come out that Stennis had put up no fight when asked for his wallet, watch, and Phi Beta Kappa gold key, but that once he had surrendered the items, one of the boys said, "Now we're going to shoot you anyway."[20]

When Nixon later spoke with Colson, he found a way to tie it all into race and busing.[21] The Mississippi Democrats in Congress clamored for a constitutional amendment restoring the legality of capital punishment.[22] The media thought this finally was the magic moment for the Congress to pass effective gun control legislation.[23]

The next day—the final day of January 1973—Nixon was preoccupied with planning for a press conference he would give at 11:30 AM. Because Ehrlichman was at *US News and World Report* giving an interview, Nixon called speechwriter Pat Buchanan to prepare for questions on Watergate, especially now that the trial in Judge Sirica's room had ended with guilty verdicts. "On the Watergate thing," Nixon said to Buchanan, "let me say that, first, since the defendants have indicated they are going to appeal, my position can very justifiably be that I am not going to comment on the case while it is still in the courts and on appeal. You get my point?" Buchanan agreed. "I think you've already stated that this stuff has no place in the political process," Buchanan added.[24]

"But my point is, they will try to say, 'What about higher-ups, do you think the court proceedings were adequate and so forth?'" Nixon asked. Buchanan seemed to have been out of the Watergate loop and had little to add on this subject, so Nixon began to pose his own questions for Buchanan to consider. "What about Stans and Mitchell? Do you favor the Ervin investigation? And what if they call White House people, including Mr. Haldeman, to testify before Ervin, would you assert executive privilege?" Again, Buchanan appeared uncomfortable with expressing an opinion. Finally, Buchanan defaulted and suggested that it might be easiest if the president pointed to an internal investigation conducted by White House Counsel John Dean, which had uncovered no criminal activity within the White House.

Nixon thought that might be a good idea. He had first mentioned the so-called "Dean Report" at a press conference at San Clemente in late August 1972, and it seemed to deflect some of the press scrutiny.

The problem was that there never was an internal investigation by Dean.[25] Nixon's continuing reliance on this phantom report as a Watergate shield would eventually become one of the pressure points that would drive Dean away from the president and into the prosecutors' arms in April 1973. By then, Dean saw very clearly that he was fast becoming the scapegoat for the scandal.

But that was down the road.

When it came time for the press conference on January 31, 1973—the twenty-ninth of Nixon's presidency—there wasn't one question asked by the press about Watergate. Nixon was shocked.

Instead, the president faced questions about Vietnam, gun control, impoundment of funds, Kissinger's upcoming trip to Hanoi, and a possible visit by Nixon to the European capitals in 1973. Nixon started the press conference in a very statesmanlike way, discussing his likely meeting with President Thieu in the spring and his firm support for US financial help in the reconstruction of both South and North Vietnam, "so they will have a tendency to turn inward to works of peace rather than turning outward to works of war."[26]

But he could not restrain himself when he was asked about healing the wounds of war within the United States itself, including the possibility of considering amnesty for those who had fled the country to avoid the draft. This was throwing raw meat before a ravenous dog.

"Well, it takes two to heal wounds," Nixon snipped, "and I must say, when I see that the most vigorous criticism or, shall we say, the least pleasure out of the peace agreement comes from those who were the most outspoken advocates of peace at any price, it makes one [question] whether some want the wounds healed." Then he blatantly lied about his administration intention to heal domestic wounds, saying, "We do."[27]

He was just getting started. He displayed just a tad too much emotion as he continued his answer, revealing the bile that lay just beneath the surface. "I know it gags some of you to write the phrase 'peace with honor,'" he said, "but it is true, because it would be peace with dishonor had we—what some have used, the vernacular—'bugged out' and allowed what the North Vietnamese wanted: the imposition of a Communist government or a Communist coalition government in South Vietnam. That goal they have failed to achieve. Consequently, we can speak of peace with honor and with some pride that it has been achieved."[28]

And about amnesty Nixon said, "Certainly I have sympathy for those who make mistakes. We all make mistakes. But also, it is a rule of life, we all have to pay for our mistakes." He went on at some length about the subject, concluding, "Those who served paid their price. Those who deserted must pay their price, and the price is not a junket in the Peace Corps, or something like that, as some have suggested. The price is a criminal penalty for disobeying the laws of the United States. If they want to return to the United States, they must pay the penalty. If they don't want to return, they are certainly welcome to stay in any country that welcomes them."[29] He had stuck it to them.

Later that afternoon he called Pat Buchanan to get his reaction to the amnesty remarks. "That was a fine job," Buchanan said. "Had to be done," Nixon said. "You know this double standard, here these poor devils come back, you know, and . . ."

Buchanan interrupted: "Well, I think you've got the country with you on this; it was just right."

Nixon said, "Well, if anybody wants to desert, they have to pay the price." Buchanan yukked it up over Nixon's mention of a "junket in the Peace Corps" for draft dodgers. "Well that's what people have suggested," Nixon replied. "Let them serve two years in the Peace Corps. Now wouldn't that be just ducky," he said. "Send them down to Brazil for a little vacation for two years with the natives? Hell no. They're gonna go to jail."[30]

Buchanan laughed. "OK," Nixon said, "you can save [the Watergate talking points Buchanan had created] for the next one—all that crap we didn't use. Fine job, though."[31]

Nixon met with John Connally for a couple hours late in the afternoon. The press was full of stories that Nixon favored Connally for president in 1976.[32] There was talk he would rejoin the Nixon administration (he had been secretary of the treasury) and change his party affiliation from the Democratic Party to the Republican Party. He eventually bolted to the Republican Party in May 1973. Though he was discussed as a potential choice to replace Agnew when he resigned in October 1973, Nixon picked Gerald Ford instead. By then, Nixon had neither the stomach nor the political strength to fight with Democrats in the Senate over the confirmation of a man who was considered by some to have been a traitor to his party.

That evening, Nixon held a state dinner for the prime minister of Japan, Eisaku Sato, and his wife. After escorting his guests to the North Portico to bid them good night, Richard Nixon, Pat Nixon, and Julie Nixon Eisenhower all returned to the second-floor residence to retire for the night.[33]

Across town, John Stennis was out of surgery and resting, but his condition was considered "very serious."[34]

January 1973 was over.

Stennis would eventually recover, and in October 1973, as Nixon's presidency was in a free fall, Nixon would call on Stennis to listen to and verify transcripts of certain tapes being sought by special prosecutor Archibald Cox. Cox rejected the so-called "Stennis compromise," not just because Stennis was notoriously hard of hearing but because he, Cox, believed he needed to hear the tapes himself—transcripts prepared by the president's secretary, Rose Mary Woods, were no substitute.

As a result, Nixon had Cox fired on October 20, 1973, during an unforgettable night that would become known as the "Saturday Night Massacre." Nixon's then–attorney general, Elliot Richardson, refused Nixon's order to fire Cox, and he resigned. Richardson's assistant attorney general, William Ruckelshaus, also declined to carry out the president's directive and was either fired or resigned before being fired—it has never been exactly clear which happened first.

It was left to the solicitor general, Robert Bork, to pull the trigger.

Nixon never recovered from the outcry that followed. He resigned from his office on August 9, 1974. Chuck Colson, Bob Haldeman, John Ehrlichman, John Mitchell, John Dean, Jeb Magruder, and a host of others went to jail. They paid for their mistakes. It's a rule of life.

Richard Nixon took a pardon. Now isn't that just ducky.

EPILOGUE

The Blessings of Simultaneity

The complex structure for peace so meticulously negotiated by Henry Kissinger and his team of experts did not hold up. On February 10 Kissinger started a three-day visit to Hanoi, the outskirts of which still resembled a lunar landscape from the intense bombing in December.[1] Yet in South Vietnam the violence continued, and next door fighting escalated in Laos and Cambodia, prompting the United States to send B-52s on major bombing runs to try to force a cease-fire there.[2] Despite it all, peace abroad remained elusive.

Nor did the healing at home that Kissinger had hoped for come to pass. As a result of the power struggle Nixon kicked off with the Democratic Congress—resulting from the December bombings, his impoundment of funds, and his attack on the Great Society—the Senate voted in the first week of February 1973 to create a special select committee to investigate Watergate and related allegations of espionage in the 1972 campaign. Senator Sam Ervin of North Carolina was chosen to head the committee. He promised to "summon various presidential advisers for questioning on espionage operations when the hearings begin."[3]

The myth of Judge Sirica was born. He alone was credited with asking the tough questions that Earl Silbert and his prosecution team did not ask. "There was motive," Walter Rugaber of the *New York Times* wrote. "While the Government did not need to establish one in order to convict the defendants, Judge Sirica said repeatedly that the jury—and by implication the public—would want to know why the defendants had carried out wiretapping and espionage activities at the Democratic headquarters at the Watergate building, and against Democratic Presidential candidates."[4]

Earl Silbert's proofs were limited; ultimately he argued that the defendants were "off on an enterprise of their own." The strong perception was that Silbert was pressured by his bosses at the Department of Justice to avoid a rigorous inquiry into the extent and purpose of the conspiracy.[5] The reality was he was probably just being a conservative lawyer, feeling more anxiety about the need to win a conviction in the biggest case of his young career than heat from his superiors to look the other way. But there is no question he had to have been watching over his shoulder, and this likely explains his failure to thoroughly interrogate and challenge Jeb Magruder, whose alibi, even to Magruder, seemed facially weak. John Mitchell was given a complete pass by an awed and intimidated Silbert.

Yet Silbert was promoted to US attorney for the District of Columbia in the summer of 1974, nominated by President Richard Nixon not long before he was run out of office. Silbert was confirmed despite an intense battle before the Senate Judiciary Committee.[6]

Kenneth Lay, CEO of Enron, hired Silbert in 2002 to represent him in the criminal case arising out of Enron's fraud.[7]

The rush to canonize Sirica ran into some bumps. The *New York Times* had to retract an editorial that lauded Sirica's questioning of Hugh Sloan. "Thanks to the courage and tenacity of Chief Judge John S. Sirica of the United States District Court who presided at the Watergate trial, the public now has on record sworn testimony that former Attorney General John N. Mitchell, the President's campaign manager, and former Secretary of Commerce Maurice H. Stans, his chief money-raiser, personally approved the disbursement of $199,000 to one of the convicted defendants to carry out the espionage," the *Times* wrote at trial's end.[8] A few days later the editors were forced to apologize. "A reading of the actual transcript of the trial shows that the testimony of Hugh W. Sloan, Jr., former treasurer of the committee, was less conclusive than had first appeared to us on the basis of news accounts," they sheepishly wrote. "The *Times* regrets the erroneous statement in our editorial of Feb. 1."[9]

Sirica went public days after the jury's verdict to express his skepticism that the trial had uncovered the truth. "I have not been satisfied, and I am still not satisfied, that all of the pertinent facts that might be available have been produced before an American jury," he said.[10]

His instincts were correct, even though his methods were atrocious. He was a blunt instrument, trampling on the rights of the defendants to due process and a fair trial—to say nothing of impartial and proportionate sentencing. More prosecutor than judge, his actions were as tyrannical as the ones he hoped to expose with his judicial crusading. He was not the referee at a prizefight; he became one of the sluggers. Somehow justice was stained in the process.[11]

But John Sirica was not to be denied. He ordered Earl Silbert to continue to pursue the matter in front of a grand jury and said he hoped the Senate's investigation would pick up where the trial had left off. He remained unapologetic for his aggressive tactics. "I don't think a Federal judge should sit up on a bench—particularly in a case like this one, with great public interest in it—I don't think we should sit up here like nincompoops," he defiantly asserted.[12]

Before a second Watergate trial in the fall of 1974, one in which Mitchell, Haldeman, and Ehrlichman, among others, were found guilty and sent off to jail, Sirica was hailed as *Time*'s Man of the Year for 1973.[13]

What has been all but lost in history is the close interconnectedness of the Watergate drama and the conclusion of the Vietnam War. The two danced together in a mutually dependent political ballet. Despite penetrating coverage of the Watergate scandal prior to the election by the *New York Times* and the *Washington Post*, and the intrepid reportage of journalists like Bob Woodward and Carl Bernstein, Richard Nixon scored an unambiguous victory in his reelection in November 1972. Watergate was well known, and the voters did not care.

But then Nixon poked a stick in the eye of a Democratically controlled Congress that was already chafing under the condescension of his imperial presidency. Sam Ervin and other senators had filed suit over the president's refusal to spend monies authorized by Congress, and he, Majority Leader Mike Mansfield, and others found Nixon's vast reorganization plan for the executive branch to be a direct threat to the power exercised by congressional oversight committees.[14]

It was the Christmas bombing, however, that was the final straw. Along with the Watergate burglars' trial itself, it was a critical spark to the Senate's Watergate investigation. The constitutional balance of power was seriously out of whack, and it had to be rectified. Congress was unwilling to continue as the stepchild of the executive. The Senate was in a mood to reassert itself.

Nixon and Kissinger's penchant for total secrecy placed the public on the sidelines, left to guess what was going on.[15] "Some of the most ardent supporters of Mr. Nixon's conduct of the war professed dismay that he had given no public or private accounting for the most recent developments," the *New York Times* wrote on January 6. "Senator John C. Stennis of Mississippi, the Democratic chairman of the Armed

Services Committee, said that a White House explanation would 'help clear the atmosphere.' "[16] But no public statement explaining the bombing was forthcoming until January 23, when peace was declared.

Nixon seemed to recognize the vulnerability he had created for himself as a result of his hiding behind closed doors over the course of the bombing and during the international furor that followed. He kept justifying his silence in his speech announcing the accords and in the succeeding days and months, but it was too little, too late.[17] His failure to build broad public support for his acts of war would prove to be a fatal miscalculation.

And in this intricate ballet, as one dancer grew stronger and the other became weaker, Nixon's ability to enforce the peace agreement in Vietnam sharply diminished as his presidency came under increasing attack from the Ervin Watergate Committee. James McCord, unwilling to spend most of the rest of his life in prison for a third-rate burglary, finally snapped in March. Nixon knew McCord was a weak reed. John Ehrlichman told him on March 20 that McCord, out on bail pending sentencing, "has a hang-up about jail; he didn't like it when he was in there at all."[18]

The date set by Judge Sirica for sentencing was March 23, 1973.

Two days earlier, on March 21, John Dean, the White House Counsel, had warned Nixon that there was a "cancer within, close to the presidency, [and it's] growing." He tried to get the president to end the hush-money payments to Hunt and the others, suggesting that he, Dean, and other White House insiders appear before a secret grand jury to take their lumps so that the presidency could survive. Nixon came close to accepting Dean's recommendation, but he eventually recoiled at the thought of people like Bob Haldeman going to jail. He decided to hunker down and tough it out.[19] Hunt and his lawyer, Bill Bittman, received another large payment that evening.[20]

On the morning of the sentencing, Sirica dramatically read a letter that McCord had delivered to him a few days earlier. McCord wrote that there had been political pressure on the defendants to plead guilty and remain silent. Perjury had occurred during the trial. Others had been involved in the operation.[21]

The floodgates had opened.

John Dean eventually broke with the president and found his own lawyer, Charlie Shaffer, another of Bobby Kennedy's Department of Justice lawyers who helped put Jimmy Hoffa behind bars. He and Shaffer utterly outmaneuvered the White House and its lawyers over the next few months, with Dean testifying in June before the Ervin Committee in damning detail about his conversations with Nixon. Though the nation was mixed about whom to believe, things turned Dean's way when White House aide Alexander Butterfield revealed the existence of the White House taping system to the Senate panel in July. The fight over the tapes saw the firing of Special Prosecutor Archibald Cox in October 1973 and a ruling from Warren Burger's Supreme Court in the summer of 1974 that Nixon had to turn over the tapes.

When the tapes were produced, Dean's testimony was corroborated; Nixon resigned on August 9, 1974.

In June 1973, at the same time that Dean was testifying against Nixon, Congress passed resolutions forbidding the president from using any funds to enforce the peace agreement, through bombing or any other military activities, in Laos or Cambodia.[22] The United States was left powerless to punish the North Vietnamese for blatant violations of the accords. Kissinger wrote bitterly, "That, and not the legal terms of the agreement, ensured the collapse of Indochina."[23]

Kissinger saw Watergate as the culprit. "Nixon took it for granted that the conclusion of the Paris accords implied the right to enforce them—as has been the case in every previous and subsequent conflict in which Americans have sacrificed their lives," he wrote. "But Watergate undermined what was left of national cohesion and altered the previous equilibrium between the executive and legislative branches."[24]

Even renewed cease-fire talks between Kissinger and Le Duc Tho in Paris in June 1973, with the execution of yet another cease-fire agreement, proved meaningless.[25] On April 30, 1975, Communist North Vietnamese and Vietcong overwhelmed South Vietnamese forces, and Saigon finally fell.[26] Among the mementos saved in the chaos from the American embassy was an inscribed color portrait of President Richard M. Nixon and his family.[27] In Paris, representatives of the Provisional Revolutionary Government announced that Saigon had been renamed Ho Chi Minh City.[28]

As it turned out, it all had come down to the withdrawal of American forces for the return of prisoners, joyful as those events were for the nation and the families involved.

Daniel Ellsberg, the man who leaked the Pentagon Papers and was the reason for the existence of the White House Plumbers, told John Dean years later that he believed Dean's testimony saved another 50,000 American lives when it resulted in Nixon's removal from office.[29]

Chuck Colson, with a touch of irony, would plead guilty to a felony count that he attempted to obstruct justice and influence the trial of Daniel Ellsberg, a case that was being handled by a federal judge other than John Sirica.[30] The charges against Colson in the Watergate cover-up case before Sirica and the Ellsberg psychiatrist break-in matter were dropped in return. Colson would be spared the vengeance of Judge Sirica.

Colson emerged from his seven months of incarceration as a born-again Christian. He founded Prison Fellowship, a successful ministry outreach program for inmates and their families, in 1976.[31] "I went to prison, voluntarily," he later said. "I deserved it."[32]

But there is something even more profound to take away from the burst of simultaneity in January 1973. It was not just that Watergate and Vietnam were tightly connected, playing off one another. Nor was it that the deaths of two Cold War ex-presidents, coinciding as they did with the end of the Vietnam War, symbolically marked the end of a particular time of American hubris. Because of America's global military triumphs in the Second World War and the development of atomic and then nuclear weaponry, Americans had come to believe that their country was, and would forever remain, omniscient and omnipotent in foreign conflicts and foreign wars. Vietnam shattered that illusion, though sadly 9/11 would cause many to "unlearn" this lesson.

These things were assuredly genuine and true about the happenings of January 1973—they were all oddly linked, associated, and coupled, like an aspen grove of trees. How else to explain Sarah Hughes, the judge who swore in LBJ on Air Force One in Dallas in November 1963, being the same person who later served on the three-judge panel in the lower court that decided *Roe v. Wade*? Her appearance in both pivotal moments, which would find ultimate expression in one day—January 22, 1973—seems improbable, to say the least.

Or what about the fact that Larry Hammond left the Supreme Court as Lewis Powell's law clerk to go to work for the Watergate Special Prosecution Force in June 1973?

But there is something deeper.

The events of January 1973, which seemed to have been so sublimely synchronized, also represented the starting point of a particularly divisive battle for the political soul of America. Though Richard Nixon may have lost his skirmish in the short run, he presided over and helped establish a new political order that still holds sway today.

Roe v. Wade, probably surprisingly to Nixon, would play an essential role in transforming the American polity, expanding on what Nixon had begun.

There is no doubt that Nixon and Colson thought they were establishing, to use their term, a "New Majority." Nixon spoke with Harry Dent of the need for a new party the day after he was elected president for the second time. Dent, who made his start in politics with Strom Thurmond of South Carolina, agreed with Nixon that the term *Republican* was anathema in the South. Something novel was needed.

Nixon and Colson's bible was a book titled *The Real Majority*, written by Richard Scammon and Ben Wattenberg. The authors showed that, statistically, the typical voter in 1970 was "the forty-seven-year-old wife of a machinist in suburban Dayton, Ohio."[33] Her politics, they wrote, would be quite different from "a twenty-four-year-old instructor of political science at Yale University."[34]

Put crudely, Scammon and Wattenberg found that, demographically speaking, most voters were "unyoung, unpoor, and unblack."[35] The authors posited that in national elections, "demography is destiny." Make the pitch appeal to this "real majority" and national electoral success was sure to follow.

This anti-intellectual, blue-collar, patriotic, Southern-based coalition was not the Republican Party of Nelson Rockefeller or even Barry Goldwater. It was an entirely new political creature—a party in which Nixon saw a Southern conservative Democrat like John Connally as his successor. And for a time, Colson even wooed big labor to join the get-together. The hardhats, as the Nixon people called them, were triggered to support Nixon as a result of his conduct of the war and his disdain for the draft-dodging, drug-taking, elitist, pampered youth on the college campuses—the ones who provoked the violence at Kent State.

The "real majority" coalesced around a backlash against a federal government that seemed hell-bent on being the definer, provider, and protector of economic, political, and social rights. Starting with the New Deal and continuing through the Great Society, these rights proliferated and became more and more controversial and the source of voter alienation: civil rights (including affirmative action); economic rights (not just broad-based programs like Social Security and Medicare but also welfare and federal food and housing programs for the poor and underprivileged); and social rights (student rights and, most critically, women's rights). The perceived usurpation by the federal government in these areas was the reason for the counterrevolution. Individual freedom and liberty were felt to be at stake.

It was time, Nixon said in his second inaugural, to "turn away from the condescending policies of paternalism—of 'Washington knows best.'"

Watergate exposed how these counterrevolutionaries viewed their political opponents as enemies rather than persons with different political views. This was a war. Where LBJ declared a war on poverty, Nixon declared a culture war.

He did this because that is what would win elections in the new era that was dawning. Scammon and Wattenberg were "tide watchers." They looked at the data to detect not just ripples or waves in election results but the ebb and flow of American political tides. "There *are* political tides," they asserted, "but they are sometimes not discernible for years."[36]

Examining the last century of American politics, Scammon and Wattenberg recognized the principal tidal voting issue as mainly economic: "the issue of prosperity with order."[37] They saw in 1970 another tide rising, this one quite different from the past. "Suddenly," they wrote, "some time in the 1960s, 'crime' and 'race' and 'lawlessness' and 'civil rights' became the most important domestic issues in America."[38] The new Voting Issue, as they called it, was "the Social Issue." It was a complex set of concerns that converged all at once, "beating ripples into waves and perhaps moving waves into a tide that will be politically observable for decades to come." The Social Issue, as they saw it, was made up of several parts: crime, race, "kidlash," the Vietnam protest movement, and lax values (the rise of pornography and permissiveness in sexual codes).[39]

The average voter felt threatened, fearful. The Social Issue was described as "a set of public attitudes concerning the more personally frightening aspects of disruptive social change."[40]

Or, as the authors so succinctly put it, "Most voters felt they gained little from crime, or integration, or wild kids, or new values, or dissent." This "antidissent dissent" became the core of the Nixon/Colson New Majority.[41]

What *Roe* added to this mix was a powerful accelerant: religion. The struggle now literally became life and death. The Religious Right to be sure had become activated politically over the "race" issue.[42] The early founders of the Moral Majority and the Heritage Foundation—Paul Weyrich and Jerry Falwell—began organizing over another

Supreme Court case, *Coit v. Green*, which established that private schools like Bob Jones University in Greenville, South Carolina, could not retain their tax-exempt status if they discriminated in their admissions practices on the basis of race.[43] It was not until 1979 and the start of the Reagan years that abortion became an explosive political issue in national elections.[44] When the issue of abortion finally caught hold, though, it generated incredible energy in support of the Nixon counterrevolution.[45]

It was, first off, a better theme to organize around than rallying on behalf of segregationist institutions. The opponents of abortion would become more akin to the abolitionists of the nineteenth century, concerned about basic human rights, not the deniers of the same. And this movement brought with it an astonishing grassroots potential— in pulpits around the country, ministers and priests decried abortion and the politicians who supported it. Tapping into this network was waking a sleeping giant in American politics.

But once awakened, the movement eventually veered off in the direction of "no compromise," which has become the hallmark of current politics. The Religious Right became frustrated by the end of the 1990s. "They fumed that they had been used and abused, like some cheap date," a reporter wrote in 1998. "In one election after another, they said, conservative foot soldiers had dutifully worked the phone banks, walked the precincts and turned out masses of voters for Republican candidates who had promised action on issues like abortion, pornography, and homosexuality. And the Republicans, they complained, had consistently failed to deliver."[46]

The problem for the Religious Right: "They say they have run out of patience as they watch their social agenda pushed to the back burner year after year, or bargained away in legislative deals," a *Times* reporter wrote.[47] Compromise was something that was impossible when life was at stake. Political opponents were evil, not just wrongheaded. They were not to be bargained with.

By the time of the Tea Party—an offshoot or descendant of the Religious Right and the Nixon counterrevolution, depending on one's perspective—compromise was simply no longer acceptable. Deadlock in Congress became a form of "antidissent dissent." A system built on checks and balances now had only checks.

And Nixon and Colson actually foresaw one of the mechanisms that would assist in the counterrevolution. In a call on December 27, 1972, the two spoke about the need for revenge against CBS, which had been scathing in its reporting about the Christmas bombings. "Whatever we can do to them, they deserve," Colson said. "That's right," Nixon replied. "One thing we are going to do is to go all out for cable. I think cable hurts all the networks. That'll really stir them up."[48]

He had no idea.

This, then, is the legacy of January 1973. The "me generation" found its voice, religion became a political force, poverty and civil rights became someone else's problem, and the national will for concerted action for the common good of all its citizens was scattered into "a thousand points of light."

At some point, perhaps those scattered lights will re-form and reunite to give birth to a rededicated nation, one that includes a place for everyone, opportunity for all, and help for those who need it. After all, it only takes a moment in time and some simultaneity. As Lyndon Johnson so aptly observed in his greatest speech—the "We Shall Overcome" speech—there are times in America when "history and fate meet at a single time in a single space to shape a turning point in man's unending search for freedom."[49]

Let us hope such a time is nearing.

ACKNOWLEDGMENTS

There are some key people who I must acknowledge for helping me bring this book to life. First, my wife, Joanna Connors, who patiently guided me as I explained the project and then endlessly listened to me reading drafts of chapters to her. She is an accomplished writer and her guiding hand has been loving and edifying. She was particularly important to me with respect to the issue of women's reproductive rights.

Second, I need to say a huge thank you to John Dean. John and I have taught an ethics course on Watergate for the past few years and travelled widely, leaving a lot of time to discuss this project. The book has its origins in our ethics course, as I discovered the concurrence of the great events of January 1973 when we were preparing a second version of our Watergate seminar. While John would not read chapters until the book was finished, he answered innumerable questions, about Watergate, Richard Nixon, Henry Kissinger, and all the players in the Watergate saga. He also was of immense assistance in helping me to understand how to find conversations and otherwise use the Nixon Tapes, even occasionally checking to see if my transcriptions on key passages had been accurate. He is a careful scholar and good friend. I could not ask for a better mentor when it comes to researching and writing history.

My former law associate Mark Gamin is next. Mark took an interest in the project and carefully edited each chapter as it was completed. He is a fantastic writer himself and has a good eye for pithy writing. He asked critical questions that helped me to clear up passages that were unclear or that needed more explanation. He was also expert in his copyediting.

Another former law partner, Charles Freed, gave me assistance in researching the Blackmun Papers at the Library of Congress. Chuck also batted around some of my central theories and themes of the book and helped me refine and understand them better.

I need to thank Blackmun biographer Linda Greenhouse for pointing me in the direction of the Lewis Powell Papers, which are online at the Washington and Lee University School of Law website.

Additional readers include Brian Lamb, David Hooker, Bruce Hearey, Tom Aldrich, Matt Liebson, and Tony Rospert.

I also thank Larry Hammond who allowed me to interview him and answered some questions by e-mail. The inside perspective was helpful, although I must emphasize that he carefully followed the rules set down by Justice Powell: Larry was free to discuss his dealings with Justice Powell but Powell asked him not to comment on other justices. Larry also never sought to edit any of my writings in any way. He is a delightful human being who has practiced law with an eye towards helping the underprivileged.

Thanks to my agent Jane Dystel, the ultimate professional. She combines a no-nonsense attitude with a willingness to be available whenever needed. She is very wise.

And thanks to Chicago Review Press and Jerry Pohlen who provided guidance throughout the writing and early editing of the book. He has been a real pleasure to work with.

NOTES

Introduction: A Stand of Aspen

1. Michael C. Grant, "The Trembling Giant," *Discover Magazine*, October 1993, http://discovermagazine.com/1993/oct/thetremblinggian285#.UxMFckJfFf8.
2. Marshall L. Michael, *The Eleven Days of Christmas, America's Last Vietnam Battle* (San Francisco: Encounter Books, 2002); "Linebacker II," *Air Force Magazine Online*, November 1997. Military people referred to these planes as "BUFFs," or "Big Ugly Fat Fuckers" (or "Fellows" in the cleaner version).
3. Richard Nixon, Presidential Daily Diary, December 18, 1972, Nixon Library Online, http://www.nixonlibrary.gov/virtuallibrary/documents/dailydiary.php# Diary.
4. Edmund Morris, *The Rise of Theodore Roosevelt* (New York: Coward, McCann & Geoghegan, 1979), 228–34, 261–71.
5. Jason Ripper, *American Stories, Living American History*, vol. 2, *From 1865* (New York: M. E. Sharpe, Inc., 2008), 72; Thomas Mallon, "Washingtonienne," *New York Times*, November 18, 2007.
6. "Mrs. Longworth's Daughter Dies," *New York Times*, January 28, 1957; Stacey A. Cordery, *Alice: Alice Roosevelt Longworth, from White House Princess to Washington Power Broker* (New York: Viking, 2007).
7. "Alice Longworth, 85, Gets Nixons' Best Wishes," *New York Times*, February 13, 1969; "Tricia Nixon Takes Vows in Garden at White House," *New York Times*, June 13, 1971 ("The most famous Presidential bride of all, 87-year-old Alice Roosevelt Longworth, daughter of Theodore Roosevelt, was another guest. Her opulent wedding took place on the same spot as Mrs. Robb's in 1906.").
8. "Family Residence Dining Room," White House Museum Online, http://www.whitehousemuseum.org/floor2/private-dining-room.htm.
9. Tape 153-01 (November 13, 1972, Nixon and Longworth), White House Tapes, Nixon Library Online, http://www.nixonlibrary.gov/forresearchers /find/tapes/tape153/153-001.mp3.
10. Tape 34-114 (December 17, 1972, Nixon and Kissinger), White House Tapes, http://www.nixonlibrary.gov/forresearchers/find/tapes/tape034/034-114.mp3.
11. Ibid.
12. Tape 34-125 (December 17, 1972, Nixon and Kissinger), White House Tapes, http://www.nixonlibrary.gov/forresearchers/find/tapes/tape034/034-125.mp3.

13. Jay Winik, *April 1865: The Month That Saved America* (New York: Harper-Collins, 2001), xiv–xv.

14. Ibid.

Prelude: "The Very Thought of Losing Is Hateful to Americans"

1. Vietnam Conflict Extract Data File of the Defense Casualty Analysis System (DCAS) Extract Files, as of April 29, 2008, National Archives.

2. Richard M. Nixon, *RN: The Memoirs of Richard Nixon* (New York: Grosset & Dunlap, 1978), 369.

3. Memorandum of Conversation, February 21, 1970 (morning session), Document 189, *Foreign Relations of the United States, 1964–1968*, ed. Edward C. Keefer and Carolyn Yee, vol. 6, *Vietnam, January 1969–July 1970*.

4. Ibid.

5. Henry Kissinger, *White House Years* (New York: Simon & Schuster, 1979), 440.

6. Ibid., 443.

7. "Le Duc Tho, Top Hanoi Aide, Dies at 79," *New York Times*, October 14, 1990.

8. Kissinger, *White House Years*, 441.

9. Ibid., 444; Memorandum of Conversation, February 21, 1970 (afternoon session), Document 190, *Foreign Relations of the United States, 1964–1968*, ed. Edward C. Keefer and Carolyn Yee, vol. 6, *Vietnam, January 1969–July 1970* (Washington, DC: United States Government Printing Office, 2008), http://history.state.gov/historicaldocuments/frus1969-76v06/d190.

10. Kissinger, *White House Years*, 446.

11. Ibid., 448–57.

12. Ibid., 457–63.

13. Ibid.

14. Ibid., 470.

15. "Warren-Johnson Letters," *New York Times*, June 27, 1968.

16. "Ex-Justice Abe Fortas Dies at 71; Shaped Historic Rulings on Rights," *New York Times*, April 7, 1982.

17. "Ideology Isn't What Sank the Fortas Nomination," *New York Times*, October 17, 1987; "Fortas Approved by Senate Panel; Filibuster Looms," *New York Times*, September 18, 1972.

18. "Life Says Fortas Received and Repaid a Wolfson Fee," *New York Times*, May 5, 1969. John Dean has written a detailed account of these events in *The Rehnquist Choice*. John W. Dean, *The Rehnquist Choice: The Untold Story of the Nixon Appointment That Redefined the Supreme Court* (New York: The Free Press, 2001).

19. "Fortas Quits the Supreme Court, Defends Dealings with Wolfson," *New York Times*, May 16, 1969.

20. "Haynsworth: It Was Not a Total Loss for Nixon," *New York Times*, November 23, 1969.

21. "Carswell Attacked and Defended as Senate Opens Debate on Nomination," *New York Times*, March 17, 1970. Republican senator Roman Hruska helped

to seal Carswell's fate with an off-handed quip to reporters during the confirmation battle: "There are lots of mediocre judges and people and lawyers," Hruska said. "They are entitled to a little representation, aren't they, and a little chance? We can't have all Brandeises, Frankfurters and Cardozos."

22. Nixon, *Memoirs*, 422; "President Bitter," *New York Times*, April 10, 1970.
23. "Blackmun Approved 94–0; Nixon Hails Vote by Senate," *New York Times*, May 13, 1970.
24. Linda Greenhouse, *Becoming Justice Blackmun* (New York: Times Books, 2005), 42–71.
25. Memorandum of Conversation, April 4, 1970, *Foreign Relations of the United States, 1964–1968*, ed., Edward C. Keefer and Carolyn Yee, vol. 6, *Vietnam, January 1969–July 1970*.
26. Ibid.
27. Memorandum from the President's Assistant for National Security Affairs (Kissinger) to President Nixon, April 6, 1970, *Foreign Relations of the United States, 1964–1968*, ed., Edward C. Keefer and Carolyn Yee, vol. 6, *Vietnam, January 1969–July 1970*.
28. Richard Nixon, Presidential Daily Diary, April 4, 1970, Appendix B, Nixon Library Online.
29. Nixon, Daily Diary, April 5, 1970, Appendix A.
30. "Visits Granddaughter," *New York Times*, April 5, 1970 (photo caption).
31. Nixon, Daily Diary, April 5, 1970.
32. H. R. Haldeman, *The Haldeman Diaries: Inside the Nixon White House* (New York: G. P. Putnam's Sons, 1994), 147.
33. Ibid.
34. Ibid., 148.
35. The United States had almost 550,000 troops in Vietnam when Nixon came into office. He started staged withdrawals in 1969 and by April 1970, 115,000 troops had already been "redeployed." Kissinger, *White House Years*, 475.
36. Haldeman, *Diaries*, 148–50; Kissinger, *White House Years*, 475–79.
37. Haldeman, *Diaries*, 148. The leak worked: "A definite time was not set for the President's report in which he is expected to announce plans for further reducing the number of Americans in Vietnam, probably by 50,000." "Apollo 13 Brings Delay in Nixon's Troop Talk," *New York Times*, April 16, 1970.
38. "President Bitter, Pledges to Nominate Third Conservative to the Court Soon," *New York Times*, April 10, 1970.
39. Nixon, Daily Diary, April 9, 1970.
40. Ibid.
41. Greenhouse, *Becoming Justice Blackmun*, 46–50.
42. Haldeman, *Diaries*, 149.
43. Nixon, Daily Diary, April 10, 1970.
44. National Aeronautics and Space Administration, *Apollo 13, Technical Air-to-Ground Voice Transcriptions* (Houston, Texas, Test Division, Apollo Spacecraft Program Office, April 1970), 160.
45. Haldeman, *Diaries*, 149–50.
46. "Nixon Is Briefed on Apollo Crisis," *New York Times*, April 15, 1970.
47. Haldeman, *Diaries*, 150.

48. "Cambodia Appeals to World for Arms," *New York Times*, April 15, 1970.

49. Haldeman, *Diaries*, 150–51.

50. "Judge Blackmun of Minnesota Nominated to Supreme Court Seat By the President," *New York Times*, April 15, 1970.

51. Haldeman, *Diaries*, 151.

52. "Nixon, In Hawaii, Joins Astronauts and Honors Them," *New York Times*, April 19, 1970.

53. Haldeman, *Diaries*, 151.

54. Kissinger, *White House Years*, 484.

55. "Nixon 'Wound Up' by Apollo Trip," *New York Times*, April 28, 1970.

56. Haldeman, *Diaries*, 152.

57. Nixon, *Memoirs*, 448.

58. "Transcript of President's Address to the Nation on Vietnam," *New York Times*, April 21, 1970.

59. "TV: Nixon's Vietnam Talk Assayed by Networks, Uncertainty on Strategy Is Apparent Reaction," *New York Times*, April 21, 1970.

60. Haldeman, *Diaries*, 152.

61. Memorandum from President Nixon to his Assistant for National Security Affairs (Kissinger), April 22, 1970, *Foreign Relations of the United States, 1964–1968*, ed., Edward C. Keefer and Carolyn Yee, vol. 6, *Vietnam, January 1969–July 1970*; Nixon, *Memoirs*, 448–49.

62. Haldeman, *Diaries*, 153.

63. Kissinger, *White House Years*, 491.

64. Ibid., 491–92.

65. Nixon, *Memoirs*, 449.

66. Kissinger, *White House Years*, 495.

67. Ibid., 498.

68. Nixon, Daily Diary, April 25, 1970.

69. Kissinger, *White House Years*, 498.

70. Ibid., 499.

71. Nixon, *Memoirs*, 450.

72. "Rogers and Laird Termed Doubtful," *New York Times*, May 6, 1970; Haldeman, *Diaries*, 155.

73. Nixon, Daily Diary, April 30, 1970.

74. Nixon, *Memoirs*, 451. Per the Presidential Daily Diary, the senators included Mike Mansfield, Edward Kennedy, Robert Byrd, John Stennis, J. William Fulbright, Robert Griffin, Margaret Chase Smith, Milton Young, and George Aiken. The House leaders included Hale Boggs, Gerald Ford, John Anderson, and Carl Albert. Haldeman confirms the standing ovation in Haldeman, *Diaries*, 158.

75. Nixon, *Memoirs*, 452.

76. "Nixon Puts 'Bums' Label on Some College Radicals," *New York Times*, May 2, 1970.

77. "4 Kent State Students Killed by Troops," *New York Times*, May 5, 1972.

78. "A Memo to Mr. Nixon," *New York Times*, May 7, 1978.

79. "Nixon Says Violence Invites Tragedy," *New York Times*, May 5, 1970.

80. Haldeman, *Diaries*, 159.

81. "Administration Will Permit Rally Today at Ellipse, South of the White House," *New York Times*, May 9, 1970.

82. "In the Nation: The Dead at Kent State," *New York Times*, May 7, 1970.

83. "Rogers and Laird Termed Doubtful," *New York Times*, May 6, 1970; "Hickel's Advisers Tell Why He Acted," *New York Times*, May 8, 1970; "Nixon Faces a Divided, Anguished Nation," *New York Times*, May 10, 1970.

84. Haldeman, *Diaries*, 161.

85. Nixon, *Memoirs*, 459.

86. "Nixon Defends Cambodia Drive as Aiding Students' Peace Aim," *New York Times*, May 9, 1970.

87. Nixon, *Memoirs*, 459.

88. Nixon, Daily Diary, May 9, 1970.

89. "Nixon, in Pre-Dawn Tour, Talks to War Protesters," *New York Times*, May 10, 1970.

90. Ibid.

91. Haldeman, *Diaries*, 163.

92. "War Foes Here Attacked by Construction Workers," *New York Times*, May 9, 1970.

93. Ibid.

94. David J. Garrow, *Liberty and Sexuality* (Berkeley, California: University of California Press, 1994), 440–44.

95. "Blackmun Approved 94–0; Nixon Hails Vote by Senate," *New York Times*, May 13, 1970.

1: "We've Got to Still Shoot Some Sparks"

1. "Truman's Body Lies in State in His Library," *New York Times*, December 28, 1972.

2. "The Economy: A Gilt-Edged Year of the Stock Market," *Time*, January 8, 1973. The Dow Jones Industrial closed at 1020, up 130 points for the year 1972, a remarkable 15 percent gain.

3. "Man of the Year: Judge John J. Sirica: Standing Firm for the Primacy of Law," *Time*, January 7, 1974.

4. Tape 829-1 (January 1, 1973, Nixon and Bull), White House Tapes, http://www.nixonlibrary.gov/forresearchers/find/tapes/tape829/829-001.mp3.

5. The Dolphins beat the Steelers in the early game on Sunday. The Dolphins' win came just one week after the Steelers had stunned the Oakland Raiders on a miraculous last-minute touchdown, dubbed the "Immaculate Reception," in which rookie Franco Harris scooped up a sailing football that had ricocheted off colliding players several yards away and ran it in for a score with just seconds left on the clock. The play would become one of the most famous in all of NFL history.

6. Tape 829-7 (January 1, 1973, Nixon and Bull), White House Tapes, http://www.nixonlibrary.gov/forresearchers/find/tapes/tape829/829-007.mp3. At the time, the NFL policy was to black out all home games regardless of whether the games were sellouts. Nixon tried to intervene to get at least playoff games exempted but was rebuffed by NFL commissioner Pete Rozelle.

"NFL Nixed Nixon Bid on TV Blackouts," *USA Today*, February 12, 2012, http://usatoday30.usatoday.com/sports/football/nfl/story/2012-02-12/NFL -TV-blackout-President-Nixon/53060586/1.

7. "Stephen B. Bull: The Man in the Middle," *Washington Post*, February 3, 1974.

8. Tape 829-9 (January 1, 1973, Nixon and Bull), White House Tapes, http:// www.nixonlibrary.gov/forresearchers/find/tapes/tape829/829-009.mp3.

9. In *Plain Speaking*, an oral biography by Merle Miller, Truman identified Nixon as one of two men that he hated in his political life. "I've told you, all the time I've been in politics there's only two people I hate, and he's one," Truman told Miller. "He not only doesn't give a damn about the people; he doesn't know how to tell the truth. I don't think the son of a bitch knows the difference between telling the truth and lying." Merle Miller, *Plain Speaking: An Oral Biography of Harry S. Truman* (New York: G. P. Putnam's Sons, 1973), 135. The other person Truman "hated" was a former governor of Missouri, Lloyd C. Stark. Ibid., 178.

10. Tape 829-9 (January 1, 1973, Nixon and Bull), White House Tapes, http:// www.nixonlibrary.gov/forresearchers/find/tapes/tape829/829-009.mp3.

11. "Dean Sayre, who a few days before had led a peaceful walk to the White House in protest against the bombing . . ." "Nixon's Self-Made Trap," *New York Times*, January 10, 1973.

12. "Wilson Grandson Born in White House," *New York Times*, January 18, 1915; "White House Baby Francis," *New York Times*, January 21, 1915.

13. "In the Capital, Sermons on Courage in Selma," *New York Times*, March 15, 1965; "Mourning is Led by President; Marches and Services Are Held," *New York Times*, April 8, 1968.

14. "Dr. King Hints He'd Cancel March if Aid Is Offered," *New York Times*, April 1, 1968.

15. Martin Luther King Jr., "Remaining Awake Through a Great Revolution," March 31, 1968, in Clayborne Carson and Peter Holloran, eds., *A Knock at Midnight: Inspiration from the Great Sermons of Reverend Martin Luther King, Jr.* (New York: Warner Books, 1998). Also available at http:// mlk-kpp01.stanford.edu/index.php/kingpapers/article/remaining_awake _through_a_great_revolution/.

16. "Johnson Says He Won't Run; Halts North Vietnam Raids; Bids Hanoi Join Peace Moves," *New York Times*, April 1, 1968.

17. Kissinger, *White House Years*, 1,406, 1,449.

18. Nixon, *Memoirs*, 715–17.

19. "Transcript of Speech by McGovern," *New York Times*, November 8, 1972.

20. Tape 33-60 (November 8, 1972, Nixon and Kissinger), White House Tapes, http://www.nixonlibrary.gov/forresearchers/find/tapes/tape033/033-060.mp3.

21. Tape 33-59 (November 8, 1972, Nixon and Rockefeller), White House Tapes, http://www.nixonlibrary.gov/forresearchers/find/tapes/tape033/033-059.mp3.

22. Charles Colson, *Born Again*, rev. ed. (Grand Rapids, Michigan: Chosen Books, 1976; rev. 2008), 17–22.

23. Tape 33-63, 64 (Manolo Sanchez to White House mess), White House Tapes, http://www.nixonlibrary.gov/forresearchers/find/tapes/tape033/033-063.mp3.

24. Tape 33-62 (November 8, 1972, Nixon and Hubert Humphrey), White House Tapes, http://www.nixonlibrary.gov/forresearchers/find/tapes/tape033/033-062 .mp3.

25. "Hanoi Says U.S. Backs Off After an Accord in Paris," *New York Times*, October 27, 1972.

26. Kissinger, *White House Years*, 1,380–1,406.

27. "New Talk Needed," *New York Times*, October 27, 1972.

28. Nixon, *Memoirs*, 691–707.

29. "Nixon Elected in Landslide; McGovern Is Beaten in State; Democrats Retain Congress," *New York Times*, November 8, 1972; "A Vote for More of the Same," *New York Times*, November 12, 1972; "Democrats Gain 2 Seats and Have 57–43 Majority," *New York Times*, November 9, 1972 ("Joseph R. Biden, who will not become 30 and thus eligible to serve until November 20, upset another Republican veteran, Senator J. Caleb Boggs, by fewer than 3,000 votes out of 230,000 cast").

30. "Empty Landslide," *New York Times*, November 9, 1972.

31. "Thurmond Given Praise and Scorn," *New York Times*, September 17, 1964.

32. "Thurmond Joins Goldwater Drive," *New York Times*, September 18, 1964.

33. "Harry Dent, the Southern Strategist," *New York Times*, December 30, 2007.

34. Tape 33-69 (Nixon and Harry Dent), White House Tapes, http://www.nixon library.gov/forresearchers/find/tapes/tape033/033-069.mp3.

35. Ibid.

36. Ibid.

37. Kissinger, *White House Years*, 1,408.

38. Richard M. Nixon, *Six Crises* (New York: W. H. Allen, 1962).

39. Kissinger, *White House Years*, 1,407–408. Nixon's book *Six Crises* is aptly named.

40. Robert Blake, *Disraeli* (New York: St. Martin's Press, 1967).

41. Nixon told an interviewer after the 1972 election that he wanted to be thought of as a "Disraeli conservative," meaning a national leader "with a strong foreign policy, strong adherence to basic values that the nation believes in, combined with reform, reform that will work, not reform that destroys." "Richard Nixon: An American Disraeli," *Time*, November 27, 1972. Nixon reads from Blake's book on Tape 819-2, Part C (24 minutes into the tape), recorded on Monday, December 11, 1972. Nixon had been carrying around Blake's bulky biography of Disraeli, which he was poring through just after the election. In the Oval Office he read aloud to Bob Haldeman and John Ehrlichman from Blake's book (at pages 504–06). He compared the establishment elite from Disraeli's time to the "Georgetown crowd" in his own. "They were rich, grand, tolerant, often eccentric, not infrequently dissipated," he read. Blake described these elites as the "traditional aristocracy with their country cousins, the squirearchy"—here Nixon interjected: "This is Georgetown." Like the McGovernites, the Georgetown elites talked about morals, Nixon said, "but they really don't care." Instead, he said, they run away from problems and were "not fit to govern." Tape 819-2, Part C (December 11, 1972, Nixon, Ehrlichman and Haldeman), White House Tapes, http://www.nixonlibrary .gov/forresearchers/find/tapes/tape819/819-002c.mp3.

42. Haldeman, *Diaries*, 532.
43. "Bold Steps Hinted," *New York Times*, November 9, 1972.
44. Kissinger, *White House Years*, 1,406–07.
45. Tape 829-5 (January 1, 1973, Nixon dictating), White House Tapes, http://www.nixonlibrary.gov/forresearchers/find/tapes/tape829/829-005.mp3.

2: "You Have Shown You Are Not Someone to Be Trifled With"

1. Tape 829-12 (January 1, 1973, Nixon and Colson), White House Tapes, http://www.nixonlibrary.gov/forresearchers/find/tapes/tape829/829-012a.mp3.
2. Diane Sawyer joined the Nixon White House in 1970 as an assistant to Gerald Warren, the deputy press secretary. She was quickly promoted up the ranks.
3. Tape 829-12 (January 1, 1973, Nixon and Colson), White House Tapes, http://www.nixonlibrary.gov/forresearchers/find/tapes/tape829/829-012a.mp3.
4. Kissinger, *White House Years*, 1,409–10.
5. Oriana Fallaci, "Kissinger: An Interview with Oriana Fallaci," *The New Republic*, December 16, 1972, 20.
6. Haldeman, *Diaries*, 538.
7. Tape 33-106 (November 19, 1972, Nixon and Haldeman), White House Tapes, http://www.nixonlibrary.gov/forresearchers/find/tapes/tape033/033-106.mp3.
8. Haldeman, *Diaries*, 538-39 (November 19, 1972).
9. Ibid., 539 (November 20, 1972).
10. Ibid.
11. Ibid.
12. Haldeman, *Diaries*, 545–46.
13. Tape 34-2 (November 29, 1972, Nixon and Haldeman), White House Tapes, http://www.nixonlibrary.gov/forresearchers/find/tapes/tape034/034-002.mp3. Haldeman reported to Nixon about Haig's observations. During this evening call, Nixon is clearly drinking as he sits in his easy chair in the Lincoln Sitting Room, chewing on ice cubes with martial music playing on a record player in the background (likely the score from *Victory at Sea*, his favorite). His call to Haig immediately following the Haldeman call shows a further deterioration—heavy breathing and slow speech. Tape 34-5 (November 29, 1972, Nixon and Haig), White House Tapes, http://www.nixonlibrary.gov/for researchers/find/tapes/tape034/034-005.mp3.
14. Kissinger, *White House Years*, 1,410.
15. "Nixon, on Visit to City, Greets 'Old Friends,'" *New York Times*, November 25, 1972.
16. Haldeman, *Diaries*, 539–40.
17. Haldeman, *Diaries*, 535–40. Rumsfeld was the third director of the Office of Economic Opportunity and later assistant to the president.
18. Kissinger, *White House Years*, 1,419.
19. Nixon, *Memoirs*, 718; Kissinger, *White House Years*, 1,412.
20. Tape 34-69 (December 13, 1972, Nixon and Haig), White House Tapes, http://www.nixonlibrary.gov/forresearchers/find/tapes/tape034/034-069.

mp3. Nixon said that his intuition was to "get the goddamn thing going," meaning the resumption of heavy bombing of North Vietnam. Haig agreed.

21. Tape 823-1, Part A (December 14, 1972, Nixon, Kissinger, Haig), White House Tapes, http://www.nixonlibrary.gov/forresearchers/find/tapes/tape823/823-001a .mp3. This is one of the most important tapes from the Nixon presidency. It shows that Kissinger, along with Haig, pushed hard for renewed bombing, and that Nixon was fully on board. "I think this is so important we ought to sit and talk about it," Nixon said as Kissinger entered the Oval Office. "We may talk all day today, by God, because we're going to do the right thing. And it's going to be at a high cost, one way or another. But the main thing is: this is going to end."

Nixon asserted that they had gotten to the point of a settlement through hard work and deft moves. He pointed to the influence of "the great initiatives: China, Russia." Now was the time to settle it, he said. "We will take no crap from people who say we should have settled before the election." There would be no second-guessing. The past was irrelevant. "You can't look back. It's like Cambodia." Nixon even talked of making a show of military might at the upcoming inauguration. There would be no peace theme; "we will have a war theme—have the goddamn cannon down there, a few nuclear bombs, it will scare the shit out of people, they will be going crazy."

22. Ibid.

23. Ibid.

24. Tape 823-1, Part B (December 14, 1972, Nixon, Kissinger, Haig), White House Tapes, http://www.nixonlibrary.gov/forresearchers/find/tapes/tape823 /823-001b.mp3.

25. Ibid.

26. Ibid.

27. "Vietnam Delenda Est," *New York Times*, December 23, 1972 ("To send B-52's against populous areas such as Haiphong and Hanoi can have only one purpose: terror"); "Nixon and Kissinger and the Collapse of the Paris Peace Talks, *New York Times*, December 20, 1972; "New Bombing Revives Antiwar Protests," *New York Times*, December 23, 1972; "Madness in Great Ones," *New York Times*, December 30, 1972.

28. "Madness in Great Ones," *New York Times*, December 30, 1972.

29. Tape 35-2 (December 26, 1972, Nixon and Colson), White House Tapes, http://www.nixonlibrary.gov/forresearchers/find/tapes/tape035/tape035-002 .mp3. "The important thing is to say nothing," Nixon told Colson he said to Kissinger before he went to Palm Springs.

30. "Trial by Fire for the North," *New York Times*, December 31, 1972.

31. Kissinger, *White House Years*, 1,446–57. "Trial by Fire for The North," *New York Times*, December 31, 1972; James Reston, "Nixon's Power Without Pity," *New York Times*, December 27, 1972; "U.S. Aides Differ Sharply Over Value of the Raids," *New York Times*, December 31, 1972 ("According to The Associated Press, Telford Taylor, the former prosecutor at the Nuremberg war crimes trial who is now a law professor at Columbia University, reported that the Bach Mai hospital in Hanoi had been 'blown to smithereens, blown to bits,

completely destroyed, and hit more than once on successive days.'"); Telford Taylor, "Hanoi Under the Bombing: Sirens, Shelters, Rubble and Death," *New York Times*, January 7, 1972. Colson's observation that the nation was not particularly concerned about the bombing can be found on Tape 35-17 (December 27, 1972, Nixon and Colson), White House Tapes, http://www .nixonlibrary.gov/forresearchers/find/tapes/tape035/035-017.mp3. "The mood of the country is not very concerned, Mr. President," Colson said. In fact, he reported, support for the bombing increased as the bombing went on. Colson said his instincts were that the administration wasn't "getting a bad bounce" over the bombing. He was delighted.

32. Tape 35-2 (December 26, 1972, Nixon and Colson), White House Tapes, http://www.nixonlibrary.gov/forresearchers/find/tapes/tape035/035-002.mp3.

33. Ibid.

34. Ibid.

35. Tape 35-3 (December 26, 1972, Nixon and Colson), White House Tapes, http://www.nixonlibrary.gov/forresearchers/find/tapes/tape035/035-003.mp3.

36. Tape 35-7 (December 26, 1972, Nixon and Colson), White House Tapes, http://www.nixonlibrary.gov/forresearchers/find/tapes/tape035/035-007.mp3.

37. Nixon, Daily Diary, December 27, 1972.

38. Tape 35-19 (December 27, 1972, Nixon and Kissinger), White House Tapes, http://www.nixonlibrary.gov/forresearchers/find/tapes/tape035/035-019.mp3.

39. Ibid.

40. James Reston, "Nixon and Kissinger," *New York Times*, December 31, 1972.

41. Tape 35-40 (December 31, 1972, Nixon and Colson), White House Tapes, http://www.nixonlibrary.gov/forresearchers/find/tapes/tape035/035-040 .mp3. Colson's theory about why Kissinger leaked to Reston was as follows: "If you put yourself in Henry Kissinger's shoes, he's going to have to spend a good part of the remainder of his life justifying why 'peace was at hand,' but then it wasn't later. And bear in mind, he's [*sic*] always has to have an enemy, he has to blame someone; he can't blame himself."

Nixon: "So?"

Colson: "So now what happens? You have to have an alibi, you've got to have a reason why when he went before the American people—and thought he was winning the election, when he was doing just the reverse—and said 'peace is at hand,' and then it isn't, we've always known that that, I always felt that was an Achilles' heel with him negotiating—I mean murderous. Because the Orientals are damn sly and they know that he stuck his damn neck out."

Nixon: "And then he had to give anything in order to prove it."

Colson: "That's precisely the case."

Nixon: "The moment he said it was at hand, he had no bargaining position."

42. Ibid.

43. Tape 829-12 (January 1, 1973, Nixon and Colson), White House Tapes, http:// www.nixonlibrary.gov/forresearchers/find/tapes/tape829/829-012a.mp3.

3: "Human Adversaries Are Arraigned Against Me"

1. Tape 829-12, Part B (January 1, 1973, Nixon, Colson, Bull, George Allen), White House Tapes, http://www.nixonlibrary.gov/forresearchers/find/tapes /tape829/829-012b.mp3.

2. "In Nicaraguan Refugee Town, Thousands Wait Uncertainly for Aid," *New York Times*, December 29, 1972.

3. "Clemente, Pirates' Star, Dies in Crash of Plane Carrying Aid to Nicaragua," *New York Times*, January 2, 1973.

4. E. Howard Hunt with Greg Aunapu, *American Spy: My Secret History in the CIA, Watergate & Beyond* (Hoboken, New Jersey: John Wiley & Sons, Inc., 2007), 156–64.

5. Nixon, *Memoirs*, 508–09.

6. Haldeman, *Diaries*, 299–300.

7. Ibid., 299–305.

8. "Ellsberg Is Ordered to Stand Trial on the Coast," *New York Times*, August 6, 1971.

9. *Impeachment Inquiry Before the House Committee on the Judiciary*, Hearing Before the Committee on the Judiciary House of Representatives, 93rd Cong., Book 3, 200–03 (Colson testimony, July 15, 1974).

10. Egil Krogh, "The Break-In That History Forgot," *New York Times*, June 30, 2007.

11. Hunt, *American Spy*, 157–58.

12. Ibid., 48–49.

13. Ibid., 245.

14. Ibid., 200, 235–36.

15. "Ex-G.O.P. Aide Is Linked to Political Raid," *New York Times*, June 20, 1972 ("Cuban sources identified him as E. Howard Hunt, who became a consultant to Charles W. Colson, special counsel to President Nixon and to other high White House officials").

16. Hunt, *American Spy*, 178–85, 212.

17. Ibid., 254–55.

18. "Anthony Ulasewicz, 'Bagman' of Watergate, Is Dead at 79," *New York Times*, December 20, 1997.

19. Ibid.

20. *Impeachment Inquiry*, 281–84 (Affidavit of Joan Hall, April 13, 1973; Colson Exhibit 13, Colson testimony, July 15, 1974).

21. Ibid.

22. Ibid., 289.

23. Ibid., 291–96 (Colson Exhibit 14, transcript of phone conversation between Colson and Hunt).

24. Colson-Hunt Dictabelt, dated November 13, 1972, by John Dean, in John W. Dean III, *Blind Ambition* (New York: Simon and Schuster, 1976), 153–55; Impeachment Inquiry, 291–94 (Colson Exhibit 14).

25. Dean, *Blind Ambition*, 157–61.

26. Obstruction of Justice, 18 U.S.C. § 1503 ("Whoever . . . corruptly or by threats or force, or by any threatening letter or communication, influences, obstructs, or impedes, or endeavors to influence, obstruct, or impede, the due administration of justice, shall be punished . . ."); *Impeachment Inquiry*, 289–97 (Colson Exhibit 14); Dean, *Blind Ambition*, 162–68.

27. "Text of Memorandum Hunt Wrote After Break-In," *New York Times*, November 5, 1974. The memo was uncovered during the Watergate cover-up trial after Nixon had resigned. Fred Emery, *Watergate: The Corruption of American Politics and the Fall of Richard Nixon* (New York: Times Books, 1994), 226–28.

28. The memo approving the Ellsberg psychiatrist covert operation, dated August 11, 1971, was from Egil "Bud" Krogh and David Young, co-heads of the White House Special Investigative Unit, to John D. Ehrlichman. It is a status report on the "Pentagon Papers Project." Krogh and Young recommended "that a covert operation be undertaken to examine all the medical files still held by Ellsberg's psychoanalyst covering the two-year period he was undergoing analysis." Ehrlichman initialed the memo and added in his own handwritten proviso, "if done under your assurance that it is not traceable." Senate Hearing Before the Select Committee on Presidential Campaign Activities of the United States Senate, 93rd Cong., Book 6 SSC 2643–45, (Exhibit 90 to Ehrlichman's July 24, 1973, testimony).

29. National Transportation Safety Board, Aircraft Accident Report, Report Number NTSB-AAR-73-16, adopted August 29, 1973.

30. Ibid., 3.

31. "46 Aboard Jet Die When It Crashes on Chicago Homes," *New York Times*, December 9, 1972.

32. "Watergate Figure's Dead Wife Had $10,000 to Invest, He Says," *New York Times*, December 11, 1972.

33. NTSB, Aircraft Accident Report, 13.

34. Carl Oglesby, *The Yankee and Cowboy War: Conspiracies from Dallas to Watergate* (New York: Berkley Publishing Corp., 1977), 236–40. (Letters reprinted in full.)

35. NSTB, Aircraft Accident Report, 31–32.

36. Nixon, Daily Diary, December 8, 1972.

37. Tape 157-026 (December 9, 1972, Nixon and Colson), White House Tapes, http://www.nixonlibrary.gov/forresearchers/find/tapes/tape157/157-026.mp3.

38. Ibid.

39. Tape 819-2, Part B (December 11, 1972, Nixon and Haldeman), White House Tapes, http://www.nixonlibrary.gov/forresearchers/find/tapes/tape819 /819-002b.mp3.

　　　For a partial transcript, see Stanley I. Kutler, *Abuse of Power: The New Nixon Tapes* (New York: Touchstone, Simon & Schuster, 1997), 180–82.

40. "Watergate Figure's Dead Wife Had $10,000 to Invest, He Says," *New York Times*, December 11, 1972.

41. Ibid.

42. Tape 819-2, Part B (December 11, 1972, Nixon and Haldeman), White House Tapes, http://www.nixonlibrary.gov/forresearchers/find/tapes/tape819/819 -002b.mp3.

43. William F. Buckley Jr., foreword to *American Spy: My Secret History in the CIA, Watergate & Beyond*, by E. Howard Hunt (Hoboken, New Jersey: John Wiley & Sons, Inc., 2007), ix–xii.

44. Transcript, United States v. George Gordon Liddy et al., 348 F. Supp. 198 (D.C. 1972) (No. 1827-72). This transcript, like several during the Liddy case, was sealed by Judge Sirica. In 2009 Professor Luke Nichter of Texas A&M University petitioned the court to release the sealed proceedings. Chief Judge Royce Lamberth of the District Court for the District of Columbia, in an opinion issued on November 2, 2012, granted Nichter's petition and directed the National Archives to release many of the sealed proceedings. The Unsealed Materials from *U.S. v. Liddy* can be found online at the National Archives website: http://www.archives.gov/research/investigations/watergate/us-v-liddy.html.

45. Transcript, *U.S. v. Liddy*, 72–73.

46. Ibid., 73.

47. Two Letters Dated January 2, 1973, and January 3, 1973, from Two Physicians Pertaining to Defendant Hunt, Unsealed Materials from *U.S. v. Liddy*. The psychiatrist was Dr. George D. Weickhardt, MD, a 1939 graduate of George Washington Medical School; the neurologist was Dr. Charles E. Law of Alexandria, Virginia.

48. Senate Hearing Before the Select Committee on Presidential Campaign Activities of the United States Senate, 93rd Cong., Book 9 SSC 3892 (Exhibit 153, Hunt's letter to Colson, December 31, 1972).

49. Senate Hearing Before the Select Committee on Presidential Campaign Activities of the United States Senate, 93rd Cong., Book 3 SSC 1,233 (Exhibit 34-28, John Dean testimony, June 26, 1973).

4: "The Abortion Cases"

1. Tape 35-50 (January 2, 1973, Nixon and the White House operator), White House Tapes, http://www.nixonlibrary.gov/forresearchers/find/tapes /tape035/035-050.mp3. One of the wonders of the presidency has always been the White House operators, seemingly able to locate anyone, anytime, anywhere, within minutes of a request.

2. Tape 35-51 (January 2, 1973, Nixon and Burger), White House Tapes, http:// www.nixonlibrary.gov/forresearchers/find/tapes/tape035/035-051.mp3.

3. Miller v. California, 413 U.S. 15 (1973). *Miller* did redefine the definition of obscenity from the "utterly without socially redeeming value" standard to the "lacks serious literary, artistic, political, or scientific value" standard. The jury was to apply a community standard in making its decision.

4. "Cover-Up and Privacy in Nixon vs. ABC," *New York Times*, October 6, 1989.

5. Time, Inc. v. Hill, 385 U.S. 374 (1967).

6. Tape 35-51 (January 2, 1973, Nixon and Burger), White House Tapes, http:// www.nixonlibrary.gov/forresearchers/find/tapes/tape035/035-051.mp3.

7. "Black a Champion of the Under Dog," *New York Times*, August 15, 1937. ("Social justice is no recently acquired idea with Senator Hugo L. Black, the new nominee to the Court.")

8. John W. Dean, *The Rehnquist Choice: The Untold Story of the Nixon Appointment That Redefined the Supreme Court* (New York, Touchstone, 2001), 32–33.

9. "One Supreme Court," *New York Times*, November 17, 1975.

10. "Justice Black Dies at 85; Served on Court 34 Years," *New York Times*, September 26, 1971.

11. "Nixon Attends Funeral in the Capital for Justice Black," *New York Times*, September 29, 1971. ("Mr. Nixon and Attorney General John N. Mitchell, who sat beside him at the cathedral, are said by their staffs to be searching for two strict constructionists to fill the Court vacancies created by the retirements of Justices Black and John M. Harlan.")

12. Tape 829-9 (January 1, 1973, Nixon and Bull), White House Tapes, http://www.nixonlibrary.gov/forresearchers/find/tapes/tape829/829-009.mp3. Bull remarked that he thought Sayre was "right out of a[n] Allen Drury novel," referring to the novelist and popular Washington journalist.

13. Tape 829-31 (January 2, 1973, Nixon and Rose Mary Woods), White House Tapes, http://www.nixonlibrary.gov/forresearchers/find/tapes/tape829/829-031.mp3.

14. "Harlan Dies at 72; On Court 16 Years," *New York Times*, December 30, 1971.

15. Haldeman, *Diaries*, 147.

16. Dean, *Rehnquist Choice*, 42.

17. Ibid., 104, 179.

18. Ibid., 113.

19. Ibid.

20. Ibid., 104, 113.

21. "Potential High Court Nominees," *New York Times*, October 14, 1971.

22. Dean, *Rehnquist Choice*, 117–19.

23. Ibid., 159.

24. Ibid., 175.

25. Ibid., 179–82; Kevin McMahon, *Nixon's Court: His Challenge to Judicial Liberalism and Its Political Consequences* (Chicago: University of Chicago Press, 2011), 158.

26. "President Asks Bar Unit to Check 6 for High Court," *New York Times*, October 14, 1971; "Potential High Court Nominees," *New York Times*, October 14, 1971. The six were Judge Sylvia Bacon, Senator Robert Byrd, Judge Charles Clark, Hershel Friday, Judge Mildred Lillie, and Judge Paul H. Roney. The Byrd selection was a feint. He had never practiced law and was a Democrat. Nixon liked the idea of forcing Senate Democrats to face the prospect of calling one of their own "undistinguished," "mediocre," and "unqualified."

27. Dean, *Rehnquist Choice*, 160–62

28. "Kennedy and Bayh Assail Nixon's Way of Filling Court Vacancies," *New York Times*, October 16, 1971.

29. "Court Nominees Termed Nixon's Stand-by Choices," *New York Times*, October 23, 1971.

30. Ibid.

31. Dean, *Rehnquist Choice*, 192–240.
32. Ibid., 199.
33. Ibid., 191.
34. Ibid., 129.
35. "Powell Is Seeking to Avoid Clashes over Court Seat," *New York Times*, October 26, 1971; John C. Jeffries Jr., *Justice Lewis F. Powell, Jr.* (New York: Charles Scribner's Sons, 1994), 210–42.
36. "White House Concedes Nixon Spoke to Powell," *New York Times*, November 3, 1971; Dean, *Rehnquist Choice*, 199–220.
37. "Court Nominees Termed Nixon's Stand-by Choices," *New York Times*, October 23, 1971; Dean, *Rehnquist Choice*, 221–64; Jeffries, *Justice Lewis F. Powell, Jr.*, 228.
38. "Early Vote Asked," *New York Times*, October 22, 1971.
39. Dean, *Rehnquist Choice*, 217; Tape 11-155 (October 19, 1971, Nixon and Powell), White House Tapes.
40. Linda Greenhouse, *Becoming Justice Blackmun, Harry Blackmun's Supreme Court Journey* (New York: Time Books, Henry Holt Company, 2005), 80.
41. David J. Garrow, *Liberty and Sexuality: The Right to Privacy and the Making of Roe v. Wade* (Berkley: University of California Press, 1994, new epilogue 1998), 521–22.
42. Rehnquist was confirmed on December 10, 1971 (68–26); Powell on December 6, 1971 (89–1).
43. "Early Vote Asked," *New York Times*, October 22, 1971.
44. Tape 35-51 (January 2, 1973, Nixon and Burger), White House Tapes, http://www.nixonlibrary.gov/forresearchers/find/tapes/tape035/035-051.mp3.
45. Ibid.

5: "I Just Feel the Torture You Are Going Through on Vietnam"

1. Tape 393-1 (January 2, 1973, Nixon and Colson), White House Tapes, http://www.nixonlibrary.gov/forresearchers/find/tapes/tape393/393-001.mp3.
2. Tape 35-64 (January 2, 1973, Nixon and Bull), White House Tapes, http://www.nixonlibrary.gov/forresearchers/find/tapes/tape035/035-064.mp3.
3. Tape 36-60 (January 2, 1973, Nixon and Bull), White House Tapes, http://www.nixonlibrary.gov/forresearchers/find/tapes/tape830/830-006a.mp3.
4. "Mike Mansfield, Longtime Leader of Senate Democrats, Dies at 98," *New York Times*, October 6, 2001.
5. "Mansfield in Line for Leader's Post," *New York Times*, August 19, 1960.
6. "Mike Mansfield, Longtime Leader of Senate Democrats, Dies at 98," *New York Times*, October 6, 2001; "Kennedy Confers on Action in Laos if Truce Bid Fails," *New York Times*, April 28, 1961.
7. "Civil Rights Bill Passed, 73–27," *New York Times*, June 20, 1964.
8. Tape 830-002 (January 2, 1973, Nixon and Mansfield), White House Tapes, http://www.nixonlibrary.gov/forresearchers/find/tapes/tape830/830-002.mp3. Nixon talked football with the press present. He told the photographers that Mansfield had been a linebacker in college, and a good one. Nixon said he also had been on the team at Whittier College when he was a freshman and

claimed that there were only eleven eligible men on the team (meaning they had to play both offense and defense). At a game against Pomona, he recalled that one of the Whittier linemen, a center, rolled his ankle in the fourth quarter and wanted to leave the game. "We wouldn't let him," Nixon told the photographers. "God, we almost killed that guy!" Huge laugh from the photographers.

9. Ibid.
10. Ibid.
11. Ibid.
12. Ibid.
13. Tape 830-004 (January 2, 1973, Nixon and Timmons), White House Tapes, http://www.nixonlibrary.gov/forresearchers/find/tapes/tape830/830-004.mp3.
14. Ibid.
15. Tape 830-006, Part A (January 2, 1973, Nixon and Colson, call to LBJ), White House Tapes, http://www.nixonlibrary.gov/forresearchers/find/tapes/tape830/830-006a.mp3.
16. Tape 35-66 (January 2, 1973, Nixon and White House operator), White House Tapes,http://www.nixonlibrary.gov/forresearchers/find/tapes/tape035/035-066.mp3.
17. Tape 35-67 (January 2, 1973, Nixon and Lyndon Johnson), White House Tapes, http://www.nixonlibrary.gov/forresearchers/find/tapes/tape035/035-067.mp3.
18. "Plane with Hale Boggs Aboard Missing in Storm," New York Times, October 17, 1972.
19. "Agnew, Mrs. Nixon and Johnsons Attend Mass for Boggs," New York Times, January 5, 1973.
20. Ibid.
21. Tape 830-006, Part A (January 2, 1973, Nixon and Colson, call to LBJ), White House Tapes, http://www.nixonlibrary.gov/forresearchers/find/tapes/tape830/830-006a.mp3.
22. Recording of Telephone Conversation between Lyndon B. Johnson and Everett Dirksen, November 2, 1968, 9:18, Citation #13706, Recordings and Transcripts of Conversations and Meetings, LBJ Library. Robert Parry, "LBJ's 'X' File on Nixon's 'Treason,'" Consortiumnews.com, March 3, 2013, http://consortiumnews.com/2012/03/03/lbjs-x-file-on-nixons-treason/.
23. Rick Pearlstein, "America's Forgotten Liberal," New York Times, May 26, 2011. "Was Humphrey really as hawkish as all that? Johnson didn't think so; he actually preferred that Nixon win the election. He didn't trust Humphrey to hold firm on the war."
24. "Mr. Humphrey and the Bombing," New York Times, February 2, 1972.
25. Max Frankel, "Johnson Says He Could Have Won in 1968," New York Times, December 27, 1968. "Former President Lyndon B. Johnson says he has no doubt whatever that he could have been re-elected last year and thinks Hubert H. Humphrey's defeat was largely due to the Vice President's mid-campaign concessions to the dovish sentiment on the war in Vietnam."
26. "Johnson Backs McGovern Despite Their Differences," New York Times, August 17, 1972.

27. "Poor Health Limits Johnson's Aid to McGovern," *New York Times*, October 15, 1972.

28. Nixon, *Memoirs*, 755.

29. Nixon, *Memoirs*, 739.

30. "Congressional Critics of War Threaten to Fight Funding," *New York Times*, January 3, 1973.

31. Ibid.

32. Ibid.

33. "Senate Democrats, 36–12, Back Action to End War," *New York Times*, January 5, 1973.

34. "Pullout Sought, Mansfield to Move to Force 'Complete Disinvolvement,'" *New York Times*, January 4, 1973.

35. Nixon, Daily Diary, January 2, 1973.

36. Tape 35-69 (January 2, 1973, Nixon and Colson), White House Tapes, http://www.nixonlibrary.gov/forresearchers/find/tapes/tape035/035-069.mp3.

6: "Every Tree in the Forest Will Fall"

1. Dean, *Blind Ambition*, 205–06. Air Force One, tail number SAM 27000, resides today inside the Air Force One Pavilion at the Ronald Reagan Library in Simi Valley.

2. Senate Select Committee on Presidential Campaign Activities, 93rd Cong., 3 SSC 973 (June 25, 1973, John Dean testimony).

3. Ibid.

4. Ibid.

5. Bittman had just returned from his holiday vacation in Florida the night before, on January 2. He took his family on vacation from December 22 to January 2. *Impeachment Inquiry Before the House Committee on the Judiciary*, 93rd Cong., Book 2, 20 (1974) (Bittman testimony, July 9, 1974).

6. House Committee on the Judiciary, *Impeachment Inquiry Before the House Committee on the Judiciary*, 93rd Cong., Book 3, 300–12 (1974) (Colson testimony, July 15, 1974).

7. *Impeachment Inquiry Before the House*, Book 3, 305–08 (Colson testimony); *Impeachment Inquiry Before the House*, Book 2, 21–23 (Bittman testimony).

8. "Hoffa Convicted on Use of Funds; Faces 20 Years," *New York Times*, July 27, 1964; "U. S. Attorneys Praised," *New York Times*, July 27, 1964. ("Attorney General Robert F. Kennedy issued a brief statement today, praising the Government attorneys who prosecuted the Hoffa case in Chicago.")

9. "A Fighting Prosecutor," *New York Times*, January 30, 1967.

10. Ibid.

11. Senate Select Committee on Presidential Campaign Activities, 93rd Cong., 3 SSC 973 (1973) (Dean testimony); Dean, *Blind Ambition*, 211.

12. *Impeachment Inquiry Before the House*, Book 3, 309–10 (Colson testimony).

13. *Impeachment Inquiry Before the House*, Book 2, 36 (Bittman testimony).

14. Hunt, *American Spy*, 272; Senate Select Committee on Presidential Campaign Activities, 93rd Cong., 3 SSC 974 (1973) (Dean testimony). ("[Colson] also

said that he told [Bittman] that clemency generally came up around Christmas and a year was a long time.")

15. "Nixon Commutes Hoffa Sentence, Curbs Union Role," *New York Times*, December 23, 1971 (Hoffa served four years and nine months of his thirteen-year sentence); Senate Select Committee on Presidential Campaign Activities, 93rd Cong., 3 SSC 973 (1973) (Dean testimony); Dean, *Blind Ambition*, 211–16; "Jury Hears Tape of Nixon Backing Hunt Clemency," *New York Times*, November 19, 1974.

16. Ibid.

17. Tape 831-006, Part B (January 3, 1973, Nixon and Haldeman), White House Tapes, http://www.nixonlibrary.gov/forresearchers/find/tapes/tape831/831-006b.mp3.

18. *Impeachment Inquiry Before the House*, Book III, 244–50 (Colson testimony, Exhibit 9, June 20, 1972 memo to file); Gordon Liddy, *Will: The Autobiography of G. Gordon Liddy* (New York: St. Martin's Press, 1996), 211; United States v. John M. Mitchell, No. 74-110 (D.D.C. 1974) Tr. 9,363–64 (Colson testimony, December 5, 1974). ("I called Magruder. I said, Hunt and Liddy stopped by, complaining that they have been doing a lot of work drawing up a security and intelligence plan and they had not been able to find anyone who would listen to them or give them a hearing or consideration. Why don't you get off your duff over there, Jeb, and do something instead of having these people running around getting up plans—listen to them and make a decision.")

19. John Dean, interview with the author, September 14, 2013; Jeb Stuart Magruder, *An American Life: One Man's Road to Watergate* (New York: McClelland and Stewart Ltd., 1974), 305–06.

20. Tape 831-006, Part B (January 3, 1973, Nixon and Haldeman), White House Tapes, http://www.nixonlibrary.gov/forresearchers/find/tapes/tape831/831-006b.mp3.

21. Ibid.

22. Ibid.

23. Sheppard v. Maxwell, 384 U.S. 333 (1966) ("The fact is," Justice Tom Clark wrote in the 8–1 opinion, "that bedlam reigned at the courthouse, hounding most of the participants in the trial, especially Sheppard." Sheppard was subsequently acquitted in a retrial); "A Most Wanted Attorney," *Orlando Weekly*, October 5, 2000.

24. "An Apology for My Lai, Four Decades Later," *New York Times*, August 24, 2009.

25. Senate Select Committee on Presidential Campaign Activities, 93rd Cong., 1 SSC 294 (1973) (Gerald Alch testimony).

26. Senate Select Committee on Presidential Campaign Activities, 93rd Cong., 1 SSC 125–26 (1973) (McCord testimony).

27. Senate Select Committee on Presidential Campaign Activities, 93rd Cong., 1 SSC 126–32 (1973) (McCord testimony).

28. Earl Silbert, Diary, Part 2, 4 (entry of Saturday, September 16, 1972).

29. Senate Select Committee on Presidential Campaign Activities, 93rd Cong., 1 SSC 250–53 (1973) (Caulfield testimony).

30. Ibid.

31. Ibid.; "Jack Caulfield, Bearer of a Watergate Message, Dies at 83," *New York Times*, June 21, 2012.

32. Senate Select Committee on Presidential Campaign Activities, 93rd Cong., 1 SSC 253 (1973) (Caulfield testimony).

33. Senate Select Committee on Presidential Campaign Activities, 93rd Cong., 1 SSC 194 (1973) (McCord testimony).

34. Senate Select Committee, 1 SSC 254 (Caulfield testimony).

35. Senate Select Committee, 1 SSC 194 (McCord testimony).

36. Senate Select Committee, 1 SSC 254 (Caulfield testimony).

37. Senate Select Committee, 1 SSC 194–95 (McCord testimony). "By this time, I was also convinced that the White House had fired Helms in order to put its own man in control at CIA, but as well to lay the foundation for claiming that the Watergate operation was a CIA operation, and now to be able to claim that 'Helms had been fired for it.'"

38. "A.E.C. Chief to Replace Helms as C.I.A. Director," *New York Times*, December 22, 1972.

39. Senate Select Committee, 1 SSC 195 (McCord testimony).

40. Senate Select Committee, 1 SSC 974, 1,235 (Dean testimony) (Exhibit 34-29, McCord note to Caulfield as transcribed by Dean's assistant, Fred Fielding).

41. Ibid.; Dean, *Blind Ambition*, 212–13.

42. Senate Select Committee, 1 SSC 256 (Caulfield testimony).

43. Ibid.

44. Senate Select Committee, 1 SSC 195 (McCord testimony).

45. Tape 35-078 (January 3, 1973, Nixon and Colson), White House Tapes, http://www.nixonlibrary.gov/forresearchers/find/tapes/tape035/035-078.mp3.

46. Ibid.

47. Ibid.

7: "The Pregnant Woman Cannot Be Isolated in Her Privacy"

1. Tape 35-051 (January 2, 1973, Nixon and Burger), White House Tapes, http://www.nixonlibrary.gov/forresearchers/find/tapes/tape035/035-051.mp3.

2. Nixon actually said Knowland swore him in in 1956; he had the year wrong. Nixon likely couldn't remember his second swearing-in as vice president because it was complicated. January 20, 1957, fell on a Sunday, so Eisenhower and Nixon were sworn in by Earl Warren during private ceremonies in the White House. The oaths were repeated the next day in the public ceremonies. "Some Took Oath Late: Hayes First To Be Sworn In Ahead of Time," *Los Angeles Times*, January 21, 1985. ("No further scheduling problem arose until Sunday, Jan. 20, 1957, when Chief Justice Earl Warren swore in Dwight D. Eisenhower and his vice president, Richard M. Nixon, for a second term at a private White House ceremony following church services. They took the oath publicly the next day at the Capitol.")

3. U.S. Const., art. II, § 1.

4. The present oath repeated by the vice president of the United States, senators, representatives, and other government officers has been in use since 1884.

The oath reads, "I do solemnly swear [or affirm] that I will support and defend the Constitution of the United States against all enemies, foreign and domestic; that I will bear true faith and allegiance to the same; that I take this obligation freely, without any mental reservation or purpose of evasion; and that I will well and faithfully discharge the duties of the office on which I am about to enter: So help me God."

5. David J. Garrow, *Liberty and Sexuality: The Right to Privacy and the Making of* Roe v. Wade (Berkeley: University of California Press, 1994, Preface and Epilogue, 1998), 528–38.

6. Garrow, *Liberty and Sexuality*, 443, 517. ("The hearing had been Weddington's first courtroom experience ever as a practicing attorney, and hence, 'I was petrified' during that part of the proceeding, she later explained.")

7. Garrow, *Liberty and Sexuality*, 439–44.

8. Roe v. Wade, 410 U.S. 113 (1973).

9. Garrow, *Liberty and Sexuality*, 451–54.

10. Doe v. Bolton, 410 U.S. 179 (1973) (Appendix A).

11. Ibid.

12. Garrow, *Liberty and Sexuality*, 444–50.

13. Linda Greenhouse, *Becoming Justice Blackmun: Harry Blackmun's Supreme Court Journey* (New York: Times Books, Henry Holt and Company, 2005), 80–83.

14. Garrow, *Liberty and Sexuality*, 533–34.

15. Ibid.

16. Ibid.

17. Greenhouse, *Becoming Justice Blackmun*, 82.

18. Garrow, *Liberty and Sexuality*, 389–96.

19. Ibid.

20. Sarah Weddington, *A Question of Choice* (New York, G. P. Putnam's Sons, 1992), 18, 26–45.

21. "1970 Abortion Law: New York Said Yes, Stunning the Nation," *New York Times*, April 9, 2000. One New York legislator remembered the time in this way: "We were living in a time of enormous change. There was the war. There was the women's movement, which was really bringing the abortion issue to a crescendo. It was the end of the civil rights era, and we viewed this as a civil right. In '65, we had repealed the death penalty, which people thought was impossible. There was a sense that extraordinary things were possible." Ibid.

22. Griswold v. Connecticut, 381 U.S. 479 (1965).

23. Ibid.

24. Ibid., 482.

25. A good definition of *penumbra* is "a space of partial illumination (as in an eclipse) between the perfect shadow on all sides and the full light."

26. *Griswold*, 484.

27. Ibid., 485.

28. Roy Lucas, "Federal Constitutional Limitations on the Enforcement and Administration of State Abortion Statutes," *North Carolina Law Review* 46 (June 1968): 730.

29. Garrow, *Liberty and Sexuality*, 371–72.

30. Tom C. Clark, "Religion, Morality, and Abortion: A Constitutional Appraisal," *Loyola of Los Angeles Law Review* 2 (1969): 1.
31. Garrow, *Liberty and Sexuality*, 394; Sarah Weddington, *A Question of Choice* (New York: G. P. Putnam's Sons, 1992), 22.
32. Garrow, *Liberty and Sexuality*, 396–97; Weddington, *A Question of Choice*, 48–49.
33. United States v. Vuitch, 402 U.S. 62 (1971).
34. Bernard Schwartz, *The Unpublished Opinions of the Burger Court* (Oxford: Oxford University Press, 1988), 116 (Blackmun's first draft of *Roe*).
35. Memorandum to the Conference, 18 May 1972. Harry A. Blackmun Papers, Manuscript Division, Library of Congress, Box 151; Thurgood Marshall Papers, Manuscript Division, Library of Congress, Box 99.
36. Blackmun was no doubt influenced in his *Doe* draft by the reaction from Brennan and Douglas after his *Roe* draft was circulated. Both wrote notes delicately pushing Blackmun to reach the constitutional privacy issue. Douglas had provided Blackmun with a draft of *Doe* he created not long after oral arguments in December 1971. See Bernard Schwartz, *The Unpublished Opinions of the Burger Court* (Oxford: Oxford University Press, 1988), 89. ("There is a note in Douglas's hand, dated March 6, 1972, indicating that a copy of the Douglas draft had been 'sent . . . to HB several weeks ago.'")

  Douglas's draft offered a *Griswold*-style privacy argument applied to abortions. But Douglas also recognized the duality of interests that Blackmun would make the centerpiece of his draft. "The woman's health is part of the concern; and the life of the fetus after quickening is another concern," Douglas had written. See Douglas to Brennan, December 22, 1971, with draft attached, William J. Brennan Papers, Manuscript Division, Library of Congress, Box 281; William O. Douglas Papers, Manuscript Division, Library of Congress, Box 1589. The May 1972 Brennan and Douglas letters to Blackmun after the first *Roe* draft are as follows: Brennan to Blackmun, May 18, 1972; Douglas to Blackmun, May 18, 1972 ("I would prefer a disposition of the core constitutional question"); Douglas to Blackmun, May 19, 1972 ("I believe I gave you, some time back, my draft opinion in the Georgia case. I see no reason for reargument on that case"); and Blackmun to Douglas, May 22, 1972 (Blackmun acknowledges that Douglas's *Doe* draft was "very helpful"), Brennan Box 282, Douglas Box 1589, Marshall Box 99. Both Douglas and Brennan emphasized their belief that the Texas and Georgia statutes should be struck down "save as they require that an abortion be performed by a licensed physician within a limited time after conception." Douglas to Blackmun, May 19, 1972, Marshall Box 99.
37. Ibid.
38. Brennan to Blackmun, May 18, 1972, Brennan Box 282; Douglas to Blackmun, May 19, 1972, Douglas Box 1589.
39. Memorandum to the Conference, May 25, 1972, Blackmun Papers, Blackmun Box 151.
40. Ibid.
41. Schwartz, *Unpublished Opinions of the Burger Court*, 120–40.
42. Ibid., 129; see also Roe v. Wade, 410 U.S. 113, 159 (1973).

43. Schwartz, *Unpublished Opinions of the Burger Court*, 129.

44. Ibid.

45. Blackmun, Memorandum to the Conference, May 31, 1972, Marshall Box 99.

46. Lewis Powell, Memorandum to the Conference, June 1, 1972, Marshall Box 99 ("It may be that I now have a duty to participate in this decision, although from a purely personal viewpoint I would be more than happy to leave this one to others"); William Rehnquist, Memorandum to the Conference, June 1, 1972, Marshall Box 99. The other votes for reargument were Burger, White, and Blackmun.

47. Brennan to Blackmun, May 31, 1972; Douglas to Blackmun, May 31, 1972, Brennan Box 282 ("The important thing is to get them down," meaning announce the opinions. "But you have a firm 5 and the firm 5 will be behind you in these two opinions until they come down."); Marshall to Blackmun, May 31, 1972, Marshall Box 99; Garrow, *Liberty and Sexuality*, 553–56 (Stewart being upset over Burger's handling of the reargument issue).

48. Warren Burger, Memorandum to the Conference, May 31, 1972, Marshall Box 99. Burger was right that the arguments in December 1971 were woeful. The truth is that neither side covered itself in laurels. The arguments can be listened to at http://www.oyez.org/cases/1970-1979/1971/1971_70_18.

49. Douglas memorandum, June 13, 1972, Marshall Box 99.

50. Douglas to Blackmun, May 25, 1972 (two letters), Marshall to Blackmun, May 25, 1972, Brennan to Blackmun, May 25, 1972, Marshall Box 99. Stewart called Blackmun on Monday, May 29, 1972, to say he would join in *Doe*. See also Garrow, *Liberty and Sexuality*, 552; Stewart to Blackmun, May 30, 1972, Marshall Box 99.

51. "Abortion Cases Creating Friction on High Court," *New York Times*, July 5, 1972. Articles in the newspapers cited unnamed sources reporting internal dissent over the reargument during the summer of 1972, but the facts as relayed by the newspapers were muddled. Though the Douglas dissent was noted, the papers knew nothing of the details of Blackmun's draft opinions or the legal bases upon which they rested. The articles placed more emphasis on Burger's decision to assign the cases and the fact that he was in the minority when he did so. On the Douglas dissent, the *Times* simply wrote, "He reportedly left a dissenting opinion to be filed if the Court decided to delay the cases, detailing the behind-the-scenes events that led up to the delay. It was not filed and efforts to reach him [in Goose Prairie, Washington] were unsuccessful." The nation did not know how close the justices had come to issuing very different and limited opinions in *Roe* and *Doe*.

8: "Harry's Lovely Farewell"

1. Tape 831-3 (January 3, 1973, Nixon and Ziegler, later Kissinger), White House Tapes, http://www.nixonlibrary.gov/forresearchers/find/tapes/tape831/831-003 .mp3.

2. Ibid.

3. "Senate Democrats, 36–12, Back Action to End War," *New York Times*, January 5, 1973; "Talking Tough—Or Just Louder?" *New York Times*, January 7,

1973. ("The United States Congress, like Carl Sandburg's fog, has grown accustomed to creeping into the capital on little cat feet. Thus, it seemed that, comparatively speaking at least, the new 93d Congress had pounced on Washington last week with the fury of a January storm.") The Democrats in the House voted 2–1 on Tuesday, January 2, and 3–1 in the Senate on Thursday "to call for legislation to bring an 'immediate' end to American involvement in Indochina. The opponents of the war as much as set a deadline of January 20—Inauguration Day—for the president to obtain a negotiated truce before they would move in earnest to try to halt combat appropriations for Southeast Asia."

4. Mansfield admitted that the resolutions passed by the congressional Democrats were not likely to "be transformed into legislation soon." Money for military expenses had already been appropriated through the end of June. "Any legislation withdrawing those appropriations could be vetoed by the President, and it would require a two-thirds majority of both houses of Congress to override the veto." Though Mansfield and others conceded they did not have the supermajorities to override a veto, they believed "that their strength may increase if a settlement has not been negotiated by Inauguration Day, Jan. 20." "Senate Democrats, 36–12, Back Action to End War," *New York Times*, January 5, 1973.

5. Tape 831-3 (January 3, 1973, Nixon and Ziegler, later Kissinger), White House Tapes, http://www.nixonlibrary.gov/forresearchers/find/tapes/tape831/831-003.mp3.

6. "New Summary and Index," *New York Times*, January 6, 1973. "[The lead legislator] said the Saigon administration believed that the coming cease-fire negotiations in Paris could last at least two months."

7. Tape 831-3 (January 3, 1973, Nixon and Ziegler, later Kissinger), White House Tapes, http://www.nixonlibrary.gov/forresearchers/find/tapes/tape831/831-003.mp3. "Senate Democrats, 36–12, Back Action to End War," *New York Times*, January 5, 1973; "Congress Opens with Democrats Planning Actions Against the War," *New York Times*, January 4, 1973. "The seriousness of the Congressional mood may have been illustrated by the seriousness of the White House response to the burgeoning calls for a legislated end to the war. Ronald L. Ziegler, the White House press secretary, urged the Democrats in Congress to be wary of taking any steps that would jeopardize the private peace negotiations scheduled to resume Monday in Paris. At the same time, the President invited members of both parties in Congress to breakfast at the White House on Friday and scheduled a reception for new members of both houses Friday evening."

8. "Report of Damage to Hanoi Hospital Confirmed by U.S.," *New York Times*, January 3, 1973 ("Mr. Friedman said he was not sure whether the damage had been caused by bombs, by downed American or North Vietnamese aircraft or by falling antiaircraft missiles").

9. Tape 832-10 (January 3, 1973, Nixon and Kissinger), White House Tapes, http://www.nixonlibrary.gov/forresearchers/find/tapes/tape832/832-010a.mp3. Nixon came back three times to the pilot-punishment question, getting more heated with each pass. "What in the name of God has our press

come to?" he said to Kissinger. "Of course they are not going to be punished," Nixon said. "They didn't do it deliberately."

10. Ibid.

11. Tape 832-10, Part B (January 3, 1973, Nixon and Kissinger), White House Tapes, http://www.nixonlibrary.gov/forresearchers/find/tapes/tape832/832-010b .mp3.

12. "Tribute to Harry Truman," 93rd Cong., Congressional Record–Senate, S 744 (January 17, 1973) (Senator Harrison A. Williams, D-N)(quoting from Sayre memorial).

13. "Truman Honored by World Notables at Cathedral Rites," New York Times, January 6, 1973.

14. "Harry's Lovely Farewell," New York Times, January 7, 1973.

15. Joe Kraft, "Twelve Days of Bombing," Washington Post, January 4, 1973.

16. Tape 160-02, White House Tapes, http://www.nixonlibrary.gov/forresearchers /find/tapes/tape160/160-002.mp3.

17. Tape 160-04, White House Tapes, http://www.nixonlibrary.gov/forresearchers /find/tapes/tape160/160-004.mp3.

18. Tape 160-06, White House Tapes, http://www.nixonlibrary.gov/forresearchers /find/tapes/tape160/160-006.mp3.

19. Tape 832-10 (January 3, 1973, Nixon and Kissinger), White House Tapes, http://www.nixonlibrary.gov/forresearchers/find/tapes/tape832/832-010a .mp3.

20. "Pullout Sought: Mansfield to Move to Force 'Complete Disinvolvement,'" New York Times, January 4, 1973.

21. "The Congress: Talking Tough—Or Just Talking Louder," New York Times, January 7, 1973.

22. Nixon, Memoirs, 745. The tape of Colson's conversation is Tape 394-3. The conversation took place just after noon in the president's Executive Office Building hideaway. The conversation is difficult to hear, mainly because of the ticking of the clock on the desk, but Colson and Nixon clearly talked about Hunt's personal tragedy (his wife's death) as a basis for clemency. Nixon is also told of the pressure being applied by the US attorney to Hunt and the others.

9: "I Wanted the Young Prosecutor to Know Just How Whitewashers Are Engineered"

1. Unsealed Materials from U.S. v. Liddy, National Archives and Records Administration, per November 2, 2012, Order and Memorandum Opinion of Judge Royce Lamberth of the United States District Court for the District of Columbia, In re Petition of Luke Nichter, Misc. No. 12-74 (RCL) 2012 WL 5382733 (D.D.C. Nov. 2, 2012), no. 135 Proceedings, Pre-Trial Conference, December 4, 1972, re various pretrial tasks, 6–9. Judge Lamberth issued a second opinion, May 13, 2013, Ex parte Order and Memorandum, releasing additional materials. See http://www.archives.gov/research/investigations /watergate/us-v-liddy.html. (Hereafter "Unsealed Materials.")

2. John S. Sirica, To Set The Record Straight: The Break-In, the Tapes, the Conspirators, the Pardon (New York, W. W. Norton & Company, 1979), 58.

3. Allen used a Mexican subsidiary of Gulf Resources to deliver the money to Ogarrio. His commitment was $100,000, but $11,000 was paid in cash directly to the Committee to Re-Elect. The balance, $89,000, was run through Ogarrio's Mexican bank. Allen also said that he was raising the money on behalf of other Texas contributors, but those contributors have never been identified. As seen in subsequent entries, Allen asked for his money back after the Watergate investigation exposed his identity.

4. Emery, *Watergate*, 188–94, 206, 214; Bob Woodward and Carl Bernstein, *All the President's Men* (New York: Simon & Shuster, 1974), 36–44; "Nixon Committee Returns $665,000 to 3 Big Donors," *New York Times*, March 10, 1973. ("Mr. Allen told Mr. Stans [in a letter asking for the money back] that because he made his contributions on April 5, 1972—two days before the new Federal disclosure law took effect—'I felt, and still do, that under the law I had every right to expect and enjoy the right of privacy and full anonymity.'")

5. The indictment on September 15, 1972, contained seven counts: (1) conspiracy in violation of 18 U.S.C. 371; (2 and 3) burglary in violation of DC Code section 1801(b); (4 and 5) illegal interception of oral and wire communication, in violation of 18 U.S.C. 2511; and (6 and 7) possession of illegal communication interception device in violation of 23 DC Code section 5439(a).

6. Unsealed Materials from *U.S. v. Liddy*, no. 135 Proceedings, Pre-Trial Conference, December 4, 1972, re various pretrial tasks, 6–9.

7. Transcript from Unsealed Materials, December 4, 1972; "Watergate Trial Judge Indicates Political Aspects of Case Will Be Examined," *New York Times*, December 5, 1972.

8. Sirica, *To Set the Record Straight*, 57.

9. "The Prosecutors: Good Guy, Bad Guy, Chief," *New York Times*, May 3, 1973; "Earl J. Silbert, Soon to be Sworn In as U. S. Attorney, Reflects on His Days as Prosecutor in Watergate Case," *New York Times*, October 16, 1975.

10. Sirica, *To Set The Record Straight*, 34–36.

11. Ibid., 17–39.

12. Ibid., 49. Typically a case is assigned on a random basis to one of the several judges in the district. Bittman wrote a letter on October 4, 1972, asking Sirica to recuse himself because he had been the judge who oversaw the grand jury investigating Watergate and as such had made rulings, and been exposed to evidence and issues that the sitting judge normally would not have encountered. Sirica denied the request on October 10. "Judge Sirica Refuses to Withdraw in Trial of 7 Charged in Bugging," *New York Times*, October 11, 1972. "I have the time to give it the attention it needs," Sirica said.

13. Sirica, *To Set the Record Straight*, 58; Unsealed Materials from *U.S. v. Liddy*, no. 135 Proceedings, Pre-Trial Conference, December 4, 1972, re various pretrial tasks, 13.

14. Ibid.

15. Watergate Part 04 of 101, FBI Vault, 39, accessed September 2, 2014, http://vault.fbi.gov/watergate/wategate-part-03-04-of-1/view. A June 26, 1972, FBI teletype identified an ex-FBI agent, Richard Maher, who had been contacted by Jim McCord "in regard to possible employment as personal body guard for Martha Mitchell and other security type positions on April twenty five last.

McCord advised Maher that he obtained Maher's name from ex-agents association, New York City. McCord stated five ex-FBI agents being considered for job. Job requirements were: age-late thirty's or early forty's with athletic background. Maher had personal interview and then declined the job offer."

16. Watergate Part 18 of 101, FBI Vault, 4–5, accessed September 2, 2014, http://vault.fbi.gov/watergate/watergate-part-17-18-of-1/view. (FBI interview of Kristen Forsberg, July 6, 1972).

17. "Security Tight in Capital after Blast in Pentagon," *New York Times*, May 20, 1972. Bill Ayers, famously linked to Barack Obama in his 2008 presidential campaign, admitted in his book *Fugitive Days*, which was serendipitously released on September 10, 2001, that he was involved in the 1972 Pentagon bombing. "Considering the Excesses of Protest," *New York Times*, November 15, 2012.

18. Most of the narrative about Baldwin and his activity is taken from transcripts of tapes of the interview Baldwin gave to Jack Nelson and Ronald Ostrow of the *L.A. Times* on the night of October 3, 1972, much to Earl Silbert's annoyance and over his vehement objection. The transcripts of the tapes of Baldwin's interview, which were turned over by the *L.A. Times* but sealed by Judge Sirica on January 17, 1973, were released on October 3, 1980, by the court (hereafter "Baldwin Tapes"). *U.S. v. Liddy*, Case No. 1827-72, unsealed Baldwin Tapes and Transcripts, Judge Bryant (October 3, 1980), 30, 33-3, National Archive and Record Administration, http://www.archives.gov/research/investigations/watergate/59162111.pdf.

19. Baldwin, in justifying his belief that his wiretapping activities were somehow authorized, pointed out to the *L.A. Times* that, around this same time, the US Supreme Court issued an opinion about the legality of warrantless domestic wiretapping, generally disapproving of it except in circumstances of a threat from a foreign "subversive group." United States v. U.S. District Court, 407 U. S. 297 (1972) (known as the "Keith case" because the federal district court judge was Damon Keith). The opinion was released on June 19, 1972, the Monday following the second Watergate break-in, which had resulted in the arrests of McCord and the Miamians. Baldwin said he considered McGovern to be "subversive, in a sense." Baldwin Tapes, 42.

20. Baldwin's memory of the first break-in over the Memorial Day weekend was fuzzy, as was so much of his testimony. The date he gave the *L.A. Times* and that he later testified to in court was Friday, May 26. This conflicts with the date identified by Hunt and Liddy. Hunt and Liddy both wrote that the first break-in was on Sunday night, May 28, not Friday the 26th. Liddy, *Will: The Autobiography*, 228–33; Hunt, *American Spy*, 210–19.

Hunt and Liddy's dates are likely correct. On Friday night, Hunt, Liddy, and the Miamians held a fake banquet dinner in the Continental Room at the Watergate Hotel, arranged by Hunt, with the hope that they could gain access to the Watergate office building through an exit door in the Continental Room. The exit door opened into a corridor in the office building that had an elevator that could take them to the sixth floor, where the DNC headquarters were located. The banquet came to be known as the Ameritas Banquet, because it was booked in the name of Ameritas, a company that Bernard Barker had established in Miami. This is the night Hunt says that he and one of the Cubans were locked into the Continental Room by a guard at 11:00 PM, and this ended the plan to gain access through the Continental Room. Hunt and Liddy said that it wasn't until Sunday night that they gained access, this time going through an underground parking garage passageway.

21. Transcript, *U.S. v. Liddy*, January 16, 1973, 722–23. Washington metropolitan police officer Carl M. Shoffler testified as follows:

A. Across the street at the Howard Johnson's I noticed a man standing on the balcony paying attention.

Q. What drew your attention over there?

A. The fact that we were in plainclothes and I had my weapon drawn, I was concerned with the fact that he may call the police and report a man with a gun.

22. Baldwin Tapes, 50–51.
23. Baldwin Tapes, 74.
24. Watergate Part 01 of 101, FBI Vault, 68–70 (FBI teletype, June 21, 1972).
25. "Judge John Cassidento Dies at 47," *The Morning Record* (Meriden, Conn.), June 12, 1974; Emery, *Watergate*, 159. The attorneys representing the DNC and O'Brien were from Edward Bennett Williams's firm, Williams, Connolly & Califano, the same firm that represented the *Washington Post*. One of the lawyers working for the firm on the case was Joseph Califano, LBJ protégé and future secretary of the Department of Health, Education, and Welfare. A young attorney working with Williams and Califano, Alan Galbraith, revealed in 2012 that forty years earlier, in August 1972, Williams dispatched him "to Connecticut to interview Alfred C. Baldwin, a Watergate conspirator who'd cooperated with the FBI in exchange for immunity from prosecution." Per Galbraith, "Baldwin's lawyer had indicated that Baldwin was willing to talk, provided he didn't have to reveal his name." Galbraith also claimed that he tipped off Carl Bernstein about Baldwin's role on September 10. "Galbraith Recalls Watergate," *St. Helena Star*, July 26, 2012. According to the *St. Helena Star*, "Baldwin's information led the DNC's attorneys to allege 'a grand conspiracy' involving many Nixon campaign officials." For corroboration, see Joseph A. Califano Jr., *Inside: A Public Life and Private Life* (New York: Perseus Books Group, 2004), 271–72.
26. "O'Brien Says His Phone Was Tapped Before Raid," *New York Times*, September 8, 1972.
27. Baldwin Tapes, 144 (Mitro speaking). Remarkably, Mitro risked the attorney-client privilege by divulging to the *L.A. Times* his confidential communications with his client, Baldwin.
28. Baldwin Tapes, 151–56.
29. Jeb Stuart Magruder, *An American Life: One Man's Road to Watergate* (New York: Atheneum, 1974), 262.
30. Earl Silbert, Diary (June 1972 to July 1973), Records Group 460, Records of the Watergate Prosecution Force, National Archives and Records Administration (College Park: Maryland), (entry for August 15, 1972), 1–10.

31. Magruder, *An American Life*, 273.

32. Ibid., 266–67.

33. Silbert, Diary (entry for August 15, 1972), 1–12.

34. Silbert, Diary (entry for December 12, 1972), 3–62.

35. "2 Nixon Ex-Aides Among 7 Indicted in Raid in Capital," *New York Times*, September 16, 1972. Silbert's public relations person, John W. Hushen, said, "We have absolutely no evidence to indicate any others should be charged."

36. Tape 779-2 (September 15, 1972, Nixon, Haldeman, and Dean), White House Tapes, http://www.nixonlibrary.gov/forresearchers/find/tapes/tape779/779-002 .mp3.

37. "Ex-FBI Agent Named as Bugging Case Witness," *New York Times*, September 17, 1972.

38. Silbert, Diary (entry of September 8, 1972), 1–26. "O'Brien Says His Phone Was Tapped Before Raid," *New York Times*, September 8, 1972. The tap on Oliver Spencer's phone was not found until September 13. "Bug Reported in Phone," *New York Times*, September 14, 1972. The FBI had missed it, and when a secretary complained about trouble with the phone line, the Democrats themselves brought in the phone company and discovered it. This led to an investigation into whether the Democrats had planted the bug—a silly charge and one that Silbert discounted. "A New Explanation of Watergate," *New York Times*, November 11, 1984.

39. Silbert, Diary, (entry of September 8, 1972), 1–26.

40. Silbert, Diary, (entry of September 9, 1972), 1–28.

41. They had talked to *Newsweek* earlier but backed away from a full interview because it involved the payment of money, and Baldwin's lawyers, after talking to Silbert, decided that if Baldwin sold his story it would hurt his credibility. Silbert, Diary, 6 (entry of September 14, 1972), 2–4. "Ex-FBI Agent Named as Bugging Case Witness," *New York Times*, September 17, 1972 (source is *Newsweek* story, which was supposed to appear the next week).

42. "Interview with Man Who Says He Helped in Bugging of Democrats," *Los Angeles Times*, October 5, 1972.

43. Silbert, Diary, (entry of October 5, 1972), 1–39.

44. "L.A. Times Asked to Produce Tapes on Key Witness in Watergate Trial," *New York Times*, December 12, 1972.

45. "Los Angeles Times Gives Judge Tapes," *New York Times*, December 22, 1972.

46. Hunt, *American Spy*, 274.

47. Tape 394-021, Part A (Nixon and Colson), White House Tapes, http://www .nixonlibrary.gov/forresearchers/find/tapes/tape394/394-021a.mp3.

48. Tom Gregory was the nephew of Bob Bennett, the president of Mullen & Company, where Hunt worked. Gregory was discovered by one of the prosecutors (Campbell) through a deeper search of Hunt's phone records as they drew closer to trial. See Silbert, Diary (entry of December 21, 1972), 3–10. Bob Bennett later worked for billionaire Howard Hughes and became a US senator from Utah (1993–2011).

49. Tape 394-021, Part A (January 8, 1973, Nixon and Colson), White House Tapes, http://www.nixonlibrary.gov/forresearchers/find/tapes/tape394/394 -021a.mp3.

10: "We Celebrated the President's Birthday Today by Making a Major Breakthrough in the Negotiations"

1. Kissinger, *White House Years*, 1,335.
2. "Hanoi Negotiator, Arriving in Paris, Takes Rigid Stand," *New York Times*, January 7, 1973.
3. "Kissinger Meets Tho for 4 ½ Hours as Talks Resume," *New York Times*, January 9, 1972. ("The North Vietnamese, as the hosts today, took care to avoid any of the displays of affability—televised smiles and handshakes— that frequently marked the previous two rounds of talks, in November and December. These gestures had provoked waves of hope and gloom around the world.")
4. Kissinger, *White House Years*, 1,463.
5. Tape 833-11, Part A (January 9, 1973, Nixon, Kissinger, Moore, Laird, and Kennedy), White House Tapes, http://www.nixonlibrary.gov/forresearchers /find/tapes/tape833/833-011a.mp3.
6. Back-Channel Message from the Ambassador to Vietnam (Bunker) to the President's Assistant for National Security Affairs (Kissinger), Kathmandu, December 31, 1972, National Archives, Nixon Presidential Materials, NSC Files, Box 413, Backchannel Messages (Top Secret, Sensitive, Exclusively Eyes Only). Bunker was in Kathmandu to visit his wife, Carol C. Laise, ambassador to Nepal.
7. Tape 833-011, Part A (Nixon, Kissinger, Moore, Laird, Rogers, and Kennedy), White House Tapes, http://www.nixonlibrary.gov/forresearchers/find /tapes/tape833/833-011a.mp3. Memorandum of Conversation, January 4, 1973, National Archives, Nixon Presidential Materials, NSC Files, Box 1026, Presidential/HAK MemCons (Secret, Sensitive). The Office of the Historian for the U.S. Department of State cleaned up Nixon's language in the official Memorandum of Conversation, with Nixon saying, "Let me say that if anyone is punished for the hitting of that hospital, I'll fire someone."
8. Memorandum of Conversation, January 3, 1973, National Archives, Nixon Presidential Materials, NSC Files, Box 859, For the President's Files (Winston Lord)—China Trip/Vietnam, Sensitive Camp David, vol. 23 (Top Secret, Sensitive, Exclusively Eyes Only). The meeting was held in Kissinger's office in the White House.
9. Memorandum of Conversation, January 5, 1973, National Archives, Nixon Presidential Materials, NSC Files, Box 859, For the President's Files (Winston Lord)—China Trip/Vietnam, Sensitive Camp David, vol. 23 (Top Secret, Sensitive, Exclusively Eyes Only). The meeting was held in Kissinger's office at the White House. The participants in the meeting were Kissinger; Tran Van Do, former foreign minister of the Republic of Vietnam; Bui Diem, former ambassador to the United States from the Republic of Vietnam; Tran Kim Phuong, ambassador to the United States from the Republic of Vietnam; and Winston Lord, NSC staff.
10. Memorandum of Conversation, January 3, 1973, National Archives, Nixon Presidential Materials, NSC Files, Box 859. Kissinger to Ambassador Phuong: "I have told you a thousand times and it does no good."

11. Memorandum of Conversation, January 5, 1973, National Archives, Nixon Presidential Materials, NSC Files, Box 859. See this interesting resemblance to Colonel Nathan R. Jessup's (Jack Nicholson's) monologue in the 1992 film *A Few Good Men*: "We use words like *honor, code, loyalty*. We use these words as the backbone of a life spent defending something. You use them as a punch line. I have neither the time nor the inclination to explain myself to a man who rises and sleeps under the blanket of the very freedom that I provide, and then questions the manner in which I provide it. *I would rather you just said thank you, and went on your way.* Otherwise, I suggest you pick up a weapon, and stand a post. Either way, I don't give a damn what you think you are entitled to." "You Can't Handle the Truth!—A Few Good Men (7/8) Movie CLIP (1992) HD," YouTube video, 2:38, from the film *A Few Good Men* (Burbank, California, 1992), posted by MOVIECLIPS, October 12, 2012, https://www.youtube.com/watch?v=9FnO3igOkOk.

12. Memorandum of Conversation, January 5, 1973, National Archives, Nixon Presidential Materials, NSC Files, Box 859.

13. Memorandum of Conversation, January 5, 1973, National Archives, Nixon Presidential Materials, NSC Files, Box 859.

14. Memorandum from the President's Assistant for National Security Affairs (Kissinger) to President Nixon, January 8, 1973, National Archives, Nixon Presidential Materials, NSC Files, Kissinger Office Files, Box 28, HAK Trip Files, HAK Paris Trip Tohak 67–146 (Top Secret, Sensitive, Exclusively Eyes Only). A stamped notation on the first page reads, "The President has seen."

15. Spencer C. Tucker, *Vietnam* (London: UCL Press, 1999), 79–87.

16. Backchannel Message from the Ambassador to Vietnam (Bunker) to the President's Assistant for National Security Affairs (Kissinger), Saigon, December 30, 1972, Library of Congress, Manuscript Division, Kissinger Papers, Box TS 45, Geopolitical File, Vietnam, Cables (Top Secret, Operational Immediate, Sensitive, Exclusively Eyes Only).

17. Ibid.

18. Back-Channel Message from the President's Assistant for National Security Affairs (Kissinger) to the Ambassador to Vietnam (Bunker), January 5, 1973, Library of Congress, Manuscript Division, Kissinger Papers, Box TS 45, Geopolitical File, Vietnam, Cables (Top Secret, Immediate, Sensitive, Exclusively Eyes Only). Written on January 4.

19. Henry Kissinger, *Ending the Vietnam War: A History of America's Involvement in and Extrication from the Vietnam War* (New York: Simon & Shuster, 2003), 404.

20. Kissinger, *Ending the Vietnam War*, 422.

21. Message from the President's Assistant for National Security Affairs (Kissinger) to President Nixon, January 9, 1973, National Archives, Nixon Presidential Materials, NSC Files, Box 859, For the President's Files (Winston Lord), China Trip/Vietnam, Sensitive Camp David, vol. 23 (Top Secret, Flash, Sensitive, Exclusively Eyes Only). Sent via Kennedy.

22. Tape 836-008, (January 9, 1973, Nixon and Richard Kennedy), White House Tapes, http://www.nixonlibrary.gov/forresearchers/find/tapes/tape836/836-008.mp3.

23. Tape 836-009, Part B (January 9, 1973, Nixon and Haldeman), White House Tapes, http://www.nixonlibrary.gov/forresearchers/find/tapes/tape836/836-009b .mp3.

24. Ibid.

25. Ibid.

26. Ibid.

27. Nixon, *Memoirs*, 747; Tape 836-009, Part B, White House Tapes, http://www .nixonlibrary.gov/forresearchers/find/tapes/tape836/836-009b.mp3.

28. Tape 35-107 (January 9, 1973), Nixon and White House Operator), White House Tapes, http://www.nixonlibrary.gov/forresearchers/find/tapes/tape035 /035-107.mp3.

29. Tape 35-108 (January 9, 1973, Nixon and Hope), White House Tapes, http:// www.nixonlibrary.gov/forresearchers/find/tapes/tape035/035-108.mp3.

30. Ibid.

31. Nixon, *Memoirs*, 746.

32. Tape 836-6 (January 9, 1973, Nixon and Haldeman), White House Tapes http://www.nixonlibrary.gov/forresearchers/find/tapes/tape836/836-006.mp3.

33. Ibid.

34. Tape 836-006, White House Tapes, http://www.nixonlibrary.gov/forresearchers /find/tapes/tape836/836-006.mp3.

35. Nixon, Daily Diary, January 9, 1973.

36. "Nobel Prize Awarded; King Olav Jeered; Oslo Students Demonstrate," *New York Times*, December 11, 1973.

11: "He Can Renew It After the Opening Statement Is Made"

1. The courthouse was named for DC Circuit appellate judge E. Barrett Prettyman in 1997. "A Tribute to a Champion of the Law, U.S. Courthouse Named After Longtime Appellate Judge," *Washington Post*, March 27, 1997. The courthouse is referred to in this article as a "nondescript gray building."

2. "Truman Deplores Totalitarianism," *New York Times*, June 28, 1950.

3. Army Department Teletype Conference, June 25, 1950, Naval Aide Files, Truman Papers, Truman Library, National Archives, Documents Online at http:// www.trumanlibrary.org/whistlestop/study_collections/koreanwar/documents /index.php?documentdate=1950-06-00&documentid=ki-21-5&pagenumber=1.

4. United Nations Security Council Resolution, June 25, 1950, President's Secretary's Files, Truman Papers, Truman Library, National Archives, Documents Online at http://www.trumanlibrary.org/whistlestop/study_collections /koreanwar/documents/index.php?documentdate=1950-06-25&documentid =ki-17-4&pagenumber=1.

5. Notes Regarding Meeting with Congressional Leaders, June 27, 1950, Harry S. Truman Administration File, Elsey Papers, Truman Library, National Archives, Documents Online at http://www.trumanlibrary.org/whistlestop /study_collections/koreanwar/documents/index.php?documentdate=1950-06 -27&documentid=ki-2-40&pagenumber=1.

6. Transcript, *U.S. v. Liddy*, Unsealed Materials, January 9, 1973, 2, http://media .nara.gov/research/watergate-sealed-court-records/DOCID-59162128.PDF.

7. Ibid., 2–4.

8. Silbert said he was relying on 5th Circuit Federal Court of Appeals precedent, United States v. Kelly, 464 F.2d 709 (5th Cir. 1972). In *Kelly*, the court ruled that Kelly could be compelled to testify before a grand jury after his conviction so long as he was given proper immunity from future prosecution. Thus, Silbert's plan was to take Hunt's plea, allow him to be sentenced, then immunize him and put him back in front of the grand jury. If Hunt refused to testify, he could be held in contempt and threatened with further sentencing for the contempt charge. See also Kastigar v. United States, 406 U.S. 441 (1972) (following the government's grant of immunity from prosecution, it can compel a witness to testify over his or her assertion of the Fifth Amendment privilege against self-incrimination).

9. Transcript, *U.S. v. Liddy*, Unsealed Materials, January 9, 1973, 4–5, http://media.nara.gov/research/watergate-sealed-court-records/DOCID-59162128 .PDF.

10. Ibid., 6.

11. Ibid.

12. Ibid., 6–8.

13. Ibid.

14. "Jury Is Completed for Trial of 7 in the Watergate Case," *New York Times*, January 10, 1973.

15. "The Prosecutors: Good Guy, Bad Guy, Chief," *New York Times*, May 3, 1973.

16. Silbert, Diary (entry for December 21, 1972), 3–9; Watergate Part 39 of 101, FBI Vault, 28–37 (Salt Lake City Reporting Office to Washington, December 22, 1972). In his diary, Silbert records that he confronted Robert Bennett for failing to tell him about Tom Gregory. Bennett had been extensively interviewed about Howard Hunt, who worked for him, but said nothing about his nephew in any of his interviews. Silbert, Diary (entry for December 21 and 22).

Acccording to Silbert's statement to the court during Gregory's testimony, he met with Gregory in his office on December 26—the day Truman died—and Gregory identified photos of Hunt, Liddy, and others. Tr. *U.S. v. Liddy*, January 11, 1973, 233–34 (testimony of Thomas Gregory).

17. *Newsweek*, July 15, 1974, 29. (According to a report prepared by Howard Baker, Robert R. Mullen & Co. had been used as an overseas cover for CIA activity from 1959 to mid-1972.)

Robert Mullen, though not a Mormon, had represented the Church of Jesus Christ of Latter-day Saints with his public relations firm and was a campaign press secretary for Dwight D. Eisenhower in 1952. "Robert R. Mullen Dead at 77; Eisenhower's Aid in '52 Race," *New York Times*, March 20, 1986.

18. Watergate Part 39 of 101, FBI Vault, 30 (Synopsis Report of James D. Downey, Salt Lake City Office, re Thomas James Gregory, December 22, 1972).

19. Transcript, *U.S. v. Liddy*, January 10, 1973, 15–67 (Silbert opening).

20. Hunt, *American Spy*, 206.

21. Silbert, Diary (entry for December 8 and 9, 1972), 2–46. In his opening, to shock the jury about how expensive these hotels were, Silbert said, "They went out to California. They stayed in first-class hotels there—the Beverly Wilshire, a $100 a day suite." Transcript, *U.S. v. Liddy*, 30.

22. Transcripts, *U.S. v. Liddy*, January 10, 1973, 15–67 (Silbert's Opening Statement).
23. Transcripts, *U.S. v. Liddy*, January 10, 1973, 76–81 (Defense Opening Statements).
24. Tape 838-17 (January 11, 1973, Nixon and Zeigler), White House Tapes, http://www.nixonlibrary.gov/forresearchers/find/tapes/tape838/838-017.mp3.

12: "Only Kings, Monarchs, Dictators, and United States Federal Judges"

1. Tape 837-003, Part D (January 10, 1973, Nixon, Rose Mary Woods, and Bob Haldeman), White House Tapes, http://www.nixonlibrary.gov/forresearchers /find/tapes/tape837/837-003d.mp3.
2. U.S. Const. art. III, § 1. "The judicial Power of the United States, shall be vested in one supreme Court, and in such inferior Courts as the Congress from time to time ordain and establish. The Judges, both of the supreme and inferior Courts, shall hold their Offices during good Behaviour, and shall, at stated Times, receive for their Services, a Compensation, which shall not be diminished during their Continuance in Office." See Michael Mazza, "A New Look at an Old Debate: Life Tenure and the Article III Judge," *Gonzaga Law Review* 39, no. 1 (2003/04): 131.
3. "New Rule on Judges Urged," *New York Times*, June 3, 1971; "Reviewing Judges," *The Spokesman Review*, August 12, 1971 (Spokane, Washington) ("Unfortunately, it appears that Sen. Byrd's proposal grows out of his disagreement with the actions of certain federal judges in the South in relation to integration, or school busing, or both").
4. Tape 837-003, Part D (January 10, 1973), White House Tapes, http://www .nixonlibrary.gov/forresearchers/find/tapes/tape837/837-003d.mp3.
5. "Reviewing Judges," *The Spokesman Review*, August 12, 1971 (Spokane, Washington).
6. Harry F. Byrd Jr., "Has Life Tenure Outlived Its Time?" *Judicature* 59, no. 10 (1976): 266.
7. Law clerks assist the justices in writing opinions, typically producing drafts that the justices edit. As a result of this privilege, they assume incredible power and authority as very young and very inexperienced lawyers. As Justice Rehnquist put it: the justices' chambers, including their clerks, are "a collection of nine autonomous opinion-writing bureaus." Adam Liptak, "A Sign of the Court's Polarization: Choice of Clerks," *New York Times*, September 10, 2010.
8. "Hammond Receives Justice for All Award," *Arizona State University College of Law News*, June 3, 2013, http://www.law.asu.edu/News/CollegeofLawNews. aspx?NewsId=4499.
9. *Peregrinus* was a term used for free subjects of the early Roman Empire who were not Roman citizens. Literally, the Latin term means "foreigner, one from abroad."
10. Larry Hammond (partner, Osborn Maldedon, P.A., Phoenix, Arizona), interview with the author, November 20, 2013. See http://tarlton.law.utexas.edu /exhibits/utlaw-mascot/keeper.html. "At present the student inducted into the Chancellors with the fourth-highest grade point average receives the honorary title Keeper of the Peregrinus and serves as an officer of the society. Until

the late 1950s, and for a brief period in 1965, and the early 1970s, the title came with serious responsibilities. The Keeper was charged with protecting the body and honor of the Peregrinus from defacement and theft—especially from engineering students [engineers]. Traditionally, only the Keeper knew Perry's location at any given time. While some Keepers chose to stow Perry safely in a glass case in Townes Hall or the dean's office, others went a step further and stashed the mascot in their apartments or closets. On rare occasions when the physical presence of the Peregrinus was necessary, such as the installment of new chancellors, the Keeper of the Peregrinus would escort the mascot to and from the event, assuring his safety."

11. "Carl McGowan Dies; A Senior U.S. Judge on Court of Appeals," *New York Times*, December 22, 1987.

12. Nixon v. Sirica, 487 F.2d 700 (1973).

13. "Nixon Loses Legal Appeal on Release of Secret Tapes," *New York Times*, February 10, 1982.

14. William E. Nelson et al., "The Liberal Tradition of the Supreme Court Clerkship: Its Rise, Fall, and Reincarnation," *Vanderbilt Law Review* 62, no. 6 (2009): 1,749, 1,756–57 (2009).

15. Ibid.

16. Todd C. Peppers, "Justice Hugo Black and His Law Clerks: Match-Making and Match Point," *Journal of Supreme Court History* 36, no. 1 (2011): 49–50.

17. Ibid.

18. Ibid.

19. Hammond, in discussion with author, November 20, 2013. Hammond said he also became a champion shuffleboard player at a local pub on Pennsylvania Avenue.

20. Jeffries, *Justice Lewis F. Powell, Jr.*, 293–94. Jay Wilkinson was the clerk Powell brought with him; Hammond and William C. Kelly were holdover clerks.

21. Jeffries, *Justice Lewis F. Powell, Jr.*, 335.

22. Powell, Memorandum to the Conference, June 1, 1972, Lewis F. Powell Jr. Papers, Docket 70-18, Powell Supreme Court Case Files Online, Powell Archives, Washington and Lee University School of Law (hereafter "Powell Files Online"); Blackmun, Memorandum to the Conference, 31 May 1972, Powell Roe Files Online, http://law.wlu.edu/deptimages/powell%20 archives/70-18_RoeWade.pdf.

23. From *Roe* opinion: briefs of amici curiae were filed by Gary K. Nelson, attorney general of Arizona; Robert K. Killian, attorney general of Connecticut; Ed W. Hancock, attorney general of Kentucky; Clarence A. H. Meyer, attorney general of Nebraska; and Vernon B. Romney, attorney general of Utah. Such briefs were also filed by Joseph P. Witherspoon Jr., for the Association of Texas Diocesan Attorneys; Charles E. Rice for Americans United for Life; Eugene J. McMahon for Women for the Unborn et al.; Carol Ryan for the American College of Obstetricians and Gynecologists et al.; Dennis J. Horan, Jerome A. Frazel, Jr., Thomas M. Crisham, and Dolores V. Horan for Certain Physicians, Professors and Fellows of the American College of Obstetrics and Gynecology; Harriet F. Pilpel, Nancy F. Wechsler, and Frederic S. Nathan for Planned Parenthood Federation of America, Inc., et al.; Alan F. Charles for

the National Legal Program on Health Problems of the Poor et al.; Marttie L. Thompson for State Communities Aid Assn.; [410 U.S. 113, 116] Alfred L. Scanlan, Martin J. Flynn, and Robert M. Byrn for the National Right to Life Committee; Helen L. Buttenwieser for the American Ethical Union et al.; Norma G. Zarky for the American Association of University Women et al.; Nancy Stearns for New Women Lawyers et al.; the California Committee to Legalize Abortion et al.; and Robert E. Dunne for Robert L. Sassone.

24. Hammond, interview with the author, November 20, 2013. Hammond had an absolute recollection of creating a thirty-page memo, but it is not in the files in the Powell Papers.
25. Powell, Mark-Up of Blackmun's May 25, 1972, First Draft of Doe v. Bolton, Lewis F. Powell Jr. Papers, Docket 70–40, October 2, 1972, Powell Supreme Court Case Files Online, Powell Archives, Washington and Lee University School of Law (hereinafter "Powell Doe Files Online"), http://law.wlu.edu/deptimages/powell%20archives/70-40_DoeBolton.pdf.
26. Powell Memorandum to Hammond, October 6, 1972, Powell Roe Files Online.
27. Abele v. Markle, 342 F. Supp 800 (D. Conn. 1972).
28. Abele v. Markle, 351 F. Supp. 224, 225 (D. Conn. 1972); Powell Notes on *Abele* Opinion, September 10, 1972, Powell Roe Files Online. Powell, Mark-Up of Abele v. Markle op. of September 20, 1972, October 10, 1972, Powell Roe Files Online, District Court Judgment, http://law.wlu.edu/deptimages/powell%20archives/70-18_RoeWadeOpinionDistrict.pdf.
29. Andrew D. Hurwitz, "Jon O. Newman and the Abortion Decisions: A Remarkable First Year," *New York Law School Law Review* 46, no. 1 (2002–2003): 231, 238–39, n55. "The author received some small inkling of the influence of *Abele II* on the Court's thinking in the fall of 1972, when interviewing for clerkships at the Supreme Court. Justice Powell devoted over an hour of conversation to a discussion of Judge Newman's analysis, while Justice Stewart (my future boss) referred to me as 'the clerk who wrote the Newman opinion.' I assume that the latter was based on Judge Newman's generous letter of recommendation, a medium in which some exaggeration is expected."
30. Hammond, Bench Memo to Powell, October 9, 1972, 10, Powell Roe Files Online.
31. Hurwitz, "Jon O. Newman and the Abortion Decisions," 237.
32. Eisenstadt v. Baird, 405 U.S. 438 (1972)(establishing the right of unmarried people to possess contraception). Justice Brennan snuck in a line filled with meaning in the abortion debate, noting: "If the right of privacy means anything, it is the right of the individual, married or single, to be free from unwarranted governmental intrusion into matters so fundamentally affecting a person as *the decision whether to bear or beget a child.*" 405 U.S. at 453 (emphasis added).
33. Hurwitz, "Jon O. Newman and the Abortion Decisions," 237.
34. Abele v. Markle, 351 F. Supp. 224, 225 (D. Conn. 1972); Powell Notes on *Abele* Opinion, October 10, 1972, 15 Powell Roe Files Online, District Court Judgment.
35. Hammond, Bench Brief to Powell, October 9, 1972, Powell Roe Files Online.

36. Powell Mark-Up of *Abele*, October 10, 1972, Powell Roe Files Online, District Court Judgment.

37. Garrow, *Liberty and Sexuality*, 568–72. Powell only asked questions during the *Doe* argument, and it was only concerning the hospitalization issues. There was no clue he was thinking about the viability standard. Note that Garrow wrote about Hammond in an anonymous way, likely based on his interviews with the Weddingtons. "Sarah and Ron [Weddington] had a sympathetic friend, a 1970 University of Texas Law School graduate, who was clerking for Powell and working on *Roe* and *Doe*, but that alone was no reason to consider Powell a likely backer." Hammond told the author that he had no contact with the Weddingtons during the pendency of the case.

38. Oyez website: http://www.oyez.org/cases/1970-1979/1971/1971_70_18. Sarah Weddington only mentioned Judge Newman's opinion in *Abele* as new authority on the constitutional right to an abortion. She did not point out the viability discussion at all. "Part of the lang—in that case," she said, "that three-judge Court held the Connecticut statute, a slightly revised statute for the second time, to be unconstitutional, and part of the language of that case pointed out that 'no decision of the Supreme Court has ever permitted anyone's constitutional right to be directly abridged to protect a state interest which is subject to such a variety of personal judgments' and, certainly, the amicus briefs before the Court showed a variety of personal judgments that come to bear on this particular situation. To oppose such a statute, the Court said, would be to permit the state to impose its view of the nature of a fetus upon those who have the constitutional right to base an important decision in their personal lives upon a different view." Indeed later in her argument, Weddington noted that there are states that have adopted time limits, but that was not the case with Texas. "Those have not yet been challenged and, perhaps, that question will be before this Court," she said. Clearly no one had in mind at oral argument the line drawing that Blackmun would invent.

39. Blackmun, Memorandum to the Conference, November 21, 1972, Powell Roe Files Online, http://law.wlu.edu/deptimages/powell%20archives/70-18 _RoeWade.pdf.

40. Blackmun noted that the Hippocratic oath varied according to the translation. One translation reads, "I will neither give a deadly drug to anyone if asked for it, nor will I make a suggestion to this effect. Similarly, and in like manner I will not give a woman an abortion remedy." Powell, Mark-Up on Blackmun's November 22, 1972 2nd Draft of Roe, November 25, 1972, Powell Roe Files Online, http://law.wlu.edu/deptimages/powell%20archives/70-18_RoeWade Opinions2nd1.pdf.

41. Greenhouse, *Becoming Justice Blackmun*, 90.

42. Blackmun Memorandum to the Conference, November 21, 1972, and second drafts of *Doe* and *Roe*, Powell Files Online.

43. Hammond memo to Powell, November 27, 1972, Powell Files Online. It is prescient that Hammond, as a matter of judicial restraint, cautioned against any line drawing at this point. He wrote: "As a political matter, it is my guess that if the opinion does not draw any line most states will adopt a statute like

the NY statute which draws the line at 20 to 24 weeks. We may eventually get a case involving a 'first trimester' statute but I would have the Ct await that event and not anticipate it in advance." Hammond memo, 4–5. Hammond was also disdainful of Blackmun's pro-doctor bias: "Doesn't it seem that this language overstates the doctor's role and undercuts the woman's personal interest in the decision?"

44. Powell Letter to Blackmun, November 29, 1972, Powell Roe Files Online.
45. Randal P. Bezanson, Memo to Blackmun, November 29, 1972, Blackmun Papers, Manuscript Division, Library of Congress, Box 151.
46. Blackmun Letter to Powell, December 4, 1972, Powell Roe Files Online, http://law.wlu.edu/deptimages/powell%20archives/70-18_RoeWade.pdf.
47. Powell Handwritten Note to Blackmun, December 11, 1972, Blackmun Papers. Linda Greenhouse, Blackmun's biographer, says the note was passed down at argument. Greenhouse, *Becoming Justice Blackmun*, 96–97.
48. Blackmun, Memorandum to the Conference, December 11, 1972, Powell Roe Files Online, http://law.wlu.edu/deptimages/powell%20archives/70-18_RoeWade.pdf.
49. William O. Douglass Letter to Blackmun, December 11, 1972, Powell Roe Files Online.
50. Thurgood Marshall Letter to Blackmun, December 12, 1972, Powell Roe Files Online.
51. William Brennan to Blackmun, December 13, 1972, Powell Roe Files Online. There is a letter from Powell to Blackmun, dated December 13, 1972, in the Powell Papers that has handwriting on it that says, "We are not certain the original of this letter was even sent to J. Blackmun or circulated to the Conference." The letter is Powell's response to Blackmun's December 11 request for comments on viability. It is a lens into Powell's mind-set and Hammond's influence. Powell argues that viability is "a more logical and defensible time for identifying the point at which the state's overriding right to protect potential life becomes evident." He also expanded on the "practical" argument that young and poor women needed more time than just the first trimester to decide on an abortion. "My guess is that older women, married women and others who are experienced and sophisticated will know when they are pregnant and be willing to acknowledge it," he wrote. "They will know where abortions can be obtained (*e.g.* in New York), and how to go about arranging for them." In contrast, "women who most need the benefit of liberalized abortion laws are likely to be young, inexperienced, unsure, frightened and perhaps unmarried. It may well be that many in this category either would not know enough to be sure of pregnancy in the early weeks, or be too embarrassed to seek medical advice prior to the expiration of the first trimester. If there is a constitutional right to an abortion, there is much to be said for making it effective where and when it may well be needed most." He concluded by expressing his agreement with Judge Newman's *Abele* opinion, about which agreement he notes, "I believe I mentioned at Conference," though he doesn't say which conference.
52. Hammond Memo to Powell, December 11, 1972, Powell Roe Files Online. In fact, Marshall's response came the day after Hammond's December 11 memo

to Powell. Upon reading it, Hammond thought that Powell should simply join in Marshall's comments. "Judge," Hammond handwrote on Marshall's December 12 letter, "this is the substance of the note I suggested to you yesterday. You might now simply indicate your concurrence with TM [Thurgood Marshall]. LAH." Marshall letter to Blackmun, December 12, 1972, with Hammond's handwriting, Powell Roe Files Online.

53. Hammond Memo to Powell, December 12, 1972, Powell Roe Files Online.
54. Blackmun Memorandum to the Conference, December 15, 1972, Powell Files Online.
55. Burger Letter to Blackmun, December 13, 1972, Powell Roe Files Online.
56. Blackmun, Third Draft of Roe, December 21, 1972, Powell Roe Files Online, http://law.wlu.edu/deptimages/powell%20archives/70-18_RoeWadeOpinions3rd.pdf.
57. Woodward and Armstrong, *The Brethren: Inside the Supreme Court* (New York: Simon & Schuster, 1979), 275–89.
58. Lewis Powell to Larry Hammond, January 3, 1973, Powell Roe Files Online.
59. Hurwitz, "Jon O. Newman and the Abortion Decisions," 244, n83.
60. "Senate Confirms Appellate Judge, Rebuffing Critics," *New York Times*, June 12, 2012.

13: "We May Be Doomed to Come to an Agreement Today"

1. The United States and North Vietnam would sign a separate two-party agreement that would mention the PRG. But, as Kissinger repeatedly pointed out to the South Vietnamese, the agreement would have no legal effect on South Vietnam. Kissinger saw it as window dressing for the North Vietnamese. The four-party agreement was to be the true operative agreement ending the war.
2. National Archives, Nixon Presidential Materials, NSC Files, Kissinger Office Files, Box 28, HAK Trip Files, HAK Paris Trip Tohak 1–66, January 7 to 14, 1973 (Top Secret, Sensitive, Exclusively Eyes Only). Sent via the White House Situation Room, Guay, and Lord.
3. Tape 837-04, Part B (January 10, 1972, Nixon and Haldeman), White House Tapes, http://www.nixonlibrary.gov/forresearchers/find/tapes/tape837/837-004b.mp3.
4. Ibid.
5. National Archives, Nixon Presidential Materials, NSC Files, Kissinger Office Files, Box 28, HAK Trip Files, HAK Paris Trip Hakto 1–48, January 7 to 14, 1973 (Top Secret, Flash, Sensitive, Exclusively Eyes Only). Sent via Kennedy.
6. Tape 35-123 (January 10, 1973, Haldeman and Nixon), White House Tapes, http://www.nixonlibrary.gov/forresearchers/find/tapes/tape035/035-123.mp3.
7. National Archives, Nixon Presidential Materials, NSC Files, Kissinger Office Files, Box 28, HAK Trip Files, HAK Paris Trip Tohak 67–146, January 7–14, 1973. Top Secret; Sensitive; Exclusively Eyes Only. Sent via Guay. Written on January 10.
8. Ibid.
9. Haldeman, *Diaries*, January 10, 1973, reprinted in the Department of State, Office of the Historian, *Foreign Relations of the United States*, 1969 to 1976,

Volume IX, Vietnam, October 1972 to January 1973, Document 259, http://history.state.gov/historicaldocuments/frus1969-76v09/d259.

10. National Archives, Nixon Presidential Materials, NSC Files, Kissinger Office Files, Box 28, HAK Trip Files, HAK Paris Trip Hakto 1–48, January 7 to 14, 1973 (Top Secret, Sensitive, Exclusively Eyes Only). Sent via Guay and Kennedy.

11. Tape 838-11, Part A (January 11, 1973, Nixon and Kennedy), White House Tapes, http://www.nixonlibrary.gov/forresearchers/find/tapes/tape838/838-011a.mp3.

12. Ibid.

13. National Archives, Nixon Presidential Materials, NSC Files, Kissinger Office Files, Box 28, HAK Trip Files, HAK Paris Trip Tohak 67–146, January 7 to 14, 1973 (Top Secret, Flash, Sensitive, Exclusively Eyes Only). Sent via Guay.

14. National Archives, Nixon Presidential Materials, NSC Files, Kissinger Office Files, Box 28, HAK Trip Files, HAK Paris Trip Hakto 1–48, January 7 to 14, 1973 (Top Secret, Flash, Sensitive, Exclusively Eyes Only). Sent via Guay and Kennedy.

15. National Archives, Nixon Presidential Materials, NSC Files, Box 866, For the President's Files (Winston Lord)—China Trip/Vietnam, Camp David Memcons, January 8 to 13, 1973 [January 23, 1973] (Top Secret, Sensitive, Exclusively Eyes Only). The meeting took place at an American-owned villa, La Fontaine au Blanc, in the Paris suburb of Saint-Nom-la-Bretèche.

16. Ibid.

17. Ibid.

18. Ibid.

19. Ibid.

20. Ibid.

21. Haldeman, *Diaries*, January 12, 1973, reprinted in the Department of State, Office of the Historian, *Foreign Relations of the United States*, 1969–1976, Volume IX, Vietnam, October 1972 to January 1973, Document 270, http://history.state.gov/historicaldocuments/frus1969-76v09/d270.

22. National Archives, Nixon Presidential Materials, NSC Files, Kissinger Office Files, Box 28, HAK Trip Files, HAK Paris Trip Hakto 1–48, January 7 to 14, 1973 (Top Secret, Sensitive, Exclusively Eyes Only). Sent via Guay.

23. Nixon, *Memoirs*, 747–48. Nixon noted that Eisenhower had the same difficulty openly praising someone.

24. Kissinger, *White House Years*, 1,468–69.

25. Nixon, Daily Diary, January 14, 1973.

26. "1972 Miami Dolphins visit President Obama, White House," *Washington Post*, August 20, 2013. Two months earlier, when the 2012 Baltimore Ravens visited the White House for their win in Super Bowl XLVII, retired center Matt Birk refused to attend based on his opposition to abortion. "Baltimore Ravens Center Matt Birk Boycotts White House Visit," *Los Angeles Times*, June 7, 2013.

14: "LBJ Got Very Hot"

1. Tape 835-8, Part A (January 8, 1973, Nixon and Haldeman), White House Tapes, http://www.nixonlibrary.gov/forresearchers/find/tapes/tape835/835-008a.mp3.
2. "George Christian, 75, Aide to President Dies," *New York Times*, November 29, 2002.
3. "Cartha D. DeLoach, No. 3 in F.B.I., Is Dead at 92," *New York Times*, March 15, 2013.
4. Tape 835-8, Part B (January 8, 1973, Nixon and Haldeman), White House Tapes, http://www.nixonlibrary.gov/forresearchers/find/tapes/tape835/835-008b.mp3.
5. Transcript, *U.S. v. Liddy*, January 11, 1973, 106–25 (Hunt guilty plea).
6. Ibid.
7. Ibid., 140–57.
8. Ibid., 211–99 (testimony of Thomas Gregory); "Student-Spy May Lose Credits for Political Job," *New York Times*, January 11, 1973.
9. Ibid., January 12, 1973, 303 (proceedings on Rothblatt dismissal as lawyer for the Miamians).
10. "More Guilty Pleas Hinted Amid Watergate Secrecy," *New York Times*, January 13, 1973.
11. Transcript, *U.S. v. Liddy*, January 12, 1973, 303–04 (proceedings re: dismissal of Rothblatt).
12. Ibid., 305–07.
13. Ibid.
14. Ibid., 308–09.
15. Ibid.
16. "More Guilty Pleas Hinted Amid Watergate Secrecy," *New York Times*, January 13, 1973.
17. Transcript, *U.S. v. Liddy*, January 12, 1973, 317–28 (proceedings re: dismissal of Rothblatt).
18. Ibid. 328–38.
19. Ibid., 338–48.
20. Ibid., 349–54.
21. Tape 838-18, Part B (January 8, 1973, Nixon and Haldeman), White House Tapes, http://www.nixonlibrary.gov/forresearchers/find/tapes/tape838/838-018b.mp3.
22. Ibid.
23. Tape 395-25 (January 12, 1973, Haldeman and Nixon), White House Tapes, http://www.nixonlibrary.gov/forresearchers/find/tapes/tape395/395-025.mp3.
24. For a fascinating review of what Johnson knew as of October 30, 1968, listen to his call on that day with Senator Richard Russell, the Georgia senator who had been Johnson's trusted mentor in the Senate (and a member of the Warren Commission). LBJ describes how his people had heard through some Wall Street businessmen, who had met with Nixon to discuss the economy, that Nixon intended to block the efforts to get the South Vietnamese to Paris. Johnson identified the "subterranean" efforts of candidate Nixon through Mrs.

Chennault, revealing that he had information of her calls to the South Vietnamese ambassador in Washington. (He does not expressly say he wiretapped the South Vietnamese embassy but says knowingly to Russell, "You know, I have my ways.") Recording of Telephone Conversation between Lyndon B. Johnson and Richard Russell, October 30, 1968, 10:25A, Tape 13612, Recordings and Transcripts of Conversations and Meetings, LBJ Library.

25. Haldeman, *Diaries*, Friday, January 12, 1973. The deleted material in Haldeman's diaries would have been designated as such before all the LBJ phone tapes became available.

26. The other taped conversations about Mrs. Chennault's treachery were with Richard Russell, Dean Rusk, Everett Dirksen, Hubert Humphrey, and a summarizing phone conference with Clark Clifford, Dean Rusk, Walt Rostow, and Jim Jones on November 4, 1968, the day before the election in which LBJ's advisors counseled him not to make what he knew public for fear of destabilizing a Nixon presidency. See http://www.lbjlib.utexas.edu/johnson /archives.hom/dictabelt.hom/highlights/may68jan69.shtm.

Though scholars have analyzed and written about these various calls, none, except Ken Hughes, have focused on the postelection calls between LBJ and DeLoach. These calls tie most of the pieces together and present a compelling picture that the Nixon camp was in fact communicating a stop request to Thieu through Chennault. Ken Hughes, *Chasing Shadows: The Nixon Tapes, the Chennault Affair, and the Origins of Watergate* (University of Virginia Press, 2014).

27. "Secret Tapes Offer Inside Scoop on Personality of LBJ," *Dallas Morning News*, September 19, 1993.

28. "Papers on Kennedy Assassination Are Unsealed, and '63 Is Revisited," *New York Times*, August 24, 1993.

29. "Secret Tapes Offer Inside Scoop on Personality of LBJ," *Dallas Morning News*, September 19, 1993.

30. The CIA had also installed a bug in President Thieu's office in Saigon. So they knew the information from both ends.

31. Recording of Telephone Conversation between Lyndon B. Johnson and Cartha "Deke" DeLoach, November 12, 1968, 8:30P, Tape 13730, Recordings and Transcripts of Conversations and Meetings, LBJ Library; Recording of Telephone Conversation between Lyndon B. Johnson and Cartha "Deke" DeLoach, November 13, 1968, 5:15P, Tape 13733, Recordings and Transcripts of Conversations and Meetings, LBJ Library. See also Cartha D. DeLoach, *Hoover's FBI: The Inside Story by Hoover's Trusted Lieutenant* (New York: Regnery Publishing, 1995): 400–05.

32. Recording of Telephone Conversation between Lyndon B. Johnson and Cartha "Deke" DeLoach, November 13, 1968, 5:15P, Tape 13733, Recordings and Transcripts of Conversations and Meetings, LBJ Library. In an oral history with the LBJ Library, given January 11, 1991 (before the LBJ tapes became known), DeLoach tried to protect Nixon by asserting there was no evidence that he or Agnew were involved in the affair and that the calls from Agnew's plane were not made to "the Department of State," when in fact his phone call with LBJ on November 13, 1968, shows that he reported to LBJ

that a call had been placed from Agnew to Dean Rusk, the secretary of state, on November 2. Cartha "Deke" DeLoach, in Oral History Interview, January 11, 1991, Johnson Library, 17–20, http://www.lbjlib.utexas.edu/johnson /archives.hom/oralhistory.hom/DeLoach/Deloach1-san.PDF.

DeLoach's dissembling or lying about the call to Rusk in his oral history was obviously an attempt to hide or obscure Nixon and Agnew's likely role. Compare the DeLoach interview with the LBJ Library in 1991—"And I did [inquire of the phone company of the calls placed by the Agnew plane]. There had been five calls made by Agnew's plane, none to the South Vietnamese Ambassador, none to the Department of State and I advised the White House that there hadn't been any in that regard and that's all there was to it. This matter was blown up all out of proportion. Somehow it was leaked—and I know in my own mind who did it—that the President had asked us to put a microphone on Mr. [Nixon's] plane"—with his actual call to LBJ, as recorded on a Dictabelt on November 13, 1968—"One of the phones on the plane had been used five times. The first call was made at 11:59 AM, a personal call from Agnew to Rusk that lasted 3 minutes." See id., Tape 13733, November 13, 1968.

33. For LBJ's call with Dean Rusk confirming the Agnew call, see Recording of Telephone Conversation between Lyndon B. Johnson and Dean Rusk, November 3, 1968, 8:45P, Tape 13711, Recordings and Transcripts of Conversations and Meetings, LBJ Library.

34. Recording of Telephone Conversation between Lyndon B. Johnson and Cartha "Deke" DeLoach, November 13, 1968, 5:15P, Tape 13733, Recordings and Transcripts of Conversations and Meetings, LBJ Library.

35. Ibid.

36. Recording of Telephone Conversation between Lyndon B. Johnson and Everett Dirksen, November 2, 1968, 8:19P, Tape 13706, Recordings and Transcripts of Conversations and Meetings, LBJ Library.

37. Nixon, Daily Diary, January 12, 1973.

15: "And We Shall Overcome"

1. Jay Sharbutt, "Final LBJ Interview," *Reading Eagle* (Reading, PA), January 24, 1973.

2. "C.B.S. to Present Johnson TV Series," *New York Times*, July 8, 1969.

3. Max Holland, "The Assassination Tapes," *Atlantic Monthly*, June 2004, http://www.theatlantic.com/magazine/archive/2004/06/the-assassination -tapes/302964/.

4. Transcript, Arthur Krim Oral History Interview VI, October 13, 1983, by Michael Gillette, 36, LBJ Library. Online: http://www.lbjlib.utexas.edu /johnson/archives.hom/oralhistory.hom/Krim-A/Krim6.pdf. (September 11, 2014).

5. Leo Janos, "The Last Days of the President," *Atlantic Monthly*, July 1973.

6. "Civil Rights Leaders of the 1960's Call Upon Nixon to Lead a New Movement," *New York Times*, December 12, 1972.

7. "It Seemed So Very Long Ago," *New York Times*, December 17, 1972.

8. "Civil Rights Leaders of the 1960's Call Upon Nixon to Lead a New Movement," *New York Times*, December 12, 1972.

9. Ibid.
10. Remarks by Former President Lyndon Johnson at a Civil Rights Symposium, Austin, Texas, December 12, 1972, https://www.youtube.com/watch?v =RJKq18m0oYs (accessed September 11, 2014).
11. "Johnson Had Heart Attack, Is Resting," *New York Times*, April 9, 1972.
12. "Lyndon Johnson Ill; Out for This Session," *New York Times*, July 2, 1955.
13. "Johnson Had Heart Attack, Is Resting," *New York Times*, April 9, 1972.
14. David Shribman, "L.B.J.'s Gettysburg Address," *New York Times*, November 24, 2013.
15. Transcript, Jewell Malechek Scott Oral History Interview I, December 20, 1978, by Michael Gillette, 26, LBJ Library. Online: http://www.lbjlib.utexas .edu/johnson/archives.hom/oralhistory.hom/Malechek/scott%20web%201. pdf (accessed September 11, 2014).
16. Richard Goodwin, February 2, 1999, Renee Garrelick Oral History Program, http://www.concordlibrary.org/scollect/Fin_Aids/OH_Texts/goodwin _richard.html.

    Goodwin coined the phrase "Great Society" but broke with Johnson later in 1965 over the war. "It was very difficult to break with him," he told oral historian Renee Garrelick. "When the war came in 1965, it effectively froze everything that I was working on—the great society, civil rights. . . . The issue of the war ended our relationship forever."
17. Remarks by Former President Lyndon Johnson at a Civil Rights Symposium, Austin, Texas, December 12, 1972, https://www.youtube.com /watch?v=RJKq18m0oYs (accessed September 11, 2014).
18. In his interview with Walter Cronkite, Johnson said he thought Nixon was a good listener and would entertain a delegation of civil rights leaders. He encouraged the rights leaders to follow a process. "I think we ought to go to the leadership of the Congress and say to them, 'Here is a big problem that represents a cancer on the society of this country and we want to do something about it. And here's what we want to get done: one, two, three. And here is the way to go about it, here's the legislation.' And then if the leaders couldn't get legislation, then they should call on the president's people and say 'We would like to talk to someone in the White House about it.' And if it wasn't corrected, they should appeal to highest officer of the land, the president himself." Lyndon Johnson, interview by Walter Cronkite, January 12, 1973, CBS.
19. Lyndon Johnson, interview by Walter Cronkite, January 12, 1973, CBS.
20. "Johnson Mediates a Rights Dispute," *New York Times*, December 13, 1972.
21. "It Seemed So Very Long Ago," *New York Times*, December 17, 1972.
22. Jay Sharbutt, "Final LBJ Interview," *Reading Eagle* (Reading, PA), January 24, 1973.
23. Transcript, Jewell Malechek Scott Oral History Interview II, May 30, 1990, by Michael Gillette, 20, LBJ Library. Online: http://www.lbjlib.utexas.edu /johnson/archives.hom/oralhistory.hom/Malechek/scott%20web%202.pdf (accessed September 11, 2014).
24. Haldeman, *Diaries*, January 12, 1973.

16: "I Want to Do This Job That Lincoln Started"

1. Chapter 12, misc. endnotes; Blackmun, Memorandum to the Conference, December 11, 1972, Powell Roe Files Online, http://law.wlu.edu/deptimages /powell%20archives/70-18_RoeWade.pdf.

2. Chapter 12, misc. endnotes; Douglass letter to Blackmun, December 11, 1972, Powell Roe Files Online, http://law.wlu.edu/deptimages/powell%20 archives/70-18_RoeWade.pdf.

3. Chapter 12, misc. endnotes; Marshall letter to Blackmun, December 12, 1972, Powell Roe Files Online, http://law.wlu.edu/deptimages/powell%20 archives/70-18_RoeWade.pdf.

4. Recording of Telephone Conversation between Lyndon B. Johnson and Thurgood Marshall, July 7, 1965, 1:30 P, Tape 8307, Recordings and Transcripts of Conversations and Meetings, LBJ Library.

   President Johnson: But I want to do this job that [Abraham] Lincoln started and I want to do it the right way.

   Marshall: Well, could I have a day or so?

   President Johnson: Yes, yes. You can have all the time you want. And you think it over, and you evaluate it, and—

   Marshall: Right.

   President Johnson: This is a non-political job. It just determines what goes before that court and then you present it, at least all you want to and then have other people—Archie Cox will be going back to Harvard; he could stay. I could ask him to stay. But I want this man to . . . I think you could see what I'm looking at.

   Marshall: [*Unclear.*]

   President Johnson: And I want to be the first president that really goes all the way.

5. Johnson had an opportunity to nominate Marshall to the court just a few weeks after he named him as solicitor general. Johnson had induced Justice Arthur Goldberg to step down from the court to succeed Adlai Stevenson as the US ambassador to the United Nations. He thought it too soon to turn to Marshall for the Supreme Court and instead nominated his friend Abe Fortas—the person whom Nixon later would run off the court, resulting in Harry Blackmun's nomination. Johnson's conversations with John Kenneth Galbraith on July 20, 1965, confirms his thinking on Marshall:

   President Johnson: And I'm going to appoint Thurgood Marshall to the [Supreme] Court. Not to succeed him [Goldberg], but after he's Solicitor [General] for a year. After he's Solicitor [General] for a year or two, the first vacancy I have. I haven't told anybody that and I don't want you to, but I brought him here. They kept him for a year and wouldn't confirm him, but he had 32 cases before the Supreme Court; he won 29 of them. And now he'll have 20 or 30 more, a variety of cases for the government. And at the end of a year or two no one can say that he's not one of the best-qualified men that has ever [been] appointed. And then I'm going to appoint him.

   Recording of Telephone Conversation between Lyndon B. Johnson and John Kenneth Galbraith, July 20, 1965, 12:06 P, Tape 8362, Recordings and Transcripts of Conversations and Meetings, LBJ Library.

6. Transcript, Tom Clark Oral History Interview I, October 7, 1969, by Joe B. Frantz, 9, LBJ Library. http://www.lbjlib.utexas.edu/johnson/archives.hom/oralhistory.hom/Clark-T/Clark-T.PDF.
7. "Texan, 39, Chosen," *New York Times*, March 1, 1967; "Justice Retiring," *New York Times*, March 1, 1967.
8. "Senate Confirms Marshall as the First Negro Justice," *New York Times*, August 30, 1967. The vote was 69–11. Marshall's nomination to the Second Circuit was in 1962. "Thurgood Marshall, Confirmed By Senate, 54-16, for Judgeship," *New York Times*, September 12, 1962.
9. Tom C. Clark, "Religion, Morality, and Abortion: A Constitutional Appraisal," *Loyola of Los Angeles Law Review* 2 (1969): 1.
10. Doe v. Bolton, 410 U.S. 179, 217–18 (1973).
11. Remarks by Former President Lyndon Johnson at a Civil Rights Symposium, Austin, Texas, December 12, 1972, https://www.youtube.com/watch?v=RJKq18m0oYs (accessed September 11, 2014).
12. Marshall letter to Blackmun, December 12, 1972, Powell Roe Files Online, http://law.wlu.edu/deptimages/powell%20archives/70-18_RoeWade.pdf.
13. Randal P. Bezanson memo to Blackmun, December 14, 1972, Blackmun Papers. Bezanson became a beloved law professor at the University of Iowa and later the dean of the Washington and Lee School of Law, where Justice Powell's papers had been donated and reside. He died on January 26, 2014, at sixty-seven, after a long bout with cancer.
14. Rehnquist dissent in *Roe*, first draft, January 11, 1973, Powell Roe Files Online, http://law.wlu.edu/deptimages/powell%20archives/70-18_RoeWade OpinionsDissent.pdf .
15. White dissent, Doe v. Bolton, 410 U.S. 179, 221–24 (1973).
16. Haldeman, *Diaries*, January 13, 1973.
17. Ibid.
18. Ibid.
19. Senate Select Committee on Presidential Campaign Activities, 93rd Cong., Book 1, 250–53 (1973) (Caulfield testimony, May 22 to 23, 1973). Caulfield became the acting assistant director for enforcement, Bureau of Alcohol, Tobacco, and Firearms.
20. Ibid., 254–55.
21. Ibid., 256. Caulfield testified, "His plan, simply, was as follow: On two occasions, one in September 1972 and the other in October 1972, Mr. McCord told me that he had called telephone numbers at foreign embassies in Washington and he stated he was sure these embassies were subjects of national security wiretaps. On both occasions he had stated that he was a man involved in the Watergate scandal and, without giving his name, had inquired as to the possibility of acquiring visas and other traveling papers necessary to travel to these foreign countries."
22. "4 Watergate Defendants Reported Still Being Paid," *New York Times*, January 14, 1973.
23. St. George's story would eventually be published in a "high adventure" men's magazine in August 1974, the month Nixon resigned. Andrew St. George, "Confessions of a Watergate Burglar," *True*, August 1974.

24. "4 Watergate Defendants Reported Still Being Paid," *New York Times*, January 14, 1973.
25. Nixon, Daily Diary, January 14, 1973; Haldeman, *Diaries*, January 14, 1973.
26. Haldeman, *Diaries*, January 14, 1973.

17: "We Should Wait for His Formal Reply Before Popping Corks"

1. Transcript, *U.S. v. Liddy*, January 15, 1937, 370.
2. Ibid., 357–60.
3. Ibid., 360–62.
4. Ibid., 362–64.
5. Ibid., 365–66.
6. Ibid.
7. Ibid., 366–70.
8. Ibid., 370–87.
9. Ibid., 391–97.
10. Ibid., 397–98.
11. Ibid., 398–99.
12. Ibid., 399–401.
13. Ibid., 402–03.
14. Ibid., 404–17.
15. Andrew St. George, "Confessions of a Watergate Burglar," *True*, August 1974. Sturgis expounded on his dismissive comments about Barker: "When he is around Hunt, or anybody that's over him, Barker is like a valet. Servile—you know what I mean? 'Sit here, Mr. Hunt, the sun won't bother you.' It's disgusting. 'Yessir, Mr. Hunt, let me refresh your drink, sir.' Enough to make you puke."
16. Transcript, *U.S. v. Liddy*, 422.
17. Nixon, *Memoirs*, 748–49. In his diary that day, Nixon wrote, "It is ironic that the day the news came out stopping the bombing of North Vietnam, the Watergate Four plead guilty." He actually appreciated the cover that the imminent peace agreement provided to the Watergate trial. "I realized what the press would have done if they had not had another story that would override it." He went on to note, "Obviously the judge is going to throw the book at them and this will present quite a problem when it comes to a pardon."
18. "President Halts All Bombing, Mining, Shelling of North; Points to 'Progress' in Talks," *New York Times*, January 16, 1973; "A World Waits—In Hope and Fear," *New York Times*, January 14, 1973.
19. Ibid.
20. "Text of White House Briefing on the War," *New York Times*, January 16, 1973.
21. Haldeman, *Diaries*, multimedia edition, January 14, 1973.
22. Kissinger, *White House Years*, 1,469.
23. National Archives, Nixon Presidential Materials, NSC Files, Box 860, For the President's Files (Winston Lord)—China Trip/Vietnam, Sensitive Camp David, vol. 24 (no classification marking). Haig was to personally hand the letter to Thieu when the two met in Saigon on January 16. Letter from President

Nixon to South Vietnamese President Thieu, January 14, 1973, *Foreign Relations of the United States, 1969–1976*, ed., John M. Carland, vol. 9, *Vietnam, October 1972–January 1973*, http://history.state.gov/historicaldocuments/frus 1969-76v09/d278.

24. National Archives, Nixon Presidential Materials, NSC Files, Box 860, For the President's Files (Winston Lord)—China Trip/Vietnam, Sensitive Camp David, vol. 24 (Top Secret, Flash, Sensitive, Exclusively Eyes Only); Back-Channel Message from the Vice Chief of Staff of the Army (Haig) to the President's Assistant for National Security Affairs (Kissinger), January 16, 1973, Document 279, *Foreign Relations of the United States, 1969–1976*, ed., John M. Carland, vol. 11, *Vietnam, October 1972–January 1973*, http://history.state.gov /historicaldocuments/frus1969-76v09/d279.

25. National Archives, Nixon Presidential Materials, Kissinger Telephone Conversations, Box 17, Chronological File (no classification marking). Nixon was in Key Biscayne, Florida; Kissinger was in Washington. Transcript of a Telephone Conversation between President Nixon and the President's Assistant for National Security Affairs (Kissinger), Document 280, *Foreign Relations of the United States, 1969–1976*, ed., John M. Carland, vol. 9, *Vietnam, October 1972–January 1973*, http://history.state.gov/historicaldocuments/frus 1969-76v09/d280.

26. "Haig, in Saigon, Begins Talks with Thieu," *New York Times*, January 17, 1973.

27. "Two Nixon Writers, One 'Thoughtful' and One 'Tough,' Worked on Speech," *New York Times*, August 16, 1973.

28. Haldeman, *Diaries*, January 16, 1973.

18: "I'm Going to Be with the Rich Cats Tonight"

1. Garrow, *Liberty and Sexuality*, 586; "Questions Left Unanswered by Ruling on Abortion," *New York Times*, January 23, 1973. (Four state laws appeared to conform to the opinions: New York, Hawaii, Alaska and Washington; all others needed to be changed.)

2. Warren Burger Letter to Harry Blackmun, January 16, 1973, Powell Roe Files Online, http://law.wlu.edu/deptimages/powell%20archives/70-18_RoeWade.pdf.

3. Harry Blackmun, Memorandum to the Conference, January 16, 1973, Powell Roe Files Online.

4. Ibid., attached to the January 16, 1973 Memorandum to the Conference.

5. Beckwith went on to have his share of controversy during his career. He became Dan Quayle's press secretary in 1988. See also Matt Glazer, "David Beckwith Pack Your Bags," *Burnt Orange Report*, January 29, 2008 ("Beckwith's history of yap first, think second has absolutely gotten him into trouble") (*Burnt Orange Report* is a Texas political blog written from a progressive/liberal/ Democratic perspective), http://www.burntorangereport.com/diary/6170/.

6. Garrow, *Liberty and Sexuality*, 588; Jeffries, *Justice Lewis F. Powell, Jr.*, 343–46; Larry Hammond, interview with the author, November 20, 2013. ("I do regret the leaks," Hammond said.)

7. Transcript, *U.S. v. Liddy*, 426–84.

8. Ibid., 498–500.

9. Ibid., 456.

10. Ibid., 442–557.

11. Ibid., 722–24. (Officer Carl Shoffler testified that he noticed "a man standing on the balcony paying attention.")

12. Ibid., 726–27

13. Ibid., 752–55.

14. National Archives, RG 218, Records of the Chairman, Records of Thomas Moorer, Box 59, CINCPAC General Service Messages, January 1973 (Top Secret, Immediate, Specat, Exclusive). Repeated to Meyer, Weyand, Clarey, and Clay. Message From the Commander in Chief, Pacific (Gayler) to the Chairman of the Joint Chiefs of Staff (Moorer), January 17, 1973, Document 284, *Foreign Relations of the United States, 1969–1976*, ed., John M. Carland, vol. 9, *Vietnam, October 1972–January 1973*.

15. Library of Congress, Manuscript Division, Kissinger Papers, Box TS 45, Geopolitical File, Vietnam, Chronological File, 1969–75 (Top Secret, Flash, Sensitive, Exclusively Eyes Only); Backchannel Message from the Vice Chief of Staff of the Army (Haig) to the President's Assistant for National Security Affairs (Kissinger), January 17, 1973, Document 285, *Foreign Relations of the United States, 1969–1976*, ed., John M. Carland, vol. 9, *Vietnam, October 1972–January 1973*.

16. Nixon refers to "intercepts" and "bugs" that the United States was using to monitor the South Vietnamese in South Vietnam. Tape 36-21 (January 20, 1973 Nixon and Kissinger), White House Tapes, http://www.nixonlibrary.gov/forresearchers/find/tapes/tape036/36-021.mp3.

17. National Archives, Nixon Presidential Materials, NSC Files, Box 860, For the President's Files (Winston Lord)—China Trip/Vietnam, Sensitive Camp David, vol. 24 (Top Secret, Flash, Sensitive, Exclusively Eyes Only); Backchannel Message from the Vice Chief of Staff of the Army (Haig) to the President's Assistant for National Security Affairs (Kissinger), January 17, 1973, Document 286, *Foreign Relations of the United States, 1969–1976*, ed., John M. Carland, vol. 9, *Vietnam, October 1972–January 1973*.

18. National Archives, Nixon Presidential Materials, Kissinger Telephone Conversations, Box 17, Chronological File (no classification marking). Nixon was in Key Biscayne, Florida; Kissinger was in Washington. Transcript of a Telephone Conversation Between President Nixon and the President's Assistant for National Security Affairs (Kissinger), January 17, 1973, Document 289, *Foreign Relations of the United States, 1969–1976*, ed., John M. Carland, vol. 9, *Vietnam, October 1972–January 1973*.

19. Ibid.

20. Ibid.

21. National Archives, Nixon Presidential Materials, NSC Files, Box 860, For the President's Files (Winston Lord)—China Trip/Vietnam, Sensitive Camp David, vol. 24 (Top Secret, Flash, Sensitive, Exclusively Eyes Only); Backchannel Message from the President's Assistant for National Security Affairs

(Kissinger) to the Ambassador to Vietnam (Bunker), January 17, 1973, Document 290, *Foreign Relations of the United States, 1969–1976*, ed., John M. Carland, vol. 9, *Vietnam, October 1972–January 1973*.

22. Ibid.

23. "Duration Unsure: Statement Is Issued After Nixon Talks to Aides by Phone," *New York Times*, January 19, 1973.

24. "Transcript of Briefing by Ziegler on the Private Peace Talks," *New York Times*, January 19, 1973.

25. Nixon, Daily Diary, January 18, 1973.

26. Howard Hunt, *American Spy*, 277–78.

27. Tape 394-021, Part A, White House Tapes, http://www.nixonlibrary.gov/for researchers/find/tapes/tape394/394-021a.mp3.

28. Senator Edward M. Kennedy, "It's Time to Normalize Relations with Cuba," *New York Times*, January 14, 1973.

29. Howard Hunt, interview by William F. Buckley, *Firing Line*, January 21, 1973, Southern Educational Communications Association, Hoover Institution, Stanford University, http://hoohila.stanford.edu/firingline/programView2.php ?programID=564. Hunt appeared a second time on *Firing Line* in 1974.

30. Ibid.

31. Tape 36-006 (January 19, 1973, Nixon and Julie Eisenhower), White House Tapes, http://www.nixonlibrary.gov/forresearchers/find/tapes/tape036/036-006 .mp3.

32. Nixon, Daily Diary, January 19, 1973.

33. The Eisenhower Theater was named in honor of President Dwight D. Eisenhower, who signed the National Cultural Center Act in 1958, which helped finance a structure dedicated to the performing arts.

34. Tape 36-016 (January 20, 1973, Nixon and Haldeman), White House Tapes, http://www.nixonlibrary.gov/forresearchers/find/tapes/tape036/036-016. mp3. Nixon later bragged about his musical prowess when talking with Chuck Colson about the Ormandy concert. "Being somewhat of the student of music, I played Grieg when I was a sophomore in high school," he told Colson. "Well, I was quite advanced at music at an early age." It actually was somewhat unusual for Nixon to brag about himself on the tapes. He is a lot of things in these tapes: serious, vengeful, strategic, racist, sexist, repetitive, obsessive-compulsive, rambling. But boastful he is not. Tape 36-018 (January 20, 1973, Nixon and Colson), White House Tapes, http://www.nixonlibrary. gov/forresearchers/find/tapes/tape036/036-018.mp3.

35. Tape 36-18 (January 20, 1973, Nixon and Colson), White House Tapes, http://www.nixonlibrary.gov/forresearchers/find/tapes/tape036/036-018.mp3.

36. "Concerts Reflect Moods of Divided Washington," *New York Times*, January 20, 1973.

37. The F Street Club is also known as the Steedman-Ray House or the Alexander Ray House and is today the official residence of the president of George Washington University.

38. "Kissinger and Mitchells Enliven a Party," *New York Times*, January 20, 1973.

19: "In Our Own Lives, Let Each of Us Ask—Not Just What Government Will Do for Me, But What I Can Do for Myself"

1. Tape 36-18 (January 20, 1973, Nixon and Colson), White House Tapes, http://www.nixonlibrary.gov/forresearchers/find/tapes/tape036/036-018.mp3.
2. Antal Dorati, a Hungarian-born conductor and composer, was principal conductor of the National Symphony from 1970 to 1977. He is credited with saving the orchestra from bankruptcy and a players' strike.
3. Ibid.
4. Nixon, *Memoirs*, 752.
5. Mike Curb, with the encouragement of Ronald Reagan, went on to become lieutenant governor of California. He started a recording company and became a NASCAR car owner.
6. "The defense of freedom is everybody's business—not just America's business," Nixon said in an address to the nation on November 3, 1969. "And it is particularly the responsibility of the people whose freedom is threatened. In the previous administration, we Americanized the war in Vietnam. In this administration, we are Vietnamizing the search for peace." "Text of President Nixon's Address to the Nation on U.S. policy in the War in Vietnam," *New York Times*, November 4, 1969. This speech was also known as the "Silent Majority" speech. See also "The Nixon Doctrine," *New York Times*, February 19, 1970.
7. Nixon, in talking to Ron Ziegler on Sunday, January 21, lamented that the press did not understand the real historic significance of his inaugural—applying the Nixon Doctrine at home as well as abroad. "Such lines as, 'instead of asking what will government do for me, what can I do for myself'—that's very different thing from what Kennedy was saying—totally different." Tape 36-31 (January 21, 1973, Nixon and Ziegler), White House Tapes, http://www.nixon library.gov/forresearchers/find/tapes/tape036/036-031.mp3.

    The press did get it: "The Second Inaugural: Nixon Stresses Less Government, Self-Reliance, Limits on Foreign Role," *New York Times*, January 21, 1973.
8. Tape 36-18 (January 20, 1973, Nixon and Colson), White House Tapes, http://www.nixonlibrary.gov/forresearchers/find/tapes/tape036/036-018.mp3.
9. Before concluding, Nixon and Colson took stock of their "New Majority" with an appalling exchange. With big labor moving quickly to Nixon's banner, Colson said he and [election analyst] Dick Scammon intended to write a memo on the shifting demographics of the electorate before Colson left the White House. "The numbers are on our side," Colson said. "On the other side [meaning the Democratic Party]," Colson said, "you have a coalition of labor, blacks and poor, but the labor you've broken away. So you've got the blacks and the poor." "And the intellectuals," Nixon added. "Right," Colson agreed, "and the intellectuals—the New Left. And as Dick [Scammon] says, the lavender shirt mob, what he calls the New Left—the homos and queers—and he said that's the bunch that now makes up the Democratic Party." Tape 36-18 (January 20, 1973, Nixon and Colson), White House Tapes, http://www.nixon library.gov/forresearchers/find/tapes/tape036/036-018.mp3. Scammon, as seen

later, was the coauthor of *The Real Majority: An Extraordinary Examination of the American Electorate.*

10. Tape 36-19 (January 20, 1973, Nixon and Haldeman), White House Tapes, http://www.nixonlibrary.gov/forresearchers/find/tapes/tape036/036-019.mp3. Nixon was bothered about why Robert Finch was not attending the inaugural. He had asked Haldeman to look into it. "It's not a very smart thing for him to miss the inauguration," Nixon said. Finch had run Nixon's 1960 campaign against Kennedy, and Nixon appointed him the secretary of health, education and welfare in 1969, before Finch was pushed out for being too liberal, whereupon he became counselor to the president. Finch left the White House in December 1972, having avoided any taint from Watergate. Haldeman reported that Finch was in the Caribbean at some previously scheduled meeting and on a vacation he had promised his wife, Carol. Nixon was both peeved and concerned enough to call Haldeman about it at two in the morning on the day of his inauguration. "Robert Finch, 70, Nixon Aide and Former Secretary of Health," *New York Times*, October 12, 1995.

11. Nixon, Daily Diary, January 20, 1973.

12. Nixon, *Memoirs*, 752.

13. Ibid. A copy of the Emancipation Proclamation is maintained in the Lincoln Bedroom in a display on an antique desk.

14. Richard Scammon and Ben Wattenberg, *The Real Majority: An Extraordinary Examination of the American Electorate* (New York: Coward-McCann, Inc., 1970). The inside cover of the book summarizes some of its authors' findings: "Using crystal-clear facts drawn from polls and surveys of the American voter, his tastes and his habits, they brilliantly dissect that enigmatic and elusive group, the American electorate. And the portrait they paint will surprise and confound. They reveal how he responds to events like riots, dissent, war, student revolt, and racial turmoil. They describe and discuss the deep concerns of moderate, decent Americans who are seeking moderate, decent government in the White House, in city hall, and at political way stations in between. It is the political center, then, which emerges from this study as the only viable political position in American life. Any candidate who foolishly wanders in the hinterlands of the extreme left or right must ultimately be defeated."

15. Tape 36-18 (January 20, 1973, Nixon and Colson), White House Tapes, http://www.nixonlibrary.gov/forresearchers/find/tapes/tape036/036-018.mp3.

16. Tape 36-21 (January 20, 1973, Nixon and Kissinger), White House Tapes, http://www.nixonlibrary.gov/forresearchers/find/tapes/tape036/036-021.mp3.

17. National Archives, Nixon Presidential Materials, NSC Files, Box 1020, Alexander M. Haig Special File, Gen. Haig's Vietnam Trip, Haigto 1–26 and misc. memos, January 14 to 21, 1973 (Top Secret, Flash, Sensitive, Exclusively Eyes Only). In Tohaig 72/WHS 3081, January 19, 1630Z, Kissinger informed Haig of the following: "I have just talked to the President and he has asked me to tell you that you must be sure to tell Thieu that no delay is possible. The President will definitely go ahead and initial the agreement. If he cannot say that he is going ahead together with the South Vietnamese the Congressional actions foreshadowed in the Stennis and Goldwater comments which we sent to Bunker may start Wednesday, January 24, and the President would not be

able to give assurances that he now plans to make in his speech." (National Archives, Nixon Presidential Materials, NSC Files, Box 860, For the President's Files (Winston Lord)—China Trip/Vietnam, Sensitive Camp David, vol. 24.); Document 310, *Foreign Relations of the United States, 1969–1976*, ed., John M. Carland, vol. 9, *Vietnam, October 1972–January 1973*.

18. National Archives, Nixon Presidential Materials, NSC Files, Box 860 For the President's Files (Winston Lord)—China Trip/Vietnam, Sensitive Camp David, vol. 24 (Top Secret: Operational Immediate, Sensitive, Exclusively Eyes Only); Document 311, *Foreign Relations of the United States, 1969–1976*, ed., John M. Carland, vol. 9, *Vietnam, October 1972–January 1973*.

19. Ibid., Tape 36-21 (January 20, 1973, Nixon and Kissinger), White House Tapes, http://www.nixonlibrary.gov/forresearchers/find/tapes/tape036/036-021 .mp3.

20. Ibid.

21. "Nixon Inaugurated for His Second Term; Sees World on Threshold of Peace Era," *New York Times*, January 21, 1973.

22. John Dean, in conversation with the author, March 21, 2014.

23. Tape 36-28 (January 20, 1973, Nixon and Robert H. Taylor), White House Tapes, http://www.nixonlibrary.gov/forresearchers/find/tapes/tape036/036-028 .mp3; "Robert H. Taylor," *New York Times*, March 14, 1981. (Taylor, who served under five presidents, died at fifty-four from cancer in 1981.) "War Scored by Thousands in Protests in the Capital," *New York Times*, January 21, 1973.

24. Document 313, *Foreign Relations of the United States, 1969–1976*, ed., John M. Carland, vol. 9, *Vietnam, October 1972–January 1973*. The essence of Kissinger's "lawyer's argument" can be found in the draft note that was to be delivered to Thieu once the accords were signed. The argument was (1) the North Vietnamese never acknowledged that they had troops in the South; (2) the Communist "leopard spots" in the South were composed of refugees from the South—and their children—who had gone to the North and returned as freedom fighters; (3) therefore the North never made a claim to the legitimacy of having its troops in the South. Because this was the case, any troops that truly were from the North were there illegitimately and in violation of the many paragraphs that called for respect of the sovereignty of the South, a peaceful political solution to its future, and a ban of further reinforcement of outside forces or resupply of the same. The entire argument rests on the false premise that the North claimed no right to have its troops in the South. The reality was that there were anywhere from 140,000 to 300,000 North Vietnamese troops in the South that would remain as a result of the cease-fire in place.

25. Ibid.

26. Document 313, *Foreign Relations of the United States, 1969–1976*, ed., John M. Carland, vol. 9, *Vietnam, October 1972–January 1973*.

27. Tape 36-30 (January 21, 1973, Nixon and Kissinger), White House Tapes, http://www.nixonlibrary.gov/forresearchers/find/tapes/tape036/036-030.mp3.

28. National Archives, Nixon Presidential Materials, NSC Files, Box 1041, For the President's Files—China/Vietnam Negotiations, Original Letters from

Thieu to RN, November 1972 to January 1973 (no classification marking); Document 320, *Foreign Relations of the United States, 1969–1976*, ed., John M. Carland, vol. 9, *Vietnam, October 1972–January 1973*.

29. Tape 36-37 (January 21, 1973, Nixon and Haig), White House Tapes, http://www.nixonlibrary.gov/forresearchers/find/tapes/tape036/036-037.mp3.
30. Nixon, Daily Diary, January 21, 1973.
31. "Congressmen Hail Theme but Ask for More Details," *New York Times*, January 21, 1973.
32. "McGovern Warns of One-Man Rule; Exhorts Liberals," *New York Times*, January 22, 1973.
33. Ibid.

20: January 22, 1973

1. "The Sexes: Abortion on Demand," *Time*, January 29, 1973.
2. Tape 399-001 (January 22, 1973, Nixon), White House Tapes, http://www.nixonlibrary.gov/forresearchers/find/tapes/tape399/399-001.mp3.
3. Tape 399-002 (January 22, 1973, Nixon and Kissinger), White House Tapes, http://www.nixonlibrary.gov/forresearchers/find/tapes/tape399/399-002.mp3.
4. Transcript, Jewell Malechek Scott Oral History Interview II, May 30, 1990, by Michael Gillette, 20-21, LBJ Library. Online: http://www.lbjlib.utexas.edu/johnson/archives.hom/oralhistory.hom/Malechek/scott%20web%202.pdf (last checked September 11, 2014).
5. "Johnson Takes Trip to Mexico for Rest," *New York Times*, July 21, 1960; "LBJs Take Acapulco Vacation," *Daytona Beach Morning Journal*, January 22, 1970.
6. James "Mike" Howard, YouTube interview on KXAN, April 14, 2011, https://www.youtube.com/watch?v=b7RM9-g7xN8.
7. Malechek, Oral History Interview 2, 27–28.
8. Weddington, *A Question of Choice*, 142–46.
9. Tape 36-37 (January 22, 1973, Nixon and Haig), White House Tapes, http://www.nixonlibrary.gov/forresearchers/find/tapes/tape036/036-037.mp3.
10. Ibid.
11. Greenhouse, *Becoming Justice Blackmun*, 101.
12. Weddington, *A Question of Choice*, 146.
13. Garrow, *Liberty and Sexuality*, 600–01.
14. Weddington, *A Question of Choice*, 162.
15. Ibid., 588.
16. Jeffries, *Justice Lewis F. Powell, Jr.*, 344.
17. Transcript, *U.S. v. Liddy*, 1,064–65.
18. Transcript, *U.S. v. Liddy*, 1,088–91.
19. Tape 36-59 (January 22, 1973, Nixon and Rebozo), White House Tapes, http://www.nixonlibrary.gov/forresearchers/find/tapes/tape036/036-059.mp3.
20. James "Mike" Howard, YouTube interview; "Stricken at Home, Apparent Heart Attack Comes as Country Mourns Truman," *New York Times*, January 23, 1973.

21. "Retired Secret Service Agent from McKinney Recalls Protecting Family," *Dallas Morning News*, November 22, 2013.

22. "Retired Secret Service Agent Talks About Day of Kennedy Assassination," *Dallas Morning News*, June 3, 2013, http://www.dallasnews.com/news/jfk50 /reflect/20130603-retired-secret-service-agent-talks-about-day-of-kennedy -assassination.ece.

23. "Trials: The Spy in the Cold," *Time*, January 29, 1973.

24. Hunt used the exact same line that he did on the Buckley program. " 'When they identified me as a former CIA officer right after the Watergate arrests,' he says, 'they abrogated our agreement of confidentiality.' " Ibid.

25. Tape 400-11 (January 22, 1973, Nixon and Colson), White House Tapes, http://www.nixonlibrary.gov/forresearchers/find/tapes/tape400/400-011a .mp3. Tape 36-44 (January 22, 1973, Nixon and Ziegler), White House Tapes, http://www.nixonlibrary.gov/forresearchers/find/tapes/tape036/036-044 .mp3. Jerrold L. Schecter had been *Time*'s Moscow bureau chief before becoming a White House correspondent in 1971.

26. Tape 36-44 (January 22, 1973, Nixon and Ziegler), White House Tapes, http:// www.nixonlibrary.gov/forresearchers/find/tapes/tape036/036-044.mp3.

27. Tape 36-46 (January 22, 1973, Nixon and Ziegler), White House Tapes, http:// www.nixonlibrary.gov/forresearchers/find/tapes/tape036/036-046.mp3.

28. Tape 36-49 (January 22, 1973, Nixon, Haldeman, Tkach), White House Tapes, http://www.nixonlibrary.gov/forresearchers/find/tapes/tape036/036-049 .mp3. Although parts of the conversation are difficult to make out, Nixon can be heard talking about "the people who have been in this office." Nixon says something about Kennedy taking pills.

"He had real problems," Haldeman says in response. "He really had problems."

Nixon then says, "Eisenhower was always afraid, and with good reason, too." Haldeman says, "He had real problems. So did Johnson."

Nixon continues on Eisenhower: "But he's [*sic*] was also a hypochondriac— Eisenhower was always worried about his health, even before he had his heart attack. Johnson was *unbelievable*. And I guess anyone who has had a heart attack maybe always [becomes] one."

29. Ibid.

30. Tape 36-50 (January 22, 1973, Haldeman and Tkach), White House Tapes, http://www.nixonlibrary.gov/forresearchers/find/tapes/tape036/036-050 .mp3.

31. Tape 36-51 (January 22, 1973, Haldeman and Tkach), White House Tapes, http://www.nixonlibrary.gov/forresearchers/find/tapes/tape036/036-051.mp3.

32. "Notes on LBJ's Death from His Closest Aide," *The Daily Beast*, January 22, 2013, http://www.thedailybeast.com/articles/2013/01/22/notes-on-lbj-s -death-from-his-closest-aide.html.

33. Ibid.; "Cronkite announces death of LBJ," YouTube video, 4:05, from a CBS news broadcast televised on January 22, 1973, posted by "robatsea2009," August 12, 2009, http://www.youtube.com/watch?v=zxHsSnEgk-A.

34. Tape 36-53 (January 22, 1973, Nixon and Haig), White House Tapes, http:// www.nixonlibrary.gov/forresearchers/find/tapes/tape036/036-053.mp3.

35. Tape 36-55 (January 22, 1973, Nixon and Haldeman), White House Tapes, http://www.nixonlibrary.gov/forresearchers/find/tapes/tape036/036-055.mp3.
36. Ibid.
37. Ibid.
38. Tape 36-61 (January 22, 1973, Nixon and Colson), White House Tapes, http://www.nixonlibrary.gov/forresearchers/find/tapes/tape036/036-061.mp3. The last time there had been a sitting president and no former president alive was during the period between January 5, 1933, and March 4, 1933, when Hoover was in office. Coolidge died on January 5, 1933, and FDR was inaugurated on March 4, 1933—thirty-nine years earlier. http://en.wikipedia.org /wiki/Living_Presidents_of_the_United_States.
39. Greenhouse, *Becoming Justice Blackmun*, 101.

21: "The Sun Is Shining in Paris This Afternoon"

1. "William White, 88, Reporter and Author," *New York Times*, May 1, 1994. He retired in 1973.
2. Tape 36-63 (January 23, 1973, Nixon and William S. White), White House Tapes, http://www.nixonlibrary.gov/forresearchers/find/tapes/tape036/036-063 .mp3; William S. White, *The Professional: Lyndon B. Johnson* (Boston: Houghton Mifflin, 1964).
3. William S. White, "Fullest Measure of 'Pity,'" *Spartanburg Herald-Journal* (Spartanburg, SC), January 27, 1973.
4. *Amour-propre* means "self-love" in French.
5. National Archives, Nixon Presidential Materials, NSC Files, Box 860, For the President's Files (Winston Lord)—China Trip/Vietnam, Sensitive Camp David, vol. 24 (Secret, Operational Immediate, Sensitive, Exclusively Eyes Only). Sent via Guay and Scowcroft; Document 328, *Foreign Relations of the United States*.
6. Kissinger, *White House Years*, 1,472.
7. Document 328, *Foreign Relations of the United States*.
8. "Kissinger and Tho End Talks with Handshakes and Smiles," *New York Times*, January 24, 1973.
9. Kissinger, *White House Years*, 1,472.
10. Tape 36-76 (January 23, 1973, Haldeman and Timmons), White House Tapes, http://www.nixonlibrary.gov/forresearchers/find/tapes/tape036/036-076 .mp3. In a conversation with Ziegler later in the day, Nixon said that he didn't need to make the peace announcement against a dramatic congressional backdrop. The announcement, he said, was powerful enough itself that he "could do it in the men's room." Besides, television coverage would just allow the cameras to focus "on those sitting on their hands—like the Kennedys and the others and the rest." Tape 36-83 (January 23, 1973, Nixon and Ziegler), White House Tapes, http://www.nixonlibrary.gov/forresearchers/find/tapes/ tape036/036-083.mp3.
11. "Thousands at Johnson Bier," *New York Times*, January 24, 1973.
12. "Vatican's Radio Criticizes Abortion Ruling by Court," *New York Times*, January 23. 1973.

13. "Statements by 2 Cardinals," *New York Times*, January 23, 1973; "Cardinals Shocked—Reaction Mixed," *New York Times*, January 23, 1973.

14. Ibid.

15. Ibid.

16. Ibid.

17. Larry Hammond, interview with the author, November 20, 2013.

18. "Respect for Privacy," *New York Times*, January 24, 1973.

19. "National Guidelines Set by 7-to-2 Vote," *New York Times*, January 23, 1973.

20. "The Sexes: Abortion on Demand," *Time*, January 29, 1973.

21. Nixon wrote in his memoirs that he was happy Pat Nixon didn't kiss him after he was sworn in at his second inaugural. "Mrs. Agnew kissed Agnew—Pat did not kiss me," he wrote. "I am rather glad she didn't. I sometimes think these displays of affection are very much in place, as was the case election night. Other times, I don't think they quite fit and on this occasion I didn't really think it fit." Nixon, *Memoirs*, 753.

22. Tape 36-81 (January 23, 1973, Richard Nixon and Pat Nixon), White House Tapes, http://www.nixonlibrary.gov/forresearchers/find/tapes/tape036/036-081 .mp3.

23. Tape 404-26 (January 23, 1973, Nixon and Colson, EOB), White House Tapes, http://www.nixonlibrary.gov/forresearchers/find/tapes/tape404/404-026a .mp3.

24. Tape 36-86 (January 23, 1973, Nixon and Ziegler), White House Tapes, http:// www.nixonlibrary.gov/forresearchers/find/tapes/tape036/036-086.mp3.

25. The Brando caricature is on the January 15, 1973, cover of *Time*.

26. Haldeman, *Diaries*, January 29, 1973. "He's very distressed with *Time*," Haldeman wrote, "especially since they did the Marlon Brando cover on Inauguration Week instead of covering the Inaugural as the cover story."

27. Tape 407-018 (January 23, 1973, Nixon and Colson), White House Tapes, http://www.nixonlibrary.gov/forresearchers/find/tapes/tape407/407-018.mp3.

28. Ibid. Though the tape is hard to hear at this point, Nixon seems to add something about a woman seeing a doctor, telling him she is only three months pregnant, and getting an abortion from the doctor, who discovers she was much later in her term. "Oh, Shit," Nixon mocks as the doctor, "I thought you told me three months." The woman says, "I thought I was."

29. Ibid.

30. Ibid.

31. Kissinger, *White House Years*, 1,473. Tape 36-89 (January 23, 1973, Nixon, Kissinger, and Ziegler), White House Tapes, http://www.nixonlibrary.gov/for researchers/find/tapes/tape036/036-089.mp3.

32. Haldeman, *Diaries*, January 23, 1973, 572.

33. Nixon, Daily Diary, January 23, 1973.

34. Tape 839-006 (January 23, 1973, Nixon address to the nation in the Oval Office), White House Tapes, http://www.nixonlibrary.gov/forresearchers/find /tapes/tape839/839-006.mp3.

35. Tape 841-10 (January 24, 1973, Nixon, Ziegler, and Haldeman), White House Tapes, http://www.nixonlibrary.gov/forresearchers/find/tapes/tape841/841-010

.mp3. Ninety-four million tuned in. Haldeman said it was twenty million more viewers than Nixon had ever had.

36. "Transcript of Address by President on Vietnam," *New York Times*, January 24, 1973.

37. Nixon would say several times in his calls on this night that he was also describing himself in these remarks about LBJ—for he too had suffered the vilification of the critics.

38. Nixon, *Memoirs*, 756.

39. "Congress United in Relief but Some Voice Worry," *New York Times*, January 24, 1973.

40. Andrew F. Smith, *Rescuing the World: The Life and Times of Leo Cherne* (Albany: State University of New York Press, 2002) (forward by Henry Kissinger). The sculptor Leo Cherne was also a prominent economist, lawyer, businessman, and chairman of the International Rescue Committee.

41. Tape 36-91 (January 23, 1973, Nixon and Ray Price), White House Tapes, http://www.nixonlibrary.gov/forresearchers/find/tapes/tape036/036-091.mp3.

42. Tape 36-94 (January 23, 1973, Nixon and Colson), White House Tapes, http://www.nixonlibrary.gov/forresearchers/find/tapes/tape036/036-094.mp3.

43. Tape 36-101 (January 23, 1973, Nixon and Haldeman), White House Tapes, http://www.nixonlibrary.gov/forresearchers/find/tapes/tape036/036-101.mp3. Haldeman provided Nixon with a much more balanced report on the country's reaction to the speech. He tried to blunt Nixon's wallowing about CBS and played up the positives, including the reaction to his touching tribute to President Johnson. Nixon seemed surprised.

44. Tape 36-94 (January 23, 1973, Nixon and Colson), White House Tapes, http://www.nixonlibrary.gov/forresearchers/find/tapes/tape036/036-094.mp3.

45. Kissinger, *White House Years*, 1,475–76.

46. Tape 36-99 (January 23, 1973, Nixon and Kissinger), White House Tapes, http://www.nixonlibrary.gov/forresearchers/find/tapes/tape036/036-099.mp3.

47. "Thieu Is Cautious," *New York Times*, January 24, 1973.

48. "End of Nightmare," *New York Times*, January 24, 1973.

49. "Thousands File by the Johnson Bier," *New York Times*, January 24, 1973.

50. "Johnson Lies in State in Capitol Rotunda," *New York Times*, January 25, 1973.

51. "Moyers Hospitalized Before Johnson Rites," *New York Times*, January 26, 1973.

52. Ibid.

53. "Transcript of Kissinger's New Briefing to Explain Vietnam Cease-Fire Agreement," *New York Times*, January 25, 1973.

54. "Reconciliation and Reconstruction," *New York Times*, January 28, 1973.

55. Tape 841-10 (January 24, 1973, Nixon, Haldeman and Ziegler), White House Tapes, http://www.nixonlibrary.gov/forresearchers/find/tapes/tape841/841-010.mp3.

56. Haldeman, *Diaries*, January 24, 1973; Nixon, *Memoirs*, 757–58.

57. "Washington Pays Final Tribute to Johnson," *New York Times*, January 26, 1973.

58. Tape 36-107 (January 24, 1973, Nixon and Rebozo), White House Tapes, http://www.nixonlibrary.gov/forresearchers/find/tapes/tape036/036-107.mp3.

59. "Johnson Buried at Texas Ranch," *New York Times*, January 26, 1973.

60. Tape 842-8 (January 25, 1973, Nixon, Rabin, and Kissinger), White House Tapes, http://www.nixonlibrary.gov/forresearchers/find/tapes/tape842/842-008a .mp3; Nixon, Daily Diary, January 25, 1973.

61. "Nixon Budget Reflects Use of 3 Tactical Rules," *New York Times*, February 4, 1973. Among the Great Society programs to be cut or slashed were a quarter of the programs in the Office of Education, including projects for drug abuse education and emergency school assistance programs, and vocational training programs; Model Cities, urban renewal, and most federal housing subsidies; the Neighborhood Youth Corps and Community Action programs of the Office of Economic Opportunity; and a number of health programs, including one-third of programs operated by the National Institutes of Health. "Fight in Prospect, Democrats Worried by Plans to End Some of the Social Programs," *New York Times*, January 27, 1973.

62. Tape 36-109 (January 24, 1973, Nixon and Haldeman), White House Tapes, http://www.nixonlibrary.gov/forresearchers/find/tapes/tape036/036-109.mp3.

63. Nixon, Daily Diary, January 26, 1973.

64. "Kissinger Vows a Congressional Role in Aid for Hanoi," *New York Times*, January 27, 1973.

65. Ibid.

66. National Archives, Nixon Presidential Materials, NSC Files, Box 341, Subject Files, HAK/President Memos (Eyes Only) ("Personal" and "Eyes Only" are written on the first page in an unknown hand); Document 355, *Foreign Relations of the United States*.

67. Haldeman, *Diaries*, multimedia edition, January 27, 1973.

68. Ibid.

69. "Tho Is Leaving for Hanoi Today," *New York Times*, January 26, 1973.

70. "Vietnam Peace Pacts Signed; America's Longest War Halts," *New York Times*, January 28, 1973; "The Settlement: Paris Peace in Nine Chapters," *Time*, February 5, 1973.

71. Ibid.

72. Ibid.

73. "Widow of Johnson and Two Daughters Pay Visit to the Grave," *New York Times*, January 27, 1973.

74. Lt. Colonel William B. Nolde, forty-three, of Mount Pleasant, Michigan, is considered the last official American combat casualty in the Vietnam War. He died from shellfire on January 27, 1973, eleven hours before the truce began. "An Army Colonel from Michigan Is Last American to Die in War," *New York Times*, January 29, 1973.

　　Al Haig attended Nolde's burial with full military honors at Arlington on February 5, 1973. The family met with President Nixon at the White House after the burial. "Last American Killed Before the Truce Is Buried in Arlington," *New York Times*, February 6, 1973.

75. "Leaders: Lyndon Johnson: 1908–1973," *Time*, February 5, 1973.

22: "Now Your Client Is Smiling"

1. Transcript, *U.S. v. Liddy*, 1,149–50.
2. Ibid.; "Judge Queries Watergate Witness Whom Can't Recall to Who He Sent Wiretap Data," *New York Times*, January 23, 1973.
3. Transcript, *U.S. v. Liddy*, 1,400–23.
4. Sirica, *To Set the Record Straight*, 74.
5. Magruder, *An American Life*, 308.
6. Ibid., 307.
7. Transcript, *U.S. v. Liddy*, 1,423–30.
8. Sloan was played by actor Steven Collins in the movie. Meredith Baxter played Sloan's nervous spouse, Debbie Sloan.
9. "Mitchell Linked to $199,000 Fund," *New York Times*, January 24, 1973.
10. Transcript, *U.S. v. Liddy*, 1,460–65.
11. "Watergate Conviction," *New York Times*, February 1, 1973.
12. "Mitchell Linked to $199,000 Fund," *New York Times*, January 24, 1973.
13. Tape 841-007 (Part B) (January 24, 1973, Nixon and Haldeman), White House Tapes, http://www.nixonlibrary.gov/forresearchers/find/tapes/tape841/841-007b .mp3. The two discussed the testimony the day before. Haldeman said it was a big day for the White House—all "our people" were on the stand. Haldeman thought it had gone well and was pleased that it coincided with a day of other news—the peace announcement that night and LBJ's upcoming funeral in Washington. "You couldn't have picked a better day," Haldeman said, "except today."
14. Excerpt of transcript of proceedings, Wednesday, January 24, 1973, 1,490–1,500, ordered sealed, and released.
15. Transcript, *U.S. v. Liddy*, 1,468. ("THE COURT: Members of the Jury, I have an announcement to make. As you probably know, the President has declared a day of mourning for President Johnson. The President has also declared Thursday a holiday for the Executive Departments. This Court feels that it should not be in session Thursday, so you will have the day off to relax, and so that will be it.")
16. Ibid., 1,658–67; "Watergate Judge Assails Argument by Defense," *New York Times*, January 25, 1973.
17. Transcript, *U.S. v. Liddy*, 1,719–23; "Jury Is Told Nixon Aides Knew of Watergate Fund," *New York Times*, January 27, 1973. Liddy always believed that Sirica would create some fatal error during the trial that would result in his conviction being overturned on appeal. His smiling that morning could have been an indication that he thought Sirica's decision to read Sloan's testimony was just such an error. Certainly including all of the bench conferences with counsel was error.
18. Transcript, *U.S. v. Liddy*, 1,457.
19. Ibid., 1,746.
20. Ibid., 1,889–94.
21. Jeffries, *Justice Lewis F. Powell, Jr.*, 344–45; Larry Hammond, interview with the author, November 21, 2013.

22. Jeffries, *Justice Lewis F. Powell, Jr.*, 344–45.

23. Nixon, Daily Diary, January 27, 1973; "Nation Celebrates Peace in Prayer and Muted Joy," *New York Times*, January 28, 1973.

24. Nixon, Daily Diary, January 28, 1973; "Text of Nixon's Radio Address on His Plans for the Federal Budget," *New York Times*, January 29, 1973; "Nixon Urges Public to Seek Budget Lid," *New York Times*, January 29, 1973.

25. Nixon, Daily Diary, January 29, 1973.

26. "Now It's in a Mood for a Real Fight," *New York Times*, January 28, 1973.

27. "Agnew Is Off for Saigon on 7-Nation Asia Tour," *New York Times*, January 29, 1973.

23: "It Is a Rule of Life"

1. Transcript, *U.S. v. Liddy*, 1,897–1,900.

2. Ibid.

3. "Letters to the Editor," *New York Times*, January 25, 1973. Another editorial, "The Judge," praised Sirica for his toughness in questioning Hugh Sloan and then sharing Sloan's testimony with the jury. "Everyone objected more or less strenuously, but the judge, not for the first time, had his way. The 68-year-old jurist was appointed by President Eisenhower in 1957, following a career as a lawyer in private practice, a Congressional investigator and Government prosecutor. As a young man he was, not so incidentally, an amateur fighter." "The Judge," *New York Times*, January 28, 1973.

4. Transcript, *U.S. v. Liddy*, 1,967–71.

5. Lt. Joseph P. Kennedy Institute of Catholic Charities in Washington, DC, today part of the District of Columbia Association for Special Education (DCASE).

6. Transcript, *U.S. v. Liddy*, 1,958–59.

7. Ibid.

8. Ibid., 2,062–66.

9. Ibid., 2,076–2,160.

10. Ibid., 2,232.

11. Ibid., 2,246–52.

12. Ibid.; "Liddy and McCord Are Guilty of Spying on the Democrats," *New York Times*, January 31, 1973.

13. "Henry Kissinger Riding High," *Time*, February 5, 1973.

14. Tape 844-003(a) (January 30, 1973, Nixon and Haldeman), White House Tapes, http://www.nixonlibrary.gov/forresearchers/find/tapes/tape844/844-003a.mp3.

15. Ibid.

16. "The Georgetown Blacking Factory," *New York Times*, January 30, 1973; Tape 36-126 (January 30, 1973, Nixon and Colson), White House Tapes, http://www.nixonlibrary.gov/forresearchers/find/tapes/tape036/036-126.mp3.

17. Tape 36-126 (January 30, 1973, Nixon and Colson), White House Tapes, http://www.nixonlibrary.gov/forresearchers/find/tapes/tape036/036-126.mp3.

18. Tape 36-127 (January 30, 1973, Nixon and Kissinger), White House Tapes, http://www.nixonlibrary.gov/forresearchers/find/tapes/tape036/036-127.mp3.

19. Tape 36-130 (January 30, 1973, Nixon and Coy Hines Stennis), White House Tapes, http://www.nixonlibrary.gov/forresearchers/find/tapes/tape036/036-130.mp3.

20. "Senseless Shooting . . ." *New York Times*, February 3, 1973.

21. Tape 36-139 (January 30, 1973, Nixon and Colson), White House Tapes, http://www.nixonlibrary.gov/forresearchers/find/tapes/tape036/036-139.mp3.

22. "Because He Was There," *New York Times*, February 4, 1973.

23. Ibid.

24. Tape 43-4 (January 31, 1973, Nixon and Buchanan), White House Tapes, http://www.nixonlibrary.gov/forresearchers/find/tapes/tape043/043-004.mp3.

25. John W. Dean, *The Nixon Defense: What He Knew and When He Knew It* (New York: Viking, 2014).

26. "Transcript of the President's News Conference on Foreign and Domestic Matters," *New York Times*, February 1, 1973.

27. Ibid.

28. Ibid.

29. Ibid.

30. Tape 43-10 (January 31, 1973, Nixon and Buchanan), White House Tapes, http://www.nixonlibrary.gov/forresearchers/find/tapes/tape043/043-010.mp3.

31. Ibid.

32. "Nixon Reported to Favor Connally in '76," *New York Times*, January 31, 1973.

33. Nixon, Daily Diary, January 31, 1973.

34. "Stennis's Condition Called 'Very Serious,'" *New York Times*, February 1, 1973.

Epilogue: The Blessings of Simultaneity

1. "Kissinger Arrives in Hanoi for Talks on Postwar Roles," *New York Times*, February 11, 1973.

2. "B-52s Bomb Laos Less Than a Day After the Truce," *New York Times*, February 24, 1973; "Rogers Hails Laos Cease-Fire, Voices Concern on Cambodia," *New York Times*, February 22, 1973.

3. "Kennedy Panel Says Government Inquiry on Bugging Was Limited," *New York Times*, February 2, 1973; "Senators Pressing Watergate Inquiry," *New York Times*, February 6, 1973; "Ervin Vows Justice in Watergate Case," *New York Times*, February 7, 1973.

4. "Still No Real Answers," *New York Times*, February 4, 1973.

5. Ibid.

6. "A Promotion for Earl Silbert?" *Washington Post*, July 11, 1974.

7. "Enron's Many Strands: Legal Counsel; Top Defense Lawyer with Low Profile Represents Enron's Former Chief," *New York Times*, February 8, 2002.

8. "Watergate Conviction," *New York Times*, February 1, 1973.

9. "Watergate (Cont.)," *New York Times*, February 3, 1973.

10. "Watergate Judge Wants New Inquiry," *New York Times*, February 3, 1973.

11. For an exceptionally thoughtful analysis of Judge Sirica's role in the trial, see Anthony J. Gaughan, "Watergate, Judge Sirica, and the Rule of Law," *McGeorge Law Review* 42, no. 2 (2011): 343. "The rule of law rests on the means used to achieve justice. A fair trial requires strict adherence to the procedural and

constitutional protections afforded to criminal defendants. To a remarkable degree, the Watergate trial failed to meet those basic requirements, particularly with regard to the right of criminal defendants to remain silent. Just as the Watergate scandal challenged the resilience of the American political system, the burglars' trial tested the limits of the American criminal justice system."

12. Ibid.

13. "Man of the Year: Judge John J. Sirica: Standing Firm for the Primacy of Law," *Time*, January 7, 1974. "One judge, stubbornly and doggedly pursuing the truth in his courtroom regardless of its political implications, forced Watergate into the light of investigative day."

14. "Talking Tough—Or Just Louder?" *New York Times*, January 7, 1973.

15. Ibid.

16. Ibid.

17. "Transcript of the Speech by the President on Vietnam," *New York Times*, January 24, 1973; "Ex-P.O.W.'s Cheer," *New York Times*, May 25, 1973. ("'Let me be quite blunt,'" Nixon said [to a group of POWs]. Had there not been secrecy and security in negotiation, "'You men would still be in Hanoi today rather than in Washington.'")

18. Tape 885-01 (March 20, 1973, Nixon and Ehrlichman), White House Tapes, http://www.nixonlibrary.gov/forresearchers/find/tapes/tape885/885-001.mp3.

19. Tape 886-06 (March 21, 1973, Nixon and Dean), White House Tapes, http://www.nixonlibrary.gov/forresearchers/find/tapes/tape886/886-008a.mp3.

20. Emery, *Watergate*, 267; Tape 422-033 (March 22, 1973, Nixon, Dean, Ehrlichman, Haldeman, and Mitchell), White House Tapes, http://www.nixonlibrary.gov/forresearchers/find/tapes/tape422/422-033a.mp3.

21. Emery, *Watergate*, 269–70.

22. "Moving Toward a Showdown," *New York Times*, June 3, 1973; "Moment of Truth," *New York Times*, June 28, 1973.

23. Kissinger, *Ending the Vietnam War: A History of America's Involvement in and Extrication from the Vietnam War* (New York: Simon & Schuster, 2003), 455.

24. Ibid., 457.

25. "A Frail 'Fresh Hope,'" *New York Times*, June 14, 1973.

26. "Communists Take Over Saigon; U.S. Rescue Fleet Is Picking Up Vietnamese Who Fled in Boats," *New York Times*, May 1, 1975.

27. Ibid.

28. Ibid.

29. John Dean, interview with the author, March 2014. In an e-mail Dean confirmed the exact location where he remembers having the conversation with Dan Ellsberg: in Washington as the two men crossed Connecticut Avenue.

30. "Colson Pleads Guilty to Charge in Ellsberg Case," *New York Times*, June 4, 1974.

31. "Charles W. Colson, Watergate Felon Who Became Evangelical Leader, Dies at 80," *New York Times*, April 21, 2012.

32. Ibid.

33. Is there any significance in the fact that war hero, returned POW, and Arizona senator John McCain chose Dayton, Ohio, to introduce Sarah Palin as his vice-presidential candidate in 2008?

34. Richard Scammon and Ben Wattenberg, *The Real Majority: An Extraordinary Examination of the American Electorate* (New York: Coward-McCann, Inc., 1970), 46.

35. Ibid., 45.

36. Ibid., 29.

37. Ibid., 27–34.

38. Ibid., 39.

39. Ibid., 40–43.

40. Ibid., 43.

41. Ibid.

42. Randall Balmer, *Thy Kingdom Come: How the Religious Right Distorts the Faith and Threatens America, an Evangelical's Lament* (New York: Basic Books, 2006).

43. Ibid.; Coit v. Green, 404 U.S. 997 (1971).

44. "Abortion Foes, at Conference, Plan Strategy of Political Activism," *New York Times*, January 21, 1980; Jill Lepore, "Birthright: What's Next for Planned Parenthood," *The New Yorker*, November 14, 2011. ("Nothing even remotely resembling party discipline on the issue of abortion can be identified on Capitol Hill before 1979.")

45. "Rev. Falwell Inspires Evangelical Vote," *New York Times*, August 20, 1980.

46. "Religious Right, Frustrated, Trying New Tactic on G.O.P.," *New York Times*, March 23, 1998.

47. Ibid.

48. Tape 035-017 (December 27, 1972, Colson and Nixon), White House Tapes, http://www.nixonlibrary.gov/forresearchers/find/tapes/tape035/035-017.mp3. Nixon had just returned that evening from Truman's services in Independence, Missouri.

49. "Transcript of the Johnson Address," *New York Times*, March 16, 1965.

INDEX